DISTANCE EDUCATION:
INTERNATIONAL PERSPECTIVE

Distance Education:
International Perspectives

Edited by
DAVID SEWART, DESMOND KEEGAN
and BÖRJE HOLMBERG

CROOM HELM
London & Sydney

ST. MARTIN'S PRESS
New York

© 1983 D. Sewart, D. Keegan and B. Holmberg
Croom Helm Ltd, Provident House, Burrell Row,
Beckenham, Kent BR3 1AT
Croom Helm Australia Pty Ltd, Suite 4, 6th Floor,
64-76 Kippax Street, Surry Hills, NSW 2010, Australia
Reprinted 1985

British Library Cataloguing in Publication Data

Distance education.
    1. Correspondence schools and courses
    II. Sewart, David   II. Keegan, Desmond
    III. Holmberg, Börje
    371.3   LC5915
    ISBN 0-7099-1525-X

Library of Congress Cataloging in Publication Data

Distance education.
    Bibliography: p.
    Includes index.
    1. Distance education—Addresses, essays, lectures.
I. Sewart, David.   II. Keegan, Desmond.   III. Holmberg
Börje.
LC5800.D57   1983   371.3   83-4973
ISBN 0-312-21319-0 (St. Martin's Press)

Printed and bound in Great Britain
by Billing & Sons Limited, Worcester.

CONTENTS

PREFACE

In 1971 Ossian MacKenzie and Edward L. Christensen published The changing world of correspondence study: international readings through the Pennsylvania State University Press. It presented a comprehensive overview of education at a distance up to the end of the 1960s.

Enormous changes have taken place since their publication.

Distance education, for long the cinderella of the educational spectrum, emerged in the 1970s and early 1980s as a valued component of many national educational systems in both developed and developing countries. The foundation of the Open Universities, developments in communications technology and in audio-, video- and computer-based learning, a new sophistication in the design of print-based materials and better support systems for the student learning at a distance, have all contributed to the availability and quality of distance education programmes.

In this book we chronicle these developments and seek to provide a new scholarly basis for the theory and practice of education at a distance. The articles selected come from leading writers in many countries. Some have been specially translated for this volume and appear in English for the first time. Others come from sources not generally available to educationists or from the journals Distance Education, Epistolodidaktika and Teaching at a Distance which are not yet held by even the most comprehensive educational libraries.

The introductions place the articles in their context and draw the reader's attention to the outstanding issues in the literature, giving references to further studies which it did not prove possible to include in this volume.

ACKNOWLEDGEMENTS

Keegan, D., "On defining distance education", Distance Education, 1,1 (1980), 13-36. Reprinted by permission.

Perraton, H., "A theory for distance education". Article from Prospects, Vol.11, No.1 copyright Unesco 1981. Reproduced by permission of Unesco.

Sewart, D., "Distance teaching: a contradiction in terms?", Teaching at a Distance, 19, 8-18. Copyright 1981 The Open University Press. Reprinted by permission.

Moore, M.G., "On a theory of independent study", ZIFF - Papiere 16, November 1977 (Hagen: Fernuniversität). Reprinted by permission.

Peters, O., "Distance teaching and industrial production: a comparative interpretation in outline", translation of "Fernstudium und industrielle produktion: skizze einer vergleichenden interpretation", pp.47-63 of Ökonomische theorie und wirtschaftliche praxis - festschrift zum 65. geburtstag von Rolf Hansehmann (Herne/Berlin: Verlag Neue Wirtschafts-Briefe, 1981). Reprinted by permission.

Wedemeyer, C., "Backdoor learning in the learning society", pp.199-205, 215-219, 239-240 of Learning at the backdoor (Madison: University of Wisconsin Press, 1982). Reprinted by permission.

Sandburg, C., extract from The People, Yes (New York: Harcourt Brace Jovanovich Inc., 1936). Reprinted by permission.

Escotet, M., "Adverse factors in the development of an open university in Latin America", PLET, 17,4 (1980), 262-270. Reprinted by permission.

Pagney, B., "What advantages can conventional education derive from correspondence education?", translation of "Quels advantages l'enseignement á distance peut-il offrir á l'enseignement formel?" (EHSC Conference 1980). Reprinted by permission.

McIntosh, N., Woodley, A., & Morrison, V., "Student demand and progress at the Open University - the first eight years", <u>Distance Education</u> 1,1 (1980), 37-60. Reprinted by permission.

Smith, K.C., "External studies at New England - a silver jubilee review, 1955-1979", pp.viii-ix, 33-41. (Armidale: the University of New England, 1979). Reprinted by permission.

Rekkedal, T., "Research and development activities in the field of distance study at NKI-Skolen, Norway", <u>Epistolodidaktika</u> 2 (1978), 29-38. Reprinted by permission.

Bates, A.J., "Trends in the use of audio-visual media in distance education systems", pp. 8-15, Daniel, J.S., Stroud, M.A., & Thompson, J.R., eds., <u>Learning at a distance: a world perspective</u>. (Edmonton: Athabasca University/ICCE, 1982). Reprinted by permission.

Beare, H., "Education by satellite: Australian possibilities", <u>Unicorn</u> 6,3 (1980), 334-342. Reprinted by permission.

Sparkes, J.J., "On choosing teaching methods to match educational aims", ZIFF - Papiere 39, January 1982. (Hagen: Fernuniversität). Reprinted by permission.

Bååth, J., "A list of ideas for the construction of distance education courses", pp.63-80 of Holmberg,B., & Bååth,J., <u>Distance education: a short handbook</u>, (Malmö: Liber-Hermods, 1982). Reprinted by permission.

Ljoså, E., & Sandvold, K., "The student's freedom of choice within the didactical structure of a correspondence course", <u>Journal of Correspondence Education</u> Vol.1/EHSC Autumn 1976 workshop paper. Reprinted by permission.

Jenkins, J., "Tell me how to write", pp.227-229 of Daniel, J.S., Stroud M.A., & Thompson, J.R., (eds), <u>Learning at a distance: a world perspective</u> (Edmonton: Athabasca University/ICCE, 1982). Reprinted by permission.

Clenell, S., Peters, J., & Sewart, D., <u>Teaching for the Open University</u> pp.5-10, 17-24. (Milton Keynes: the Open University, 1977). Reprinted by permission.

Daniel, J.S., & Marquis, C., "Interaction and independence: getting the mixture right", <u>Teaching at a Distance</u>, 14, 29-44. Copyright 1977. The Open University Press. Reprinted by permission.

Schwarz, R., "The consultation in the process of distance education". This translation of Dr. Schwarz's (1975) speech "Die Konsultation im Studienprozess des Fernstudiums" was authorised by Prof. Dr. H. Möhle, Leipzig, and is published with his permission.

Wagner, L., "The economics of the Open University revisited", <u>Higher Education</u> 6 (1977), 359-381. Reprinted by permission.

Snowden, B.L. & Daniel, J.S., "The economics and management of small post-secondary distance education systems", <u>Distance Education</u> 1, 1 (1980), 68-91. Reprinted by permission.

Rumble, G., "Economics and cost structures", pp.220-234 of Kaye, A., & Rumble, G. (eds.), <u>Distance teaching for higher and adult education</u> (London: Croom Helm, 1981). Reprinted by permission.

We are grateful to the above authors, publishers and editors of periodicals. Without their permission, assistance and support it would not have been possible to carry forward a project of this sort.

I am also deeply indebted to my secretary, Miss Gillian Brown and Miss Fiona Sewell for her editorial assistance. Both have provided unstinting support and notable patience in the face of the numerous problems and set-backs which have been met and overcome.

David Sewart

DISTANCE EDUCATION:
INTERNATIONAL PERSPECTIVE

SECTION 1: THE CONCEPT OF DISTANCE EDUCATION

INTRODUCTION

The term distance education

Distance education is a fairly new term. It denotes the forms of study not led by teachers present in class-rooms but supported by tutors and an organisation at a distance from the student. This brief description allows an interpretation which equates distance education with correspondence education. The reason why the term distance education has come into being is that the word correspondence is felt to be associated exclusively with the written word, whereas usually audio recordings and often radio, TV, telephone communication and other media nowadays supplement the written word in what is here called distance education. Sometimes, particularly in the USA, independent study is used as a synonym.

Correspondence education can be and often is taken to denote this multi-media approach. This is for instance the interpretation of the Association of British Correspondence Colleges. Others reserve the term correspondence education for the types of distance education which are entirely based on printed courses and communication in writing.

The characteristics of distance education

Distance education, whether concerned with elementary, university, informal, occupational or professional study, regularly includes three types of activity on the part of the organisation that administers it, i.e.

- the development of self-instructional study material, i.e. courses printed and/or recorded which may either be self-contained or of a study-guide type relying on set texts

- teaching at a distance by comments in writing, on the telephone or on audio cassettes on students' work submitted

- counselling and general support of students' work by

the same distance-study media

For the students this implies interaction with the course material, with tutors and counsellors. The study is an individual activity, however, and the students basically work on their own. It is possible to supplement these non-contiguous activities by on-campus tutorials, lectures, laboratory work, counselling sessions and other face-to-face interaction with tutors and fellow-students. This is regarded as essential in some systems, as marginal in others.

Distance education mainly belongs to adult education, but special forms of supervised distance study have been developed for primary and secondary education in sparsely inhabited areas. Distance education is usually a cost-effective type of education which compares favourably with conventional study.

Distance education as related to teaching and learning in general

Ripley Sims, who has contributed a valuable study of distance-education processes, has found one clear border line between distance education (which he calls correspondence education) and conventional education. The basic difference, he says,is in the means of communication:

> In the contiguous learning environments, communication is personal and face-to-face; in the non-contiguous environments communication may be personal and face-to- face for limited periods of time, but it is largely written, mechanical, electronic or some other means of communicating at a distance......Learning is fundamentally an individual process and each person enters the process with techniques and levels of achievement uniquely his own. The method of correspondence study provides simultaneously an educational device for individualization in three distinct senses - student ability, variety of course offerings and flexibility for time and place of study.

Otto Peters, who is also concerned with what constitutes the basic difference between distance education and conventional education, has developed a consistent view of distance education as an industrialised form of teaching and learning. On his approach see Section 2.

Seven models of learning and teaching influential in general educational work, among them such extremes as on the one hand Skinner's behaviour-control model, on the other hand Roger's model for facilitation of learning, have been studied by Bååth with a view to finding out to what extent they are applicable to distance study.

For each of the models Bååth has investigated its general applicability to distance study, the implications for the development of course material, for non-contiguous two-way communication and for the supplementing of this

2

two-way communication by face-to-face contacts. Further, he has analyzed some special relations between these various models and distance study (Bååth 1979).

This study is important in that it expressly relates generally accepted principles of teaching and learning to distance education. It is a useful basis for further theoretical and practical work.

Delineating the concept of distance education

In the 1970s some fruitful attempts have been made to stake out the discipline of distance education. This applies to a process model developed by Delling featuring eight dimensions of distance education (society, the student, the distance, the information carrier, the study aim, the study matter, the learning result and the supporting organisation), by means of which it should be possible to describe all distance -education processes (Delling 1971), and to Graff's cybernetic approaches based on decision theory which, however, lead to the conclusion that the great problems are to be found 'beyond the calculation'.

My German monograph on distance education as a scholarly discipline surveys various theoretical approaches, among them my own theory of the guided didactic conversation, suggests a systems description and tries to pin-point the tasks of this academic discipline. Its theoretical function is to understand and *explain* what occurs in distance education. One consequence of such understanding and explanation will be that hypotheses can be developed and submitted to falsification attempts. This will lead to insights telling us what in distance education is to be expected under what conditions and circumstances, thus paving the way for corroborated practical methodological applications. The discipline of distance education would thus meet Popper's dictum that the task of scholarship is on the one hand theoretical, to bring about explanation, and on the other hand practical, to provide for application of technology.

At the beginning of the 1980s three new important contributions have been made by Desmond Keegan, Hilary Perraton and David Sewart to the discussion of the character and essence of distance education. The three papers concerned are reprinted in this section. They illuminate the present debate and views on the concept of distance education. Keegan's paper has caused a discussion in the Australian journal Distance Education, in which it was published. There John Bååth questions whether two of the alleged characteristics of distance education listed by Keegan are really typical. This objection concerns the inclusion of occasional face-to-face meetings and the participation in an industrialized form of education under the main elements of distance education. Bååth points out that high-quality distance education *can* be provided - and sometimes *is* provided - ent-

3

irely at a distance in courses where there is no possibility of additional face-to-face meetings. He further argues that although most distance teaching can be characterised as industrialised teaching, there certainly are forms of distance education - e.g. a number of small-scale projects at the university level - that cannot be described in this way but rather as teaching of a 'handicraft' type.

The two contributions by Perraton and Sewart are of a different character. Perraton lists fourteen relevant statements on the characteristics of distance education representing external and internal influences, and Sewart discusses the theory and practical experience between the basic components of distance education, the course package and student support.

The papers by Keegan, Perraton and Sewart reprinted in this section reflect present-day awareness of the necessity to attain some sort of agreement on what can be called the philosophy of distance education. Charles Wedemeyer engages in this discussion in his comprehensive new book Learning at the back-door (1981), which analyses the conditions, tasks and procedures of 'non-traditional' learning. My book of 1981, Status and trends of distance education, reflects the same tendency by devoting one chapter to the distance-study concept and another to the philosophy of distance education.

There seem to be at least two different schools of thought on distance education, one stressing individual study and individual, non-contiguous tutoring on the basis of course materials produced for large groups of students, the other aiming at parallelism with resident study and usually including class or group teaching face-to-face as a regular element. Whereas the former represents the type of industrialisation leading to rationalisation and economy of quantity discussed by Peters and considers distance education to be basically different from face-to-face eduation, distance education is to the latter merely a form of distribution for which even the same tutor-student ratio for distance study and on-campus study is considered acceptable and even advantageous. The former represents a large-scale approach of the Open University and traditional correspondence school types, the latter a small-scale approach, for which the Australian University of New England can be regarded as a prototype (Smith 1979). In Sweden, which has more than eighty years' favourable experience of the large-scale type of distance education, a successful application of the small-scale type now occurs at the universities (Willén 1981). The Canadian University of Waterloo cassette-teaching system, which addresses classes rather than individuals, is a modified application (Leslie 1979).

Börje Holmberg

References

Bääth, J.A. (1979) Correspondence education in the light of a number of contemporary teaching models. Malmö: LiberHermods

Bääth, J.A. (1980) Postal two-way communication in correspondence education. London: Gleerup

Bääth, J.A. (1981) On the nature of distance education. Distance Education 2, 2, pp. 212-219

Holmberg, B. (1978) Fernstudiendidaktik als wissenschaftliches Fach. Hagen: FernUniversität, ZIFF

Holmberg, B. (1981) Status and trends of distance education. London: Kogan Page

Leslie, J.D. (1979) The University of Waterloo model for distance education. Canadian Journal of University Continuing Education VI, 1, pp. 33-41

Peters, O. (1971) Theoretical aspects of correspondence instruction. In: MacKenzie, O. & Christensen, E.L. (eds.), The changing world of correspondence study. University Park: Pennsylvania State University Press

Peters, O. (1973) Die didaktische Struktur des Fernunterrichts. Untersuchungen zu einer industrialisierten Form des Lehrens und Lernens. Tübinger Beiträge zum Fernstudium 7. Weinheim: Beltz

Popper, K. (1972) Conjectures and refutations. The growth of scientific knowledge. London: Routledge & Kegan Paul

Sims, R.S. (1977) An enquiry into correspondence education processes: Policies, principles - and practices in correspondence education systems worldwide. (unpublished ICCE-UNESCO report)

Smith, K.C. (1979) External studies at New England. Armidale, NSW: The University of New England

Wedemeyer, C. (1981) Learning at the back door. Reflections on non-traditional learning in the lifespan. Madison, Wis.: The University of Wisconsin Press

Willén, B. (1981) Distance education at Swedish universities. Uppsala: Almqvist & Wiksell International

ON DEFINING DISTANCE EDUCATION

Desmond J. Keegan

The term 'distance education' covers the various forms of study at all levels which are not under the continuous, immediate supervision of tutors present with their students in lecture rooms or on the same premises, but which, nevertheless, benefit from the planning, guidance and tuition of a tutorial organisation.

(Holmberg, 1977:9)

Distance education is education which either does not imply the physical presence of the teacher appointed to dispense it in the place where it is received or in which the teacher is present only on occasion or for selected tasks.

(Loi 71.556 du 12 juillet 1971)

Distance teaching/education (*Fernunterricht*) is a method of imparting knowledge, skills and attitudes which is rationalised by the application of division of labour and organisational principles as well as by the extensive use of technical media, especially for the purpose of reproducing high quality teaching material which makes it possible to instruct great numbers of students at the same time wherever they live. It is an industrialised form of teaching and learning.

(Peters, 1973:206)

Distance teaching may be defined as the family of instructional methods in which the teaching behaviours are executed apart from the learning behaviours, including those that in a contiguous situation would be performed in the learner's presence, so that communication between the teacher and the learner must be facilitated by print, electronic, mechanical or other devices.

(Moore, 1973:664)

Introduction

The growing literature on distance education contains many

complaints about the lack of unanimity on the terminology used in the field. This is especially true of the English-speaking world where each of the following terms is used extensively: correspondence study, home study, independent study, external studies, distance teaching and distance education.

There is also confusion about the place of distance education within education as a whole and whether it is identical to or to be differentiated from such areas as correspondence education, non-traditional education, off-campus education and open learning.

The need for more theoretical analysis (Bååth, 1978) and for an intellectualisation of distance education recurs from time to time. Moore (1973:661), for instance, writes as follows:

> As we continue to develop various non-traditional methods for reaching the growing numbers of people who cannot, or will not attend conventional institutions but who choose to learn apart from their teachers, we should divert some of our resources to the macrofactors: describing and defining the field, discriminating between the various components of this field, identifying the critical elements of the various forms of learning and teaching, in short, building a theoretical framework which will embrace this whole area of education.

This article addresses the questions of terminology, definition and identification in an effort to contribute to the theory of distance education. The method used is an analysis of generally accepted definitions in an attempt to highlight what can be regarded as essential elements of any definition. A presentation of what can and what cannot be regarded as distance education follows and a concluding section suggests that 'distance education' is the most satisfactory solution to the problem of terminology.

There are some educators who feel that terminology is unimportant and that there is little need to divert resources for analysis. 'Let's all do more of it without worrying too much about what it is' is not really a caricature of some distance educators. This article does not subscribe to such views. Some of the reasons for urgent attention to a theoretical analysis of distance education will become apparent from the discussion of Peters' definition in the section which follows.

Four definitions

It is easier to devise a definition than to accept someone else's. It is not the purpose of this study to devise yet another definition of distance education but to highlight those elements which are essential to any definition.

Of the many definitions of distance education which have been prepared in the last decade four have been chosen for analysis. An attempt has been made to make them as representative as possible.

Holmberg is from Sweden, works in the Federal Republic of Germany and often writes in English. The French definition is from official government sources which formulate policy on the administration of distance education. After a long association with the Deutsches Institut für Fernstudien an der Universität Tübingen, Peters worked in Berlin before becoming foundation president (*Gründungsrektor*) of the Fernuniversität-Gesamthochschule in Hagen. Moore has worked extensively in the United States of America and today is senior counsellor in the Southern Region of the Open University of the United Kingdom.

It will be seen at once that three of the definitions (Holmberg, the French Law, Moore) are descriptive. Peters, however, presents a new philosophical analysis of distance education as 'an industrialised form of teaching and learning'. If Peters' definition, or any elements of it, is accepted, a radical separation of distance education from other forms of education is effected.

Holmberg

Basic to Holmberg's definition are two elements both of which can be considered essential:

- the separation of teacher and learner

- the planning of an educational organisation.

The separation of teacher and learner is fundamental to all forms of distance education whether they be print-based, audio/radio-based, video/television-based, computer-based or satellite-based. This separation differentiates distance education from all forms of conventional, face-to-face, direct teaching and learning. (Holmberg, 1974, 1978).

The structuring of learning materials and the linking of these learning materials to effective learning by students through an educational organisation differentiates distance education from private study, learning from interesting books or cultural television programmes.

The French law

On 12 July 1971 the French Government passed a law regulating the conduct of distance education in its territories. This law contained the definition of distance education translated at the beginning of this article.

Again two elements are basic to this definition:

- the separation of teacher and learner

- the possibility of occasional seminars or meetings between student and teacher.

The separation of teacher and taught is underlined as it is in Holmberg's definition and it can be accepted that no one would wish to propose a definition of distance education which did not include the possibility of face-to-face contact 'on occasion or for selected tasks'. The wording of the law can be challenged in that it is so broad that it could encompass certain forms of conventional education.

Moore

Moore's definition highlights three elements:

- the separation of teaching behaviours and learning behaviours
- the use of technical media
- the possibility of two-way communication.

His analysis separates teaching into two areas: in normal face-to-face teaching the teacher's preparation is done apart from his students and he teaches in the presence of students. In distance education both the preparation and the teaching are done apart from students.

The emphasis on technical media and two-way communication (Bååth and Flinck, 1973) are valuable additions to what has already been presented. It is important for Moore (1975, 1977) that the system should allow the learner to initiate this communication.

Moore's definition was further elaborated by Rune Flinck (1975, 1978) who presents it as follows:

Distance education is a learning system where the teaching behaviours are separate from the learning behaviours. The learner works - alone or in a group - guided by study material arranged by the instructor who together with the tutors is in a location apart from the students, who however have the opportunity to communicate with a tutor/tutors with the aid of one or more media such as correspondence, telephone, television, radio. Distance education may be combined with various forms of face-to-face meetings.

This development of Moore's thought is more comprehensive and introduces the notion that the teaching role may be shared and that different study situations are possible for the learner.

Peters

The three definitions so far considered can probably be accommodated within any basic theory of education. The major theoretical formulation of distance education so far published, Otto Peters' Die didaktische Struktur des Fernunterrichts. Untersuchungen zu einer industrialisierten Form des Lehrens und Lernens (1973) takes quite a different position. It merits careful study.

Peters begins the theoretical part of his analysis with a description which coincides quite readily with the three considered so far:

> Distance education is a form of indirect instruction. It is imparted by technical media such as correspondence, printed materials, teaching and learning aids, audiovisual aids, radio, television and computers. (1973:104)

Basic to this description are two of the elements already identified; separation between the teacher and the learner, and the use of technical media. Peters' analysis, however, proceeds (1973: 157-205) much further than the others considered and leads him to the conclusion that the didactical structure of distance education can best be understood from industrial principles especially those of productivity, division of labour and mass production. The mechanisation and automation of teaching methodology and the dependence of teaching effectiveness on prior planning and organisation (rather than on teaching ability) lead him to posit a radically different role for the teacher in distance education from that exercised in the lecture hall or seminar room.

This leads Peters to the definition quoted at the beginning of this article. The definition can be queried in the emphasis that it places on the course production process. Many would consider this as only the start of the learning process and expect some reference to tuition and teacher/-learner exchanges.

Peters next (1973:207) considers other theories of distance education and gives a comprehensive listing of those that have been proposed:

- a fringe form of ordinary teaching

- an institutionalised form of individual study

- education through teaching aids

- expanded form of teaching by correspondence with feedback

- special type of mass education.

He is led to the conclusion that all are inadequate as explanations of the phenomenon described.

Peters concludes (1973:295) with an attempt to define the relationship between teacher and taught in a distance education system. He characterises this relationship as being controlled by technological rules (and not social norms as in face-to-face teaching), maintained by emotion- free language (and not interactional speech), based on a limited possibility of analysing students' needs and giving them

10

directions (not on expectations built on personal contact) and achieving its goal by efficiency (and not through personal interaction).

In earlier writings (1965,1971:225) Peters had laid the ground for his theory of distance education:

> Correspondence instruction is the most industrialised form of instruction, and the usual theoretical criteria for the description of traditional instruction do not help very much in analysing correspondence instruction. (This) has suggested the introduction of *new categories* taken from those sciences investigating the industrial production process. It is, in fact, astounding to see how much better these criteria help to understand and describe the institutional process in correspondence instruction. Some of the suggested criteria are: division of labour (on the side of teachers); mechanisation; automation; application of organisational principles; scientific control; objectivity of teaching behaviour; mass production; concentration and centralisation.

This brief presentation cannot do justice to Peters' attempts to show that distance education is based on a new academic theory which is quite alien to traditional didactics. He is quite convinced that distance education has its own laws of didactical structure, great teaching potential, serious didactical flaws and that it presents opportunities and dangers to both teachers and students which are not yet fully studied. Anyone professionally involved in education, he maintains, must presume the existence of two forms of education which are strictly separable: traditional education based on personal communication and distance education based on industrialised and technological communication.

There have always been those who have objected to such a presentation and two of the objections will be considered briefly here. In 1968 Mackenzie, Christensen and Rigby wrote:

> Much confusion stems from the popular misconception that correspondence instruction is somehow different in kind from resident or institutional instruction. This simply is not so. Correspondence instruction shares the same goals and the same educational philosophy as many different methods of instruction. It differs from them primarily in the means, in the method itself. (1968:17)

Similar views are often encountered in Australia where an 'integrated mode' of distance education is practised in many universities and colleges. In the 'integrated mode' a lecturer is given responsibility both for a group of conventional, on-campus students and for a group of distance education students, known as external students. Learning materials are usually developed in close parallel with the lecturer's lecture-room course and the same assignments and examinations are provided for both on-campus and external students. (Smith,1978)

It is in this context that some Australian educationalists (Foks, 1979; Hopper, 1979) can write of 'the blurred demarcation between on-campus and off-campus studies':

> External studies, off-campus studies, or distance education, as it is variously called, is no more than a method of teaching. . . I believe that we shall move much more to the provision of carefully prepared learning materials and study guides for our students and to much more flexible attendance patterns. If this occurs, it will become virtually impossible to designate students as on-campus or off-campus students, or to designate institutions which are teaching in the off-campus mode. (Hopper,1979:74)

This is not the place to debate whether distance education should be integrated within or separated from conventional face-to-face programmes (Perry 1976, Daniel and Smith 1979). The contention is, however, that what is said here of distance education should be applicable mutatis mutandis to the distance education segment of an integrated programme.

The second objection to the claim of a radical separation in didactic structure between distance education and conventional education is based on the idea that Otto Peters, and many educational philosophers with him, have misinterpreted what occurs in conventional education, especially at university level. Typical of the position that is challenged is R.S. Peters' statement (1972:104) of what is central to the learning process:

> At the culminating stages of education there is little distinction between teacher and taught; they are both participating in the shared experience of exploring a common world. The teacher is simply more familiar with its contours and more skilled in handling the tools for laying bare its mysteries and appraising its nuances. Occasionally in a tutorial this exploration takes the form of a dialogue. But more usually it is a group experience. The great teachers are those who can conduct such a shared exploration in accordance with rigorous canons, and convey, at the ame time, the contagion of a shared enterprise in which all are united by a common zeal.

There is clearly a huge gulf between this statement and the industrialised process that Otto Peters describes. The counter argument runs that it is incorrect to say that in traditional education learning takes place in the lecture room and that the teacher's role is therefore of crucial importance. Good adult education, the objection claims, is essentially self-education by the learner based on private study in libraries, audio-visual carrels and laboratories. Those who support the view that distance education is radically to be differentiated from conventional education would point out that access to the university's library and carrels is not often possible for students who study at a distance from the institution and that the use of indirect teaching methods (see below) in face-to-face instruction does not make it identical with distance education.

In spite of these objections one can grant to Otto Peters that he has highlighted a characteristic of distance education that should form part of any definition:

- it is the most industrialised form of education.

Nature of distance education

It must also be conceded that Peters has attempted to get to the nature of distance education and that the two objections just quoted, and many others like them, seem to neglect certain fundamental aspects of distance education. There are five reasons for this:

1   In traditional education a teacher teaches. In distance education an institution teaches. This is a radical difference. In traditional education the teacher is present in the lecture room with students and his success often depends on the rapport he can build up with students: personality and even idiosyncracies may be central. In distance education the teacher prepares learning materials from which he hinself may never teach. Another teacher may use the materials and evaluate students' work. The pedagogical structuring of the learning materials, instructional design and execution may be assigned to others. Personality needs to be played down, idiosyncracies eliminated. The teaching becomes institutionalised. Different skills are needed as even part of the content of what is taught may be contributed by others.

2   In distance education the goal of linking of learning materials to learning is at the centre of the organisational structure. In conventional education the 'intersubjectivity that R.S. Peters saw as central to the teaching/learning process is automatically set up. In distance education this 'intersubjectivity' is lacking and there can be no guarantee that anything will happen once learning materials have been developed and dispatched to the student.
    Administrators of distance education systems who consider that distance education is merely a 'fringe form of traditional education' often forget to provide this linking. They feel that once the learning materials have been developed and dispatched to the student the

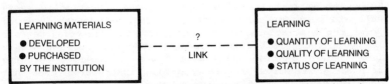

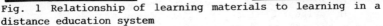

Fig. 1 Relationship of learning materials to learning in a distance education system

job is done: learning will occur. In distance education there is no basis for this unless a successful linking system is provided. Even then questions on the quantity of learning, the quality of the learning and the status of the learning remain for solution.

3   From the student's point of view there are important differences between the two systems of education. The distance system gives a radical new meaning to the concept of the independence of the adult learner. In this system he is responsible for initiating the learning process and, to a large extent, for maintaining it throughout. Questions of motivation and skill acquisition, of a specifically different kind to those required in traditional education, need to be tackled to combat the phenomena of non-starters and drop-outs that have been a feature of this type of education throughout the last one hundred years.

4   Management skills that are more akin to those found in industrialised enterprises are needed in distance education. The distance system has daily preoccupations with lead times, deadlines, print runs, job schedules, type-faces, warehousing, delivery and dispatch and planning decisions on educational priorities that must take place two, three or more years before teaching is to take place. Such pre-occupations are not normally characteristic of educational administrators.

5   Distance education is a form of education that can easily become depersonalised both for staff and students. Students are not invited to Milton Keynes nor to many of the distance education institutions throughout the world. There is little doubt that the absence of students can create a strained atmosphere for lecturers. The constant process of writing creatively for distance students, whether alone or in a course team framework, poses problems, which are not fully resolved even in those institutions where the lecturer has some responsibilities for on-campus students as well. The marking of distance students' work, even when relieved by face-to-face seminars, telephone tuition and work for radio or

14

television has a definite propensity for staff disillusionment.
Much has been written, from Marx to today, on alienation in the workforce. In an industrialised form of education where division of labour is necessary, where organisational planning and scheduling of a precise kind are essential and where educational decisions may be controlled by mechanised and automated processes the possibility of alienation among the workforce is real. It is even more real when the workforce is composed of academics whose qualifications and training have not prepared them for work in the most industrialised form of education.

Summary

From the examination of the four representative definitions of distance education in this section the following characteristics have been highlighted. All six are to be regarded as essential for any comprehensive definition:

- separation of teacher and student

- influence of an educational organisation especially in the planning and preparation of learning materials

- use of technical media

- provision of two-way communication

- possibility of occasional seminars

- participation in the most industrialised form of education.

The next stage is to show what forms distance education may take and why certain kinds of non-traditional education do not fall within its scope.

Forms of distance education

Distance education has been in existence for about one hundred years. The elements of a definition that have been established in the previous section do not therefore exist as abstractions; they must correspond to the reality. This section focuses on forms of education that are included within the concept of distance education; what is excluded is treated in the next.
    Three different approaches to identifying the forms of distance education are presented: the medium on which the learning materials are based, institutional type and didactic model.

Choice of medium

The different forms of distance education can be identified

15

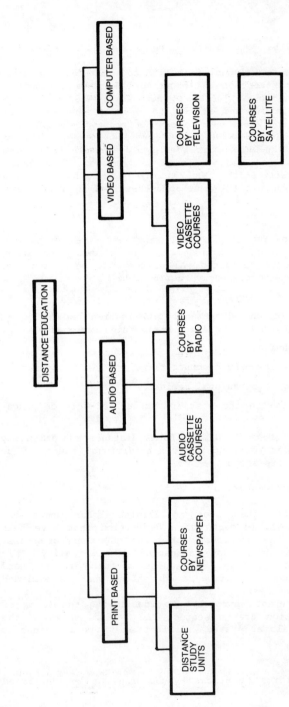

Fig. 2 Forms of distance education distinguished
by the medium which is the basis of the learning
materials.

by their

   - use of technical media

as the basis for the learning materials.

A possible presentation of the bases of the learning materials is given schematically on the previous page.

Print-based. By far the great majority of distance education programmes are print-based. The teaching basis of the Open University of the United Kingdom, for example, is approximately 80% print-based, 10% broadcasting (radio and television) and 10% face-to-face seminars and summer schools.

A real disservice has been done to the field of distance education by overemphasis on terms like 'University of the Air'. Educators, administrators and politicians, not only in developing countries but also in developed countries where finance for education is now being limited, should realise that the vast majority of distance education courses are print-based and will remain so.

Exceptions to this in the foreseeable future will come only with populations for whom literacy is a problem and perhaps in those regions where there is traditional reticence about correspondence-type programmes. Higher education in the United States of America is an area where an attempt to transfer emphasis to videotape-based or computer-based programmes might be worth considering because of the population's interest in technology and dislike of correspondence study.

An interesting variant on print-based programmes are the courses by newspaper developed under the leadership of Martin N. Chamberlain, Dean of University Extension at the University of California, San Diego. The Deutsches Institut für Fernstudien at Tübingen has recently introduced a similar programme in the Federal Republic of Germany.

Audio-based courses in which the educational content is carried by audio-cassettes or transmitted over radio and to which printed materials are peripheral, if used at all, have been used by distance educators. They are frequently cost-effective, can be used by people with literacy problems and may be a successful method of teaching languages. The University of Waterloo in Ontario is an extensive user of this method.

Video-based. Distance education can be video-based when the basic educational content of the course is broadcast on television or contained on video-cassettes. Some printed materials containing background, further reading and assessment procedures often are supplementary to the course. The development of cable television and the possibility of home ownership or rental of VCRs make this an area of interest in some cultures.

17

Series of programmes for television have already been developed by a number of groupings in America and elsewhere and a series of programmes based on video-cassettes is offered for credit by the independent study division of the University of Minnesota. Such programmes are to be regarded as distance education when they satisfy the characteristics outlined in the first section of this article.

A variant of both audio and video-based programmes is the educational use of satellites. Daniel (1978) presented an evaluation of the first attempts at satellite-based programmes to the 11th World Conference of the I.C.C.E. at New Delhi. Interest has also been aroused by the educational programmes of the Appalachian Area Satellite Project.

Computer-based. A computer can be the medium on which educational programmes that fall within the definition of distance education are based. A number of institutions have developed computer-based distance education programmes and the Fall 1978 Catalogue of courses published by the Control Data Education Company lists over 300 computer-based courses already developed for the PLATO system. They range from Accounting Fundamentals to Zeiss - a model Planetarium. It is known that in America negotiations are in progress for the accreditation of some of these computer-based programmes for college and university credit.

No evaluation of the relative merits of the media described nor of the possibility of developing a multi-media system by combinations of the various components is offered here. Nor can consideration be given to whether it is possible or desirable to combine distance education with on-campus education. That is the work of other studies.

Institutional type

When consideration is given to the

- influence of an educational organisation especially in the planning and preparation of learning materials

two major groupings of institutions can be distinguished: those that are privately sponsored and those that are publicly supported.

Private, proprietary correspondence schools have made valuable contributions to this field of education since the last century. In recent years standards have been set by affiliation to national accrediting bodies: the National Home Study Council of the U.S.A., the Association of Accredited Correspondence Colleges of the United Kingdom. Some of these institutions are non-profit making and a number receive some government support (Weinstock 1976:411) and they are found throughout the world.

Government sponsored schools, colleges and universities have played a role in distance education for the last seventy years. Many of these institutions are specially structured for distance education: Athabasca University, Edmonton; the Open College of Further Education, Adelaide; the Centre National de Télé-enseignement in France; the Fernuniversität-Gesamthochschule in Hagen. Many other colleges and universities have a department which concentrates on the distance students : the independent study department of the University of Minnesota, Minneapolis; the external studies department of the University of Queensland, Brisbane.

The Open University at Milton Keynes in the United Kingdom founded only ten years ago, has already made an impressive contribution to research, theory and practice in the field of distance education.

This wide range of institutional type, incorporating both public and private operations, makes the defining of the limits of the educational field within which all lie a difficult task. It is felt, nevertheless, that all institutions in this area because of the separation of their students from their teachers are engaged in the planning or purchase of learning materials and possess or have access to an integrated range of technical media, by which the student is given the possibility of two-way communication, not only when beginning but throughout the course. These institutions are representatives of the most industrialised form of education.

Didactic model

Three forms of didactic structure characterise distance education institutions, especially when considered under the headings:

- provision for two-way communication and

- possibility of occasional seminars.

Variations of the three models presented here are to be found employed by the different institutional types considered above in their effort to link learning materials to learning.

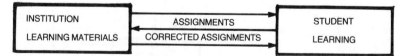

Fig. 3 A Correspondence school model of distance education

The correspondence schools send learning materials by post to the student, the student studies the materials and posts assignments back to the institution which marks and comments upon them and posts them back to the student.

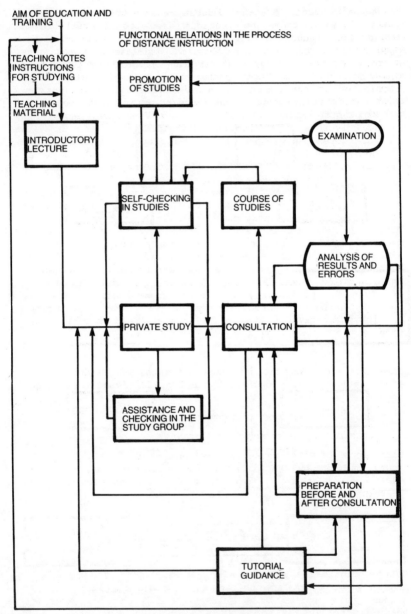

Fig. 4 A Central European model

Source: Möhle (ed) Hoch-und Fachschuffernstudium in der DDR und in Entwick-lungsländern Afrikas

The correspondence element in distance education is here reduced to a minimum and once the learning materials have been developed and distributed to the students, the emphasis is placed on compulsory fortnightly two-to-three hour consultations. At these, groups of students meet their tutor for evaluation of their home study and for explanation and preparation of the next stage of learning materials. In the third and fourth year of study the frequency of the consultations is greatly diminished.(Schwarz.,1978).

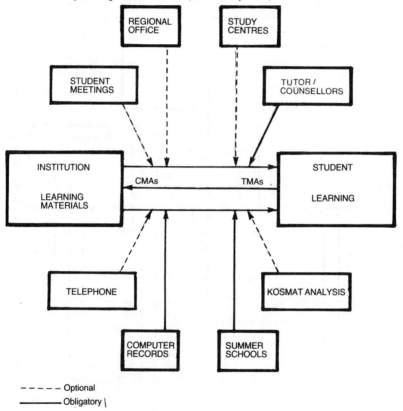

Fig. 5 **An Open University-type model**

In a system similar to that of the Open University of the United Kingdom the link between learning materials and learning is promoted by as coherent a structure as possible. The student is supported by a wide range of activities, most of them optional unless the course team has decided otherwise. This tends to strengthen the possibility that learning takes place and that unnecessary drop-outs are prevented.

Forms that are not distance education

From time to time (Perry, 1975) distance education is described as 'the opposite of face-to-face education'.

This statement needs to be taken further as there are
many forms of what may be considered the 'opposite of
face-to-face' education that are not distance education, as
the following diagram shows:

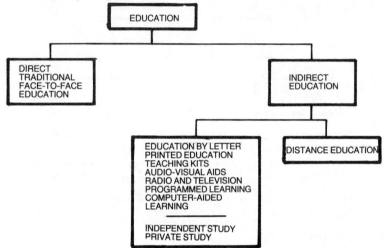

**Fig. 6 Relationship of distance education to other forms of
indirect education**

Indirect education

This distinction is again based on an idea of Peters (1973:-
101) and merits attention because of the importance in
definition of what is excluded. Each of the following forms
of indirect education lacks one or more of the characteristics of distance education that were outlined in Section 1.

Education by letter. From Plato and Paul to Erasmus letters have been used for instructional purposes and the
practice, doubtless, continues today. They lack the structuring of an educational institution that is a characteristic
of distance education.

Printed education. Pamphlets, books and teach-yourself
manuals fall into this category. The lack of an educational
organisation is again the major factor which distinguishes
these from distance education, together with the impossibil-
ity of two-way communication. It is clear that many people
learn a great deal from these means, even though they may
lack didactical structuring or even an educational goal.

Teaching kits. In increasing use in face-to-face teaching are kits of various kinds containing samples, games and

specimens on which students are invited to work without supervision.

Audio-visual aids. When a lecturer communicates with a student by means of audio-visual aids: slides, film, audio and video-tapes, he is teaching indirectly.

Depending on the structure of the programme within which they are being used, these forms of indirect teaching can form part either of face-to-face instruction or of a distance education programme.

Radio and television. Many people learn a great deal from radio and television and sometimes those media are used in distance education programmes. Kenneth Clarke's <u>Civilisat ion</u> or Jacob Bronowski's <u>The Ascent of Man</u> were not conceived as part of a distance education programme. Nevertheless they have become part of both on-campus and distance education programmes when offered for credit with accompanying didactically structured assignment, reading and assessment materials.

Programmed learning, which was popular in the 1960s, is a form of indirect teaching which has many similarities to distance education. Both demand extensive preparation of learning materials, careful sequencing and tend towards the individualising of learning.

Computer-aided learning is a recent form of indirect education and is used extensively in many conventional teaching programmes.

Mention is made here of independent study and private study as two forms of education with similarities to the above.

Independent study. There are many forms of independent study amongst which can be classed study guided by a governess, tutor or counsellor and many contract, independent or external degree programmes in American colleges.

Private study can be seen as neither a form of direct, classroom education nor of indirect off-campus studies. It is widespread and devoid of institutional linkages, though it may be based on materials developed for use within an institution either for traditional classroom students or distance learners.

Programmes with some similarities to distance education

There are certain forms of education which have some similarities to distance education but are not identical with it. Four of the most important are here presented for consideration: extension programmes, University Without Walls, experiential learning, the external degree. Three more general terms: 'non-traditional learning', 'off-campus studies' and 'open learning' are first considered briefly.

One cannot define 'non-traditional learning' without first defining 'traditional learning' and that is clearly beyond the bounds of this article. It seems at times that in the United States any educational programme that is not a four-year, residential, university degree programme can be regarded as non-traditional learning, though there are clearly more restricted usages. 'Non-traditional learning' is to be regarded as a vague, generalised term of which distance education is one example. 'Off-campus studies' is another general term for any programme which does not take place on the central university or college campus - distance education is one possibility.

Wedemeyer (1977a:2117) gives an accurate analysis of 'open learning':

> It is difficult to find a common definition for the many experimental programmes that call themselves *open* . However, all open schools have one principle in common: they are to a greater or lesser extent efforts to expand the freedoms of learners. Some are open only in a spatial sense . . . while others provide freedoms in more significant dimensions - in admissions, selection of courses, individual adaptation of the curriculum and time, goal selection and evaluation.

'Open learning' therefore, is a term that is not to be used in an administrative context; rather its context is philosophical to describe, for instance, colleges with 'open' administration policies or a special spirit like Paris VIII at Vincennes, *l'Université Ouverte* (Debeauvais,1976). Some of these are face-to-face institutions, others teach at a distance.

Extension programmes are ways of extending the expertise of a university or college to new populations. The term can imply offering the same programmes as for full-time, day-time students by different means, at different locations or at different times. An extra-mural department usually has a similar function of extending the expertise of the university to a broader community. Some of these programmes are for credit, others not.

The range of extension and extra-mural programmes is very extensive and distance education can be regarded as one grouping of a number of possibilities of providing education outside the normal lecture room. Extension, especially as used in the United States, is a much broader term which can include part-time, day or night, conventional lectures on campus.

University Without Walls implies the design of an individualised programme based on a learning contract for students with clear learning objectives who cannot realise their whole educational aspirations through existing programmes. A University Without Walls programme can include experiential learning credits, ordinary lectures, distance education elements, learning from community sources or job-related activities, all of which can be evaluated towards a college or university degree.

Experiential learning programmes are those which give credit for prior learning which did not take place in a lecture room setting and was not sponsored by an educational institution, but was acquired through work experience including volunteer work, co-operative education or self-study.

The external degree was defined in 1978 by the U.S. Department of Health, Education and Welfare:

> A degree programme which can be completed in the following manner: a student entering the programme with the minimum entrance qualifications can complete it with less than 25 percent of the required work taking the form of campus-based classroom instruction.

(Sosdian and Sharp, 1977:1)

In the attempt to place some conceptual order around the wide range of study programmes that are associated with non-traditional and distance education, the question of whether or not the external degree should be included within the concept of distance education is the one which poses the most precise definitional and research problems. (Houle 1974; Sosdian, 1978; Sosdian and Sharp, 1978).

In so far as the external degree serves to describe the programmes whose primary function is to recognise education and attribute to it an appropriate qualification, it does not fall within the concept of distance education as it has been presented in this study. If, on the other hand, it is used to describe programmes whose function is to provide education for students, then it may be identified with distance education providing it agrees with the descriptors given in the first section of this article.

One hundred and eighty-three college and university degree programmes are classified as external in the American study referred to above. The Ed.D. programme from Nova University, Fort Lauderdale, Florida which has been at the centre of the controversy about the external degree in the United States in recent years is not mentioned. (Ashworth, 1978, Cowden and Jacobs, 1979).

The Nova doctoral programme consists of class meetings known as clusters which meet for eight hours once per month; reading requirements; written assignments and a major applied research paper.

Do the Nova Ed.D. and similar external degrees lie within the field of distance education as described? When attempting to formulate an answer one is faced with the fact that any doctoral programme contains large elements of private research and little face-to-face tuition.

Clearly the dividing line between the Nova cluster system and the consultation system of the German Democratic Republic is a thin one. This study tends to exclude the former because of its lack of emphasis on the pedagogical structuring of learning materials by the educational institution and because it is a less industrialised and technological form of education and tends to include the latter.

Terminology

The term 'distance education' has been used in this article.

It is meant to designate the cluster of educational organisations which are usually referred to as *Fernstudium* in German, *télé-enseignement* in French, *educación a distancia* in Spanish and *teleducacão* in Portuguese but for which a number of different terms are used in the English-speaking world.

Other languages

In German there is an awkward status question of whether *Fernstudium* 'distance study' refers only to higher education at a distance (universities and university-oriented colleges) and *Fernunterricht* 'distance teaching' refers to further education at a distance (technical and vocationally-oriented institutions). There seems to be some indication that *Fernstudium* will become the established term for all levels in the Federal Republic of Germany, as it is in the German Democratic Republic.

Télé-enseignement 'distance teaching' is an influential term in French because of its use in the titles of the Centre National de Télé-enseignement, (C.N.T.E.), the Centres de Télé-enseignement Universitaire (C.T.U.) and the Télé-université de Québec. It should be noticed however, that the law of 12 July 1971 uses the term *enseignement à distance* 'teaching at a distance'. There are some who would argue that *formation à distance* 'education at a distance' reflects more closely modern pedagogical theories.

The problem with *télé-enseignement* is that many do not realise that the root of *'télé'* is the Greek word *têle* 'from afar', 'from a distance' and does not refer to television. *Télé-enseignement* appears to be the generally accepted term.

The words *educatión a distancia* in Spanish and *teleduc-acão* in Portuguese seem to be gaining acceptance as terms for 'distance education', side by side with the spread of influence of this type of education in Spanish and Portuguese speaking countries.

English terminology

In English there are at least six major terms: correspondence study/education, home study, independent study, external studies, distance teaching, distance education.

Two propositions underlie what follows:

- neologisms are unnecessary in an area where there is

26

already a multiplicity of terms

- 'distance education', although not perfect, is the most suitable term and should be used.

Correspondence study is not a suitable word for what has been described as 'distance education' in this article. It cannot describe radio-based programmes like *Ensemble*, tele-vision-based programmes like *The Great Plains*, computer-based programmes in the PLATO series nor the Appalachian Satellite programme.

Communications theory experts tell us that words get tired and if they do then 'correspondence study' is a tired word. It is significant that when the directors of the correspondence schools of the United States of America came together in 1926 to form an association the title chosen the National Home Study Council and not the National Corres-pondence Study Council. Charles A. Wedemeyer (1976b) was chairman of a committee of the International Council for Correspondence Education (I.C.C.E.) to consider a change of name as many felt its present title was inappropriate if the organisation wished to remain a major influence in the field.

'Correspondence study' is a correct designation of that subgroup of the print-based areas of distance education in which student contact is not encouraged. It should continue to be used for such programmes and only for such programmes.

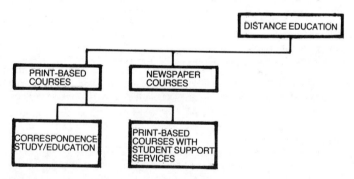

Fig. 7 Relationship of correspondence study/education to distance education

'Correspondence study/education' institutions have frequently a philosophy which suggests that students enrol with them because they 'want to be left alone', that student support services can infringe learner autonomy or the independence of the adult learner. They claim that student seminars do not add to student learning from a correspondence study system.

Home study is used mainly in the United States of America and is there confined to further and technical education. The 1979 listing of approved members of the National Home Study Council contain 94 institutions, most of them proprietary.

When the universities of the United States of America which teach at a distance wanted to form an association it is significant that they rejected the title 'Home Study' and chose instead 'Independent Study'.

'Home study' is thus unsuitable as a generic term for the wide range of teaching-learning activities which have been described.

Independent study is the term used in higher education in the U.S.A. The 1979 Guide to independent study through correspondence instruction lists 68 members of the Independent Study Division of the National University Extension Association. Nearly all of these are correspondence sections of extension departments of American universities. In addition to programmes for degree credit, many of the courses are at high school or certificate level. (Childs and Wedemeyer, 1961).

Charles A. Wedemeyer has been the proponent of the term 'independent study' both in his writings and during a lecture tour of Australia which he undertook in 1977:

> Independent study in the American context is a generic for a range of teaching-learning activities that sometimes go by separate names (correspondence study, open education, radio-television teaching, individualised learning). In several European countries such systems are clustered under the term *distance education* or are still perceived as separate programmes without any basic, generic relationship. (1977a:2115)

He feels that the term 'independent study' has the capacity to encompass a wide range of activities and defines it as:

> Independent study consists of various forms of teaching-learning arrangements in which teachers and learners carry out their essential tasks and responsibilities apart from one another, communicating in a variety of ways, for the purpose of freeing internal learners from inappropriate class placings or patterns or providing external learners opportunity to continue learning in their own environments, and developing in all learners the capacity to carry on self-directed learning, the ultimate maturity required of the educated person. (1977a:2114)

There are elements of a philosophy of educational maturity in this statement to which most distance educators would subscribe. The term 'independent study', nevertheless, is to be rejected as a generic term.

There are three reasons for this:

- the normal understanding of 'independent study' implies a different relationship to an educational institution (see section two)

- the ideal in distance education is not necessarily independence but, as John S. Daniel wrote, 'interaction and independence: getting the mixture right'

- in the United States of America an 'independent student' is one who sets up an individual study programme on a contract basis during an interview with a faculty member. The contract may include periods of normal lectures, unguided study or distance programmes.

External studies is the term most widely used in Australia. Its use is confined to that region where it well describes the essence of the 'integrated model' of distance education as found in many Australian institutions: 'external to' but not 'separated from' the faculty staff. It can have little claim to general acceptance because of this limitation and because of confusion with the American external degree. Whether or not the American external degree, especially those associated with Antioch and Nova universities, falls within the concept of distance education has already been discussed.

Distance teaching or *Teaching at a distance* has been the term most commonly used by the Open University in the United Kingdom. Distance teaching is only half the process we are trying to describe: to distance teaching must be added distance learning. A suitable term for both together is 'distance education'.

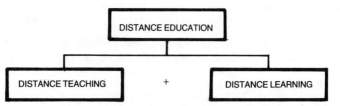

Fig. 8 Relationship of distance teaching to distance education

Conclusion

Wedemeyer's (1977:2121) study already referred to concludes:

> In Europe the term *distance education* has a usage somewhat comparable to that of *independent study* in the United States. It is increasingly used in Europe as an omnibus term to include correspondence study, open learning, instruction by radio and television - in short, all learning-teaching arrangements that are not face-to-face.

The time has come to extend the use of the term 'distance education' (Rawson-Jones, 1974) beyond Europe. It has already gained wide acceptance in Canada and Australia. In the United States of America 'home study' should be regarded as the further education section of distance education and 'independent study' as the higher education section.

Distance education is not, however, synonymous with 'all learning-teaching arrangements that are not face-to-face' (Wedemeyer) nor to be defined as 'the opposite of face-to-face education' (Perry).

The main elements of a definition of distance education are:

- the separation of teacher and learner which distinguishes it from face-to-face lecturing

- the influence of an educational organisation which distinguishes it from private study

- the use of technical media, usually print, to unite teacher and learner and carry the educational content

- the provision of two-way communication so that the student may benefit from or even initiate dialogue

- the possibility of occasional meetings for both didactic and socialisation purposes

- the participation in an industrialised form of education which, if accepted, contains the genus of radical separation of distance education from other forms.

This article has tried to delineate the field of distance education, to show what is included within the field and what is not; it has tried to suggest some unanimity about terminology.

It is not my purpose to propose yet another new definition nor any new terminology. Provided the delineators that have been identified are kept constantly in mind I am willing to accept Börje Holmberg's definition as printed at the head of this article. It is the one which pays most attention to the needs of the learner.

I feel that cumbersome neologisms should be barred from discussions among distance educators for whom, above all, clarity of expression should be of prime concern. 'Andragogical' and 'telemathics' (Delling, 1976) are two dubious terms that have appeared in the literature in recent years.

The introduction of 'andragogy' into educational discussions was unnecessary and its use by distance educators is even more so. What M.S. Knowles meant by andragogy had been good pedagogy for years. Whatever the Greek root of 'pedagogy' may have been, the word in English is a generic term for teaching at all levels. In the decade since 'telemathics' was coined it has not found general acceptance and should now be abandoned.

In conclusion I refer readers back to Peters' definition and the profound implications it has for all workers in this field. It identified distance education as a different form of education - a possibility unpalatable to many. It suggests that the 'education' of distance educators lies in packages on the shelves of warehouses until consumer demand causes it to be dispatched. It suggests too a danger of alienation in the workplace that it is not a characteristic of other forms of education and which administrators of distance systems would do well to keep in mind.

References

Ashworth, K.H. (1978) The nontraditional doctorate: time for sine cera? Phi Delta Kappan, November, 173-175

Bääth, J. and Flinck, R. (1973) Two-way communication in correspondence education. Sweden: University of Lund

Bääth, J. (1978) Research and development work in correspondence education. ICCE Newsletter, 4,9-15

Childs, G.B. and Wedemeyer, C.A. (1961) New perspectives in university correspondence study. Chicago: Centre for the Study of Liberal Education for Adults

Control Data Education Company. (1978) Fall 1978 catalog: PLATO courses. U.S.A.: Control Data Corporation

Cowden, P. and Jacobs, F. (1979) The external degree and the traditions of diversity and competition. Phi Delta Kappan, April, 559-561

Daniel, J.S. (1978) Satellites in distance education: Canadian experiments on the Hermes satellite. In Wentworth, R.B. (ed). 11th ICCE Conference papers I. London: Tuition House

Daniel, J.S. and Smith, W.A.S. Opening Open Universities: the Canadian experience. Athabasca University, mimeograph

Daniel, J.S. and Marquis, C. (1979) Interaction and independence: getting the mixture right. Teaching at a Distance, 15,29-44

Debeauvais, M. (1976) L'Université ouverte; les dossiers de Vincennes. Grenoble: Presses Universitaires

Delling, R.M. (1976) Telematic teaching? Distant study! ICCE Newsletter, 6,2, 19-20

Flinck, R. (1975) The telephone as an instructional aid in distance education. A survey of the literature. Pedagogical Reports, No. 1, University of Lund

Flinck, R. (1978) Correspondence education combined with systematic telephone tutoring. Malmö: Hermods

Foks, J. (1979) Report on ICCE conference, ASPESA Newsletter 5,2,35.

Holmberg, B. (1974) Distance education - a short handbook. Malmö: Hermods

Holmberg, B. (1977) Distance education: a survey and bibliography. London: Kogan Page

Holmberg B. (1979) Fernstudiendidaktik als Wissensscaftliches Fach. Hagen:Fernuniversität

Hopper, M. (1979) External studies. In Harman, G. (ed.) Tertiary education in the aftermath of expansion, Canberra: A.N.U.

Houle, C.O. (1974) The external degree. San Francisco: Jossey-Bass

Mackenzie, O., Christensen, E.L. and Rigby, P.H. (1968) Correspondence instruction in the United States, N.Y., McGraw-Hill

Möhle, H. (1978) Das in das einheitliche sozialistische Bildungswesen der DDR integrierte Hochschulfernstudium, seine Grundkonzeption und seine Ergebnisse. In Möhle, H. (ed.) Hoch-und Fachschulfernstudium in der DDR und in Entwicklungsländern Afrikas. Leipzig: Karl-Marx-Universität

Moore, M.G. (1973) Toward a theory of independent learning and teaching. Journal of Higher Education, 44, 661-679

Moore, M.G. (1975) Cognitive style and telemathic (distance) teaching. ICCE Newsletter, 4, 3-10

Moore, M.G. (1977) On a theory of independent study. Hagen: Fernuniversität

National Home Study Council (1978) Directory of accredited home study schools 1978-1979. Washington: NHSC

National University Extension Association (1977) Guide to independent study through correspondence instruction 1977-1979. Washington: NUEA.

Nova University (1972) Ed. D. How to earn your doctorate without giving up living. Fort Lauderdale: Nova University

Perry, W. (1975) Lessons for distance education derived from the experience of the Open University. In Granholm, G.W. (ed.) The System of Distance Education 2. Malmö: Hermods

Perry, W. (1976) The Open University. Milton Keynes: Open University

Peters, O. (1965) Der Fernunterricht. Weinheim: Beltz

Peters, O. (1971) Theoretical aspects of correspondence instruction. In Mackenzie, O. and Christensen E.L. (Eds.) The changing world of correspondence study. University Park and London: Pennsylvania State

Peters, O. (1973) Die didaktische Strukur des Fernunterrichts. Untersuchungen zu einer industrialisierten Form des Lehrens and Lernens. Weinheim: Beltz

Peters, R.S. (1972) Education as initiation. In Archambault, R.D. (ed.) Philosophical analysis and education (2nd ed.) London: Routledge and Kegan Paul

Schwarz, R. (1978) Die Konsultation in Studien prozess des Fernstudiums. In Möhle, H. (ed.) Hoch-und Fachschulfernstudium in der DDR und in Entwicklungsländern Afrikas. Leipzig: Karl-Marx-Universität

Sims, R.S. (unpublished) The correspondence educating processes. ICCE/UNESCO research project. Unedited draft

Smith, K.C. (1978) Integrated teaching in Australia. Open Line, 16, 4-6

Sosdian, C.P. and Sharp, L.M. (1977) Guide to undergraduate external degree programmes in the U.S. - Spring 1977. Washington: National Institute of Education

Sosdian, C.P. (1978) External degrees: programme and student character-istics. Washington: National Institute of Education

Sosdian, C.P. and Sharp, L.M. (1978) The external degree as a credential: graduates' experience in employment and further study. Washington: National Institute of Education

University of Minnesota (1978) Extension independent study 1978-79.

Minneapolis: University of Minesota

Wedemeyer, C.A. (1977a) Independent study. In Knowles, A.S. (ed.) The international encyclopaedia of higher education. Boston: CIHED

Wedemeyer, C.A. (1977b) Progress-response report of the ICCE 'name' committee. ICCE Newsletter, 2, 4-14

Weinstock, N. (1976) Les Cours par Correspondance du Secteur Privé en Belgique. Brussels: Centre National de Sociologie du Droit Social

A THEORY FOR DISTANCE EDUCATION

Hilary Perraton

Distance education has managed very well without any theory. It has been used to bring education, through print, radio or television, to thousands and thousands who would never get to school or college. And, as practitioners, at the British National Extension College and at the International Extension College, we have shunned theory, arguing that we were interested only in practice. Partly that is policy - though one man's policy is another's prejudice - and a desire to keep out in the wide open spaces of educational innovation rather than creep into the house of theory, seen as an annex to the ivory tower of academe. Partly it is a reflection of our intellectual tradition: 'The British were never ones for theory in any case. We have always been empiricist, anti-metaphysical in philosophy, mistrustful of theoretical systems.'[1] And partly it is a suspicion of two kinds of theory - of those which try to simplify education to a theory as grand as $E = MC^2$ and those who try to restrict it to a theory which 'is neutral with regard to ends but exhaustive with regard to means'.[2]

But questions about the theory of distance teaching will not go away. If we define distance teaching as 'an educational process in which a significant proportion of the teaching is conducted by someone removed in space and/or time from the learner',[3] legitimate, general and therefore in one sense theoretical questions arise about the circumstances in which it is relevant. These questions are important if distance teaching is to be taken seriously as a set of educational techniques. They can be answered by references to theories of education and of communication.

It follows, then, that if we are to build a house of theory for distance education, its architecture will depend on existing philosophies of education, and theories of communication or diffusion; it will not be constructed from brand-new components. Within such limits it is possible to state a theory. For the sake of formality and to stimulate disproof, it is stated in the form of fourteen statements or hypotheses.

The statements depend upon political as well as philosophical views about education. In <u>Distance Teaching for the Third World</u>[4] we quoted Nyerere:

Man can only liberate himself or develop himself. He cannot be liberated or developed by another. For Man makes himself. It is his ability to act deliberately for a self-determined purpose which distinguishes him from the other animals. The expansion of his own consciousness, and therefore of his power over himself, his environment, and his society, must therefore ultimately be what we mean by development.

So development is for Man, by Man, and of Man. The same is true of education. Its purpose is the liberation of man from the restraints and limitation of ignorance and dependency. Education has to increase men's physical and mental freedom - to increase their control over themselves, their own lives, and the environment in which they live.

The ideas imparted by education, or released in the mind through education, should therefore be liberating ideas; the skills acquired by education should be liberating skills. Nothing else can properly be called education.

We went on to argue:

In other words, education is to do with power. People without education are at the mercy of those with it, who can use what they know to their advantage and to the disadvantage of the ignorant around them. Education is a means of gaining power, and not simply the right of the better-educated minority. On this showing the case for expanding education is a simple egalitarian one.

My starting point is, therefore, expansion - the need to expand education.

But the way in which education is expanded is also important. Expansion of schooling is of limited value if it simply reinforces the ideas that learning is a valuable possession, held by the teacher or shut within the covers of a textbook, that can be acquired provided the student listens or reads diligently and respectfully.[5] Instead, with many educators, we would stress the importance of dialogue. There are, however, both weak and strong forms of the argument for making it central to a theory of education. The weak form of the argument points out that expression helps learning and that dialogue, giving an impression of human warmth and interest, encourages it. Learning is more effective if, through dialogue between student and teacher, the student can be shown how the new matter he is learning relates to what he already knows, and relates to his environment. And dialogue has an important checking function: it enables the tutor to check the student's progress, the tutor to check her method of presentation by seeing whether the student understands her, and the student to check the tutor, in case the tutor has actually got things wrong. The strong form of the argument goes much further and claims that, unless there is dialogue, education changes to indoctrination: dialogue is here seen as a necessary condition of an education which respects the humanity of student and teacher. This view is reinforced in much out-of-school education, where it is clear that the student's knowledge of the world in which he has grown up merits respect and attention along with the tutor's knowledge of her own specialism.

If those, then, are our aims - of expanding education and of stressing the importance of dialogue - then a theory of distance teaching should illuminate the ways in which it does, or does not, lead towards them.

The ways in which distance teaching is used are, of course, politically and culturally determined. If, for example, society rewards credentials and the diploma disease is rife, then it is extremely difficult for a distance-teaching institution to set off in a different direction. In Mexico, for example, *Telesecundaria*, which uses television and print to support secondary education, is successful in getting children through their examinations - but by doing so may be merely contributing to urban drift and problems of unemployment in the towns. [6] Distance-teaching institutions inevitably reflect the values of their societies. The experience of *Telesecundaria*, or of the Free University of pre-revolutionary Iran, which was seen as a device to prevent students coming together, can be contrasted with the radio campaigns of the United Republic of Tanzania, which reflect something of the political philosophy of TANU in their attempt at mass involvement. [7] The success or failure of a distance-teaching project will, therefore, depend at least as much on its political context as on its methods. Our arguments about method inevitably rest on political assumptions.

Expanding education

Experience enables us to make five hypotheses, our first five 'statements', about the way in which distance teaching can be used to maximize education. Chu and Schramm exhaustively analysed the literature on the comparative methods of different media, seeking differences between print, radio, film, television, classroom teacher and so on. Most of the research suggests that there are no significant differences between them in their educational effectiveness. [8] Trenaman similarly found in comparing radio, print and television that 'the three media communicate a wide variety of material with roughly equivalent efficiency.' While differences between students or audiences, and differences between subjects, have a major effect on how easily something is learned, differences between the media seem to be far less important.[9] Making the point very broadly, then, Statement 1 is: *you can use any medium to teach anything.* Much flows from this hypothesis; it has consequences for our methodology, considered below, and for our desire to expand education. For, if we can use a variety of media secure in the knowledge that they are comparable in their effectiveness, then we can examine how to use audio-visual media like radio and television, which enable us to reach audiences who could not get to school or college. And we can go on from considering the qualities of individual media to decisions about using a variety of media, and decisions about combining print or broadcasts with some face-to-face study.

It follows from Statement 1 that the face-to-face teacher is not unique in his/her ability to teach (though he/she may have unique qualities which we return to at Statement 7 below). And so we can depose teacher with Statement 2: *distance teaching can break the integuments of fixed staffing ratios which limited the expansion of education when teacher and student had to be in the same place at the same time.*

Traditionally the expansion of education has demanded an expansion in the number of teachers; if that constraint is removed by distance teaching then the prospects for expanding education may be enhanced, provided that distance teaching is no more expensive than teaching through orthodox methods. The prospect would, on the other hand, be no brighter if distance teaching were necessarily more expensive than orthodox education. Economic forces would then press any reasonable person into expanding ordinary schools and colleges. But distance teaching can be cheaper. With broadcasts, as with print, one teacher's words can reach a much larger audience than would ever be possible face-to-face so that economies of scale are possible. There is empirical evidence of such economies being attained. Jamison and Orivel, for example, considered twelve distance-teaching projects for which cost data are available and found that 'most of the projects studied here are less expensive than equivalent traditional methods of education.'[10] We can then make Statement 3: *there are circumstances under which distance teaching can be cheaper than orthodox education, whether measured in terms of audience reached or of learning.*

It is not always cheaper. At primary level, most teachers are paid so little that it is difficult to find any cheaper way of educating small children. At the other extreme, tertiary education is often so expensive that it is much easier to come up with a cheaper, distance, alternative. At any level it is fairly easy for distance teaching to work out as an expensive alternative if only a handful of students follow any one course or (if we are concerned with the number of students who successfully complete a course and not just with the number of enrolments) if the drop-out rate

37

is high. And at any level costs per student are sensitive to the choice of medium. This can vary widely, so that one could conceive of the costs, for the same programme, of print, radio and television being in the ratio of 1 : 10 : 100.[11] Statement 4: *the economies achievable by distance education are a function of the level of education, size of audience, choice of media and sophistication of production*

If these hypotheses are true then we have established that distance teaching can be effective and that its costs can compare favourably with those of orthodox education. Universal post, and radio with its seven-league boots, thus make it possible to increase access to education, while the social constraints on the use of telecommunications are at least slightly different from those on the use of schools. The relevance of distance teaching to the expansion of education is clear, and our key Statement 5 is: *distance teaching can reach audiences who would not be reached by orthodox means.*

Dialogue

So distance teaching may help us towards our first objective. What of the second, to encourage dialogue? We are faced with a dilemma here. If teaching through broadcasts and print is linked with face-to-face study then dialogue is, of course, possible within that face-to-face element. It is far easier to envisage dialogue, if we use the term to mean our strong form or in the sense that Freire uses it, in face-to-face discussion, than through print or broadcasts. As educators, therefore, we are constantly under pressure to increase the face-to-face component of distance teaching. But, as we saw, the economic attractiveness of distance teaching springs from the economies of scale which it makes possible; we are equally under pressure to limit the size of the face-to-face component. A central problem, therefore, concerns the balance between economic arguments, of crucial importance to us if we wish to widen access to education, and educational arguments, of equal importance if we want to emphasize dialogue. The way that dilemma is resolved, between quantity and quality, will vary from time to time and place to place; we return to it below (page 41) when considering the methods of distance teaching.

In struggling with the dilemma, it is worth remembering that much orthodox education is not based on dialogue. Children are taught to learn things by heart; much agricultural extension assumes that the farmer should simply do what the extension agent tells him. In practice we cannot learn everything, in school or out, by discovery and dialogue. The tough challenge for distance teaching, then, is to provide not merely as good opportunities for dialogue as orthodox education, but more such opportunities. Distance teaching has long been criticized for encouraging rote learning. Of its nature, correspondence education demands a respect for the printed word which is at odds with the sort of scepticism implicit in our view of education. Even a distance-teaching institution as sophisticated and generously endowed with arrangements for dialogue as the British Open University has not always overcome the problem:

In far too many of the Arts assignments questions are set which it is virtually impossible for students to answer except by regurgitating the unit material . . . Recently a mature student, just completing her Honours degree, wrote to me criticising a third level history course. 'When I learnt history at school', she said, 'and even when I've done the history blocks . . . I've been given facts, and a sequence of events to learn. Now I'm given a series of hypotheses about which no-one seems to agree.'[12]

But many correspondence-based courses, at the Open University and elsewhere, do encourage dialogue of one kind or another. The radio campaigns of the United Republic of Tanzania and Botswana set up dialogue between village learning-group members and both educators and government; Radio Éducative Sénégal has used feedback from radio groups to change government policy. [13] Students in National Extension College correspondence courses confirm that dialogue, on paper and face-to-face, forms a central part of their experience, even though they learn mainly at a distance. Despite the inherent problems, therefore, of arranging dialogue when learning is based on materials produced in advance and distributed en masse, there is empirical evidence for our key Statement 6: *it is possible to organise distance teaching in such a way that there is dialogue.*

That dialogue may be on paper, or may be through occasional face-to-face sessions between tutor and student, or may be organized through group discussion of one kind or another. But its existence suggests a change in the function of the teacher, something foreshadowed in Statement 2 about staffing ratios; the function of a teacher working in distance education is different from that of a classroom teacher. If the distance teacher is writing lessons; or making broadcast programmes, her function can be quite easily compared with that of a teacher standing before a class. But even here there are important differences: the kind of explanation which is appropriate to a class often needs to be transformed in one way or another if it is to be recorded. In just the same way as, to turn a play into a film, you need to do more than put a cine camera in the auditorium, so the teacher producing educational material needs to do something different from recording just what she says or does before a class. Once that job of recording the factual information which is to be used by students has been done, then the role of a teacher in a face-to-face session

39

for distance students becomes markedly different from that of an ordinary teacher. She is no longer the means of passing on information; rather she is there to help students learn information brought to them from outside. That Copernican revolution is one that many teachers in regular schools already welcome. And so Statement 7 is: *where a tutor meets distance students face-to-face, her role is changed from being a communicator of information to that of a facilitator of learning.*

Dialogue between a student and tutor is only one kind of dialogue. There is extensive evidence that, where distance teaching materials are available, students can help each other to solve problems which in an ordinary class they would put to their teacher. This is the normal method of working for distant students in farm forums or radio schools; more surprisingly, perhaps, children learning from television in Niger found that they could and would solve each other's learning problems when there was no adult present.[14] In formal education, then, there is a place for class work or group work, along with distance study. Group work looks even more important in adult education. A whole range of group-learning projects, from the radiophonic schools of Latin America to the farm forums of Africa and India, confirm that group learning can be effective, and can lead to group activity. The finding is buttressed by communication theory: the two-step and multi-step theories of human communication suggest that we are more likely to adopt an innovation if we discuss it with friends or colleagues than if we simply learn about it individually and passively.[15] The combination of local interest and knowledge, possessed by a group of people meeting together, and information from scholars recorded in print or on tape, is a potent one, and we can therefore make Statement 8: *group discussion is an effective method of learning when distance teaching is used to bring relevant information to the group.*

Distance teaching, then, can be effective and can stimulate dialogue. Linked with group study, it can extend education far beyond the confines of schools or colleges and can be related to community needs and interests. It can do all these things cheaply. But it will not do so cheaply if we have to provide anew the schools, the libraries or the network of teachers or extension agents which orthodox education and extension requires. We need to use what is already there. And experience of many projects suggests that, in many communities, there are resources which are under-used. Tévec, a distance teaching project in a poor area of Quebec, for example, had as an explicit aim to enable its students to make use of its resources in the community, nominally available to them, which they lacked the knowledge or confidence to take advantage of.[16] Obviously the resources available will vary immensely from place to place, from time to time, and in their relevance to any particular educational programme. But we can make a general Statement 9: *in most communities there are resources which can be used to support distance learning, to its educational and economic advantage.*

Methods

We started with 'method' in order to establish that distance teaching could face the major educational problems of access and of dialogue. But considerations of 'method' lead in another direction, too, into decisions about the best way of organizing distance teaching. If Statement 1 is accepted, and a range of media are available to us, then there is no easy way of deciding which medium to use, in what way, for which purpose. But there is evidence to believe that several media are better than one. This may simply mean that to use more than one medium makes learning more fun, and therefore, perhaps, more effective, or that it enables information presented in one medium to reinforce that in another, or that individuals learn more easily from one rather than another. There is evidence that, in the United Kingdom, if we measure the proportion of people following a course, a multi-media approach is superior to one that relies on a single medium.[17] Statement 10 follows: *a multi-media programme is likely to be more effective than one which relies on a single medium.*

This does not solve our problems of choice. Distance teaching remains, for many educators and scholars, an uncharted area. We have very few years' experience of combining print, broadcasts and face-to-face learning in contrast with the centuries of experience of orthodox teachers, working with schools and books. We cannot - for better or worse - teach just as we were taught if we are to teach in a new medium; we need to plan to do something different. Experience so far suggests Statement 11: *a systems approach is helpful in planning distance education.*

The problems of students at a distance drive us on to three further statements.

We have already stressed the importance of dialogue to the student. But the benefits to the tutor are also important, and the problems for the tutor separated from her students are different from those of classroom teachers. Unless the tutor has some means of knowing how her students are working, she has no means of helping them and she cannot discover how successful are the materials she has created. Statement 12 therefore states: *feedback is a necessary part of a distance-learning system.*

Feedback can be of various kinds: the term embraces both feedback to the student, showing where he has understood or misunderstood, and feedback to the tutor or course writer. Some of the feedback to the student is immediate - if answers to questions in a correspondence course are printed at the back of the book, for example. But some is necessarily delayed and the distant student faces particular problems in learning by himself. It is peculiarly easy not to learn when studying by correspondence, or by following broadcasts. One can concentrate on the material, feeling that one is working hard, but remembering little of what one epxeriences. Even with generous opportunities for face-to-face learning, most distance study involves individuals working their way through material, and we cannot assume that tutorials will ensure learning. To help the student learn, the materials he is to use must be designed so that he does more than read or listen to them or watch them. Statement 13: *to be effective, distance-teaching materials should ensure that students undertake frequent and regular activities over and above reading, watching or listening.*

Feedback and active learning, then, are necessary for effective distance education, but a concentration on them does not answer the opening question about which medium to use for which purpose. If we group the media roughly into three - print, broadcasts (including recordings) and face-to-face meetings of any kind - then face-to-face communication has two qualities which differentiate it from the others. It makes possible immediate feedback between student and tutor, or dialogue between student and student, and its costs rise proportionately with the number of students, whereas economies of scale are possible with both print and broadcasts. (Even if students are meeting each other in informal groups, there are costs associated with the establishment and support of such groups.) It is this which, as we saw above (page 38), leads to central problems for us in reconciling the demands of education and economy. And it therefore suggests a paradoxical criterion for choice - to concentrate on the non-distant elements in order to design good distance teaching, and make wise use of all elements in multi-media education. Statement 14 therefore claims: *in choosing between media, the key decision on which the rest depend concerns the use of face-to-face learning.*[18]

Another approach

We can look at all this another way, and state the argument more succinctly or set it out diagramatically, as in the figure. Educational media are similar in their effectiveness, but differ in the ways they can readily be distributed (box A). This makes it possible to move away from the fixed staffing ratios necessary to face-to-face study (box B), thereby changing the role of the teacher (box C) and making possible a reduction in costs (box D). It is then possible to reach audiences different from the traditional ones, through distance teaching, and to do so at a reasonable cost (box E). The equivalence of the media, however, presents us with problems of choice (box F), best resolved by a multi-

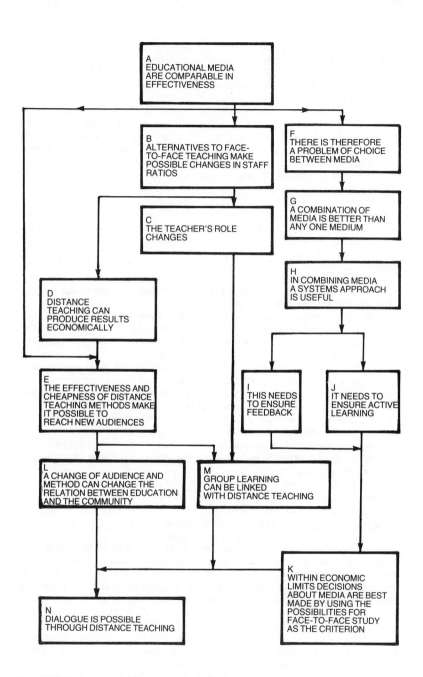

Key elements in a theory for distance education

media approach (boxes G and H) which allows for feedback (box I) and encourages active learning (box J). In working out the approach to be used, the organization of any face-to-face element is of key importance (box K) and leads us to consider how to use distance teaching to ensure dialogue (box N) - something which is facilitated if a concern with new audiences and a new relation between education and the community (box L) lead to the use of groups as a basis for adult learning (box M).

What is the use of it? And what is to be done? Is the construction of this sort of theory of any use? I'd suggest two tests for it. First, does it help anyone to see where and how distance teaching might be useful, or useless, for a particular educational job? Second, does the formulation of fourteen hypotheses suggest ways of testing them which would yield useful knowledge for practical educators?

Notes

1 Iris Murdoch 'A House of Theory', in N. MacKenzie (ed.), Conviction, p.220, London, MacGibbon & Kee, 1958.

2 J. S. Bruner. Toward a Theory of Instruction, Cambridge, Mass., Harvard University Press, 1966.

3 H. Perraton (ed.) Alternative Routes to Formal Education, Washington/Baltimore, World Bank/Johns Hopkins Press, 1980.

4 M. Young, H. Perraton, J. Jenkins and T. Dodds, Distance Teaching for the Third World, pp. 1-2, London, Routledge.

5 R. Dore, The Diploma Disease, London, Allen & Unwin, 1976, describes how education has moved from learning to credentialism.

6 Young et al., op. cit., p. 57.

7 See, for example, B. L. Hall and T. Dodds, Voices for Development, Cambridge, International Extension College, 1974.

8 G. Chu and W. Schramm, Learning from Television: What the Research Says, Stanford, ERIC, 1968.

9 J. M. Trenaman, Communication and Comprehension, p. 43, London, Longmans, 1967.

10 D. T. Jamison and F. Orivel, 'The Cost Effectiveness of Distance Teaching for School Equivalency', in H. Perraton (ed.), Alternative Routes to Formal Education, Washington/Baltimore, World Bank/Johns Hopkins Press.

11 It is convenient to separate fixed and variable costs for distance teaching so that the cost per student is calculated as AC=TC/N+V where TC is the total fixed cost, N the number of students and V the variable cost per student. In a multi-media project, using, say, radio, print and face-to-face study, one would then have a formula of the type

$$AC = \left(\frac{TC_r}{N_r}+V_r\right) + \left(\frac{TC_p}{N_p}+V_p\right) + \left(\frac{TC_f}{N_f}+V_f\right)$$

where r, p and f represent radio, print and face-to-face, and the average cost is that of a learner using all three modes of study. The relation between fixed and variable costs in distance teaching is likely to be different from that of orthodox education.

12 B. Hill, 'Regurgitation and Plagiarism', Teaching at Distance, Vol. 15, 1979, pp. 60-1.

13 H. Cassirer, Mass Media in an African Context: An Evaluation of Senegal's Pilot Project Paris, Unesco, 1974 ('Reports and Papers in Mass Communication', No.69).

14 Young, et al., op. cit., p.55.

15 Distance teaching here leans on the work of people like Elihu Katz and Peter F. Lazarfield, Personal Influence, New York, Free Press, 1955, and Everett M. Rogers and F. Floyd Shoemaker, Communication of Innovations, New York, Free Press, 1971.

16 T. Dodds, Multi-media Approaches to Rural Education, pp. 28-31, Cambridge, IEC, 1972.

17 Personal communication from Richard Freeman, National Extension College.

18 I have expanded on this in 'Is there a Teacher in the System?', Teaching at a Distance, Vol. 1, 1974, pp. 55-60.

DISTANCE TEACHING:
A CONTRADICTION IN TERMS?
David Sewart

It is sometimes said that there is nothing new about the concept of distance education, since it is possible to point to examples of the use of written material for educational purposes almost back to the beginning of written records and a clearly didactic objective is inherent in, for example, the Epistles of St. Paul. However, it is only in the twentieth century, and perhaps particularly in the last decade, that teaching at a distance has achieved international recognition and even acclaim. Consequently some have seen teaching at a distance as an industrialized form of teaching arising out of the new techniques which have been perfected in the twentieth century;[1] others, while not denying the importance of the new technologies, have seen in the recent rapid growth of this form of teaching a reflection of the increased and increasing costs of conventional teaching which is very labour intensive and to which distance teaching offers, therefore, a seductive alternative.

What makes distance teaching popular?

In both developing and developed countries the possibility of supplementing or even perhaps replacing conventional teaching methods by teaching at a distance has had wide appeal. For the developing countries, where the supply of trained and competent teachers is often severely restricted, teaching at a distance materials can be produced by a small skilled group of teachers which set a standard of excellence capable of wide dissemination, bypassing the need for training, in the first instance, a generation of teachers and thus significantly reducing the time scale for mass education.[2] An example of this can be seen in India where the central government, with technical assistance from UNESCO, has been involved in planning an open school project at the secondary level based on the Central Board of Secondary Education and following a similar syllabus to the Central Board's conventional secondary schools. Such a system would not only cater for 'drop-outs' from the conventional system - a large and increasing number forced for economic reasons to abandon full-time education and seek employment - but also 'left-outs', since the conventional secondary education system is not equipped to cater for the increasing size of the school population. In the developed countries the motives for experiments in teaching at a distance are more complex and here, perhaps, the cost of employing teachers is a more significant factor, but it is worth noting that one of the three primary objectives of the state government of Nordrhein-Westfalen in setting up the Fernuniversität in Hagen was to deal with the fact that the conventional universities could not cope with qualified potential students. However, even in developed countries the lateral expansion of knowledge - the arrival of new subjects and new disciplines - can and often has outstripped the supply of teachers and we can see, for example, in the United Kingdom that the government is now beginning to use the expertise of the Open University in the area of continuing education and for updating in subjects such as computer science and the use of computing in management where the advances have been so rapid as to deny the opportunity for training a large cohort of teachers.

Freedom and restrictions on distance students

Teaching at a distance liberates the student/teacher interface from the strait-jacket of the lecture hall or tutorial room. The student may learn when he wants, whatever the hour of the day or night; he may learn wherever he wants; he may learn at his own pace. Because of this 'freedom' allowed to the student learning at a distance, we might consider that teaching at a distance is inherently a more individualized system than the conventional face-to-face method as far as the student is concerned. In the conventional system, teaching is directed to a group and the group must learn together within the restrictions placed upon it by the abilities of those who form its membership. Its learning will therefore approximate to the mean between the extremes of the abilities of its members, and the needs and potential of the individual in learning will tend to be subservient to this mean. However, the student learning at a distance normally does so as an individual. He learns, therefore, in the way and at the pace which is most suitable to him since he controls his own learning situation. On the debit side, however, it is clear that the student learning alone and at a distance lacks the supportive atmosphere of the tutorial class. He has no-one against whom he can measure himself in the development of his learning. He does not know if he is doing well in relation to his learning. Indeed he has no framework against which to judge 'doing well'. He can of course expect to receive comments on and perhaps grading for, his work from his tutor, but this interaction is strictly between teacher and student, and the student is therefore always at a disadvantage. No comparison with the peer group is possible and the student learning at a distance lacks the usual bench marks for his self-assessment.

A variety of educational packages

Any system of teaching at a distance must concern itself with what it is teaching and how it is teaching. The variety of systems of teaching at a distance and the levels of study which they embrace are now almost legion. Most of the systems contain a package of attractively presented self-instructional materials. Printed material invariably forms the basis of this package, but it is often supplemented by audio-visual material, normally on cassettes but sometimes offered through open circuit broadcasting. In all cases a great deal of thought is customarily put into the assembly of this package and it is made as attractive as possible for the student learning at a distance. The production of such packages is usually seen as the basis on which economic calculations are made and, since the production demands complex resources, both material and human, and requires long-term planning, it often dominates the system of teaching at a distance to the exclusion of all other activities. Indeed there is a beguiling temptation to assume that the problems of teaching at a distance can all be solved by the production of an as yet merely hypothetical perfect package of material.[3]

This excessive concentration on the package is the institution-based approach to teaching at a distance and indeed it is characterized in the very use of the word 'teaching'. The student-based approach involves a more rigorous examination of learning at a distance. It is, of course, inherently more difficult since, whereas the teaching approach can start from a fixed standard package - a unified, concrete and controllable phenomenon - and tacitly assume the subordination of the needs of the individual to that package, the student approach requires a consideration of the needs of the individual in relation to the package and must involve an examination of an almost infinitely variable base which cannot be controlled or completely stabilized within a specifically de-limited area.

A student-based versus institution-based approach

Yet why is it necessary to consider the student-based approach? Can we not seek to arrive more closely at the theoretically perfect teaching package of material? Before we can begin to arrive at any answer to this question, we must define rather more clearly the relationship of the institution to the student and the flow of contacts or interchange between both parties, the one attempting to teach and the other to learn at a distance. In a simple civilization there can be a personal relationship between the individual and those who stand for the religious or secular authority. In a complex civilization, such as our own, this personal relationship, of necessity, disappears. There is a gulf between the system (for example, society, the social and medical services, the consensus, education) and the individual (for example, the citizen, patient, pupil, case study). Within this gulf in the complex civilization there has grown up a group of intermediaries - social workers, broadcasters, teachers, counsellors, etc. - who seek to adapt a system to the individual needs of people. The primary concern of the intermediaries is not for the system itself, but rather for the individuals and, although they are normally employees of the system, they seek to represent individual needs to such an extent that they force the system to take cognisance of these needs. In education this function of intermediary is embraced within a variety of roles which we refer to as teacher, tutor, advisor, counsellor, etc. The intermediary is concerned with the general welfare and support of students, but the various applications of this concern, both in breadth and depth, are almost infinite. On the one hand he may provide information on basic administrative functions; on the other hand he may offer psychological and medical advice. The reason for the variety of roles and duties lies in the variety of education itself. For each system of education we may posit a distinct supportive role.[4]

Why are intermediaries necessary?

In examining a system of teaching at a distance we must analyse the requirements of an intermediary function. To pose the question in more concrete terms we must ask ourselves whether these requirements can be met by a package of materials, that is whether the package can take the place of every essential facet of the teacher in the conventional teaching situation.

Even a cursory examination of the learning process will lead to the conclusion that the needs of the student are not wholly related to the subject that is being studied. That is not to say that such needs are solely of a psychological nature and are completely unconnected with the content of his study. His needs are of an educational kind, even of an academic kind, but they are not strictly related to a subject. This phenomenon is observable in education at all levels. The word 'teaching' is a simple definition of a complex interactive process and we might begin by dividing teaching from the point of view of the institution into the subject matter and advice/support. The subject matter would embrace the strictly academic content of the course and advice/support would embrace general study problems arising from the individual circumstances of the student or the system of teaching peculiar to the institution.[5] We might look at this in another way by saying that the subject matter is information or knowledge and the advice/support covers the way in which the student as an individual fits this new knowledge into his own peculiar pre-existing framework and into his everyday life style.

Limitations of the package

What part does the teaching package in a system of teaching at a distance play in the intermediary role? Does it or could it provide both subject matter and advice/support for individuals? While not wishing to exclude the theoretical possibility that the teaching package could perform all these functions, there are a number of reasons for suggesting that in practice it will always fall a good way short of this ideal, if only for reasons of complexity and cost. While it is possible to define and de-limit the subject matter through an institutionally centred analysis in a way which might receive general assent within the institution, advice/support, being student-centred, is by comparison almost infinitely variable. It follows therefore that any package of materials which seeks to embrace advice/support must admit of almost infinite variation. Moreover, if we were to posit the existence of such a hypothetical package of materials, the cost of production and delivery would render it completely impractical. Clearly however, a package of material need not be limited to the subject matter. It may cover some aspects of advice/support which are judged to be universal or at least common. While economic considerations will of course be of importance in that area of the package which deals with the subject matter, it is likely in practice that general agreement can be obtained on the various limits of the subject matter and therefore on its cost. The same is unlikely to be true in the case of advice/support and here the cost-benefit approach will begin to operate. All students need the subject matter, therefore this element is 'cost-effective'. Not all students can easily be seen to need some/all of what can be offered in terms of advice/support; consequently it is by comparison far less cost-effective.

I have suggested above that institutions engaged in teaching at a distance have concentrated extensively on the production of a package of materials. For obvious academic reasons these packages embrace the subject matter. For equally obvious economic and practical reasons, few of these packages embrace the function of advice/support. It does not seem unfair to suggest that there is an overwhelming tendency within the field of teaching at a distance to offer systems from the standpoint of the institution teaching at a distance, rather than from the standpoint of the student learning at a distance. The response to the individual needs of the student learning alone and at a distance has often become lost in the overriding requirement to produce a grandiose package of materials.[6]

Contexts of distance and conventional students

Perhaps this failure to recognize and concentrate on individual needs arises out of a failure adequately to appreciate the difference between the conventional student and the student learning at a distance. Conventional students, in digesting the academic pabulum of their chosen study, exist within a highly artificial and wholly supportive framework. For most of them their study is merely a further stage in an unbroken linear development which began when they were infants. The infant school class and the university lecture are generically similar in offering a group learning situation with a face-to-face teacher/student contact and the subsequent possiblility for instant feedback of an oral and visual nature. The group learning situation is itself supportive of the learning process, not only because of the potential interaction between students in relation to the academic content of the course - learning through discussion with one's peers - but also because the group learning offers a bench mark to the individual members of the group. The students might naturally expect to fall short of the comprehension of a particular subject which is demonstrated by their teacher. The bench mark of how short or 'how much of this are we expected to understand?' is provided by the group, and through the group a common denominator of success or achievement is established for all its members.

The situation of students learning at a distance is wholly different. Often they are returning to study after a number of years. For such people the concept and practice of their previous learning is somewhat clouded. They have an experience of life and work and hence a framework into which their new learning has to be set. Often the students learning at a distance are part-timers. Their work and families are of prime importance. It is not open to them as it is open to the conventional students to devote themselves entirely and with singular purpose to learning. Moreover, the process of learning at a distance is generically different from the conventional mode. The swift feedback available from the face-to-face learning model is almost entirely absent. The supportive environment of the peer group is lacking and the bench mark of achievement and, deriving from this, the maintenance of the individual's confidence, is difficult to establish.

A division of roles

It is elements of this sort, fundamental to the student learning at a distance, which the package of materials either cannot influence at all or can only influence in a marginal way. The teaching package is the raw academic pabulum of the institution for teaching at a distance; for the student learning at a distance there is need of another element, an advisory/supportive role. In conventional education the teacher can and often does perform the advisory/-supportive role while acting as the source of academic knowledge. In a system of teaching at a distance we normally find the separation of the source of academic knowledge and the advisory/support role, the former being contained in the teaching package. The separation of these activities does not, in itself, create problems. Problems will however arise if the two elements are not balanced; if the teaching package predominates to the virtual or complete exclusion of the intermediary role; if the existence of these two activities is not constantly in the minds of those involved in teaching at a distance.

Drop-out as a measure of effectiveness

No-one who has given even a cursory glance to the literature of distance teaching will have failed to note a preoccupation, almost at times approaching hysteria, with the phenomenon variously described as drop-out, wastage, withdrawal, attrition, etc. This phenomenon exists in all forms of teaching, but in distance teaching it is a major characteristic since its incidence is often many times as great as in any form of conventional teaching, and its very existence threatens the 'cost-effectiveness' which is so often listed as an advantage. The hypothesis that the face-to-face teacher and the student's peer group could not be adequately replaced in distance teaching received, until recently, almost universal credence and this belief was 'substantiated' by reference to drop-out statistics. In the last decade and particularly in the last two or three years the hypothesis has received a practical challenge from the success of the Open University in the United Kingdom. Here, instead of the ninety per cent drop-out confidently predicted in the educational press when the University first began to offer courses, we find that up to sixty per cent of finally registered students are graduating, and, moreover, that a very significant proportion of the forty per cent of 'drop-outs' is in any case unavoidable, ranging from the obvious cases of death, through movement outside the United Kingdom, significant changes in domestic circumstances and satisfaction with the completion of a part rather than the whole of a particular programme. The success of the Open University has brought it an international reputation and many attempts have been made to transplant this success to other countries and other continents. So far it would appear that none have managed to improve upon the drop-out rate and thus, in popular terms, the 'success'. Indeed the opposite seems to be the truth. None have come anywhere near reaching a success rate approaching sixty per cent. There are a number of reasons for this but, I would suggest, only one of major significance. The popular conception of the Open University, even by those who have made a careful study of it, is of a system dominated by a highly structured package of correspondence texts and broadcasts.

The method of preparation of this package by a course team has been seen as a unique development and a major contributory factor to the quality of the package. The package - particularly the course units - and its method of production, are extensively and variously copied. Yet, I would contend that this analysis of the Open University system is too superficial. The success of the Open University does not rest wholly or entirely on the highly structured teaching package. It rests rather on the inter-relationship of that package with the student as an individual through the agency of the counselling and tuition functions peculiar to the Open University. It is the combination of these elements on which the comparative success of the Open University is based. Neither is sufficient in itself.

Contrasting the Open University with Fernuniversität

The truth of this hypothesis might be supported in quasi-mathematical terms through the use of a paradigm of the Open University. The Fernuniversität in Hagen falls within the same broad ambit of Western European culture and tradition as the Open University in the United Kingdom. While the countries are not identical in geographical, cultural and economic terms they are, nevertheless, very similar. The students of the Fernuniversität are highly motivated, being self-selecting as in the Open University. In general, however, they are far better qualified than Open University students, since they must normally have achieved the Abitur, whereas forty per cent of Open University students in the last three years have less than the minimal requirements for normal entry to a degree course at universities and polytechnics in the United Kingdom.[7]

The teaching package of the Fernuniversität does not contain open circuit broadcasting, although audio and video material is often available in cassette form. In the quality of its correspondence material (course units), the Fernuniversität could fairly be seen as the equal of the Open University. The Fernuniversität does not, however, possess an integrated support system and is becoming increasingly concerned about the high drop-out rate of its students which raises the concomitant questions of economic viability.

Bases of Open University support services

If we accept that, for all practical purposes, the advice/-support function cannot be supplied through the teaching package, but see it as a vital element in the system, we can go on to consider the ways in which this might be supplied.

In practice, Open University support services are

53

offered through tutor-counsellors in some two hundred and sixty local study centres throughout the United Kingdom. In addition, students are attached to specialist tutors to deal with the specific academic content of the course and to mark their assignments. The function of the tutors is exclusively related to the teaching package. What then is the rationale behind the use of study centres and tutor-counsellors?

The use of study centres in a system of teaching at a distance might not unreasonably be seen as a contradiction in terms. Study at a distance is normally depicted as independent of time and place and these are normally claimed as characteristics and advantages for the system. But study centres impose a restriction in place; they also impose a restriction in time to a greater or lesser extent as they are not open all day for every day of the year. Are study centres per se an essential part of teaching at a distance, if it is to be successful, or are they not essential at all? If the latter is true, why do many systems of teaching at a distance use them and in particular the Open University? Since they almost invariably offer a facility for face-to-face interaction, do they therefore deny on this account the practical viability of teaching at a distance?

Radio, television and telephone supplementing print

In our earlier analysis we defined the teaching process as the transmission of subject matter and advice/support. Until the sixteenth century, the transmission of subject matter - or at any rate its wide dissemination - was through a verbal medium. Cost and time factors inherent in copying by hand placed out of court the provision of a text for students. The professors and the lecturers communicated verbally with their students as the very root of these words implies. The introduction of printing brought a dramatic change. The professors and lecturers continued to lecture to their students, but no longer was the student limited exclusively to the time and space of a lecture room. He could have as a supplement - or even as a substitute - a text book written by someone to whom he would, perhaps, not otherwise have access. Moreover, he could study this in his own time and at his own pace, re-reading whenever and wherever he thought fit. However, the text book had none of the interaction of face-to-face teaching. Teaching at a distance relies now, and for the forseeable future will continue to rely, upon the technology of printing. Other more recent technologies have supplemented this, but none have replaced it. The telephone has offered a direct substitute for student/tutor interaction. The student can receive an immediate response to his question through the telephone as in the lecture room. He lacks the non-verbal signs of normal communication, but this is not usually seen as a vital loss. However, the telephone is limited in time, since tutors and students must have their interchange at the same time and it is limited in space both by the requirement of an installation and by the cost of the link. Furthermore, telephone lectures or tutorials between one tutor and a number of students, while far less costly in tutor time, begin to pose some of the disadvantages of radio in that tutors, deprived of non-verbal signals, teach at their own pace, and their students, unwilling to contribute to a technological anarchy, refrain from interrupting. There are certain similar disadvantages attached to the use of radio. While open circuit broadcasting is restrictive in time and space, the use of audio and video cassettes can ameliorate, to some extent, these problems by offering the student an opportunity to view and listen at his own pace and in his own time, the availability of a re-play facility being the only restriction. However, the possibilty of interaction between tutor and student is virtualy non-existent within this medium. Printed material, radio and television can be used for the simple transmission of subject matter. Assuming re-play facilities, all can be used by the student in his own time and, with the wide dissemination of equipment in recent years, all are, or could be, independent of space. They are however the tools of *teaching* at a distance, not necessarily of *learning* at a distance, since they are not susceptible of an interactive mode: only the telephone offers this facility.

Education is about learning more than teaching

The view that education is primarily a learning process on the part of the student rather than an instructional process on the part of the teacher has achieved almost universal acceptance in recent years. The fact that the Ministry of Education in Italy is still called the Department of Public Instruction and that *enseignement* is still used in France can be seen as anachronisms. In Germany the use of *Fern unterricht* for 'distance teaching' has been superseded at all levels by the term *Fernstudium* (distance learning) which had originally only been used for degree level study. While recognizing this trend in educational thinking, distance teaching systems have found difficulty in its practical application. One solution has been to develop, for the printed medium, highly structured self-instructional materials in which the student is required to respond at regular intervals to the text and there follows a discussion of a variety of potential responses. Because of the wide range of possible responses, the discussion cannot be all embracing, so that this development must always fall some way short of perfection. However, the creation of this internal dialogue for the student within the material has been a significant element in changing the student from a passive to an active learner. [8]

Adding correspondence tuition and counselling

The standard teaching package, however well structured, cannot provide an individualized learning system for students. It is only the introduction of a human element which can adapt to the almost infinite variety of student needs. Hence, in distance teaching, and in particular in the Open University, we have witnessed in recent years the refinement of teaching by correspondence alongside the development of the carefully designed teaching package. The technique and the approach of the correspondence tutor are not always immediately grasped by those who have been engaged in the traditional forms of teaching. The correspondence tutor is not there to transmit information - all this is done in the package of materials. The role of the correspondence tutor is that of a facilitator. This requires two things: the ability on the part of the correspondence tutor to convey through his comments advice for further study and the ability to perceive his student's present state of knowledge and conceptual framework, so that the advice may be as relevant as possible to the individual student. The tutor must offer comments which are considered, human, constructive and supportive. The formal nature of written comment which is not susceptible of the inflection, tone and pause of speech, renders it liable to misinterpretation. Clarity is essential. While much has been done to refine the art of correspondence teaching, it is, as yet in its infancy. It is clearly not the case that the skills of the traditional teacher can be adapted for correspondence teaching; rather there is a need for the development of new skills. [9]

The Open University has combined its teaching package with an individual support system offered through correspondence tuition and a general and continuous academic support provided by a tutor-counsellor, who is responsible for the progress of the individual student from entry into the University until graduation. This general service is supplemented by specialist tuition beyond the foundation level. The interrelationship of the package of materials with the student has been achieved through the agency of tutor-counsellors and course tutors. Individual contact can be, and often is made by telephone and by post.

A rationale for study centres?

But we have still not supplied a rationale for the study centre, and indeed we seem increasingly to be isolating it as superfluous and as an anachronism in a system which, as we have seen, can probably comprehend the subject matter and advice/support. The study centre has been used for a number of functions in various distance teaching systems. In some it has been seen as a viewing centre where replay devices may be used. In others it has been seen as a library resource centre. In some it has been seen as a locus for student interaction and self-help groups, a substitute for the conventional campus. In yet others it has offered a site for practical experiments or the use of equipment, such as computing facilities, which are essential to study, but which cannot be offered to the student at home without great difficulty. Finally, there are cases where the origin of the study centre system is shrouded in complex educational politics, and study centres are seen as a tangible link between the otherwise amorphous distance teaching institution and the local community.[10]

Can we then say that the study centre is the dustbin of teaching at a distance? Is it the repository into which are emptied those functions or parts of functions which seem to be too difficult or too expensive to carry out? Is it there because we cannot feel completely confident as yet in our combination of teaching materials and correspondence tuition, because it is particularly useful in the provision of the advice/support function in which the necessity for individualization is paramount? Is the presence of study centres a denial of the practical possibility, as yet, of teaching at a distance? Might we so 'improve' teaching at a distance as to be able to dispense with study centres entirely?

We might construct cogent arguments against the use of study centres. Clearly they are a costly element. As far as can be ascertained in all systems of teaching at a distance, the use of, and need for, study centres on the part of the students falls a long way short of the use and need projected by the institution. It is clear that a large number of students either are not able, or choose not to, attend a study centre. Clearly, many students choose to study by distance teaching methods because they prefer or require, for domestic or work purposes, to be freed from the time and space constraints of conventional teaching methods.

Continuingly changing functions

I would suggest that we are being over-simplistic, if we take the view that the study centre in the Open University is merely a dustbin wherein we can deposit all the difficult functions of teaching at a distance, which we intend ultimately to carry out by other means. Indeed, I would suggest that it is entirely wrong to see study centres in the Open University solely against the background of traditional education, as places in which conventional face-to-face contact between teachers and students takes place. Within the Open University, our concept of a study centre is blinkered by our adherence to the objectives of study centres seen in the original report of the Planning Committee of the Open University.[11] The Planning Committee had initially seen two purposes for study centres. They were to be used as viewing centres and as places in which tutorials would take place. Such tutorials were envisaged as an essential element in this system of teaching at a distance. The reality, almost from the beginning, proved to be different. Over two hundred and sixty study centres were created, but within the first three years it became apparent that they were not being and could not be used as originally intended. The open circuit broadcasting of radio and television did not always match the evening opening times for study centres. Furthermore, the store of audio and video tapes, particularly the latter, became too expensive to maintain, and the replay facility provided through technicolour machines and audio-cassette devices lapsed. The increase in the number of courses after foundation level was not and could not be matched by increases in student numbers. The average post-foundation course population rapidly fell below two students per study centre. The idea of local tutorials, other than for the high population foundation level courses thus disappeared. Thus the conception of study centres as viewing centres and locations for essential tuition was not even the case, in practice, in the University's first year of operation. It is even less the case today. Yet the Open University has failed to re-define the role of study centres in its formal publications, although a significant element of their role is implicit in the functions of the tutor-counsellors.

A focus for the tutor-counsellor

Tutor-counsellors are seen in the Open University as the local and continuing support for students. The description of this support as local is given a physical presence in the study centre which is seen as the base for a tutor-counsellor's activities. The local study centre is a place in which the foundation level tutor-counsellor is able to offer face-to-face support of a strictly academic and of an advisory/supportive nature to his first year students, all of whom live in the vicinity. The tutor-counsellor is seen as weaning students from the traditional methods of face-to-face group teaching to the Open University's methods of individual and independant study. The study centre is, in reality, a traditional phase for the students in this process. For the student it has much of the appearance of the traditional classroom in that it is a physical location in which an authoritative figure, the tutor-counsellor, is present. If the similarity between the traditional and non-traditional teaching methods holds good for the physical situation, it certainly does not hold good for the educational rationale. The tutor-counsellor does not lecture or profess a subject in the traditional way. Instead he takes the academic content as given in the shape of the course units and broadcasts and sets out instead to help the student to learn from the material, either by himself or in groups. As such, therefore, we might describe the study centre as an important element for most new students in the painful early steps of adapting to learning at a distance. It is a stepping stone from group learning of the traditional sort to individual and/or group learning of the non-traditional sort. While it is possible that some students do not need such a stepping stone, it seems clear from the attendance of students themselves that most students still require this element. Moreover, the needs of the individual can be met by the service of the tutor-counsellor in the study centre. The student may take advantage of what is offered whenever and as often as he pleases. He may feel no need to attend for some time but later develop a need. Such a need is met by the regular presence of the tutor-counsellor in the study centre.

A local resource centre

It might be alleged that this argument does not hold equally true for post-foundation level tuition and this is almost certainly true. For post-foundation level students the tuition is unlikely to be as 'local', but the study centre with its face-to-face tutorials - and by this I mean tutorials in the Open University sense - does satisfy a need. The face-to-face contact provides for a large number of students a stimulus, both social and educational, to the continuing process of study. The initial strong 'local' support of the tutor-counsellor is not totally withdrawn after the first year. It exists in more rarefied form thereafter but can be tapped into by the student as and when he thinks fit.

The study centre is a place in which tutorials, day schools and self-help groups take place. Students do not use these facilities as often as the institution makes them available, but they are nevertheless essential. We know that students do not read every word of the course units or even all the course units. They sometimes - perhaps often - do not read the set books. Some students omit the radio and television broadcasts entirely, most are extremely selective. Some students do not complete all their home experiment kit activities and, indeed, a few do not even open up the boxes. It is clearly naive and certainly over-simplistic to try to use student usage as the sole determinant of the value of an element in the system, unless of course the use is that of a very insignificant minority and even here we should be careful. It is the richness and variety, the multiplicity of provision, which attracts and sustains our students. Study centres and what is offered in them are part of this richness of provision.

Are study centres an anomaly?

Are we to say that study centres are a contradiction of the feasibility of teaching at a distance? The answer for the Open University is certainly no. The confusion rests with the definition of teaching at a distance. If we consider the variety of teaching and learning processes we might see at one extreme the continuous face-to-face dialogue between one teacher and one student, a totally supportive learning situation. Further along the spectrum we find the conventional primary school in which the authoritative figure of the teacher provides a continuous contact throughout the day with a group of students. Much further along the spectrum we find a traditional university teaching system in which the authoritative figure of the teacher appears only occasionally and the students are more independent in their learning situation. At the other end of the spectrum we find a pure system of teaching at a distance in which the student is learning at a distance from those who have prepared the material and learns at his own pace, wherever he wishes to study and whenever he wishes to study. The Open University, like the conventional universities, falls somewhere between the two ends of the spectrum, although it is clearly further towards the end of pure distance teaching. Its position in the system has been determined by a number of elements. These include the varying entry qualifications of its students, their domestic and work circumstances as adults learning part-time, their previous experience of learning and their perception of what they are capable of and the support that they require. The study centres and what is provided in them are part of the total package of the Open University teaching system to which we ascribe overall the generic term of teaching at a distance. There is no contradiction between the notion of study centres and teaching at a distance. For some students who do not attend study centres, the Open University might come close to 'pure' (sic) teaching at a distance. For others it will come less close. More important, however, from the student's point of view, the Open University offers a richness of variety in opportunities for learning, such that its appeal is catholic. It is from this that its success follows, and if the University ever seeks to alter the balance of its provision or removes specific elements from the rich variety of this provision, it must do so only with extreme care and mindful of the fact that in doing so it will almost certainly be detracting somewhat from its present universal appeal.

Notes

1 Perhaps the major contribution to this debate has been provided by Otto Peters, Die didaktische Struktur des Fernunterrichts,Untersuchungen zu einer industrialisierten Form des Lehrens und Lernens, Tubingen, 1973.

2 This has been apparent in numerous countries where the educational problems seem overwhelming as was noted by K. Whitlock, (1980)

Perspectives on adult education in Latin America, Teaching at a Distance, No. 18, pages 28-33.

3 Anyone so beguiled would do well to read Abercrombie,M.L.J. (1976) Paths to learning, Teaching at a Distance, No. 5, pages 5-12.

4 For further discussion of this point see D. Sewart, Continuity of concern for students in a system of learning at a distance, Zentrales Institut für Fernstudienforschung, Papiere 22, Hagen, 1978.

5 I use the phrase 'advice/support' as a shorthand description. It should be taken as embracing not only general study problems connected with the course but also problems which are less course specific or perhaps not at all course specific, such as career planning and advice to the individual in the context of studying at a distance.

6 This is not to say that all distance teaching packages are totally concerned with teaching rather than the students' learning. Mary Thorpe, When is a course not a course? Teaching at a Distance, No. 16, pages 13-18, has recently pointed to and argued for the increasing recognition of the role of the tutor and student in the development of courses.

7 Open University experience tends to show that qualified students in general do better than non-qualified students. At the same time, this experience also shows that it is dangerous to extrapolate from such a general hypothesis to a particular individual.

8 In offering this general statement I am very conscious of the fact that our knowledge of 'dialogue' is certainly limited. Brian Lewis, Conversational man, Teaching at a Distance, No. 2, pages 68-70, suggested an intensive scrutiny of the whole topic of dialogue/conversation. To date no-one appears to have accepted the challenge.

9 For a further analysis of the role of correspondence tutor see Clennell, S. Peters, J. Sewart, D. Teaching for the Open University, 1977.

10 Some aspects of study centres in the Open University are covered by Bradford, M. Study centres: The background to the current policy review; and Kirk, P. Study centres: some impressions, Teaching at a Distance, No. 16, pages 33-41. A more comprehensive and international viewpoint is available in Gough, J.E. Study centres in distance education, University of Deakin, 1980.

11 The Open University (1969) Report of the Planning Committee to the Secretary of State for Education and Science, HMSO.

12 The 'local' nature of the study centre will clearly vary and there are some students whose homes are beyond reasonable travelling distance of a study centre. However, given the large number of study centres and the density of population in the United Kingdom, this is clearly the exception rather than the rule.

SECTION 2: THEORIES OF DISTANCE EDUCATION

INTRODUCTION

The theoretical underpinnings of distance education are frag-
ile. Most effort in this field of education has been practical or mechanical and has concentrated on the logistics of
the enterprise. Lack of accepted theory has weakened distance
education: there has been a lack of identity, a sense of
belonging to the periphery and the lack of a touchstone
against which decisions on methods, on media, on financing,
on student support, when they have to be made, can be made
with confidence.

The words of the American theorist, Wedemeyer, published
nearly a decade ago, remain true today:

> It is unfortunately true that the failure of correspond-
> ence study to develop a theory related to the mainstream
> of educational thought and practice has seriously handi-
> capped the development and recognition of this field.
> (1974:3)

The theoretical positions from which the selection for this
reader has been made can be grouped under three headings:
Theories of autonomy and independence (Rudolf Manfred Delling
- Federal Republic of Germany; Charles A. Wedemeyer - United
States of America; Michael G. Moore - United Kingdom),
Theory of industrialisation (Otto Peters - Federal Republic
of Germany) and *Theories of interaction and communication*
(Börje Holmberg - Sweden/Federal Republic of Germany; John
A. Bååth - Sweden; David Sewart - United Kingdom).

Delling takes up an extreme position. In two articles
(1975, 1976) he describes distance study as an artificial
dialogic learning opportunity in which the physical distance
between the learner and the helping organisation is bridged
by an artificial signal carrier. Delling tends to reduce the
role of the teacher and of the educational organisation to a
minimum and throw the whole emphasis of the system on the
autonomy and independence of the learner.

Wedemeyer's thought is generous and liberal, owing much
to the philosophy of Carl Rogers. It has at times been

criticised as impracticable. His thought on distance education (for which he tried to popularise the term 'independent study') has two bases: a democratic social ideal and a liberal educational philosophy. Wedemeyer considers that nobody should be denied the opportunity to learn because he or she is poor, geographically isolated, socially disadvantaged, in poor health, institutionalised or otherwise unable to place him or herself within an institution's special environment for learning.

He also considered that 'independent study' should be self-pacing, individualised and goal-free: the student should be free to pace his learning according to his own circumstances and not be bound by any mechanisms of the institution; the student should be free to follow any of several channels for learning; the learner should have freedom in the selection of the goals he wishes to aim at, the activities that will lead to these goals and the evaluation of his achievements.

Moore believes that to define independent study only in terms of distance is a mistake. He argues that the autonomy of the learner is an equally important variable in correspondence and other forms of distance education and his proposed classification of educational programmes is by the two variables of 'distance' and 'autonomy'. He recognises that learners vary in the extent to which they are able to exercise autonomy and hence there is no value judgement in the use of the terms 'autonomy' and 'distance'. There are programmes with much autonomy and dialogue and programmes with less and they vary in distance. A programme of high autonomy, Moore holds, may be as damaging as one of low autonomy. The problem is to match programmes to learners so that each learner exercises the maximum of autonomy and grows.

The German scholar, *Peters*, starts out from the position that the analysis of teaching at a distance in terms of conventional instructional theory has proved unsuccessful and unproductive and that one must therefore seek for another basis of analysis. His extensive research on distance education institutions of every kind in the 1960s led Peters to propose the hypothesis that distance education could best be analysed by comparison with the industrial production of goods. He proposed new categories for the analysis of distance education taken from economic and industrial theory.

Peters' applications of the categories of industrial theory to distance education led him to the conclusion that it was the most industrialized form of education and that the theory of industrialization was the best explanation of it. It follows that he maintains that 'whoever is professionally concerned with education today must acknowledge that there exist *two* clearly differentiated forms of teaching: traditional face-to-face teaching based on interpersonal communication and industrialised teaching based on technical and prefabricated forms of communication.' (1973:310).

Holmberg describes distance education as a guided didactic conversation. Study in a distance system is self-study, but it is not private reading, for the student is not alone. Students benefit from having a course developed for them and also from interaction with the tutors and other representatives of a supporting organisation. It is this relationship between the student and the supporting organisation which Holmberg characterises as guided didactic conversation. The conversation can either be real (by correspondence; by telephone; by personal contact) or simulated (conversational style of authors' of distance study materials; students' internalized conversation by study of a text).

Bååth's name has been associated with the concept 'two-way communication in correspondence education'. Throughout the 1970s he undertook a series of research projects on the possible forms of two-way communication in education at a distance: on the possibility of providing interaction within the materials by means of exercises, questions or self-check tests and on the central role of the tutor in providing communication with the student by mail, computer, telephone or face-to-face.

Sewart has summed up his theory of distance education as a continuity of concern for students learning at a distance. He rejects the notion that the package of materials can perform all the functions of a teacher, or holds that, if it could, it would become infinitely expensive as it would have to reflect the complex interactive process of the teacher with individual students. In this way he considers the situation of the student learning at a distance to be quite different from that of conventional students because of the absence of swift feedback and of the peer group as a benchmark. The provision of advice and support for students in a system of learning at a distance poses, for him, almost infinitely variable problems and that creates the need for an advisory and supportive role of a distance institution in addition to the provision of a teaching package.

The selections chosen for this volume come from *Moore*, as a representative of the autonomy/independence theorists; *Peters* on industrialisation; and *Holmberg* as a representative of the interaction/communication group.

The paper from Moore is the final one in a series of presentations that can be found in Convergence (1972), Journal of Higher Education (1973), Epistolodidaktika (1975) and ICCE Newsletter (1976). Moore shows how his work with Charles A. Wedemeyer at the University of Wisconsin led him to conceptualize about a 'family of instructional methods in which the teaching behaviours are executed apart from the learning behaviours'. The concept of the separation of learner and teacher led him to the concept 'distance' and an analysis of on-campus independent study led him to his

65

concept of learner autonomy. From these premises he developed the theory of independent study based on the variables 'apartness' and 'learner autonomy' which is presented in the first Reading in Section 2.

MacKenzie and Christensen's book of international readings on distance education in the 1960s and earlier, The changing world of correspondence study, contained a first presentation of Otto Peters' theory of distance education as an industrialization of the educational process. The second Reading in Section 2 was first published in German in 1981 and shows that the basic framework of the theory remains intact to today. Little modification has been introduced to what remains the most impressive theoretical formulation of distance education yet developed.

The task of translating Peters' major contribution, his 1973 book Die didaktische Struktur des Fernunterrichts. Untersuchungen zu einer industrialisierten Form des Lehrens und Lernens remains undone. Only when this work is translated will scholars who do not read German be able to assess the full presentation of the thesis. Nevertheless the 1981 article presented here gives a succint overview of Peters' thought and embraces (i) the attempt to show a historical parallel between the emergence of education at a distance 130 years ago and a growing industrialisation of society; (ii) the choice of elements of industrialisation that are said to have parallels in distance education: the importance of the planning phase; success due to scientific planning; formalisation of procedures and normalisation of product; objectivisation of processes; mechanisation introducing functional change; centralisation and monopoly leading to elimination of small operations and (iii) the dependence on the Berlin school of educational philosophy of Paul Heimann and Walter Schultz.

Holmberg has made extensive contributions to the literature of distance education from 1960 to the present. A theme which gradually establishes itself in his writings is that of 'guided didactic conversation' as the characteristic of distance education. This concept is felt by Holmberg to be normative as it is designed to suggest procedures which are expected to be effective in facilitating learning. These procedures would include course writing in a conversational style in which the personal pronouns 'I', 'you', 'we' are frequently used and in which a careful structuring of content and language distinguish distance study materials from the normal style of textbooks. (Section 2, third Reading).

Despite the work of the authors cited here, the calls of scholars like Peters, Bååth and Moore for a thoroughgoing theoretical analysis of distance education went largely unheeded during the 1970s and early 1980s.

Desmond Keegan

References

Delling, R.M. (1975) Distant study as an opportunity for learning. In Ljoså, E. (ed.) The system of distance education. Malmö: Hermods. pp. 55-59

Delling, R.M. (1976) Telemathic teaching? Distant study. ICCE Newsletter, 18-21

Peters, O. (1971) Theoretical aspects of correspondence instruction. In MacKenzie, O. and Christensen, E.L. (eds) The changing world of correspondence study. University Park: Pennsylvania State. pp. 223-228

Peters, O. (1973) Die didaktische Struktur des Fernunterrichts. Untersuchungen zu einer industrialisierten Form des Lehrens und Lernens. Weinheim: Beltz

Wedemeyer, C.A. (1974) Characteristics of open learning systems. In Open learning systems. Washington: National Association of Educational Broadcasters

ON A THEORY OF INDEPENDENT STUDY

Michael Moore

Introduction: The "Copernican Revolution" in education

In the past thirty years and especially during the past
decade there has occurred in education what U.N.E.S.C.O.'s
Henri Dieuzeide has called a "Copernican Revolution", a
transfer of the centre of gravity of educational thinking
and research from the functions and activities of teachers,
the "teacher centred mentality", to the behaviours of learners, the "pupil centred approach".[1] The change has been
described by a prominent Australian broadcaster as the "decen-
tralisation of learning".[2]

In earlier times, when the centre of the educational
universe was the teacher, emphasis in teacher training and
in research was on the identification of those actions of
the teacher that would stimulate in students the responses
thought desirable by the teacher. In such centralised learning systems it was necessary for students to cluster around
teachers in "classes", and teachers had to know how to plan
what would be learned, how to implement various strategies
supposed to promote learning, and how to test to obtain
evidence of the effectiveness of their strategies.

A distinguished British educator, Edith Moorhouse writes
of elementary school teaching as it was forty years ago:

> the emphasis in teacher training was on the techniques
> of holding the attention of a class of children: the
> question at the appropriate moment when attention began
> to lapse, the raising of an eyebrow, the quick drawing
> on the blackboard. . . . The teacher stood in front of
> the class of children of one age group who sat in
> straight rows facing the blackboard and talked to and
> questioned the children for much of the day.[3]

Teacher centred education has not been confined to the
elementary school. "Universities have existed for over a

thousand years", writes Brown, but

> From the very beginning of organised higher education, teachers and professors have presented a united front against the notion that students will learn just as much, and possibly a great deal more, if permitted to learn on their own initiative rather than as a captive audience in the classroom. At no point in the history of education have schools and universities allowed students the autonomy which is necessary in the learning process. [4]

According to observers of the British Primary School, the change to a learner centred educational universe has been due to a growing acceptance by learners and teachers of three basic principles long discussed by educators but not widely acted upon. The first of these is the recognition that each individual learns each content area or skill in different ways, and probably at different times from other learners; if learning has any one characteristic it is idiosyncracy, and the concept of a "class" of learners is therefore a foolish paradox. The second principle is that effective learning is experiential; whether interpreted in a phenomenological or behaviourist's framework, the principle is that one can best learn by experiencing. The third principle is that learning in the new world of rapid change must be lifelong, so that in youth one need not learn enough for a lifetime, but must acquire the skills to be a responsible continuing learner in adulthood.

The role of the teacher in the new learner centred educational universe, at its simplest, is not so much to "instruct" as to provide an environment in which each individual learner is able to identify what he is ready to learn, and in which he has access to a large variety of resources for learning. In particular, the school teacher tries to provide a rich supply of materials:

> Materials of every kind should be available: basic materials, such as sand, water, clay and wood; a collection of junk, boxes, containers of every size and shape in wood, cardboard and plastic; a wide variety of cardboard and paper in different shapes, sizes, thicknesses and colours; paints (water, oil and emulsion), pens, charcoal, pencils, a variety of brushes, crayons, in fact all kinds of media for making marks that a child can explore; a variety of pastes and glues that do the job expected of them; scissors that cut; benches, a vice, and tools; an assortment of materials to stroke and use - velvet, silk, satin, wool, cotton, linen, fur, nylon. Each item has a different quality that can only be fully appreciated by handling and using and coming to terms with the discipline they impose. All

these materials may be used at the child's own stage of development and maturity: one child might be at the stage of pitting his own strength against boxes and planks and yet be able to join in with a group of children of varying ages and abilities who are construct-ing a telescope or a space ship - that will hold several children - imaginative, constructive work which is the basis of mathematics.[5]

By providing a richness of materials, and being both non-dire-ctive and responsive, the learner centred educator gives the learner opportunity to learn what is important for him at a particular time in his growth, gives opportunity to learn by experience, and gives opportunity to learn to exercise choice and responsibility in making educational decisions. As a result, from the schools - not all schools, but many - is emerging a generation of new adult learners that knows how to learn, and a generation of teachers that knows how to facilitate independent study. The expectation of these learn-ers is that in adulthood, as in school, their learning will be self directed, and when they identify learning needs they will be able to call upon the sources of information and training they require to satisfy their needs.

The response of institutions of higher education to this expectation, is suggested in a report from the Univer-sity of Notre Dame:

Institutions are responding with programs to support the new learning styles emphasized by the need for lifelong learning. And those programs of continuing education seem likely, for a variety of reasons, to experience rapid growth in the years ahead. This growth will come about without any substantial changes in national policy. As a matter of course, formal educa-tional institutions will expand their offerings to accom-modate an increasing demand for external degrees, individualized off-campus study, correspondence study programs, and other modes of reaching the varied interests of students.[6]

Together with the pressure from students, the design and development of "other modes of reaching the varied interests of students" is the second development that has brought independent learners to the foreground of current educational research. At the very time that demand for learner freedom has increased, a plethora of new communications devices has made it possible for institutions to respond in efficient ways to that demand. Designed according to systems design principles, instructional programmes may now provide an effi-cient exposition by any of the world's authorities on any subject to individual learners, communicated to them by means of the computer, television, radio, video-cassette, audio tape, telephone, and in print. Using such programmes, each learner has the universe for a classroom, and an abundance of material and human resources. As a child-centred teacher provides a rich environment of learning materials, and responds to the self directed learning of the individual pupil in the classroom, the higher education institution now has the technical power to respond to each individual adult learner as, in his interaction with his adult environment, he identifies learning needs and makes them known, and enters into programmes of independent study.

Henri Dieuzeide describes two kinds of technology based educational institutions, one of which is a community educational resource centre offering

> a community service of individualized self-instruction for safe-guarding individual freedom of action - a complete self-service system adaptable to individual needs, to which the pupils would feel an allegiance based on individual involvement.[7]

By contrast with the cloisters of the traditional campus, where teachers tried to transmit knowledge to learners in an environment sheltered from the outside world, this new kind of institution is not a place to which people travel, but a resource centre from which they draw out the information and the skills they need. The material they require is communicated through appropriate media, having been prepared and packaged in advance, in anticipation of learners' demands. Learners using these systems are independent in two senses of the term, for they are physically independent of the need to be resident on a campus, and they are independent of the control of their learning by pedagogues. The institution is "teaching at a distance".

The following description is of a typical university Independent Study and Distance Teaching venture, the University Without Walls, which is a consortium of twenty-seven participating American colleges and universities.

> Each student outlines his learning objectives and designs a study program leading to goal achievement from a list of hundreds of opportunities for independent study. Among the possible options are regular course work at any of the participating institutions, internships or jobs, programmed materials, and even travel. UWW students graduate whenever they have achieved their learning objectives. [8]

Purpose of this Paper

What has been described above is a renaissance of interest in independent learning and the teaching of independent learners. We have a vast array of new research and development questions in the universe of education, some of which we will introduce for your consideration at the conclusion of this paper.

Our first task however, and the main purpose of our colloquium today, is to focus our attention upon an enterprise in which we have been engaged in recent years, namely the statement of what Independent Study and Distance Teaching are, and the construction of a conceptual framework of the field. Since 1970 we have developed the theory on the basis of a typology of programmes which was itself based on the characteristics we identified as critical elements of Independent Study and Distance Teaching programmes. In this paper we will provide a brief history of our progress in pursuit of the theory, after which we will describe, again briefly, the typology and the concepts associated with it, and in conclusion will mention one research project which has been completed, and other questions of interest for future consideration.

Towards a Theory of Independent Study

Although we had some experience of the use of correspondence and of radio and television in adult education before going to the United States in 1970 it was not until we joined Charles Wedemeyer at the University of Wisconsin that Independent Study and Distance Teaching became a major professional preoccupation. Wedemeyer was by then the leading American thinker about Distance Teaching and had recently returned from Great Britain where he had been a consultant in the establishment of the Open University. We moved together into a project to design an Open School for the State of Wisconsin [9], and a score of other projects followed, ranging from "Edsat", the use of the orbital satellite in education, and the state Educational Telephone Network, to the development of disposable slides and flimsy audio discs for correspondence students. However, this exciting and demanding work was the cause of cognitive dissonance when we held discussions with educationists in the Faculty of Education, for they usually spoke of education as synonomous with school teaching of children in classrooms, and even adult educators seemed to regard education as a social activity, almost always conducted in groups. In our academic activities we were constantly faced with the need to transpose theoretical concepts from the domain of child education to adult education, and from the classroom and the group to settings which were unnamed, but were obviously not group settings.

When we studied the research in education we read, for example, that:

"The ultimate goals of research on teaching are theories of teaching, and these in turn involve the development

of a critical language for the analysis of classroom behaviour",[10] and "researchers are becoming increasingly
concerned with what actually happens in classrooms"[11]
and, " . . . the word instruction refers to the
activity which takes place during schooling, and within
the classroom setting".[12]

Even in the literature of adult education, in an inventory
of the research compiled for the Adult Education Association
of the U.S.A., De S. Brunner, one of the senior professors
of adult education in the U.S.A., and his colleagues included
a whole chapter on "The Use of Discussion", and another on
"Group Research and Adult Education", but made no mention at
all of correspondence teaching. There were some references
to radio and television, classified as audio-visual aids,
but the bias, even of literature as prestigious as this was

"Clearly adult education will take place in groups
almost exclusively".[13]

It was clear that a vast number of adult learners were
receiving instruction in non-group settings, and we concluded
that educational theory which did not provide a place for
such learning and teaching was incomplete, and unsatisfactory. After a year, we summarised our dissatisfaction in a
paper, which included the following:

"teaching consists of two families of activity with
many characteristics in common, but different in one
aspect so important that a theory explaining one cannot
satisfactorily explain the other.

The first of these families, the older, better understood, more fully researched, includes all educational
situations where the teacher is physically contiguous
with his students, so that the primary means of communication is his voice, and in which (to use the economists'
terms) teaching is a "service" that is "consumed" simultaneously with its "production". The physical proximity
of the learners with the teacher permits each to stimulate the other, consequently teaching of this kind is
conceived as a process of "social interaction"."

After elaborating on teaching as a process of social interaction, we continued:

"The second family of teaching methods, and the subject
of our concern, includes educational situations distinguished by the separation of the teacher from his learners, so that communication has to be facilitated by a
mechanical or electronic medium. Teaching in this environment is "consumed" at a time or place different
from that at which it is "produced", and to reach the
learner it must be contained, transported, stored and

73

delivered. There may be interaction, between learner and teacher, but if so, it is so greatly affected by the delay resulting from the necessity to communicate across distance or time, that it cannot be an assured component of teaching strategy, as it may in classroom or group teaching. We refer to this as DISTANCE TEACH-ING, to distinguish it from "contiguous teaching" where teacher and student are in physical proximity".

We argued that we could anticipate a growth in distance-teaching, and stated that:

"we believe the time is appropriate for an examination of the methods now in use, in the hope of identifying the characteristics that distinguish them, and that can be used to show the relationship between them. We are of course not concerned with the "hardware" characteristics of the media, but with the educational characteristics. Our search then is aimed at bringing together into a system, the discrete observations and definitions of researchers and practitioners in a number of separate, yet we believe, related teaching methods. As we examine the methods we will ask questions like:

What learning theory is assumed, or stated, by teachers using these methods? Are there differences between teachers' assumptions about learning - within each method, and between methods?

Are there differences and similarities in goal setting? In evaluation? Is there dialogue between teacher and learner? How much provision is there for learners to contribute to programme planning and evaluation? How do leaders in each method define the nature of their method? Do these methods appeal to different kinds of adult learners? What kinds of programmes are provided?"

As the problem became clarified, we sought a method for dealing with it, and were influenced by the success of John Buskey, who had developed a typology of residential adult education programmes.

He had "focussed upon a holistic impressionistic study of programmes with a view towards sorting them into groupings of seemingly similar programmes" and we decided to focus in a similar manner on "an impressionistic study of a selected sample of literature, including descriptions of programmes, but including also theoretical papers and reported research" [14] The research question as it was defined a few months later was:

"Does an analysis of selected literature of the various methods used to instruct independent learners reveal a pattern of educational elements that can be used to differentiate the field and define it?"

Since the parameters of the universe we proposed to explore were quite unknown, it seemed best to gather as large and various a sample of literature as we could. We were assisted by a professional librarian, and received other supporting services in the University of Wisconsin Educational Satellite project. We selected eventually more than 2000 items of literature pertaining to educational programmes in which learners were not in face-to-face relationships with teachers. We prepared abstracts on postcards, and it was these that we manipulated and classified in search of the key variables which would enable us to define and describe our field.

This is not the place to describe in further detail the different attempts we made in 1971 and 1972 to build a theoretical framework from this data, for it is more important that we now proceed to consider the framework which eventually appeared. However, two further points about the past must be made before we go on, for one was a starting point, and the other a turning point.

The starting point was our early definition of the kind of educational relationship we would study; we called them "distant learning and teaching" and defined distance teaching as follows:

"Distance teaching may be defined as the family of instructional methods in which the teaching behaviours are executed apart from the learning behaviours, including those which in a contiguous situation would be performed in the learner's presence, so that communication between the teacher and the learner must be facilitated by print, electronic, mechanical or other devices".

From our present perspective it can be seen that our method, though we meant to be inductive was rather more of the kind Melvin Marx has called "functional"[15], there being a continuous interaction between conceptualisation and data. It was from the concept of separation of learner and teacher that we derived the concept Distance, which was crucial in determining the selection of data for study which in its turn eventually provided us with our theoretical framework.

Following our definition, we generated a classification of programmes where "teaching behaviours are executed apart from the learning behaviours". We classified by the variable "medium of communication".

The media we listed at that time were: radio, television, dial access tape systems, computer assisted instruction, programmed instruction, textbooks, telephone and correspondence. A persistent intruder into this classification by medium was the wealth of so-called "independent study" programmes on university campuses, characterised by separation between learner and teacher for most but not all of the relationship, but not clearly characterised by a communications medium. This was a problem we were forced to return to in time.

A next major advance in the classification by medium was the identification of two variables, Individualization and Dialogue. A programme was said to be individualized to the extent to which a learner could control the pace at which he received information and at which we was compelled to make his response, while Dialogue described the extent to which the media of a programme made it possible or impossible for a learner to interact with the teacher. Perhaps the point can be illustrated by our own experience at that time when we were leading a telephone-teaching group. We obviously were in a Distance teaching situation, which was one where dialogue was possible, since any student could respond to the distant teacher, but in which the teaching was prepared for, and directed to a typical learner, but to no particular learner. The programme was as un-individualized as the "mass" medium of radio, yet considerably more "dialogic". Using these variables, we ordered our media as follows:

LEAST
DISTANT

	Highly Individualized	independent study on campus	1
High Dialogue		individual telephone	2
		individual correspondence	3
	Less Individualized	group telephone	4
		group correspondence	5
	Highly Individualized	computer assisted instruction	6
		programmed instruction	7
Low Dialogue		dial access tape systems	8
		television	9
	Less Individualized	radio	10
		textbook	11

(Distant Learning and Teaching)

MOST DISTANT

Fig. 1 **Distant Learning and Teaching Methods classified by the Dimensions of Distance.** [16]

We concluded that in a theory of Distance Education, Distance was not to be measured in physical terms, in miles or in minutes, but in the extent to which a particular teaching - learning relationship was individual and dialogic.

The second point from the past we wish to make, is what

we previously referred to as the turning point, and arose from our attempts to organise the literature of independent study on campus environments.

As in many other countries, in American Universities for at least half a century there had been various arrangements to permit selected students to follow personal study programmes, and to prepare papers or engage in personal research projects. These programmes were once called "honours courses", since they were restricted to only the more intellectual students, but after a national conference in 1925 became known as "independent study" [17]. By 1967 independent study was available in 90% of American universities [18]. We studied numerous definitions of this kind of independent study, including Baskin's:

> "Independent Study is defined as independent work or reading, sometimes on one's own, sometimes in small groups, but with such work taking place in the absence of the teacher and in lieu of certain regularly scheduled class meetings." [19]

Alexander and Hines defined it thus, "Independent Study is learning on one's own," [20] and the National University Extension Association called it:

> "a teaching-learning process in which the student studies primarily in a non-classroom situation remote from, and independent of direct, sustained face-to-face contact with the professor during the duration of the course". [21]

What went on under the name of independent study was:

(a) carried on apart from teaching,

(b) carried on by individual learners, and therefore appeared to belong in the universe of Distance Teaching.

However other definitions of this kind of instruction introduced other significant variables. MacDonald stated that the independent student was free to pace his learning according to his own circumstances and needs, and was free to choose among various channels, or resources for learning. [22] Trump wrote that "The individual student is given responsibility for the completion of work he helps to choose for himself. It includes students setting their own rate of progress through the use of teaching machines, libraries, language laboratories, and science laboratories". [23] The more literature we searched, the more clearly the variable of Learner Responsibility became evident. Alexander and Hines wrote, "Independent Study is considered by us to be learning activity, largely motivated by the learner's own aims to learn and largely rewarded in terms of its intrinsic values" [24]. Dressel and Thomson provided the term we eventually employed in our theory, in defining independent study as:

> "The student's self directed pursuit of academic competence in as autonomous a manner as he is able to exercise at any particular time".[25]

From our study of independent study on campus, a field with considerably more literature than the distance teaching field, and only a few items of which have been mentioned here, we deduced the following characteristics of such educational programmes, in addition to (a) and (b) above:

(c)   in Independent Study the learner chooses when and where to study, at what pace, and by which methods,

(d)   the learner chooses what to study,

(e)   the learner is self motivating,

(f)   the learner is self evaluating.

We then classified programmes in our collection of literature, by the variables of Learner Autonomy.

In 1972 a typology with programmes classified by Distance and by Learner Autonomy was presented to the International Conference on Correspondence Education. What follows in the next part of this paper is the outline of that concept, with some modifications and refinements of recent rewriting.

Part 2: Summary of the Theory of Independent Study

Definition 1: Independent Study is any educational programme in which the learning programme occurs separate in time and place from the teaching programme, and in which the learner has an influence at least equal to the teacher in determining goals, resources and evaluation decisions.

As defined, Independent Study is a generic term describing a major category of educational transactions, which are classified by the differentia "distance", i.e. "the learning programme occurs separate in time and place from the teaching program," and "autonomy", i.e. "the learner has an influence at least equal to the teacher". Perhaps to those meeting it for the first time, the use of the word "Independent" is misleading, since it might suggest the student is a kind of Robinson Crusoe, cast away on an island of self-sufficiency, which is not the sense in which the term is used. The independent student is engaged in an educational programme, which by definition implies both a learner and a teacher or teachers in a transactional relationship. Thus:

Definition 2: An educational programme is the use in a learning programme of a teaching programme.

Definition 3: A learning programme is a set of learner's objectives for his change in skills, attitudes or knowledge, a set of resources and procedures for reaching the objectives and a design for measuring the achievement of the objectives.

It should be emphasised that we are distinguishing "learning" and "learning programme", which is synomous with "study". Of course all humans are learning at all times of consciousness, but such is casual learning, random, uncontrolled, usually unconscious. A learning programme is a deliberate, purposeful and planned sequence of activities, which usually makes use of agents or helpers, who may be called facilitators, instructors, or teachers.

A teaching programme is equally deliberate and carefully planned:

Definition 4: A teaching programme is a set of teacher's objectives for change in learner's skills, attitudes or knowledge, a set of resources and procedures for reaching the objectives, and a design for measuring the achievement of the objectives.

It will be argued that deliberate learning can be without teaching, and if indeed a learner can establish objectives and achieve them using no resources or procedures prepared by another, and if he can evaluate his achievement, a learning programme without teaching will occur. The self taught ornithologist who knows about birds from his years of field study must be a good example of a learning programme without teaching, though if he resorts to a guide-book he is, though still highly independent, engaged in an educational transaction, since the book was written deliberately to assist his learning, by one whom we call a teacher.

The Variables of Apartness

Definition 5: Distance, or Telemathic Teaching is a teaching programme in which, because of the physical separateness of learners and teachers, the interactions between them are conducted through print, mechanical or electronic devices.

Telemathy means "learning at a distance", and is a word formed by combining the terms "tele" and "mathy", meaning respectively "far off" or "at a distance", and "mathy" from Greek "mathein", "to learn", as used, for example in "opsimathy", to learn in later life, and in "mathematics". Telemathic teaching is teaching in support of learning "at a distance". Independent study programmes vary in the extent to which there is distance between teacher and learners. What makes a programme more distant than another, making one programme of instruction more telemathic than another, is a function of two variables in the learner-teacher relationship, which are the extent of dialogue in their communication, and the extent of structure in the teaching programme.

Communication, the sending and receiving of messages, is an essential element of every educational programme, and in non-telematic teaching programmes is achieved by speech, together with various supporting non-verbal, but observable, interpersonal interactions. Dialogue is two-way communication. Telematic teaching requires the use of electronic, print, or mechanical methods of communicating and these methods differ in the extent to which they permit two-way communication, or dialogue, between learners and teachers. In a programme in which a high degree of dialogue is possible, it can be said that distance is less than one in which little dialogue is possible. For example, in a telematic teaching programme using the Educational Telephone Network, since dialogue is easy, the learner is less distant from his teacher than one in which the FM/AM radio is the communication method, when dialogue is impossible. Even among programmes using the same communications method there are differences in the degree of dialogue permitted by the programme design, and even among teachers using the same resource, a particular correspondence course for example, there may be differences in the use' of dialogue and thus differences in "distance".

Structure is the extent to which the objectives, implementation procedures, and resources and evaluation design of a teaching programme are prepared, or can be adapted, to meet specific objectives, implementation resources and procedures, and evaluation design of individual learning programmes. While dialogue is a measure of the degree to which the communications medium in a telematic programme permits learner-teacher interactions, structure is a measure of the extent to which, whether there is dialogue or not, the programme will permit individual, personal transactions between learner and teacher. It is a measure of the extent of the responsiveness of a teaching programme to the objectives of an individual learner's programme.

To the extent that a programme "consists of pre-produced parts, at least in the form of particularized plans listing item by item the knowledge and skills to be covered by the programme," [26] the programme may not be responsive to learners' idiosyncracies, and structure is said to be high.

Koffman explains the problem of preparing a less structured programme which attempts to provide many options to the learner,

All questions must be specific by the course author as well as a set of anticipated student responses to each question. If branching is to occur, explicit instructions must be given indicating the performance criteria for a branch and the new continuation point in the programme.

> Since everything must be specified in advance, extensive time must be spent in preparing the course material for presentation. Furthermore, once programmed, this material has very little flexibility. [27]

In a highly structured programme, such as in a linear, or non-branching programmed text, no variation of the programme is possible, while a correspondence programme is likely to be somewhat less structured, but perhaps more than a computer assisted instructional programme in which the medium permits the teacher to anticipate and prepare responses to thousands of different stimuli from many learners. Among programmes using a particular medium, the degree of structure will vary.

Using the variables of dialogue and structure, telematic teaching programmes can be classified according to distance between learner and teacher.

In Figure 2 where +D represents dialogue, +S structure, -D no dialogue, and -S no structure, the most distant programmes are those of the -D-S type, and the least distant are the +D-S type. These are theoretical poles, and all programmes fall between them. The variables by which we are defining distance are qualitative, and programmes must be regarded as "more" or "less" distant. Therefore, a correspondence programme is likely to be less distant than a programmed text, since it is likely to be less structured, and certainly more dialogic. However, among correspondence programmes great variability in distance will be found, some especially being more dialogic than others, and some correspondence programmes can be no more dialogic or unstructured than programmed instruction. Thus, it is not intended to classify communications methods in this model, but only the uses to which methods are applied in educational programmes.

	Type		Programme Types	Examples
Most Distance	-D-S	1	Programmes with no dialogue and no structure	Independent reading-study programmes of the "self directed" kind
	-D+S	2	Programmes with no dialogue but with structure	Programmes in which the communication method is radio or television
	+D+S	3	Programmes with dialogue and structured	Typically programmes using the correspondence method
Least Distance	+D-S	4	Programmes with dialogue and no structure	E.g., a Rogerian type of tutorial programme

Fig. 2   Types of telematic teaching programmes

81

In a programme where distance between teacher and learner is low, because dialogue is easy and there is a minimum of structure, both teachers and learners can respond easily to the stimuli of the others. In such a programme the teaching behaviours Smith calls "admonitary acts" as well as "directive action" and "logical operations" are possible.[28] However, when dialogue is difficult, or impossible, and when structure is high, "admonitary acts" become difficult or impossible. In a programmed text, such as Mager's, a minimum of dialogue between teacher and learner is obtained by use of the branching technique. The admonitary acts, such as "ooops! You didn't follow instructions",[29] are weak by contrast to the power such statements would carry in a highly dialogic interaction. In telematic teaching "directive action" is more easily communicated, than admonition, but the teacher must assume that a large part of direction, as well as admonition, will be self administered by the learner. The less distance, the more direction will be feasible. Even the most distant teachers are able to communicate "logical operations". Whether a particular learner will benefit from a programme low in distance, or from a highly telematic programme is determined by the extent to which he benefits or is impaired by direction and admonition. This is determined by his competence as an autonomous, or "self directed" learner.

Graphic Model of Telematic Teaching

The relationship of learners in telematic teaching programmes can be depicted by use of graph theory (Figure 3). In these figures, the influence of A, the teacher, is represented by a ray ($\longrightarrow$), an open and general influence, directed at any learners who choose to be influenced. Unbroken lines from learners to the teaching of A represent the learners "hooking on to" the teaching; the broken lines represent the response of the instructor to each learner. In the dialogic teaching programmes there are numerous responses, while in the non-dialogic programmes there is only one. In programmes of less structure there are several rays, representing alternative versions of teaching provided to potential learners, and in programmes of no structure there are no rays emanating from the teacher, but only responses to the stimuli of learners.

The Variable of Learner Autonomy

Definition 6: Autonomy is the extent to which the learner in an educational programme is able to determine the selection of objectives, resources and procedures, and the evaluation design.

Fig. 3 Telemathic Teaching Types

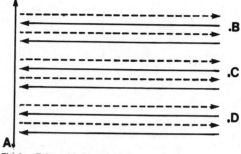

Fig. 3a—Telemathic Teaching Type +D+S
(e.g. correspondence programme)

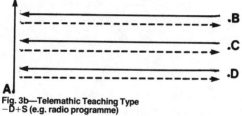

Fig. 3b—Telemathic Teaching Type
−D+S (e.g. radio programme)

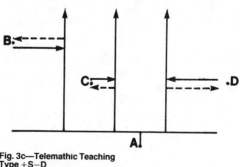

Fig. 3c—Telemathic Teaching
Type +S−D
but less structured than Fig. 2c
(e.g. programmed text)

Fig. 3   Telemathic Teaching Types (cont.)

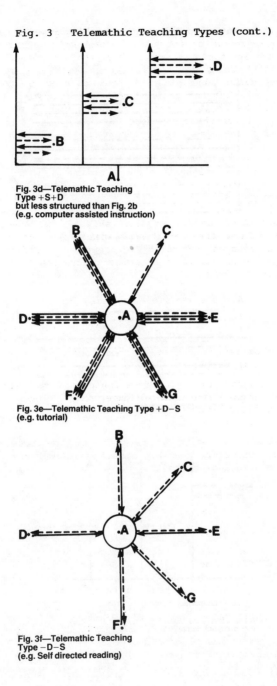

Fig. 3d—Telemathic Teaching
Type +S+D
but less structured than Fig. 2b
(e.g. computer assisted instruction)

Fig. 3e—Telemathic Teaching Type +D−S
(e.g. tutorial)

Fig. 3f—Telemathic Teaching
Type −D−S
(e.g. Self directed reading)

In the context of a programme, the term learner autonomy describes the extent to which in the learning-teaching relationship, it is the learner rather than the teacher who determines the goals, the learning procedures and resources, and the evaluation decisions of the learning programme. A fully autonomous learner is a person who identifies a learning need when he finds a problem to be solved, a skill to be acquired, or information he does not have. He is able to articulate his learning need in the form of a general goal, which is differentiated in several more specific objectives, which are accompanied, more or less explicitly, with criteria of achievement. In implementing the learning need, the autonomous learner gathers the information he desires, collects ideas, practises skills, works to resolve his problems, and achieves his goals. In evaluating, the learner judges the appropriateness of newly acquired skills, the adequacy of problem solutions, the quality of ideas, and the knowledge acquired. He reaches conclusions, accepting or rejecting the material, and eventually decides the goals have been achieved, or abandons them. This is obviously the behaviour of a mature adult.

The development in children of perceptions and response patterns having to do with dependence and independence, has been described by Heathers, who defines independence as follows: "A person is independent of others to the extent that he can satisfy his needs without requiring that others respond to him in particular ways".

> There are two kinds of independence, called instrumental and emotional. Instrumental independence means conducting activities and coping with problems without seeking help . . .

> The extent to which he persists in the task without asking for help may be taken as a measure of his instrumental independence. [30]

Emotional independence means "the absence of needs for reassurance, affection, or approval in particular situations". It includes "self assertion", in the form of the need to master tasks, which is motivated by the need for self approval on the basis of one's performance. Any behaviour motivated by the need for approval of others is symptomatic of emotional dependence, while behaviour motivated by need for self approval is symptomatic of emotional independence.

Heathers' definitions may be used to explicate the concept of the autonomous learner, who is emotionally independent when pursuing a learning programme, being motivated primarily by the need for self approval. To the extent that any of his behaviours are motivated by need to win approval of his instructor, or other external judge, he is not autonomous. He is also likely to have a high degree of instrumental independence, since he is experienced in coping with learning problems in a self reliant manner, but may be instrumentally dependent at times, for he might ask for help from many resources, and will be able to control and manage various sources of help. However, his approach to a helper is functional, not emotional, so help is used to achieve his learning objectives, not to win the approval of the helper. If he uses distant resources, several perhaps, he may have no personal relationship with a teacher, but if he has a personal teacher, will be able to control the effect and significance of teacher input in a realistic and unemotional way. He will resist teacher direction and admonition, and have a high tolerance for loneliness in learning. This description is very similar to Boyd's definition of the adult learner, a person who

> . . . can approach subject matter directly without having an adult in a set of intervening roles between the learner and the subject matter. The adult knows his own standards and expectations. He no longer needs to be told, nor does he require the approval and rewards from persons in authority. [31]

According to Knowles, such autonomous behaviour should be natural for the adult learner who, by definition, has a self concept that he is self directed. Indeed, Knowles writes "the point at which a person becomes an adult, psychologically, is that point at which he perceives himself to be wholly self-directing". Knowles says that dependency is part of the self concept of a child, who begins to see himself as having the capacity to make decisions for himself as his self identity begins to take shape. Unfortunately, however,

> . . . as the child moves up the educational ladder he encounters more and more of the responsibility for his learning being taken by the teacher, the curriculum planners, and his parents. The net effect is to freeze him into a self-concept of dependency.

For this reason, adult educators often must help learners to overcome a fear of being self directed and self reliant in learning, for "adults are typically not prepared for self directed learning; they need to go through a process of reorientation to learning as adults". [32]

Since autonomous behaviour is adult, the very nature of good adult education is the restoration and support of learners' autonomy. In all programmes, this means "great emphasis is placed on the involvement of the learners in the process of planning their own learning", "the learning-teaching transaction [is] . . . the mutual responsibility of learners and teachers", and there is a "process of self-evaluation in which the teacher devotes his energy to helping the adults get evidence for themselves about the progress they are making toward their educational goals".[33]

Similar positions have been expressed about autonomous learning by Pine and Horne[34], Landvogt[35], Maslow[36] and Carl Rogers[37], and described in an earlier paper.[38]

Classification of Independent Study Programmes by Variable of Learner Autonomy

Since learner autonomy is identified as a major characteristic of independent study, programmes can be classified according to the extent to which the learner can exercise autonomy in learning. To arrive at this classification the following questions are asked:

1   Is the selection of learning objectives in the programme that of the learner, or the teacher?

2   Is the selection and use of resource persons, of books, and other media, the sequence and pace of learning experiences, the decision of the teacher, or the learner?

3   Are the decisions about the method for evaluation and criteria to be used made by the learner or teacher?

By applying these questions a typology of teaching programmes is generated. In Figure 4 programmes range as follows:

1   Autonomous learning programmes in which the learner will use resource persons, literature, and other sources of information and skill, but decides himself what to learn, in what manner, and how to evaluate successful achievement. For example, a homemaker who feels a need to be a better cook, and sets the specific objective to be able to cook three varieties of fruit pies with a success rate of 90%, where success is determined by her family's eating the pies, who chooses to learn by using a "teach yourself" book has made all decisions about her learning herself. Her programme may be described as the AAA type. A teaching programme is used by the learner, but control and direction of the learning programme is in the learner's, not the teacher's, hands.

2   This is a class of programmes of lower autonomy, in which the learner's achievement is judged by an external agent, but the areas of competence in which he offers himself for testing, and the means he employs for achieving competence, are within his own control. In Great Britain, since 1885 it has been possible to register oneself as an external student at the University of London (though not for all degrees). Quite independently, the student in the London system may select areas of study, may study as he will, and may present himself for the evaluation of the University examiners.

		Objective Setting	Implementation	Evaluation
A = Learner	1	A	A	A
Determined	2	A	A	N
("Autonomous")	3	A	N	A
	4	A	N	N
	5	N	A	A
N = Teacher	6	N	N	A
Determined	7	N	A	N
("Non-Autonomous")	8	N	N	N

Fig. 4 Types of independent study programmes by variable learner autonomy

3   Having freely selected learning objectives, learners may surrender the direction of the use of resources to a teacher. Perhaps this is illustrated in the case of learning sports' skills, where several learners seek out a professional's instruction, but each has different criteria of achievement in mind, and each decides when he has learned enough.

4   A programme in which the learner, once having defined learning objectives he wishes to achieve, enters a controlled series of learning activities, and is evaluated by his teacher or other external agency. A person who chooses to learn the skills of driving an automobile, and enrolls with a professional instructor, has little control of the instruction, and none of the evaluation.

5 &   Programme formats, in which the learner controls, in
6   the one case implementation procedures and evaluation, and, in the other, evaluation only.

7   A common type of programme where the student has some control of the implementation procedures, but where the goals are prescribed by his teacher, and he is evaluated by an external agency. The majority of school and college independent study programmes fall into this category.

8   The common type of programme in institutions, especially where professional certification is at stake. The objectives for learning, the means, and the evaluation of achievement, are in the control of the teaching authority.

Discrimination among the various types suggested above is by the variable "learner autonomy", "the extent to which in an independent study programme the learner determines objectives, implementation procedures and resources, and evaluation".

Classification of Independent Study Programmes by Variables of Distance and Learner Autonomy

Independent study describes any educational programme where the learner has autonomy and there is distance between teacher and learner. However, since distance and learner autonomy are both qualitative variables, so is the term independent study descriptive of elements in all educational programmes rather than descriptive of an exclusive class of programmes or methods. By super-imposing Figure 2 on Figure 1, we can provide a typology of all educational programmes showing the range from most independent study to least independent study.

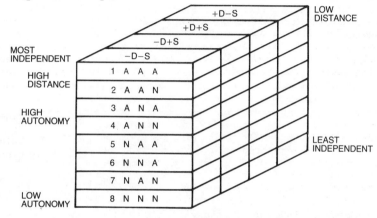

Fig 5   Suggested typology of educational programmes

In Figure 5 as in Figure 2, D represents Dialogue and S represents Structure. Programmes range from 1-D-S, which is a programme of high learner autonomy, very high distance, to 8+D-S, a programme where autonomy and distance are very low, so the learner is largely controlled by the teacher. The former programme is a high independent study programme, the latter is low. Using this typology we are able to describe any educational programme in terms of its Learner Autonomy, its Telemathy, and its Independent Study.

Part 3: The Theory in Practice

There is some disagreement in education about the nature and about the role of theory. Some educationalists have adopted a pragmatic, or functional approach to the generation and use of theory, and theirs is the position we share. We liken theory to a map, and writing it is a matter of seeking out and describing relationships about different aspects of the topography of the business of teaching and learning. The purpose of such theory is to bring order to the phenomena in which we are interested, for we cannot become scientific in our enquiries, i.e. we cannot proceed to manipulate variables, as long as we are trying to work with masses of assorted facts.

Thus the first stage in any new field consists in constructing a framework for classifying the phenomena in the field. This is not a highly empirical or positivistic concept of theory, as might be appropriate in such better developed sciences as physics, and our theory should not be tested by the criteria of such sciences. Ours has not been an experimental approach to theory building, nor has it been inhibited by concerns about operationism. We have been holistic in our concerns, nomothetic, and molar; positivists will object, in particular to our use of Hypothetical Constructs like "learner autonomy". Our defence is that this theory has been developed as a tool, not an end in itself, and its primary purpose as a tool is to define a field which was previously ignored, certainly in North American educational theory. Its significance therefore is merely as a starting place, as a heuristic device, and if it is then responsible for generating research by suggesting ideas, or even by arousing disbelief and resistance, it will have served its purpose. In this last part of our paper we will describe one major research project which was generated from the theory, and will give some examples of many other questions it suggests.

The research we conducted in Canada and the U.S.A. from 1974 to 1976 investigated the cognitive styles and the attitudes to independent study of students in one programme selected from the High Autonomy/Low Distance sector of the typology, and in another from the High Distance/Low Autonomy sector[39]. The psychological variable we selected for measurement was that known as "field independence". This was selected because it appeared to represent in one system the personality characteristics which might be expected to predict successful independent learning; it discriminates the person who is likely to define his needs independent of others, maintain his own directions, and prefers self evaluation over evaluation by external standards. Further, field independent persons are said to be task oriented and less affected than others by social stimuli, so might be expected to have a high tolerance for learning at a distance. The second variable to be studied was learners' attitudes to various aspects of independent study, which were measured by means of a semantic differential.

It was conjectured that:

1   People who decide to learn through independent study will prove to be of the field independent cognitive style.

2   In independent study programmes of high autonomy and high distance, learners will hold different attitudes to more dependent study than they will to independent study.

3   Between learners in an independent study programme of high autonomy, and one of high distance, there will be differences in learners' attitudes to independent study.

4   Among independent study learners, those with the personality attributes associated with field independence will find autonomous learning and distance teaching more satisfactory than will less field independent. Therefore, the attitudes of field independent learners to independent study will be more positive than the attitudes of field dependent learners, i.e., there is a personality X treatment interaction, where the personality characteristic is the cognitive style of field independence, the treatment is independent study methods, and the dependent variable is learner attitude.

To test the conjectures, two programmes were selected from the universe of North American independent study programmes, to represent the extremes on our typology of independent study programmes. One, referred to as the Distance programme was the University of Wisconsin's Independent Study Course A42, "Principles of Vocational, Technical and Adult Education" and typical of programmes relatively high in distance. The other, relatively high in learner autonomy, and referred to as the Autonomous programme was the programme for teaching adult education at St. Francis Xavier University in Eastern Canada. Both are programmes for professional education of practising adult educators. In the latter students have almost complete responsibility for writing their curriculum, using resources, and for self evaluation.

Students are referred to as the Distance students and the Autonomous students. The age, sex and educational distributions of students in the two programmes were similar. The conjectures were stated in the form of hypotheses, the researcher designed an "Independent Study Differential" (I.S.D.) for the measurement of attitudes, and then administered the I.S.D. and Witkin's Embedded Figures Test for the measure of field independence, in person, to each subject in both programmes. Data was analysed by t-tests and regression analysis, and the following is a summary of the findings.

(a)   Students in the more Distant form of Independent Study were significantly more field independent than the norm, (.99 level of significance), but the students in the more Autonomous programme were not.

(b)   Among Distance students there were fewer attitudes in favour of Distance teaching or autonomous learning concepts, but the Autonomous students preferred both over non-telemathic teaching and non-autonomous learning.

(c) Thus field independence might not be used as a predictor of successful participation in autonomous learning, but might be used as a predictor in distance study. As distance becomes less, a more field dependent cognitive style would seem to be desirable.

Some of the questions which are stimulated by the above research concern the field independence of students in programmes from other sectors of the typology, the field independence of "drop-outs", and the measurement of other cognitive styles. Replication of the study is desirable because there were limitations of a methodological nature in the original which the researcher is well aware of. However, apart from the value of the findings about cognitive style and attitudes of independent students, the research was of some importance, because it was derived from, and in turn contributed to the validity of, the theoretical framework which is the subject of this paper.

Conclusion

What we have presented in this paper has been a summary of the theory of Independent Study and Telemathic, or Distance, teaching. The theory was preceded by a survey of the origin and development of the theory, and was followed by a brief account of one major research project which it has operated.

It was said in our introduction that with the use of the tool of the Independent Study Theory, we could identify "a vast array" of new research and development questions. In conclusion, as a possible contribution to discussion, we will list a few which we believe to be important.

1 What is the most effective conceivable system for the production of distance teaching programmes which are truly responsive to the demands of learners?

2 What mechanisms are needed to see that learning needs are successfully articulated among individuals and communities for transmission to the distance teaching institution? How can we teach people to be more autonomous where there is need?

3 To what extent should Universities provide distance teaching in non-academic fields? (For example, teaching about Parenthood)

4 In programmes of high structure, how can we reduce it? In programmes of low dialogue, how can it be increased?

5 For which students is it desirable that programmes be of high structure and low dialogue, i.e. Distant; for

whom -D-S, i.e. most Distant; and for whom less Distant? *Is* there a relationship between Distance and Autonomy?

Questions such as these will have to be taken into account as we proceed with rebuilding old institutions and designing new ones. New and changed institutions will certainly be a consequence of the growing confidence with which the values of independent study are now asserted. Adult learning need no longer be random, for through independent study, self directed adults can expect to be served by professional resources in planning and implementing their learning, surely a significant move towards a system of lifelong education and towards the reality of a learning society.

Notes

1 Henri Dieuzeide, Educational Technology and Development of Education (Paris: UNESCO, IEY Special Unit, 1970), p.9.

2 Moss Cass, "Inaugural Address the Commonwealth Educational Broadcasting Conference", Combroad 29 (October-December 1975) p.10.

3 Edith Moorhouse, "The Philosophy Underlying the British Primary School", in Teaching in the British Primary School, ed. Vincent Rogers (New York: Macmillan Co., 1970), p.1.

4 Bartley F. Brown, Education by Appointment; New Approaches to Independent Study (West Nyack, New York: Parker Publishing Company, 1968), p.19.

5 Edith Moorhouse, in Rogers (ed) Teaching in the British Primary School, pp.8-9

6 Study on Continuing Education and the Future, The Learning Society (Notre Dame, Indiana: University of Notre Dame, 1973), p.7.

7 Dieuzeide, Educational Technology, p. 16.

8 Education Daily, 17th May, 1972.

9 Charles Wedemeyer, C. Wood and M. Moore, The Open School, Madison, State Office, 1971.

10 Richard Snow, "Brunswickian Approaches to Research on Teaching", Albert Yee (ed.), Social Interaction in Educational Settings. Englewood Cliffs, Prentice-Hall, 1971.

11 Phillip Jackson, "The Way Teaching Is", in R. Hyman (ed.), Contemporary Thought on Teaching. Englewood Cliffs, Prentice-Hall, 1971.

12 Association of Supervision and Curriculum Development. "Criteria for Assessing The Formal Properties of Theories of Instruction" in R. Hyman (ed.) Contemporary Thought on Teaching.

13 De S. Brunner et. al. An Overview of Adult Education Research (Chicago, Illinois: Adult Education Addociation of the U.S.A., 1950).

14 Michael G. Moore, "Teaching the Distant Adult Learner", Madison, University Department of Curriculum and Instruction, unpublished, 1971.

15 Melvin Marx. "The Nature of Scientific Theory Construction", in Theories in Contemporary Psychology, New York: MacMillan, 1963.

16 Michael G. Moore, "Toward a Theory of Independent Learning and Teaching", Journal of Higher Education, Ohio, American Association for Higher Education, December 1973.

17 Charles A. Wedemeyer, "Independent Study", in The Encyclopedia of Education, Vol. 4, Lee C. Deighton, Editor-in-Chief (New York: The MacMillan Co., 1971), p.550.

18 Paul L. Dressel and Mary M. Thompson, Independent Study (San Francisco: Jossey-Bass, 1973), p.15.

19 Samuel Baskin, "Quest for Quality, "New Dimensions in Higher Education", No. 7 (Washington, D.C. : U.S. Government Printing Office, 1960), p.3.

20 William Alexander and Vynce Hines, Independent Study in Secondary Schools (Gainesville: University of Florida, 1967), p.67. Report Number CRP-2969.

21 National University Extension Association, Descriptive Exposition of the Independent Study Division: National University Extension Association (Washington, D.C.: NUEA Independent Study Division, 1969), p.5.

22 James B. MacDonald, "Independent Learning: The Theme of the Conference", in The Theory and Nature of Independent Learning, ed. by Gerald T. Gleason (Scranton, Pa : International Textbook Co., 1967), p.2.

23 J. Lloyd Trump and Dorsey Baynham, Guide to Better Schools: Focus on Change (Chicago: Rand McNally, 1961). The quotation is from The Rand McNally Handbook of Education, ed. by Arthur W. Foshay (Chicago: Rand McNally, 1963), p. 242.

24 Alexander and Hines, Independent Study in Secondary Schools, p. 1.

25 Dressel and Thompson, Independent Study, p. 1.

26 Börje Holmberg, "Educational Technology and Correspondence Education", in Proceedings of the Eighth International Conference of the International Council on Correspondence Education, ed. by Renee Erdos (Paris: International Council on Correspondence Education, 1969), p. 60.

27 Elliott B. Koffman, "CAI Systems that Process Natural Language", Educational Technology, 14 (April, 1974), 38.

28 B. Othanel Smith, "A Concept of Teaching", Teachers College Record, 61 (February, 1960), 230.

29 Robert F. Mager, Preparing Instructional Objectives (Belmont, Cal. : Fearon Publishers, 1962), p. 5.

30 Glen Heathers, "Acquiring Dependence and Independence: A Theoretical Orientation", Journal of Genetic Psychology, 87 (1955), 277-291.

31 Robert Boyd, "A Psychological Definition of Adult Education", Adult Leadership, 13 (November, 1966), 180.

32 Malcolm S. Knowles, The Modern Practice of Adult Education (New York: Association Press, 1970), pp. 39-40.

33 Ibid.

34 Gerald J. Pine and Peter J. Horne, "Principles and Conditions for Learning in Adult Education", Adult Leadership. 18 (October, 1969), 109.

35 Penny L. Landvogt, A Framework for Exploring the Adult Educator's Commitment Toward the Construct of "Guided Learning" (Bethesda, Md. : ERIC Document Reproduction Service, 1970), ED 036 765.

36 Abraham Maslow, "Some Educational Implications of the Humanistic Psychologies", Harvard Education Review, 38 (Fall, 1968), 691.

37 Carl Rogers, Freedom to Learn (Columbus, Ohio: Charles E. Merrill Publishing Company, 1969), p.5.

38 Michael G. Moore, The Cognitive Styles of Independent Learners, Madison, Wisconsin, Ph.D, dissertation, 1976.

39 Ibid.

DISTANCE TEACHING AND INDUSTRIAL PRODUCTION*
A COMPARATIVE INTERPRETATION IN OUTLINE
Otto Peters

The more one attempts to grasp and explain the phenomenon of distance teaching, and especially the more one tries to identify the particular educational opportunities distinguishing this form of teaching from other forms of imparting academic knowledge, the clearer it becomes that the conventional range of educational terminology is not sufficiently comprehensive. Distance study represents facts new to education in several aspects. Compared with other forms of study it was novel in the form in which it made its first breakthrough over 90 years ago. With even greater justification it can be called novel in its present form in which it is currently spreading throughout the world, contributing towards the discovery of the educational opportunities provided by the modern media, such as radio and television. It is, above all, novel and pointing towards the future when it makes use of electronic data processing equipment and wideband cable transmission techniques. It is no coincidence that university study at a distance, in its early form of correspondence teaching, began its development only about 130 years ago, as it requires conditions that only existed from then on. One necessity, for example, is a relatively fast and regular postal and transport service. The first railway lines and the first correspondence schools were established around the same time. When one further realises how much technical support distance teaching establishments need nowadays in order to cater effectively for large groups of students, it becomes clear that distance study is a form of study complementary to our industrial and technological age. Lectures, seminars and practice sessions, on the other hand, have developed from forms of teaching derived from ancient rhetoric and practised at medieval universities; the colloquium originates from the dialogic teaching methods of the humanistic era [1]. These forms of teaching have changed little in their basic structure since the beginning of the 19th century. They proved almost completely resistant to combination with technical support facilities. In this context they can therefore be described as pre-industrial forms of study.

On account of these differences, distance study can only be described and analysed to a limited extent using traditional educational terms. They are not wholly adequate for this new form of study. This is understandable insofar as these terms developed from pre-industrial forms of teaching. If one applies them to distance study one will think in conventional concepts. To emphasise the point, one looks at a new form of study from an old perspective and has one's view of the essential structural characteristics distorted.

Industrialisation is the symbol of a new epoch in the development of man fundamentally different from all previous epochs. It is without example in history, above all, on account of the basic changes in most spheres of human existence. Academic teaching alone seems to have remained largely unscathed by industrialisation - with the exception of distance study, for this form of study is remarkably consistent with the principles and tendencies of industrialisation. For this reason, experimentally, structural elements, concepts and principles derived from the theories of industrial production are used here to interpret the distance study phenomenon. This does not mean that the teaching and learning processes occurring in distance study are equated with processes in industrial production. The comparison is purely heuristic.

A comparison of this kind between a form of teaching and processes from another sphere of life is legitimate and not without example in the history of educational theory. Amos Comenius, the "founder and virtuoso of the method of parallel comparison" [2] in his Didactica Magna, for example, compared the 'art of teaching' in unusual detail with the art of printing, also a technical process. Theodor Litt identified the nature of pedagogic thinking by comparing it with artistic creativity, technology and the processes of growth [3]. In the sixties, experiments were carried out which tried to explain the teaching and learning processes using the technical model of the feedback control system, in order to find approaches to a 'cybernetic pedagogy' [4]. Most impressive, however, was the achievement by Gottfried Hausmann who, in 1959, condensed the analogy between the dramatic arts and education into a 'dramaturgy of teaching'. In it he interprets the educational structure of teaching and learning processes in detail using the terms and principles of the dramatic art in the theatre. Paul Heimann saw the merit of this comprehensive and detailed comparison in the possibility that "it might give rise to a complete revision of our teaching and learning models" [5].

Furthermore, it may not be without significance for this planned interpretation that for another important aspect of university or college work, namely research, comparisons with the production process already exist. In 1919, Max Weber defined structural similarities between research institutes and capitalistic organisations [6], and, in 1924, Helmut Plessner pointed out that the "mechanisation, methodisation and depersonalisation of the manufacturing process equally dominate the production of economic as well as cultural goods" [7]. The following comparison between distance study and the industrial production process will prove similar consistencies.

From the start, distance study has a special relationship with the industrial production process insofar as the production of study materials in itself is an industrial process built into the whole teaching process as a constituent part, quite unlike the production of text books, for example. In the case of commercial distance teaching establishments the further question of selling the printed or otherwise duplicated study units adds calculations of applied economics to the teaching process. Even the distance teaching departments of government-financed universities are not entirely free from these considerations. It would be interesting to examine how far these facts have influenced the structure of distance teaching already.

In order to facilitate the discovery of further relationships between distance teaching and the production process, the following structural changes - essentially brought on by industrialisation - in the development of the production of goods should be noted:

1 According to the principle of rationalisation, individual work as it was traditional in the craftmen's trades, changes at an early stage to a production based on the division of labour (e.g. in factories), and this later leads to the development of assembly lines and mass production.

2 Work processes initially characterised by the use of tools are increasingly re-structured by mechanisation and, later, automation.

3 In detail, these changes lead to the following results:

    - The preparatory phase becomes increasingly important.

    - Success depends, among other things, on systematic planning and organisation. Scientific measures of control are needed.

    - Work processes must be formalised and products standardised.

    - The production process is objectified.

    - Each developmental step towards increased mechanisation leads to changes in the function of those involved in the production process.

- Small concerns are no longer able to raise the investment needed for developmental work and technical equipment. A strong tendency towards concentration and centralisation becomes noticeable.

The terms used in business studies to describe these facts will be outlined briefly and - where possible - applied to distance teaching.

Rationalisation

By rationalisation we mean all 'methodical, i.e. rationally guided measures' with the purpose of achieving 'output with a comparatively (compared to earlier situations) lower input of power, time and money'[8]. Scientific discoveries should "be evaluated for practical use in such a way as to achieve the best possible results in view of the continually necessary development and redevelopment of economic and technical processes"[9].

Applied to the practical example of the production process this means that "the entire production line, from raw material to end product, is carefully analysed to allow each single work process to be planned so as to make the most effective contribution possible towards achieving clearly formulated business tasks"[10].

Georges Friedmann emphasises that this is a dynamic process aiming at continuous improvement in quality through "continuous progress in the study of materials, accuracy and precision"[11]. Rationalisation of this type has only started to develop with increasing industrialisation at the end of the 19th century[12].

Management Science believes the reason for the considerable obstacles to rationalisation to lie in human nature itself, because "human inadequacy inhibits the motivation to gain unprejudiced views and the willingness to act according to rational convictions"[13]. Further obstacles are considered to be tradition, convention, habits and fashion.

In education, a rationalising way of thinking is nothing new. In a general form, it influences the reasoning for numerous educational decisions. For example, the introduction of lectures to larger groups of students, the use of printed books and the specialisation of university lecturers were considerable steps towards the rationalisation of the academic teaching process. Every university teacher will, when planning a lecture, choose those subjects that will help him most to fulfil the purpose of that particular lecture. In distance teaching, however, ways of thinking, attitudes and procedures can be found which only established themselves in the wake of an increased rationalisation in the industrialisation of production processes. The characteristic details are, among others, as follows:

1   In distance study the teaching process is based on the

division of labour and detached from the person of the University lecturer. It is therefore independent from a subjectively determined teaching situation, thus eliminating part of the earlier mentioned obstacles to rationalisation. The division of labour and the objectification of the teaching process allow each work process to be planned in such a way that clearly formulated teaching objectives are achieved in the most effective manner. Specialists may be responsible for a limited area in each phase.

2 The use of technical equipment (duplicating machines, organisation systems, transporting devices) makes it possible to convey the knowledge, ability and teaching skills of a university lecturer, by means of the detached objectivity of a distance study course of constant quality, to a theoretically unlimited number of students. The rationalisation effect of mass production becomes apparent here.

3 The rigorous application of organisational principles and means saves teachers as well as students unnecessary effort.

4 At some of the newer distance teaching establishments, modern means of technical support, such as film, television and electronic data processing installations, have replaced teaching staff in certain areas of their work, in particular, in the fields of giving information and assessing performance.

5 Students work through a course which has been tested prior to going to print. This prevents misunderstandings and stops students from going in the wrong direction.

6 The quality of a distance study course can be improved, because its effectiveness can be monitored at any time by scientific methods.

If the number of students required in a society outgrows the number of university teachers available, rational thinking should be able to find ways and means of changing teaching methods in such a way that the teaching resources of the university teachers available are used to the best effect, quantitatively as well as qualitatively. Distance study can be regarded as a result of such endeavours.

The division of labour

The division of labour has played an important role in the sociological theories of the last 100 years[14]. Applied to the production process it means that the work is split in the sense of "dividing one complete work process into a number of elementary procedures"[15], as described by Adam Smith at an early stage[16]. With an extensive division of labour "training periods become shorter, more people are able to carry out the work and wages can be lowered" [17].

A result of the advanced division of labour is increased specialisation. The following statement, by Adam Smith in 1776, applies to everyone involved in a production process where a division of labour exists: "Men are much more likely to discover easier and readier methods of attaining any object, when the whole attention of their minds is directed towards that single object than when it is dissipated among a great variety of things. It is naturally to be expected therefore that some one or other of those who are employed in each particular branch of labour should soon find out easier and readier methods of performing their own particular work, whenever the nature of it admits of such improvement" [18].

Just as the division of labour is a pre-condition for the mechanisation of work processes and for industrialisation as a whole, it has made university study at a distance possible. The division of labour is the main pre-requisite for the advantages of this new form of teaching to become effective. The principle of the division of labour is thus a constituent element of distance teaching.

The 'complete work process', which is split in distance teaching, consists of the teaching activity of the university lecturer, i.e. the entirety of the measures he takes in order to initiate and guide learning processes in students. Initially, the two basic functions of the university teacher, that of conveying information and of counselling, were allocated as separate responsibilities in distance teaching departments of universities or colleges. Both functions, above all however that of transmitting information, are now even further divided. If, for example, the number of students enrolled on a distance study course is high, regular assessment of performance is not carried out by those academics who developed the course. The recording of results is the responsibility of yet another unit; and the development of the course itself is divided into numerous phases, in each· of which experts in particular fields are active.

This specialisation may bring the following advantages:

- Materials required for the development of the distance study course can be assembled by leading experts in the specialist fields concerned.

- Having completed the manuscript the author can then be freed from the time-consuming processes of exact source references and of lecturing.

- Educationalists and experienced practitioners of distance teaching are able to revise the manuscripts of study units in order to make the planned teaching process more effective.

- Even colleagues from the 'academic middle tier' may be involved in the correction of exercises carried out by students. There are cases where even senior students have taken over such tasks, especially where they are concentrating on marking the exercises from a limited number of correspondence units. As in the industrial manufacturing process, the level of previous training may be lower on account of the division of labour and, as there, 'more people are able to carry out the work'. Since with extensive specialisation of this type the number of scripts one university teacher is able to mark may be much higher, this process is also cheaper.

Mechanisation

Mechanisation means the use of machines in a work process [19]. These machines replace the work done by the muscles of men or animals. In part they even take over elements of brain work. There are varying degrees of mechanisation. The pre-industrial stage is characterised mainly by craftwork making use of tools. The first level of industrialisation was reached with the use of 'dependent machines'. The second level of industrialisation led to mass production as a result of the use of 'semi-independent machines' and assembly lines. Finally, the third level of industrialisation is characterised by the spread of automation (with automatic control or feedback). The changes occurring at each level are so great that, in this context, one author has spoken about a first, second and third technical or industrial revolution [20].

In order to remain with this analogy, distance study could be ascribed to the industrial levels, as it cannot take place without the use of machines. Duplicating machines and transport systems are pre-requisites, and later forms of distance teaching have the additional facilities of modern means of communication and electronic data processing installations.

In contrast, when considering the framework of conventional study one cannot help thinking that its forms of teaching belong to the pre-industrial level. There the university teacher is comparable to a craftsman as he uses 'tools' (pictures, objects, books), without these changing the structure of the teaching process to any considerable degree.

Assembly line

Buckingham referred to the importance of the assembly line principle in connection with the use of machines. Both these factors, among others, had made mass production possible [21]. Assembly line work is characterised by the fact that the worker remains at his place of work, whilst the workpieces travel past him.

The formal similarity between distance teaching and the production process becomes particularly noticeable here. In the development of the distance study course the manuscript is passed from one area of responsibility to another and specific changes are made at each stage. The study units are printed on a large scale, stored, sent to the distance learner, completed by him, sent to the script marker who checks the work, and finally submitted to the administration, where the performance of the distance learner and the effort of the script marker (to calculate fees) are recorded. The rationalisation effect achieved by the fact that many university teachers and thousands of students do not have to meet in one place in order to participate in teaching events is at least the same as that a car manufacturer tries to achieve when, instead of sending the worker to the vehicle to be built, he transports the necessary parts to the worker. In both cases - the production process as well as distance teaching - time , energy and money are saved.

Mass production

In modern sociology the term 'mass trend' has rid itself of its negative cultural connotation, making it a largely neutral expression[22]. Mass trend nowadays merely denotes a structural characteristic of an advanced industrial society and indicates "that in a pure consumer society such as ours, the rise in the standard of living is due purely to the fact that industry produces certain consumer goods and commodities in large quantities, thus making them generally accessible"[23].

Mass production is by its nature only possible where there is a sufficiently large 'mass of consumers'. This, in turn, requires an efficient transport system providing a connection between producer and consumer who, as is typical in today's system, are geographically distant. In order to work profitably, the producer needs to research consumer requirements and find standards acceptable to all consumers for his product. He must continually improve his goods (aim at perfection), as each shortcoming is multiplied by the number of items produced.

If one equally rids the term 'consumer' of its negative cultural connotation, one can speak of the student as a 'consumer of academic education'. Quite obviously, 'demand' outstrips 'supply' at universities and colleges, and this had led to the large scale operation at our universities and colleges. As traditional forms of academic teaching originally envisaged small groups of students, and today's practice of applying methods designed for small groups to large groups must be seen as a perversion of an educational concept, (e.g. several lecture rooms with loudspeaker connection), one can understand it if various governments see distance teaching, on account of its similarity with the mass production process, as a means of providing very large groups of students more adequately with academic teaching than conventional methods would allow it.

Indeed, the multiplication effect achieved by technology and the postal delivery system mean that the university teacher and the distance learner - like producer and consumer - no longer need to live in the same geographical location.

From an economic point of view, the production of distance study courses represents mass production. Apart from reasons of profitability, the large number of courses produced forces distance teaching organisations to analyse the requirements of potential distance learners far more carefully than in conventional teaching and to improve the quality of the courses. For example, in the USSR the Public Accounts Authority complained at one time that too many students dropped out of distance study and it is suspected that this might have been the reason that led to an examination of the study materials. Most American distance study courses are revised and re-issued at regular intervals (every one to four years). As American universities charge fees to cover the greatest part of the budget allocated to distance teaching departments, the quality of distance study courses must not be allowed to deteriorate. When, on account of mass production, the University of California has more distance study courses to offer than there is demand for them, it occasionally places advertisements for students in newspapers.

Statistics prove that the number of graduates in areas without a university is lower than in areas near universities. It is possible that, according to the principle of mass production, distance teaching will one day equalise the opportunities to study, just as industrial mass production has assimilated consumer patterns in town and country. Analogous to the increase in the standard of living, this would make a general increase in the level of education possible, which might not otherwise have been achieved.

Preparatory Work

In a production situation where a division of labour prevails, economy, quality and speed of the work processes depend on the right type of preparation. This is necessary in industries producing a variety of articles and needs to be carried out by senior specialist staff in special departments (thinking departments), as workers, foremen and masters involved in the production process lack the necessary knowledge and experience. During the preparatory stages one determines how workers, machines and materials can usefully relate to each other during each phase of the production process. In addition, there are developmental and constructional tasks. The more thorough the preparation, the less is a successful production process dependent on the particular abilities of the workers involved. Consequently, workers can easily be exchanged. Normally, considerably larger sums of investment are required for preparatory work than was the case previously in the manufacture of goods.

As distance teaching institutions have to develop a great variety of distance teaching courses, the comparison with a firm producing a variety of goods comes to mind. In distance teaching too success depends decisively on a 'preparatory phase'. It concerns the development of the distance study course involving experts in the various specialist fields with qualifications also often higher than those of other teachers involved in distance study. Here too, each section of the course can be carefully planned. The use of technical support and a suitable combination of this with individual contributions from distance tutors and advisers play an important role in this. Compared to university teachers in conventional study, who are responsible for the entire teaching process, distance tutors and advisers are more easily exchangeable on account of the thorough preparatory work. Finally, the development of distance study courses also requires investment to an extent that has never before been considered at establishments of higher education.

The separation of preparatory work and individual instruction and the distribution of these functions among several persons is a particularly clear example of analogy with the production process.

Planning

An essential element of preparation is planning which needs to be far more comprehensive and detailed in the industrial manufacturing process than in manual production, as it requires the coordination of many interacting factors. By planning we mean that "system of decisions which determines an operation prior to it being carried out"[24]. In more detail this means that "all measures necessary for the economical execution of an order - from placement to delivery - must be introduced according to plan"[25].

Management Science distinguishes two methods of planning. Effective planning consists of choosing the most advantageous of several alternatives and forecasting the future development of data. Contingency planning is applied where market situations suddenly change[26].

In the developmental phase of a distance study course planning plays an important role, as the contents of correspondence units, from the first to the last, must be determined in detail, adjusted in relation to each other and represented in a pre-determined number of correspondence units. Where distance study is supplemented by residential weeks on campus or weekend seminars, planning becomes even more important; these supplementary teaching events are not intended to repeat academic contents already offered, nor have an 'enrichment' function, but should be structurally integrated in the distance study course. When combining distance teaching with other media, one has to consider carefully which type of contents suits what medium. Finally, where computers are used in distance study, preparatory planning is most advanced and demands by far the greatest expenditure as the teaching activity of the computers needs to be programmed.

In all these efforts to pre-determine and arrange the course of teaching processes as far as possible, we are dealing with effective planning. Intervention by advisers and tutors during the course of distance study, however, is regarded as contingency planning, which supplements effective planning.

Organisation

Planning largely concerns itself with the organisation of the production cycle. In organisational management terms, organisation means "creating general or permanent arrangements for purpose-orientated activity"[27]. As a consequence of the division of labour, the production process has to be rationally ordered according to organisational principles and with specially developed organisational means, since "the continuous interacting of numerous people towards a specific purpose requires organisation"[28], and furthermore, productivity depends on the type and degree of organisation. Distinguished from organisation are improvisation (preliminary and provisional regulations) and disposition (special regulations)[29].

In distance study, likewise, there is an immediate connection between the effectiveness of the teaching method and rational organisation. Organisation, for example, makes it possible for students to receive exactly pre-determined documents at appointed times, for an appropriate university teacher to be immediately available for each assignment sent in, for consultations to take place at fixed locations at fixed times, or for examinations to be held, or for a counsellor to inform himself at any time of the progress of a student or a group of students. Organisation becomes easier in large distance teaching establishments, as trained personnel and modern means of organisation are available. These enable them to supplement the organisation of distance teaching with improvisation and disposition.

The importance of organisation in distance teaching can be assessed by the fact that it is often difficult to distinguish between the operational (technical) organisation of distance study and the methodical organisation of the actual academic contents.

Scientific control methods

In recent decades the principles of scientific management have made a gradual breakthrough. According to them work processes are analysed systematically, particularly by time studies, and in accordance with the results obtained from measurements and empirical data the work processes are tested and controlled in their elementary details in a planned way, in order to increase productivity, all the time making the best possible use of working time and the staff available.[30] Frederick Winslow Taylor describes this process as the application of scientific engineering techniques to management.[31]

In distance teaching, similar tendencies can be shown. For example, some distance teaching institutions commission experts to analyse scientifically the success of their courses. Michael Young outlines the educational function of the research techniques applied by remarking that they replace the eyes and ears of academics in face-to-face teaching: they register students' reaction to the distance study course and aim at improving its effectiveness accordingly.[32]

These research techniques are not only used to determine the effectiveness of the course for individual students, but - and this is even more important - its effectiveness for the whole group of students involved. With its efforts to measure the success of a teaching method, distance teaching has doubtless introduced a hitherto neglected aspect into university teaching.

Formalisation

On account of the division of labour and mechanisation in the manufacturing process there is a much greater need to pre-determine the various phases formally than in manual production. It is only the emphasis on formality which makes the cooperation of all those involved in the production process possible, as each of them has to rely on previous work having been carried out according to plan. Most activities and interactions in an industrial set-up must therefore be determined according to agreed rules.[33]

In distance study, likewise, all the points in the cycle, from student to distance teaching establishment to the academics allocated, must be determined exactly. Communication is standardised by the use of forms. Authors of correspondence units are recommended to consider the incorporation of standard formalised aspects that have proved to be of advantage. Lecturers marking assignments also work to standard guidelines. Assessment is, in parts, largely formalised through the frequent use of multiple choice questions, where the student only has to place a cross against the right answer. In the most modern forms of distance teaching, formalisation goes as far as students marking the results of their learning on a punchcard in coded form and this is then input to a computer.

Standardisation

It is characteristic of a production situation involving the division of labour and high technology that manufacture is limited to a number of types of one product, in order to make these more suitable for their purpose, cheaper to produce and easier to replace [34]. Georges Friedmann pointed out that this does not at all represent a threat of dullness and uniformity. On the contrary, the elementary parts produced could be combined in extremely diverse ways [35].

The application of the principle of the division of labour and the use of machines, as well as the duplication of correspondence units in often large numbers, force distance teaching institutions likewise to adopt a greater degree of standardisation than is required in conventional teaching. Not only is the format of the correspondence units standardised, the stationery for written communication between student and lecturer, and the organisational support, as well as each single phase of the teaching process, but also the academic contents.

Whereas the academic giving a conventional lecture may indulge in an interesting deviation, because he sees educational advantages in this at a particular time with a certain group of students, the distance study lecturer has to be aware that he is, when writing a correspondence unit, addressing such a large group of students that situation-dependent improvisation becomes impossible. Instead he has to find a standard adequate, as far as possible, for every student admitted to the distance study course in question. This is achieved by developing a model for the course, perfecting it through the involvement of several experts and then approximating it to the required standard by testing it on a representative group of students before printing large numbers of copies. Just as the production of a branded article can only remain economical if its quality is continuously adapted to the constant needs of a large group of consumers, a distance teaching institution has to standardise the academic contents of its courses in such a way that it can be sure they appeal to all distance learners as equally as possible. The adaptation to any number of students, however large, forces the lecturer more strongly than in conventional study to consider the necessary standard that is, at the same time, realistic for as many students as possible.

Consequently, the choice of contents of a distance study course is less likely to be a reflection of the particular interests of an academic giving conventional lectures, but rather of the objective requirements of the total course profile.

Change of function

On account of the division of labour and the use of various types of machines, the function of the worker in the production process has changed considerably. Whereas it was typical for the craftsman to plan the production of a piece of work as well as acquire the necessary materials, carry out the work and finally sell the finished piece of work himself, industrialisation led to a more marked functional differentiation. When preparatory work and selling became separate from production and, within these three phases, many individual functions were allocated to different individuals, a loss of function naturally occurred for each single worker. On the other hand, new roles were created and new achievements became possible. For example, "in jobs where, due to mechanisation, the processing of the material has been taken out of the worker's hand, speed and energy of execution are no longer required; they have been replaced by accuracy and diligence; the work no longer shows quantitative but qualitative critera"[36].

As a result of the division of labour, the function of the lecturer teaching at a distance also changes. The original role of provider of knowledge in the form of the lecturer is split into that of study unit author and that of marker; the role of counsellor is allocated to a particular person or position. Frequently, the original role of lecturer is reduced to that of a consultant whose involvement in distance teaching manifests itself in periodically recurrent contributions. In order to ensure the effectiveness of the four functions mentioned, numerous support functions of an operational-technical type are particularly important, as, without them, distance study could not take place.

As tutors and consultants have largely been relieved from the task of conveying course matter, they are able to devote themselves to a considerable degree to more demanding tasks, such as aiding motivation, providing individual support, structuring course contents for students, identifying problems, establishing connections, etc. Here, too, a loss of function is compensated for by a gain in function whereby, at the same time, an otherwise almost unattainable level of quality can be achieved.

Objectification

The more the production process is determined by machines and organisational principles, the more it loses its subjective element which used to determine craftmen's work to a considerable degree. Hermann Schmidt pointed out that this process already started when man began to substitute tools provided by nature, such as hands, fists, and teeth, with tools taken from his surroundings. Objectification was not possible until the item to be objectified had become the subject of reflection [37].

Considering that, since Frederick Winslow Taylor, there has been a change over to analysing each single phase of the industrial production process with scientific means and to purposefully organising the contribution of workers and machines accordingly, it becomes clear what a high degree of objectification has been achieved. This development has found a climax in automated production where man's involvement in the course of the production process has largely been eliminated.

In this respect too, the relationship between distance study and conventional study is the same as between industrial production and mechanical fabrication. The university lecturer who lectures from his chair or leads a seminar discussion has the freedom and the opportunity to allow his subjectivity to influence his way of teaching: he is free to decide how and how much to prepare, he determines his own academic aims and methods and is able to change them spontaneously during a lecture, whereby not all the changes in his teaching method need to be reflected. In distance teaching, however, most teaching functions are objectified as they are determined by the distance study course as well as technical means. Only in written communications with the distance learner or possibly in a consultation or the brief additional face-to-face events on campus has the teacher some individual scope left for subjectively determined variants in his teaching method. In cases where a computer is used in distance study, even this opportunity is limited further.

The advantages of objectifying the teaching process in the form of a distance study course lie in the fact that the teaching process can then be reproduced, thus making it available at any time and, above all, that it can be manipulated. Without objectification distance study courses could not take place anywhere and at any time and be continuously improved.

The objectification of teaching practice in distance study is of particular importance in societies where, on account of an hierarchic structure of universities and colleges, the function of the provider of knowledge is combined in many academics with that of a holder of very great authority. As a result of this the relationship between student and lecturer is similar to that of subordinate and superior. As distance study has largely been freed from subjectivity, the process of providing knowledge is hardly affected by situations of this kind. In this context, distance study is particularly suitable for the further education of adults.

Concentration and centralisation

The investment required for mechanised mass production involving the division of labour has led to large industrial concerns with a concentration of capital, a frequently centralised administration, and a market that is not seldom monopolised.

In this context it is significant that some distance teaching establishments cater for very large groups of students. The largest universities teaching at a distance in the

USSR and in South Africa have over 40,000 students, and the Open University in England has more than 70,000. Each of these three establishments - as well as their Spanish equivalent - caters for the national demand. Obviously, a minimum number of students is necessary to make the technical installations and the establishment of an efficient organisation feasible. Economically, it is therefore more worthwhile to create a large central distance study establishment rather than 10 or 20 small regional institutions. Just as the industrial markets for certain products have long expanded beyond narrow regional frontiers, such centralised distance teaching establishments must cross the traditional areas of the responsibility of universities and the educational administration.

If all the said principles of distance teaching are rigorously applied, monopoly-like prestige positions in teaching activity are created for leading experts in various disciplines. Just as no record producer would use a mediocre singer when he can engage a Fischer-Dieskau, a distance teaching institution has to try and gain the best lecturers in their field for the development of its distance study courses. Just as in industry, however, one must ensure that such monopoly-like positions do not hinder free competition.

The possible consequences of a rigorous concentration and centralisation of distance teaching were hinted at, for the first time in 1966, in a memorandum from the British Government concerning the then proposed University of the Air[38]. In future, universities would no longer pursue the same objectives in all subjects, but specialise in some disciplines and cater for the national requirements for distance study in these.

Summary

From the above comparisons the following conclusions in relation to distance teaching may be drawn:

1   The structure of distance teaching is determined to a considerable degree by the principles of industrialisation, in particular by those of rationalisation, division of labour and mass production.

2   The teaching process is gradually re-structured through increasing mechanisation and automation.

3   These changes are the reason for the following structural characteristics to have emerged:

 - the development of distance study courses is just as important as the preparatory work taking place prior to the production process.

 - the effectiveness of the teaching process is particularly dependent on planning and organisation.

- courses must be formalised and expectations from students standardised.

- the teaching process is largely objectified.

- the function of academics teaching at a distance has changed considerably vis à vis university teachers in conventional teaching.

- distance study can only be economical with a concentration of the available resources and a centralised administration.

The result of this comparative interpretation permits the addition to recent explanations of distance study based on traditional educational concepts of a definition which is apt to point to the specific characteristics of the new forms of teaching and learning, thus structurally separating them from conventional forms of teaching and learning. This definition is as follows:

Distance study is a rationalised method – involving the definition of labour – of providing knowledge which, as a result of applying the principles of industrial organisation as well as the extensive use of technology, thus facilitating the reproduction of objective teaching activity in any numbers, allows a large number of students to participate in university study simultaneously, regardless of their place of residence and occupation.

This definition shows that, within the complex overall distance teaching activity, one area has been exposed to investigation which had regularly been omitted from traditional didactic analyses. Contrary to other attempts at definitions, new concepts are used here to describe new facts.

It was not a purpose of this comparative interpretation to pass judgements on the industrial structures which have been shown to apply to distance teaching. Presumably, the striking advantages of these structures, from a point of view of educational policy and organisation, are also connected with important educational disadvantages. This question has yet to be discussed. In this context it shall merely be hinted that it must be disadvantageous to a society if the developments outlined here have not been, or have not been fully, recognised, or are even denied. Such deep structural changes in academic teaching merit everyone's attention, no matter what hopes or fears are connected with them. If society's awareness lags behind the speedily developing technological and industrial opportunities, this is bound to lead to painful malfunctions, even in the area of academic teaching. They can be detected and remedied more easily, when the industrial structures characteristic of distance teaching are recognised and taken account of when the appropriate educational decisions are taken.

*This contribution is the revised and re-edited version of the 2nd chapter of the monograph Das Fernstudium an Universitaten und Hochschulen , which the author had published by Beltz in 1967.

Notes

1 Hausmann, G: Didaktik als Dramaturgie des Unterrichts. Heidelberg 1959, p.153.

2 Ibid. p.68 .

3 Litt, T: Führen und Wachsenlassen, Stuttgart 1958. App. 1: Das Wesen des pädagogischen Denkens, p.83ff.

4 Frank, H: Kybernetische Grundlagen des Lernens und Lehrens, Stuttgart, 1965.

5 Didaktik als Theorie und Lehre, in: Die Deutsche Schule, Heft 9, 1962; p.421.

6 Wissenschaft und Beruf, in: Gesammelte Aufsätze zur Wissenschaftslehre, 2nd ed., Tübingen 1951.pp.566-597. Quoted from Schelsky, H: Einsamkeit und Freiheit, Hamburg 1963, p.192.

7 Zur Soziologie der modernen Forschung und ihrer Organisation in der deutschen Universität, in: Scheler, M. (ed.): Versuche zu einer Soziologie des Wissens, München 1924,pp.407-425, quoted from Schelsky, H., in: Einsamkeit und Freiheit, Hamburg 1963, p.192.

8 Seischab, H. and Schwantag, K. (ed.): Handwörterbuch der Betriebswirtschaft, c.e. Poeschel Verlag, 3rd. ed., Stuttgart 1960, Vol. III, column 4530.

9 Ibid.

10 Buckingham, W: Automation und Gesellschaft, S. Fischer Verlag, Frankfurt am Main 1963. p.24f.

11 Friedmann, G: Der Mensch in der mechanisierten Produktion, Köln 1952. p. 203.

12 Seischab, H. and Schwantag, K. (ed.): as above, Vol.III, column 4531.

13 Ibid. column 4530.

14 E.g. Durkheim, E: De la division du travail social, and Die Theorie der Arbeitsteilung, by Gustav Schmoller.

15 König, R. (ed.): Soziologie, Das Fischer Lexikon, p.27. The author refers here to Adam Smith.

16 Smith, A: The Wealth of Nations, quoted from the chapter "Division of Labor" in Lewis, Arthur, D. (ed.) Of Men and Machines. A Dutton Paperback Original, New York 1963.pp.110-113.

17 König, R. (ed.): Soziologie, Das Fischer Lexikon, Frankfurt am Main, 1958, p.27. The author quotes Charles Babbage (1792-1871).

18 Smith, A: Division of Labour. In: Lewis, Arthur, D. (ed.): Of Men and Machines, A Dutton Paperback Original, New York 1963,pp.110-111.

19 Buckingham, W: Automation und Gesellschaft. S. Fischer Verlag. Frankfurt/Main 1963,pp.17-27.

20 Buckingham, W: As above, p.17.

21 Ibid. p.20.

22 König, R. (ed.): Soziologie, Das Fischer Lexikon, Frankfurt/Main 1958, p.171.

23 Ibid.

24 Seischab, H. and Schwantag, K. (ed.); as above, Vol.III, column 4341.

25 Seischab, H. and Schwantag, K. (ed.): as above, Vol.I, column 1742.

26 Seischab, H. and Schwantag, K. (ed.): as above, Vol.III, column 4348.

27 Mayntz, R: Soziologie der Organisation, rowohlt's deutsche enzyclopädie. Reinbeck near Hamburg, 1963. p.86.

28 Mayntz, R: as above, p.7.

29 Koziol, E: Grundlagen und Methoden der Organisationsforschung, Berlin 1959, p.18ff, quoted from Mayntz, R: Soziologie der Organisation, rowohlt's deutsche encyclopädie, Reinbeck near Hamburg, 1963, p.86.

30 Seischab, H. and Schwantag, K: (ed.): Vol.I, column 1055.

31 McConnell, J.W.: In Henry Pratt Fairchild. Dictionary of Sociology and Related Sciences, Littlefield, Adams, Totowa, N.J. 1966, p.268.

32 The home study review, Washington D.C. Spring 1965, p.37.

33 Mayntz, R: as above, p.86.

34 Friedmann, G: Der Mensch in der mechanisierten Produktion. Köln, 1952. p.394.

35 Ibid.

36 Ibid. p.389.

37 See Lexikon der kybernetischen Pädagogik und der Programmierten Instruktion. Schnelle, Quickborn 1966. p.133.

38 A University of the Air. Presented to Parliament by the Secretary of State for Education and Science by Command of Her Majesty. London; Her Majesty's Stationery Office, February 1966, 7 pages.

GUIDED DIDACTIC CONVERSATION IN DISTANCE EDUCATION

Börje Holmberg

Education is based on communication between *educans* and *educandus* and, in most cases, on peer-group interaction. This communication can take the form of conversation face to face. It is my contention that even when such real conversations cannot take place it is the spirit and atmosphere of conversation that should - and largely do - characterise educational endeavours.

Thinking aloud is a frequently occurring form of text elaboration which has been studied in different contexts (cf. Ericsson & Simon 1980, Chafe 1979 and 1980, Graff 1980 p.149). Elaborative processing of text, i.e. the interaction of the text content with the prior knowledge of the reader, has, in fact, proved conducive to retention (Weinstein, Underwood, Wicker & Cubberly 1979, Mayer 1980, Ballstaedt & Mandl 1982). Whereas a student who does very little elaborating does not secure the new learning matter sufficiently, those who do a lot of broad elaborating seem to risk difficulties in retracing the text information in the multitude of connections they have established. Thus moderate use of text elaboration seems profitable (Mandl & Ballstaedt 1982; cf. Ballstaedt & Mandl 1982 p.5).

Text elaboration has something of a conversational character also when it does not literally mean thinking *aloud*. Cf. Lewis, who rejects any contrasting of 'conversational activity with more solitary activities such as private reasoning and silent reading', which he characterises as 'internalised conversations'. 'As we mull things over quietly and in solitude, we are actually holding a conversation with ourselves' (Lewis 1975 p.69).

If we accept that this elaborative text processing and 'internalised conversation' represents a useful learning strategy it is logical to draw conclusions from this to a teaching strategy. In its simplest form this would imply causing students to apply an appropriate extent of text elaboration to their learning. This leads to what I have called a style of guided didactic conversation likely to influence students' attitudes and achievements favourably. The more a student is dependent on guidance, support and encouragement, the likelier is the favourable influence of the guided didactic conversation. It is the author's contention, however, that most learners, also among the most mature and autonomous students, benefit from teaching presentations based on the style of guided didactic conversation and thus conducive to appropriate text elaboration.

The gist of the concept of guided didactic conversation in distance education

Distance education can - and to some extent does - provide an application of this thinking. My theory implies that the character of good distance education resembles that of a guided conversation aiming at learning and that the presence of the typical traits of such a conversation facilitates learning. The distance-study course and the non-contiguous communication typical of distance education are seen as the instruments of a conversation-like interaction between the student on the one hand and the tutor counsellor of the supporting organisation administering the study on the other. There is constant interaction ('conversation') between the supporting organisation (authors, tutors, counsellors), simulated through the students' interaction with the pre-produced courses and real through the written and/or telephone interaction with their tutors and counsellors.

I first introduced my view of distance education as a form of guided didactic conversation in 1960. Since then the conversation concept has become important in other considerations of education. A remarkable contribution has been offered by Gordon Pask in his interpretations of learning under controlled conditions (Pask 1976, Entwistle 1978). Other applications of the concept of conversation are, for instance, found in Lewis 1975, Moran & Croker 1981, Thomas & Harri-Augstein 1977. The last-mentioned authors state:

> Effective internalization of the complete learning conversation produces the self-organized learner and the fully functioning man or woman. Such people learn from experience and continue to learn from life. Frozen internal conversations disable us as learners, and it is only when the external conversation is re-established that the frozen process can be revived. Living then becomes an ongoing opportunity for learning (p.102).

Although these approaches have some similarities with mine, they serve other purposes.

The basis

My approach is originally based on seven postulates. They are

1 that feelings of personal relation between the teach-

ing and learning parties promote study pleasure and motivation;

2 that such feelings can be fostered by well-developed self-instructional material and two-way communication at a distance;

3 that intellectual pleasure and study motivation are favourable to the attainment of study goals and the use of proper study processes and methods;

4 that the atmosphere, language and conventions of friendly conversation favour feelings of personal relation according to postulate 1;

5 that messages given and received in conversational forms are comparatively easily understood and remembered;

6 that the conversation concept can be successfully translated for use by the media available to distance education;

7 that planning and guiding the work, whether provided by the teaching organization or the student, are necessary for organized study, which is characterized by explicit or implicit goal conceptions.

Whereas postulates 1, 3, 4 and 7 are of a somewhat axiomatic character in agreement with generally accepted beliefs, numbers 2 and 6 are supported by a wealth of more or less systematized observations made by practitioners. Postulate 5 has to some extent been empirically validated.

A basic general assumption is that real learning is primarily an individual activity and is attained only through an internalizing process. This is, in my view, to be regarded as a background theory on which distance education is based. It leads us to a study of how this individual learning can be supported and facilitated.

As indicated in the postulates both the presentation of learning matter in a printed or otherwise pre-produced course *and* the two-way communication brought about by assignments (or otherwise) serve the purposes of didactic conversation. Whereas the former can pave the way for profitable interaction with the study material and thus represents a kind of *simulated* communication, the communication between student and tutor or counsellor in writing, on the telephone or by other means represents *real* communication. The two together constitute the kind of didactic conversation possible in distance education. It is the simulated communication that is above all studied in this presentation of the guided didactic conversation in distance education.

On real, non-contiguous two-way communication see Bååth

1980, Holmberg 1981a, Chapter 4, and Holmberg 1981b.

So-called self-checking exercises, review questions with model answers, inserted questions and similar components often stand out as important elements of simulated communication. They are not always necessary, however useful they are in many contexts. If a problem-learning approach is applied in the sense that the whole learning is based not on what we now know but on the problems asked by scholars of earlier times and by any serious student, then the discussion of how to put the questions, what paths to go and what procedures to use to come to a conclusion may include the conversational elements. Cf. Weingartz 1980 and 1981.

The characteristics of guided didactic conversation may be said to be:

- Easily accessible presentations of study matter; clear, somewhat colloquial language, in writing easily readable; moderate density of information.

- Explicit advice and suggestions to the student as to what to do and what to avoid, what to pay particular attention to and consider, with reasons provided.

- Invitations to an exchange of views, to questions, to judgements of what is to be accepted and what is to be rejected.

- Attempts to involve the student emotionally so that he or she takes a personal interest in the subject and its problems.

- Personal style including the use of the personal and possessive pronouns.

- Demarcation of changes of themes through explicit statements, typographical means or, in recorded, spoken communication, through a change of speakers, e.g. male followed by female, or through pauses. (This is a characteristic of the guidance rather than of the conversation).

This can - and should - be seen as an attempt to describe essential traits of good distance education and thus represent an understanding of its basic character. However, it is also a prescriptive theory in that it suggests procedures effective in facilitating learning.

The theory

A course presentation following the principles of guided didactic conversation in the sense described is assumed to be attractive to students, support study motivation and facilitate learning. This is expected to apply to most learners at all levels, but particularly to those with little or modest experience of study and limited independence. As exceptions are foreseen (a minority of students are expected to be indifferent or, in extreme cases, even negative to the style of guided didactic conversation) this is not a nomological theory.

If, as is usually assumed, children and adolescents rely more on guidance and a style of presentation adapted to estimated learning difficulties than mature adults, then the didactic conversation must be expected to appeal less to and be less effective with a target group consisting of mature adults than one consisting of less mature young people. Further, learning at an elementary stage is usually assumed to need more personal approaches and references to knowledge already acquired than highly advanced study. The didactic conversation would thus seem to suit elementary learning better than advanced study. It would also seem to suit the presentation of new learning matter where the learner is aware that he or she is covering new ground and thus needs personal guidance rather than presentations of learning matter that the student has already worked with on earlier occasions.

With these reservations I assume that if a distance-study course consistently represents a communication process felt to have the character of a conversation, then the students will be more motivated and more successful than if the course studied has an impersonal textbook character. This also concerns the use of assignments for submission: if used as a means to stimulate and facilitate conversation-type communication they are assumed to contribute considerably more to motivation and success than if used as a means to examine and evaluate students.

My main formal hypotheses based on the general postulates and the assumptions about what constitutes guided didactic conversation can therefore be summarised as follows:

- The stronger the characteristics of guided didactic conversation, the stronger the students' feelings of personal relationship between them and the supporting organisation.

- The stronger the students' feelings that the supporting organisation is interested in making the study matter personally relevant to them, the greater their personal involvement.

- The stronger the students' feelings of personal relations to the supporting organisation and of being personally involved with the study matter, the stronger the motivation and the more effective the learning.

- The more independent and scholarly experienced the students, the less relevant the characteristics of guided didactic conversation.

It would be tempting to try to test the influence of each of the characteristics of the guided didactic conversation as listed above. However, it does not seem possible to explore if each of them separately constitutes a sufficient means to bring about a type of communication which creates feelings of personal involvement. The different characteristics evidently overlap too much to make this possible. It is the united influence of the characteristics as a composite characterising quality that is tested.

The validity of the theory is tested in a way inspired by Popper, i.e. through falsification rather than verification attempts.

1 A unit of a German post-graduate course on educational planning was modified in such a way that the first part was developed according to the principles of guided didactic conversation whereas the second part was retained in the original form, which was in the style of traditional German scholarly writings. The students' attitudes to the two types of presentation were investigated by a questionnaire study (Holmberg & Schuemer 1980).

2 A post-graduate distance-study course on 'Essentials of distance education' in a British and a German version was written in the style of didactic conversation and was tried out as a training course for distance educators (from a number of different countries). Their opinions about the value, if any, of guided didactic conversation in distance education were collected (Holmberg & Schuemer 1982).

3 An English-language course on English grammar for Swedish students reviewing their school knowledge as a preparation for university study of English was re-written in the style of guided didactic conversation. On the basis of a randomised selection an experimental group of students were given the revised version whereas a control group were given the original version. The attitudes and the attainments of the two groups were analysed and compared (Holmberg, Schuemer & Obermeier 1982).

Results

The empirical investigations gave no conclusive evidence. However, the tendency apparent in all the three studies favours the theory although no consistent, statistically significant corroboration has emerged. The students taking part in the investigation state that they feel personally involved by the conversational presentations, their attitudes are favourable to them and in the third study they do

119

marginally better than the students taking the original course in their assignment attainments.

These results are statistically less supportive of the theory than expected. Nevertheless the tendential outcome does support the theory. Statistically it has not been proved wrong (has not been falsified) and is considered valid as an ad-hoc theory until one with more explanatory power has been developed and tested with more favourable results.

These conclusions are the more reasonable on account of the testing procedures used.

To test the applicability of the theory of guided didactic conversation the falsification attempts have caused particular attention to the circumstances (frame factors) which appear to weaken the predictive value of the theory. Students' attitudes to the style of didactic conversation as well as their achievements on studying a handbook presentation in relation to those following the study of a conversation-style presentation were, in consequence, analysed under circumstances as unfavourable as possible to the theory:

1 The courses used for the empirical investigations concerned the university stage, where the independence of the form of presentation and of guidance is assumed to be considerably greater than at lower stages.

2 The students concerned in the investigations were adults and therefore presumably somewhat independent in their study.

3 The course chosen for the first study (limited to research on students' attitudes) was an advanced course (on educational planning) mainly studied as a post-graduate course by teachers and others who had acquired a university degree before they enrolled for this course, by students of other universities supplementing their degree programme and by external students with particular interest in the subject.

4 The course on which the second study was based was a professional course for distance educators at post-graduate level.

5 The third study, which included an analysis of the students' achievements, was concerned with a distance-study course meant for and used as a deepening revision of a subject area (English grammar) that at lower levels the students had gone over on several earlier occasions. They could thus be expected to benefit from and be attracted to a survey of a handbook format rather than learn more effectively from and enjoy a conversation-like presentation.

If the theoretical universe of the study is taken to consist of distance study in general, these falsification attempts lead to a deviation from isomorphism between the cases tested and all relevant cases, but in such a way that the validity of the theory is strengthened through the statistical failure of the falsification. This is due to the logical certainty that non-disproved applicability of the theory of guided didactic conversation to the cases studied must be interpreted as a clear indication that it applies as much to cases of distance study at more elementary level and with less mature or advanced students than in the cases studied.

References

Bääth, J.A. (1980) Postal two-way communication in correspondence education. Lund: Gleerup

Ballstaedt, S.P. & Mandl, H. (1982) Elaborationen: Probleme der Erhebung und Auswertung. Forschungsbericht 16. Tübingen: Deutsches Institut für Fernstudien

Chafe, W.L. (1979) Creativity in verbalization and its implications for the nature of stored knowledge. In Freedle, R.O. (ed.), Discourse production and comprehension. pp. 41-55. Norwood, N.J.: Ablex

Chafe, W.L. (1979) The flow of thought and the flow of language. In Givon, T. (ed.), Syntax and semantics 12, Discourse and syntax, pp. 159-181. New York: Academic Press

Chafe, W.L. (1980) The development of consciousness in the production of a narrative. In Chafe, W.L., The pear stories. Cognitive, cultural, and linguistic aspects of narrative production. pp. 9-50. Norwood, N.J.: Ablex

Entwistle, N.J. (1978) Knowledge structures and styles of learning: a summary of Pask's recent research. British Journal of Educational Psychology 48, 255-263

Ericsson, K.A. & Simon, H.A. (1980) Verbal reports as data. Psychological Review, 87/1980, pp.215-251

Graff, K. (1980) Die jüdische Tradition und das Konzept des autonomen Lernens. Weinheim: Beltz

Holmberg, B. (1960) On the methods of teaching by correspondence. Lunds universitets årsskrift NF. Avd. 1. Bd. 54, Nr.2. Lund: Gleerup (Also translated into German: Über die Lehrmethoden im Fernunterricht. Hamburg-Rahlstedt: Walter Schultz KG 1962)

Holmberg, B. (1977) Distance education. A survey and bibliography. London: Kogan Page

Holmberg, B. (1981a) Status and trends of distance education. London: Kogan Page

Holmberg, B. (1981b) Zur medienvermittelten Zweiweg-Kommunikation im Fernstudium. ZIFF Papiere 38. Hagen: Fernuniversität

Holmberg, B. & Schuemer, R. (1980) Methoden des gelenkten didaktischen Gespräches. Ergebnisse einer Voruntersuchung. Hagen: Fernuniversität, ZIFF

Holmberg, B. & Schuemer, R. (1982) Meinungen zum Kurs 'Essentials of distance education'/'Grundlagen des Fernstudiums'. Hagen: Fernuniversität, ZIFF

Holmberg, B., Schuemer, R. & Obermeier, A. (1982) Zur Effizienz des gelenkten didaktischen Gespräches. Hagen: Fernuniversität, ZIFF

Lewis, B.N. (1975) Conversational man. Teaching at a Distance 2, 68-71

Mandl, H. & Ballstaedt, S.P. (1982) Effects of elaborations on recall of texts. In: Flammer, A. & Kintsch, W. (eds.), Discourse processing. Amsterdam: North-Holland Publishing Co.

Moran, L. & Croker, S.W. (1982) Take counsel with yourself: a self-directed counselling package. Off Campus 3, 1, 10-15

Pask, G. (1976) Conversational techniques in the study and practice of education. British Journal of Educational Psychology, 46, 12-25

Popper, K. (1959) The logic of scientific discovery. London: Hutchinson

Thomas, L.F. & Harri-Augstein, S. (1977) Learning to learn: the personal construction and exchange of meaning. In Howe, M.J.A. (ed.), Adult learning. Psychological research and applications. London: Wiley

Weingartz, M. (1980) Didaktische Merkmale selbstinstruierender Studientexte. Hagen: Fernuniversität

Weingartz, M. (1981) Lernen mit Texten. Bochum: Kamp

Weinstein, C.E., Underwood, V.L., Wicker, F.W. & Cubberly, W.E. (1979) Cognitive learning strategies: verbal and imaginal elaboration. In: O'Neil, H.F. & Spielberger, C. (eds.), Cognitive and affective learning strategies, pp. 45-75. New York: Academic Press

SECTION 3: DISTANCE EDUCATION AND SOCIETY: A RATIONALE

INTRODUCTION

The reader of this volume will already have encountered a number of justifications for the provision of education at a distance. Perraton (Section 1, second Reading) starts out from 'the need to expand education', while Sewart (Section 1, third Reading) mentions 'the new techniques which have been perfected in the twentieth century', 'the increasing costs of conventional education' and the possibility of a small expert group providing learning materials when teachers or skills are not otherwise available. Moore (Section 2, first Reading) places the emphasis on 'the demand for learner freedom' and Peters (Section 2, second Reading) is concerned with mass education.

To these reasons must be added the opening up of education to groups of students who cannot or do not wish to participate in conventional educational provision. Firstly there are those, children and adults, who live too far from the nearest educational institution and are prevented by distance from enrolment. Secondly there are those groups of students who have been traditionally barred from education by the time-tabling of classes and lectures and by the necessity of joining a learning group in order to study. Four types of students can thus be identified: (i) those in full-time employment; (ii) housewives; (iii) the institution-alized; (iv) those in certain occupations (shiftworkers, for example) that have traditionally been associated with distance study.

In a period during which the character of work and the importance it plays in people's lives is altering in a number of societies, it is important for society to provide educational possibilities for those who must remain full-time in the workforce while developing new skills which are required either for maintenance in their present employment or for a replacement for employment that becomes redundant.

Women have found distance programmes particularly attractive and many institutions report higher proportions of housewives and women caring for young children than conventional institutions. Athabasca University, for instance, had in 1980-81 61% female to 39% male undergraduates.

Distance institutions frequently take a special interest in and are sometimes given a special mandate by society for the education of the disabled; the infirm; the hospitalized; prisoners and the aged. They teach an older age group than conventional institutions with 12% of Athabasca students, 16% of UNED Spain and no fewer than 32.3% of the Open University of the United Kingdom's students being over 40 in 1981.

Every institution that teaches at a distance can provide a colourful listing of occupations that have traditionally formed part of their clientele: lighthouse keepers; itinerants; executives who spend much time in travel; fruitpickers; the army; the police; shift workers; sailors. To these must be added a growing number of students in the late 1970s and the early 1980s who choose to study at a distance even when a similar programme is available at a conventional institution convenient to them.

Initially many of the institutions incorporating these ideas were propietary institutions –privately supported and privately organised - but publicly-sponsored institutions have been active in this field for almost a century.

A new urgency for provision of distance education was witnessed in many societies in the last decade. It led to the creation of universities specifically designed to cope with the problems of providing education for students studying only at a distance: the 'open universities' or the 'distance teaching universities'. These new university structures, with their claim that they can provide university degrees and a university education on a par with conventional universities provide the ultimate rationale for education àt a distance. (Keegan and Rumble, 1982).

These new universities with their date of incorporation are: Open University of the United Kingdom (1969); UNED Spain (1973); Allama Iqbal Open University (1975); Athabasca University, Canada (1975); Fernuniversität, Federal Republic of Germany (1975); Everyman's University, Israel (1976); UNA Venezuela (1977); UEED Costa Rica (1978); Free University of Iran (1978); Open University, Sri Lanka (1980); Open University, Thailand (1981); Open University, Netherlands (1981). New foundations are being planned in Portugal, Nigeria, Japan and a number of other countries. Rumble (1982:10) has analysed the goals of the Open University of the United Kingdom and found them to include the following points of focus:

- those previously deprived of higher education through lack of opportunities rather than lack of ability;

- those qualified school leavers who, despite expansion of conventional universities, could not gain a place in such universities;

- those who had left school early (without gaining normal academic requirements) but who later realised they wanted or needed higher education;

- the many thousands of certificated non-graduate teachers who would wish to acquire graduate status;

- other significant groups of professional students interested in the University's courses;

- the university's 'unrivalled opportunity to rectify' the 'long continuing imbalance' in the number of women in further and higher education.

The state government of North-Rhine-Westphalia gave three reasons for founding the Fernuniversität in the Federal Republic of Germany:

- to increase the number of university places available

- to provide a university setting for continuing professional education

- to introduce new methodologies into university teaching.

Developments such as these have led commentators to regard distance education as the final phase in the expansion of provision of post-secondary education in the post World War II period. In both developed and developing countries it makes provision for those who cannot avail themselves of the programme provided by conventional institutions, even when this is on a part-time, night-time basis.

Besides its contribution to the educational systems of developed and developing countries of the Western World, distance education plays an important role in the socialist democracies of Central and Eastern Europe.

The rationale for distance education in socialist systems is two-fold: it provides for a democratisation of the educational process and it enables students to continue to contribute to the Gross National Product of their country's economy during the length of their study. (Gorochov, 1979:14). Distance programmes in socialist countries are often expressly linked to the workplace with paid study leave, support from the employer during the study period, a thesis on some aspect of the company's activity and - possibly - promotion to a management position at the conclusion of the study programme being characteristics of the system.

Escotet shows an awareness of many of the factors which provide a justification for education at a distance when he lists a very wide range of open and distance programmes in Latin America. He criticises, however, any rationale which would justify the importation of distance systems from outside Latin America. He feels that each culture has 'learning styles' which are related to the social and educational characteristics of the region. He queries the transfer of a system of general education into the Latin American university structure of professional degrees (*carreras*) and calls for audacity and imagination in the development of strategies suitable for Latin America.

Pagney calls for distance education to 'shed its marginal image once and for all, and be accepted as an integral part of the educational system'. He considers that its rationale is not to fill any gap in 'normal' provision but to enrich the educational process and permit it to reach its full potential. He speaks from the background of the massive, official government provision of distance education in France, now in its 43rd year. His institution, the Centre National d'Enseignement par Correspondance (formerly the Centre National de Télé-enseignement) enrolled 220,00 new students from 104 countries in 1982, in programmes ranging from primary schooling to post-graduate university level programmes (CAPES, *agrégation*). Pagney argues succinctly that those who provide for education in a national system by distributing taxpayer's monies to educational institutions are required to make provision for education at a distance.

In the extract chosen for this volume *Wedemeyer* treats distance learning, independent learning and open learning as aspects of 'non-traditional learning' and seeks to evaluate their contribution to American society and that society's reaction to such forms of learning. He claims that the 'non-traditional learner knows loneliness, not so much in a social sense, as in the sense of identity as a learner'. His choice of the brusque phrase 'back-door learning' to describe distance and non-traditional systems shows his view of society's evaluation of study at a distance.

Wedemeyer gives glimpses of the evolution of non-traditional forms of education in the U.S. from the Chatauqua movement, originally a form of summer camp for Sunday School teachers, through the land grant universities, to the 'astonishing surge of innovation at all levels of education' in the 1960s and the establishment of new institutions in the period 1969-1975. In a final section he tries to assess why the United States, which leads the world in the communications revolution, has had little success with distance education systems. The closure in 1982 of the ill-fated University of Mid-America is a good illustration.

The selections from Escotet, Pageny and Wedemeyer will give the reader an entrée into the literature, admittedly little developed, of the rationale for distance systems and a background to assess their role in the future.

Desmond Keegan

References

Gorochov, W.A. (1979) Hauptwege zur Vervolkommung des Fernstudiums in der UdSSR, in Dietze, G. (ed.) Referate und Beitrage: 4. Internationales Wissenschaftliches Seminar zum Hochschulfernstudium. Dresden: Zentralstelle für das Hochschulfernstudium

Keegan, D. and Rumble, G. (1982) The distance teaching universities: an appraisal. In Rumble, G. and Harry, K. (eds) The distance teaching universities. London: Croom Helm

Rumble, G. (1982) The Open University of the United Kingdom. Milton Keynes: OU (DERG)

Wedemeyer, C.A. (1981) Learning at the back door. Madison: Uof Wisconsin Press

BACK DOOR LEARNING IN THE LEARNING SOCIETY
(extracts)
Charles A. Wedemeyer

Carl Sandburg's advice to a youth coming of age is relevant to non-traditional, back door learners of any age.

> Tell him to be alone often and get at himself
> and above all tell himself no lies about
> himself whatever the white lies and protective
> fronts he may use amongst other people. Tell
> him solitude is creative if he is strong and
> the final decisions are made in silent rooms.
> Tell him to be different from other people if
> it comes natural and easy being different.
> Let him have lazy days seeking his deeper
> motives. Let him seek deep for where he is a
> born natural. Then he may understand Shakespeare
> and the Wright Brothers, Pasteur, Pavlov,
> Michael Faraday and free imaginations bringing
> changes into a world resenting change. He
> will be lonely enough to have time for the
> work he knows as his own.[1]

In a society in which education is dominated by traditional institution methods, and practices, the non-traditional learner knows loneliness, not so much in a social sense, as in the sense of identity as a learner.

Back door learning has been something of an embarrassment to traditional institutions. To learners, non-traditional learning is sometimes a frustrating kind of satisfaction, fulfilling to the self, but eliciting from a schooling and credential-oriented society an incomplete and distorted image of actual accomplishments. In ways characteristic of any bureaucracy, the viewpoints, policies, and procedures of traditional education have denigrated, dismissed, or downplayed the self-initiated and self-directed efforts of learners. It is almost as though such learners don't really exist; as though their achievements in learning can't be identified, measured, and compared with the achievements of traditional learners. Similarly, studies of non-traditional learning have, by and large, been ignored.

Yet by any standard, non-traditional learners and their achievements constitute the equivalent of a great natural resource in America. As the kind and quality of education a person obtains for himself becomes more urgent, non-traditional learning more and more replaces, supplements, extends or builds upon learnings acquired in traditional ways. This great but largely invisible national resource spreads and renews itself at little cost and great benefit to the nation. Even back doors to education, it appears "once opened, cannot be shut."

It is said that "forty years ago, Robert Binkely at Western Reserve University stumbled onto what he came to call the 'amateur scholar', and recognized an intelligentsia in America invisible in every way save locally."[3] Currently, Gross is studying the

serious, advanced intellectual work conducted independently . . . to call attention to the passionate pursuit of truth beyond academe, by all kinds of people in all kinds of realms: the hard sciences from microbiology to astronomy, the humanities from history to metaphysics, the social sciences from demographics to environmental activism; other realms of knowledge denigrated or undreamt of by the academy . . . utterly voluntary, pro-active, self-directed, autonomous, idiosyncratic, non-institutionalized, productive, innovative, and joyous.[4]

Non-traditional learning at the back door encompasses a broad and diverse range of activities. At one end is learning undertaken, as Gross notes, with complete autonomy and independence. At the other is learning undertaken in a transactional relationship with educational programs and institutions, but entered into by the choice of the learner on the basis of his own needs, concerns, and aspirations. Such learning employs non-traditional methods that afford opportunity and access irrespective of learner location and situation, and that in varying degrees place the learner at or near the centre of the teaching-learning relationships. Distance, independent, and open learning are terms in wide use today for certain kinds of non-traditional learning, but such terms are imprecise, ambiguous, and overlapping. Even the catch-all "non-traditional learning" is almost undefinable, and preserves myths and misunderstandings about learning.

Non-traditional learning is not new, but rests upon a long history of learning before education was institutionalized, and the vigorous effort in earlier America to bring some semblance of civilization to the settling of diverse peoples in a vast wilderness. Lyceum, Chautauqua, debating societies, subscription libraries, self-improvement societies, churches and informal study groups began the democratization of education even while schools, academies, colleges, and universities tended to preserve the elitism in education that was part of the European heritage of the America-seekers. The self-made (meaning self-educated) person was - and to some extent still is - a persistent and enduring folk model.

The societal contexts that in earlier times had produced school, college, university, and adult institutions and programs changed during the growth, industrialization, and democratization of America. Yet the educational institutions created out of those contexts did not altogether keep up with the new contexts that were evolving. Eurich, commenting on a statement by Drucker, pointed out that knowledge in earlier times was regarded as an ornament of man and society, but that in the modern world has become a meal ticket for the one and a charm against disaster for the other.[5] Before the twentieth century, to be educated meant being unproductive, a condition that society couldn't afford in too many people. But by the latter part of the twentieth century the exact opposite has become true: being educated is equated with being productive.

Of course, the pre-twentieth century education referred to as ornamental and unproductive was formal, traditional education obtained at schools, academies, colleges and universities, which had not kept up with the changing needs, circumstances, and aspirations of American society. In histories of education, little attention is given to the other kind of education obtained by Americans on their own initiative. This non-traditional education has been a significant factor in America's innovation, self-reliance, and unparalleled productivity in agriculture, science and technology, music and the arts, business and manufacturing and social-civic adaptation. If formal, traditional education was regarded as ornamental and unproductive in early America, there was alongside it an educational process that was eagerly sought for productive self and community improvement.

Long notes that in the Colonial period,

Young men, and to a lesser degree, young women of "low" birth or social station could aspire to great achievement. Perhaps more than at any earlier era, learning could produce immediate tangible results . . . Prior to the Revolution there was a kind of spirit that nurtured the idea of a learning society . . . all of society was instructive; each individual was both learner and teacher. Within three generations of the Revolution, however, a changed attitude could be noted; "learning" became the responsibility of teachers and schools, and an activity reserved for juveniles.[6]

Long comments, "It could be argued that some of what would be considered non-traditional forms of education today were more likely to have been 'traditional' two hundred years ago".[7] For example, in the colonial period "independent learning among adults was more a tradition than was dependence on 'schooling'. That condition can be contrasted with the contemporary situation where independent study is labelled 'non-traditional'. [8]

Foreign visitors to early America found things they liked and disliked, and some things that surprised them. De Tocqueville, in the 1830's, was struck by the fact that he did not find Americans culturally deprived. The American pioneer, he said, "is a highly civilized being who consents for a time to inhabit the back woods. . . It is difficult to imagine the incredible rapidity with which thought circulates in the midst of these deserts. I do not think that so much intellectual activity exists in the most enlightened districts of France." [9] These comments may be taken as an oblique reference to the vigor and effectiveness of early nineteenth-century education, especially that now called nontraditional. But de Tocqueville, it will be said, was something of a romantic, and he did not see all of America.

Charles Dickens, English novelist and social critic, visited America in 1842. Defrauded in a land scheme and appalled by the brutish toil, ill manners, violence, chicanery, and libertarian boasting of some Americans, he criticized the country in ways then thought to be severe. Yet Dickens was startled by the extent of self-education in America by persons who, in England, would have remained uneducated. In American Notes (1842) he describes the fervor of young American women (mill workers from the countryside, working twelve hours a day and living in town boarding houses) to rise above their present condition by self-initiated study, reading music, and (this really astonished Dickens) by writing and publishing a magazine.

I am now going to state three facts which will startle a large class of readers [in Britain]. Firstly, there is a joint-stock piano in a great many boarding houses. Secondly, nearly all these young ladies subscribe to circulating libraries. Thirdly, they have got up among themselves a periodical [in which] it is pleasant to find that many of its Tales are of the Mills and of those who work in them; that they inculcate habits of self-denial and contentment, and teach good doctrines of enlarged benevolence . . . feeling for the beauties of nature . . . A circulating library is a favourable school for the study of such topics . . . [10]

Dickens, the social critic, anticipates that the response of his English readers to such learning efforts will be "preposterous . . . These things are above their station." He continues, "I know no station which is rendered more endurable to the person in it, or more safe to the person out of it, by having ignorance for its associate. I know no station which has a right to monopolise the means of mutual instruction, improvement, and rational entertainment . . . ." Despite his ambivalent feelings toward America, Dickens put a discerning finger on a major educational difference between the Old World and the New: the power and popularity of self initiated learning as a means of removing class distinctions in America.

Learning had, of course, other uses. Turner, writing about the American pioneer, said that in the New World "he was forced to make old tools serve new uses; to shape former habits, institutions and ideas to change conditions; and to favour new means when the old proved inapplicable."[11] Making old tools serve new uses, shaping habits, institutions, and ideas and favoring new means all signify skill, cognitive and affective learning however and wherever initiated, sustained, evaluated, and applied. Some may call it improvising, but it should be remembered that improvisation has much in common with the trial-and-error problem solving associated with idiosyncratic learning, and that when disciplined and formalized it is part of the intellectual development of hypotheses to be tested.

As the pioneer period faded, many new problems confronted Americans, and old settlers and new immigrants responded with the same spirit that had been shown earlier. Speaking of the latter part of the nineteenth century, Gould comments:

Americans looked to themselves for solutions to the host of problems that beset them in the seventies and eighties. The Chautauqua movement [begun in 1874] lay ready to hand, and they used it. They subscribed to Chautauqua courses, copied Chautauqua forums, hired Chautauqua speakers, emulated Chautauqua ideals. . . . Chautauqua paved the way for extension courses, community colleges, adult education centers, and dozens of other educational ventures . . .[12]

But Chautauqua "lay ready to hand" because of what had gone before.

It was, fundamentally, a response to an unspoken demand, a sensitive alertness to the cravings of millions of people for "something better." It was part of that tradition of revolution without dogma that has been typical of America since the first settlers landed on our shores. One of several waves of mass enthusiasm for self-improvement, social betterment, and reform . . . it filled a vast need . . . provided a free platform for the discussion of vital issues . . . introduced . . . new educational concepts, ideas and opportunities . . .[13]

Chautauqua became a university, chartered by the New York State Legislature in 1883, signifying in a unique and unprecedented way the willingness of Americans to improvise with higher education. As Gould points out, "Certainly no one would have been hardy enough to predict that this freak among universities would put the stamp of its own uniqueness on all of American higher education. But that is what happened . . ."[1] For millions of back door learners, Chautauqua was the nearest thing they had to front door opportunity in higher education, for a while at least, until the varied programs that Chautauqua developed were replicated and institutionalized in the land grant universities and other institutions that eventually took over Chautauqua's programs.

Now, approximately a century after the "great change" wrought by Chautauqua, Gould perceives another change. "The individualism which spurred so many to learn . . . to enroll in a demanding course of study, or to swelter in a brown canvas tent for the sake of 'culture' is no longer a vital force in our lives." Gould may have been contrasting the great self-taught heroes of earlier days (Thomas A. Edison, Henry Ford, Abraham Lincoln, and many others) with the devotees of the new barbarianism, the counter-culture movements of the early sixties. He continues, "We tend to think of ourselves in terms of our membership in a social class, a union, a profession, a minority, or simply an interest group; we passively accept the group values, and thereby surrender our identity . . . we are passive observers."[15] Are we?

Perhaps. But Gould wrote his commentary on Chautauqua, an incident in the continuing American revolution, in 1961. Yet the remainder of that decade witnessed an astonishing surge of innovation at all levels of education, but most particularly in non-traditional learning for adults. In 1964, with partial funding from the Carnegie Corporation, a unique four-year experiment in the opening of higher education to persons excluded from it was inaugurated by the University of Wisconsin. This experiment, called AIM (for Articulated Instructional Media) laid the theoretical, academic, technological, and operational bases for the creation of new institutions of open, distance and independent learning.[16] The experiment ended in 1968, and the principles it had established were almost immediately applied in the new (1969) Open University of the United Kingdom. Thereafter followed an explosion of new institutions.

In 1970, the Commission on Non-Traditional Study was set up by the College Entrance Examination Board and the Educational Testing Service to study the pros and cons of non-traditional study.[17] By 1974/5, there were, in the United States alone, nearly one hundred new institutions or programs employing in a variety of ways the open, distance, and independent learning approaches.[18] Studies were underway in numerous states and foreign countries to assess the feasibility and desirability of creating new institutions of these kinds.[19] In 1975, UNESCO published a world survey of selected open learning case studies.[20] In the seven years between the end of the AIM experiment and the UNESCO report there was an upswelling of new institutions, experiments, programs, studies, reports, conferences, articles and books on non-traditional learning, such as few issues in education have ever generated. Self-initiated learning at the back door, far from declining as Gould had suggested in 1961, was proliferating at an unprecedented rate.

During these years great progress was made in several fields related to non-traditional learning: the how-to aspects of building and evaluating non-traditional programs; the design and development of instructional materials; the development of cooperative, apprentice and work-study programs; linking learning with community resources beyond the schools; different ways of organizing knowledge and relating disciplines in curriculum building, materials development, and instruction; studies of adult learning projects, which have yielded new information on the learning of adults; the place of technology in providing opportunity and access to learners; the testing and employment of new technologies and media in teaching and learning (television, the telephone, blackboard by wire, the satellite, cable, the newspaper, cassettes); demographic and marketing studies to determine learner needs; coalitions and consortia of institutions combining resources to create non-traditional programs on national or regional bases.

A whole new vocabulary relating to non-traditional learning came into being: *learning exchanges, Elderhostels, educational brokering, free universities, learners' cooperatives, self-chosen learning, learning networks,* and other terms. New periodicals on different aspects of non-traditional learning appear regularly, sponsored by a wide variety of interested groups. Their name suggests the vigor of the movement: *Second Thoughts, Basic Choices, Setting the Pace, Community Memory.* There is even a new organization, The National Alliance for Voluntary Learning, which will work against MCE (mandated continuing education), to preserve continuing education free from compulsion and to save it from the groupy blandness and other-direction of schooling.

Gould ended his 1961 book on Chautauqua with these words: "Changed times must bring new improvisations."[21] The new improvisations called non-traditional learning continue to reflect active, not passive, roles for non-traditional learners, and a healthy state of innovation in education. The purpose of this book has been to reflect the new urgency of learning that has brought about so rapid a development of non-traditional learning, to link this development with past as well as present, to suggest the significance of non-traditional learning respecting education in general, to relate non-traditional learning to general learning theory, and to the need for a lifespan view of learning.

134

A Watershed in Education

American education has reached a watershed in its development. The full democratization of education requires that all learners be treated equally, and their learnings - if they so choose - be assessed and accredited on a common basis. Learning is a vital, renewable, efficient, and economic resource, whether traditional or non-traditional. As Bok's law puts it, "If you think education is expensive, try ignorance."[22]

Non-traditional learning has worked very well in America, although short of support and recognition, something many learners need and want. When traditional academics are asked to authorize non-traditional learning, they are prone to comment that non-traditional learning "may succeed all right in minor areas in some courses, but of course it couldn't in my area." The comment is only half right. The reason it doesn't work in the traditional academic's area is that recognition has been refused in advance on an a priori presumption of inferiority, perhaps wholly on the criterion of the communication technology enjoyed. If communication is other than speech in the standard classroom format, the non-traditional program is frequently refused recognition. Traditional faculties, professional associations, and administrative and accrediting agencies have adopted rules that in many instances prohibit credit or any other recognition for courses taken by correspondence, radio, or television.

Such rulings do not rest on studies of comparative learning by different media. Instead, by fiat, learnings achieved by different methods are ruled beyond comparison. Such elitist and unscientific reasoning is unworthy of the high educational and professional standards to which academic groups generally adhere. One consequence of such blunt-axe proscriptions is that some of the very institutions which pioneered and sustained non-traditional learning have been unable properly to accredit learners who have, by standard academic assessments, achieved a quality of learning comparable to that of traditional learners. This is the original back door learning syndrome all over again - in the country that has led the world in a communications revolution.

Certainly there are non-traditional schools whose courses and programs may be below standard. And there are non-traditional learners who have not achieved a level of learning comparable to that required of traditional learners. But to refuse recognition to all non-traditional schools or learners because some do not meet standards is patently unjust. Traditional schools vary in quality also, with some falling below standards. The academic professions have dealt with such schools on an a priori presumption that they are inherently good and useful and should be helped to raise standards before they are put off-limits to learners. Furthermore, each school is considered on its own merits after careful and periodic review by a team of evaluators. There is, for traditional schools, no collective ruling against all schools in a given class of institutions because one or some of the schools have not maintained a particular standard of instruction. Learners in traditional schools are generally assumed to have some rights of choice, and most institutions have elaborate procedures for settling disagreements over instruction fairly, if not amicably.

The a priori presumption that teaching and learning are inferior by any means other than the classroom is a cognitive-affective blend perilously close to the mechanisms of racial bias. Instead of skin color, the communications mode of an instructional system is prejudged as a mark of inferiority - all evidence to the contrary notwithstanding. The failures of the few are made the burden of many, and the successes are ignored or rationalized away as nonsubstantive.

It should be immaterial whether a person has learned at the front door or the back door of the Palace of Learning. What one has learned - not where, or how, in what sequence, at what institution, or in what period of time - is the only criterion of supreme importance. Fortunately, the individual and social injustices against those who have learned via non-traditional methods have not stopped non-traditional learning. The learners involved have generally experienced personal satisfaction and improvement in quality of life, despite the slings and arrows of disparagement.

Socially, however, sharp questions have been raised about the political morality of a system of different standards for front and back door learners. The new open, distance, and independent learning institutions were a response to the unwillingness of traditionalists to recognize and accredit non-traditional learning. But, admirable and needed as they are, they cannot meet the needs of non-traditional learners without access to a sympathetic government, education profession, and unbiased accreditation. Curiously, there is some opposition to the concept of independent learning by social egalitarians who seem to fear individual enterprise, even in learning. For example, Pflüger, commenting on adult education, states that" . . . individualistic attempts to promote participation in education have no prospects of success . . . Emancipation is not an individual affair, but only definable and practicable as a solidarity struggle for freedom from dependence on society."[2][3]

The call for "solidarity" seems more a political than a learning slogan. Learning is personal, idiosyncratic. While there is a need for a more just and equitable system of assessing learning on a base common to all learners, solidarity of one group over another is what we have now. Another kind of solidarity merely creates new "ins" and "outs," and justice still may not be served. Solidarity too implies other-direction, control, and derogation of the individual - not really desirable conditions if unfettered learning is what is being talked about.

Non-traditional learning would unquestionably benefit from an assessment and accreditation system that is fully independent of traditional education; in fact, so would traditional learning. The regional accreditation associations in the United States are gradually moving toward greater independence. That trend should be accelerated. There is new willingness to review and even accredit special (non-traditional) institutions, and some progress has been made.

The other effort that needs to be made is to improve the availability of better courses for non-traditional learners - locally, regionally, nationally, and even internationally. Satellite retransmission for learning is just as feasible (already adequately demonstrated by the University of the South Pacific) as satellite transmission for international news, sports, business, and entertainment.

In view of the reluctance of traditional faculties to be involved in programs for non-traditional learners, the difficulties of sustaining dual institutional missions on a level of equal priority, and the apparent retreat of university extension from conflict with residence faculties over credit instruction, the greatest hope would seem to lie in the creation of new institutions. Community colleges and vocational-technical institutes have shown initiative. Regional consortia of institutions are being tried. Most promising at the moment are the University of Mid America, and the Educational Satellite Program of the Appalachian Regional Commission, a consortium of universities in the Appalachian region.

The University of Mid America is vigorously exploring the feasibility of becoming The American Open University. If this should come about, the learning opportunities of thousands of learners (back door and front door alike) would be immensely improved. The Appalachian program may, through access to cable systems, be able to extend its programs nationwide. To succeed, however, these innovative institutions will have to have control of curriculum and rewards for non-traditional learners, and not to be forced to depend upon traditional institutions for accreditation policy.

The argument is sometimes advanced that learning, like virtue, is its own reward, and that non-traditional learners should be satisfied with courses intended for traditional learners, but without the credit. That is specious sophistry. Non-traditional learning, to learners and to society, is too important to be dismissed in such callous fashion. There are, of course, many fully independent non-traditional learners who do not need or want any sort of credit or recognition. But there are others who do need and want credit and recognition simply because certification is forced upon them, made a requirement by the upward mobility processes of traditional institutions in education, business, government, and industry.

What non-traditional learning does not need is anything that would diminish the freedom of choice, autonomy, and independence that has kept this kind of learning vital, practical, resourceful, innovative, and humane from the beginning of this country. Non-traditional learning works for thousands of learners because they link it to their needs, concerns problems, and aspirations. A bureaucracy could not do as well on the personal learning side, but might help in the assessment of learning, which is a social problem.

Non-traditional learning is many things, but mostly it is a natural survival behavior. Roger Reynolds was seriously injured in a skydive. He writes,

A year after my fall, all the casts were off except the one from my left knee to the ankle. The ankle was weak after a bone-graft operation and the bone wasn't healing. The doctor said, "Rog, we're going to give it one more month. If it doesn't start to heal we're going to have to operate again." I was totally bottomed out emotionally.

For some time, I had been sneaking up to the medical library to read about orthopedics. I learned that in order to heal, bones need circulation and exercise. I figured I had one month to see if that would work.[24]

What Reynolds had learned about exercise worked. The learning that Reynolds did is characteristic of the kind of non-traditional learning that has helped sustain Americans and America: natural learning, intrinsically motivated, applied, and evaluated. It didn't make Reynolds an orthopedic specialist, but it solved his problem. That is the most powerful learning known. It is not schooling.

The American Dream meant the opportunity to become what one could become. For millions of Americans, that meant self-initiated learning, self-development, preparations for that better time that lay ahead. It meant catch-as-catch-can learning for mother or father, but sending the children to school, and to college, for the things the parents had to discover for themselves, and things they never had the time to learn. Perhaps the earlier way had some advantages, for then the person's own needs, concerns, purposes, and circumstances could motivate and determine the education one got for oneself. Living and learning were coterminous, with the accent on living, which supplied the need and motivation for learning. For non-traditional learners at the back door, it is still very much that way.

Will America's long, successful, but largely unacknowledged experience with non-traditional learning revitalize education ? We must all hope so, for we must all be learners throughout our lives. We must make ourselves competent generalists in the areas that affect our survival and quality of life and specialists in the areas on which we depend for our livelihoods. Formal, other-directed, and classroom-based education reflects its origins in earlier labor-intensive societies. The knowledge-intensive society we have now entered gives prominence to self-acquired learning throughout the lifespan.

Isaac Asimov foresees the time when computers, in a symbiotic relationship with learners, will greatly expand and extend learning. "When that happens . . . for the first time in history [we] will be achieving something approaching intellectual maturity. And we will look back on everything before that time as simply the childhood of the human race."[25]

If America is on the threshold of becoming a Learning Society, non-traditional learning may be its most genuine ingredient.

Notes

1 Carl Sandburg, The People, Yes (New York: Harcourt Brace and Co., 1936), pp. 18-19. Used with permission of the publisher.

2 Tom Wayman, "Longshoremen are Also Authors and Artists, "In These Times, 14-20 November 1979, p. 13.

3 "Musings," a column in Second Thoughts 2, no. 2 (October 1979): 11.

4 Ronald Gross, "The Converse of MCE (Mandatory Continuing Education)." Second Thoughts" 2, no. 2 (October 1979): 11.

5 Alvin C. Eurich, "Reflections on University Research Administration." Sponsored Research in American Universities and Colleges, ed. S.R. Strickland (Washington, D.C.: American Council on Education, 1968), pp. 1-6.

6 Huey B. Long, Continuing Education of Adults in Colonial America (Syracuse, N.Y.: Syracuse University Press Publications in Continuing Education, 1976), p.1.

7 Long, Continuing Education of Adults in Colonial America, p.3.

8 Long, Continuing Education of Adults in Colonial America, p. 75.

9 Alexis de Tocqueville, Democracy in America (New York: Alfred A. Knopf, 1944), p. 317.

10 Charles Dickens, American Notes and Pictures from Italy (New York: Oxford University Press, n.d.), pp. 80-81.

11 Frederick Jackson Turner, The Frontier in American History (New York: Henry Holt, 1921), pp. 145, 305.

12 Joseph E. Gould, The Chautauqua Movement (Albany: State University of New York Press, 1961), pp. 98-99. Used with permission of the publisher.

13 Gould, Chautauqua, pp. vii-viii.

14 Gould, Chautauqua, p. 13.

15 Gould, Chautauqua, p. 99.

16 Charles A. Wedemeyer and Robert E. Najem, AIM: From Concept to Reality, The Articulated Instructional Media Program at Wisconsin (Syracuse: Syracuse University Press Publications in Continuing Education, 1969).

17 Samuel B. Gould and K. Patricia Cross, Explorations in Non-Traditional Study (San Francisco: Jossey-Bass Publishers 1972).

18 National Association of Educational Broadcasters, Open Learning

Systems. (Washington D.C.: NAEB, March 1974).

19 For example: Charles A. Wedemeyer, Michael Moore, and Clifford Wood (ed.), The Open School (Supplement to final report of the commission. Madison, Wis: Governor's Commission on Education, 1971).

20 Norman Mackenzie, Richard Prostgate, and John Scupham, Open Learning (Paris: UNESCO Press, 1975).

21 Gould, Chautauqua, p. 100.

22 Paul Dickson, "Any Fool Can Make a Rule," Reader's Digest, March 1979, pp 99.

23 A. Pflüger, "Lifelong Education and Adult Education: Reflections on Four Current Problem Areas," in Lifelong Education: A Stock Taking, ed. A.J. Cropley (Hamburg: UNESCO Institute of Education, 1979), p. 98.

24 Roger Reynolds, "The Man Who Fell to Earth" Reader's Digest, January 1980, p. 52.

25 Isaac Asimov, "Computerized Education in a Low Birth Rate Society" Continuum, 44, no. 1 (September 1979): 13.

ADVERSE FACTORS IN THE DEVELOPMENT OF AN OPEN UNIVERSITY IN LATIN AMERICA

Miguel Angel Escotet

Introduction

In the last ten years a desire has grown in Latin America to renovate the structures and educational techniques which are considered obsolete in relation to the scientific advances in the psychology of learning and the rapid development of technology and systems of communication.

Within this renovation process, educational experiments have been designed at all levels, but the majority of them have not been completed or have not passed the threshold between theory and practice. In most of the cases the experiences have been reduced to isolated projects under the inspiration of guidance from developed countries, without possibilities of generalizing the experiments to the educational systems.

Within this concept of innovation, higher education has generated ideas and programmes inclined towards improvement of the quality of post-secondary education, orientating it towards areas of economic and human development to respond to characteristics and necessities for 'massification', to provide to 'he who learns' a type of individualized education which will be relevant and which will give opportunities for true access and permanence in the educational population (Escotet, 1976b).

These factors have made imperative research to find bolder educational innovations among which it is possible to emphasize distance and open educational systems, either through programmes within traditional institutions or in new projects which are solely orientated towards this type of methodology. Some of these experiences in Latin America, which have partially or totally achieved the goals of open education, are worthy of emphasis.

The Instituto Tecnológico y de Estudios Superiores (Institute of Technology and Higher Studies) in Monterrey, Mexico is one of the first organizations of higher education which has introduced new forms of learning such as: (a) the personalized system of instruction (PSI); (b) the micro-learning clinic for pedagogic improvement of teachers; and (c) the Open High Schools, founded on the experiences of the Open University in England.

Also in Mexico, the Universidad Nacional Autónoma (National Autonomous University) developed an Open University with great hopes in 1972, but diverse technical problems and educational policy problems have made it difficult to expand this innovation. The Instituto Politécnico Nacional (National Polytechnical Institute) has achieved relative success in the preparation of technicians in machine operation, tools, electricity and construction through this open modality. Also the Universidad Autónoma de Guadalajara (Autonomous University of Guadalajara) has been testing open learning through its Centros de Recursos de Aprendizaje y Educación Médica en la Comunidad (Resource Centers for Learning and Medical Education in the Community) (Garibay, 1976).

Costa Rica is currently developing a new university, the Universidad Estatal de la Educación a la Distancia (State University for Distance Education) with the technical assistance of the Open University of Spain and the Open University in England. Student population will be limited in the first years to 1000 students, for the purpose of making an adequate formative evaluation and at the same time to reduce the risks of the experiment.

The Universidad Nacional Abierta de Venezuela (National Open University of Venezuela), founded in 1977 after a year and a half of studies, began with 10,000 students in mid-1978. The model contains characteristics of similar universities in other regions, but also has components that are unique and important in the Latin American reality. All of the courses up to this moment have been developed in Venezuela. However, external factors, the logistics of the locations of Local Learning Centers, the time limitations between the planning and execution of the teaching/learning process, insufficient curricular evaluation, lack of human resources in production, and the initial large student population, have placed in danger the quality and maintenance of this bold project.

There also exist in Venezuela other important experiences such as 'Supervised University Studies', among which it is important to point out the Free Studies of the Simon Bolivar University, the Supervised Studies in Education of the Central University of Venezuela, the Distance Studies of the Simón Rodríguez University, and the Supervised Studies of the Zulia University. All of these experiences are coordinated by a permanent commission at the national level and the student population up to this moment has been relatively small, with important annual increases. The curricular areas that are included are concentrated in general studies, education and administration. However, the distinction of being the first Venezuelan institution to administer courses through distance education is shared by the Instituto de Mejoramiento Profesional del Magisterio (Institute for Professional Improvement of Teachers) and the Dirección de Educación de Adultos (Directory of Adult Education), both divisions of the Ministry of Education.

Colombia has had various experiences in open education, with the most important and earliest innovations in this field being the project of the Projectos de Universidades Desescolorizadas (De-Schooled University) at the University of Antioquía in Medellín and the programme called Distance University of the Javeriana University. These projects include areas of educational psychology, mathematics and Spanish. Also recently, the Universities of Del Valle and Los Andes have included in their general programme some open educational elements. On the other hand, since 1975, the Instituto Colombiano para el fomento de la educación superior - ICFES (Colombian Institute for Promotion of Higher Education) has developed a distance project, but as of this year, political and financial factors have impeded its implementation.

Brazil has various isolated experiences in distance education and currently the Ministry and the Council of Presidents of the Brazilian Universities are proposing the creation of an open university with national coverage, which, given the tremendous population and geographic extent of Brazil, could constitute a project which will function at an appropriate economic scale and would achieve success in educational promotion, particularly for adults.

Educational television has achieved certain developments in Chilean universities, especially in the Catholic University of Santiago, the University of Chile, and the Catholic University of Valparaíso. Probably Chile has the best level of advancement in educational TV in Latin America, although open education has not had any decisive projects.

Argentina has developed an important experience with the Luján University, teaching people agriculture and cattle raising through distance education, but actually the model has been distorted. On the other hand for many years the University of Buenos Aires has included in its programmes 'Free Studies', but the conception of these has been traditional and adjusted to the European lines of free studies in the university.

In Bolivia, there are programmes of tele-education such as the one at the Gabriel René Moreno University with a nonsystematized audience of 40,000 persons in education for the home, health, hygiene, and environmental cleanliness. The Cochabamba University has 10,000 students in courses of diffusion, compensation and enrichment.

After the reformation of the Peruvian education system, this country developed a project called De-Schooled Higher Education at the University of Lima and a pilot plan for an open university at the National University of Education and the Center of Teleducation at the Catholic University. The system 'extraordinary professional qualification' is a form of de-schooled education sui generis, orientated to the updating and training of the working class in Peru.

This rapid and incomplete look at distance and open education in Latin America allows us to infer that there is a great deal of interest in this educational modality. However, corroborating our initial impression, the majority of the experiments are isolated, are appendices to traditional institutions and are in the very beginning stages of experimentation. It is necessary to classify policies and objectives, to form technical groups for planning, to pay close attention to and take decisions about priorities in investment in higher education (Serna, 1976).

Maybe the success of these systems, as Carlos Tunnermann would say (1976), will depend as much on our efforts as on our imagination, loosening the reins which tie us to the traditional systems and allowing the imagination to take flight.

Transfer of technology in open education

Open education is particularly characterized by the removal of restrictions, exclusions and privileges; by the accreditation of students' previous experience; by the flexibility of the management of the time variable; and by substantial changes in the traditional relationship between professors and students. On the other hand, *distance education* is a modality which permits the delivery of a group of didactic media without the necessity of regular class participation, where the individual is responsible for his own learning (Universidad Nacional Abierta. Comisión Organizadora, 1977a).

However, there exists a similar use of both terms as a result of the transfer to Latin America of the concept which originally was produced in England, derived from the term 'University of the Air' and reinforced by other concepts such as 'lifelong learning', 'permanent education', 'continuous education', etc. The transition which the English leaders made with the terms university of the air and open university is a product of a reorientation of the objectives and media of this institution. At the beginning, the objective was orientated towards university extension and the main media were radio and/or television, but as the idea of the university began to crystallize, it orientated the development towards providing university education for adults, promoting equality of education opportunities and using all communication media (Perry, 1976), and the concept was transformed into the open university. This term orientates it in four directions: open to the population, to geographic locations, in terms of methods, and in terms of ideas.

We have here then the beginning of the transfer of

technology in open higher education for Latin America through the educational bridge with Spain, because of the creation of the Universidad Nacional de Educación a Distancia (National University of Distance Education) which comes closer to a unidirectional system (written media) at a distance than an authentic 'open' education.

All kinds of projects begin to appear in Latin America which indiscriminately use the names 'distance' or 'open' without considering the objectives, goals and media which have generated the project.This overgeneralized use of the two terms has produced confusion in both modalities with negative consequences in the administrative and philosophic framework. While open education is a strategy opposed to traditional education, distance education may or may not be the main difference; the only difference it has from existing universities is in the mode of delivery of learning. Through distance education we are going to form the same individual who might have been instructed in the regular university, but with open education the strategy of learning is different, not only in the media but also in its objectives and processes, which carry with it a different meaning in professional formation.

With this we do not wish to indicate that the projects of distance education that exist in Latin America are forming human resources similar to other institutions. That will depend on the modality of learning; more, some of the 'distance' programmes perhaps should be called 'open' and, vice versa, projects labelled 'open' education are possibly strategies for 'distance' education. It is precisely in this confusion that we establish our thesis which is that we have not seen a transfer of the concepts; rather we have seen a rather liberal or free translation of the title 'Open University'.

Another fundamental aspect of the transfer of the open education technology is in the processes of creativity of course design, the production of learning material, the distribution of the material, academic evaluation and certification.

The process of creativity and course design

There are courses which have high and low levels of cultural content. For those in which social/cultural variables do not particularly enter into the contents, such as mathematics, the process of adaptation of the courses is simple and only requires the use of universal terms.

Those courses which contain extensive interpretative content, even when cultural variables are not essential, such as logic and physics, require a semantic and conceptual adaptation. This implies the use of transcultural techniques, such as the semantic differential of Osgood which measures and defines the equivalence of those most important concepts

145

in the original materials and their adaptation to specific cultures.

At the same time it is absolutely necessary to conduct a nominal evaluation process which involves the establishment of particular and general criteria such as the use of the same techniques of formative evaluation which are used in the original material, measurement of the social/ cultural differences, linguistic development, learning style of the potential students of both cultures and the transformation of the examples, tables, etc., to the reality of the country which is transferring this learning material (Escotet, 1977b). This process of nominal validation in the case of transfer of instructional modules is more difficult and costly to prepare than it was originally because it requires formative evaluation, and because although the original prog-ramme required formal evaluation, it did not require nominal evaluation which includes both. The studies of Díaz-Guerrero and his collaborators in the evaluation of *Plaza Sésamo* (Díaz-Guerrero et al., 1975) determined that it was necessary to transform many of the scripts because, even though they were cognitive and intellectual stimuli for Mexican children, they did not produce the same effect as they did in North American children and on many occasions they distorted certain behavioural guidelines which were considered positive for the Mexican culture.

On the other hand the design of the instruction, al-though it is a neutral technique, invariably requires studies of the necessities and styles of learning of the population which will determine the form and content which is best for the instructional material in relation to that population. What are the differences between the youth and the adult in the same culture? What are the learning styles between the different socioeconomic levels of the population? What differ-ences exist between these variables and the cultural charac-teristics of the two countries (the exporting country and the importing country)?

As an example let us suggest the research on personality development which was done at the National Autonomous Univer-sity of Mexico and the University of Texas (Holtzman, Díaz-Guerrero and Swartz, 1975), which indicates as an important datum that while the North American student is competitive, the Mexican student is cooperative, and the two cognitive styles are indirectly related to the cultural guidelines of behaviour and to the educational system.

Could it not be that the design of instructional mater-ials in the United States generates more competition between students? Is this one of the objectives of Anglo- Saxon education and therefore a part of the objectives of their designers? What is the relation between pace of learning and time for learning and the increase or decrease in competitive behaviour? Is it possible to create transfer of instructional

146

material from these countries with the required nominal evaluation that would reduce cooperative behaviour in Latin America? These are only some of the many questions which have not yet been investigated, but which obviously constitute factors that are important for the use of course materials produced in highly developed countries for open education in Latin America.

Those courses which have high cultural content such as sociology, pyschology, languages, etc., cannot be transferred unless we are interested in the transformation of the more fundamental values which define us.

A fact which reinforces the suggestions which we have discussed refers to the introduction in Latin America of procedures of evaluation during the decade of the 1950s and 60s, which came from competitive systems in industrialized countries and were appropriate to the characteristics of limited demand in the labour market in those countries. From there came the scales of evaluation based on Gauss's curve of probabilities with which knowledge is measured in terms of the group and not in terms of motivation, capacity or individual efforts (normal curve). In spite of the fact that this curve is excellent as a medium to produce an individual who is well formed, the scale produces competitive individuals: a fact which is considerably distant from the generally cooperative attitude which has always been one of the most positive characteristics of the Latin American culture (Escotet,1976b).

Production of learning material

The form of presentation of the instructional modules in written and audiovisual media is another factor which generally is transplanted without effecting a transfer which involves nominal and formative evaluation.

For example, studies in Venezuela (Escotet, 1972) determined that Venezuelan learning style is idiographic and idiochromatic, that is to say, learning through representation and colour. This implies that the adaptation or elaboration of written or audiovisual materials should reinforce these factors in order to obtain better cognitive stimulation. Perhaps in other countries this will not be as relevant.

On the other hand those visual representations which include stimuli which are not directly related to a specific culture, for example snow in the tropics or a Nordic typology in the Caribbean, block identification of the learner with the material and in some cases cause his rejection of the material. From there, animated audiovisual material or unstructured figures are more appropriate for a universal representation and therefore more easily transferable from one culture to another (Díaz-Guerrero et al., 1975).

Obviously other materials exist which are not landscapes, geography, etc., which do not require a complicated transfer process except in soundtracks and one or another reinforcing stimuli which can be added for the culture to which they are being transferred.

Distribution of the material

The transfer of systems of distribution of the learning material can be reduced to certain universal administrative processes, but it is obvious that in each area each university will have to generate its own system in accord with the communication characteristics of the country. In the case of Venezuela the mail system is quite deficient, in contrast to the English or North American systems. This has meant that the organisers of the open universities must use the infrastructure of their local centres at the national level to process the distribution. On the other hand there are other systems which are more effective than the mail, for example, the newspaper distribution agencies, private distribution services, and even the distributors of soft drinks.

The transfer or reproduction of the distribution system is only justifiable when both cultures have very similar communication services.

The use of radio and television will depend both on the feasibility of the emission and coverage as well as the receptivity which these media have with the students. While in the highly developed countries television is an article of first-level necessity, in underdeveloped countries it is a luxury for the majority of the people. The schedule of transmissions of programmes, the number of receivers which exist in each household, the competitive programmes from other channels, etc., are factors which can only be studied in the culture where the project is being developed.

Academic evaluation

The processes of evaluation of students' achievement can be done at a distance or on site as the final part of the teaching/learning process. It is here where an open system should be completely synchronized with its users. However, the majority of the experiences to which we have referred in the introduction of this work have reproduced forms of evaluation without the corresponding research to verify the learning styles of the students.

On the other hand it is logical to think that if the coming material has not had nominal and formative evaluation, the process of student evaluation will be distorted even more.

If the mechanization of this process is essential to provide services to large numbers of students, an effort must be made to relate it to the group of academic counsellors who will intervene in the evaluation process. When

148

the student does those things in order to achieve the academic objectives and a relationship between students and teachers is established through experiments, lectures, consultations, study groups, use of audiovisual media, etc., the process of evaluation begins and this is where we find one of the characteristics which significantly differentiates *open* education from *distance* education.

For this reason the degree of independence or dependence of the study of the students will have an effect upon the assistance strategy both in the frequency of student/teacher contacts and in the style of the contact.

We can see that in many cases it is a fallacy to try to suggest that there will be a reduction of costs in the authentic open university in relation to the traditional university, but that is not necessarily the case with distance education.

Here also we see an interesting case of inter-institutional rather than intercultural transfer. This consists of transfer of processes from one institution to another of different instructional modality *in the same country*. The case of the Javeriana University of Bogotá is appropriate. The terms of evaluation are by semester, as a repetition of the academic periods of most universities in Colombia and other countries. However, they did not take into consideration the fact that distance processes are more complex and slower. This then obligated the university, after the first experience, to use an annual period so that it could bring about a nominal evaluation process because it was impossible to do it in a shorter time (Tunnermann, 1976).

Finally, the preparation of the objective tests requires a process of validation, reliability and fidelity, but even if this is transferred from one culture to another, it implies the application of *transcultural methods* and the analysis of semantic and conceptual equivalence of the instruments in the involved cultures. It has been demonstrated that the lack of application of these procedures produces results which are inconsistent with and different from the objectives (Sears, 1961).

Certification

The majority of the programmes of higher open education in Latin America have been inspired by the Open University of the United Kingdom. The academic success of this institution has inspired many countries to test this educational modality. It would appear that the analysis of this university which has been done by Latin American specialists has concentrated on the process of design and administration and not on the requirements for professional certification.

Study of the systems of certification will permit us to conclude that the requirements for graduation are completely different in the Latin American cases, and are also different from the bachelor's degree of the United States.

First of all, the Open University does not authorise professional degrees (engineers, administrators, economics, pyschologists, etc.) but rather certifies studies of education or general studies similar to an academic course in the Latin countries, equivalent to two-and-one-half years of study, which they administer in two years, in two courses per year during five years with a dedication on the part of the student of ten hours a week (Perry, 1976). Secondly, the student can graduate with six annual credits, (each credit is equivalent to six semester credits, approximately) or what would in Latin systems be between 36 and 50 semester credits.

However, Latin American systems require the *licenciatura* or professionalization in a determined speciality, and the successful completion of a minimum of approximately 140 semester credits for the authorisation of the title. To this one must add the intensive workshop and laboratory practice which is required for professionalization and which the Open University does not need because of the type of certification which it authorizes. The Open University uses micro-laboratories which are sent to each student to do simple experiments similar to those which are done in our basic courses of science and technology.

Even if the process of transfer could be done, the fact that the objectives differ dramatically would make difficult the implementation and maintenance of an open university, accredited along the lines of certification which are common in Latin America. Up until this time there is not an experience in the world which has produced engineers, doctors or physicists through distance or open education.

The error which has been committed has been to transfer the concept and technology of a system of general education to a system of specialized education which requires full-time dedication on the part of the student. What guarantee exists that the process would not suffer approximation towards the traditional system when it begins to offer professional studies? Will it then be possible to achieve the principles of massification, democratization, and optimization of the investment, the educational innovation and institutional complementarity which justify to a great extent the existence of this modality?

This rather significant factor carries with it a suggestion that the transfer of technology in education should be seen within the context of a *gestalt* perception, and not as one of parts or a specific transfer of technology. The Open University of Venezuela has fallen, in our viewpoint, into this narrow perception and will have to transform or reduce its expectations in order to not suffer a collapse in the execution of its programmes. Alternatively, it will have to redefine its original principles, especially in terms of cost and methodology of instruction.

Other adverse factors for the development of open universities

The limitation of time and space only allows us to mention some of the external factors which interfere in the creation and development of open universities in Latin America. Some of these are as follows:

Financial resources

To put into practice a university of this type, and to provide its initial maintenance, requires a strong investment of capital which significantly increases the budget of higher education at the national level. Except in a very small number of countries, the majority of Latin American nations have difficulties with their budgets and the order of priorities of financing is orientated to consolidate existing institutions and to keep up with immediate necessities and obligations. An example of this factor is the postponement of the creation of the Distance University in Colombia.

Political factors

As was suggested by Latapí (1978), the university and the existing power structure constitute conflict areas to the extent to which there is a bigger intervention of political power in the specification and achievement of university objectives. The financing of the university by the State, and the possibility that this will generate cultural forms opposed to the dominant social forces, constitute a common source of permanent conflict in Latin American systems. This happens with even greater intensity in educational innovations, which by their nature have instrinsic obligations to generate changes and transform patterns of behaviour. On the other hand institutionalized or established power gives more value to institutional dominance than to the generation of knowledge. In Latin America, where qualified human resources are scarce, no political party, not even any ideological tendency, could fill up a university or other institution with qualified personnel of only their political party, even when the pressure to do just that is constant and permanent. Therefore, in many cases nonqualified personnel interfere in institutional development, placing more importance on political power than intellectual power. Any educational innovation requires a concentrated effort of all the political tendencies to guarantee its natural evolution.

To these factors we must add the personal positions of political leaders and, even more grave, the lack of knowledge about the type of innovation and the tendency to take advantage of 'circumstantial power' in trying to transform or even eliminate innovations.

151

Resistance to the innovation

These factors, working against what we have presented so far, are not so much in the population as in the incapcity of the institution to reduce its resistance. Fishbein and Ajzen (1975), through their model of the relation between beliefs and attitudes, show that the resistance to an innovation is generated on the one hand by lack of information in the population, and on the other hand by reinforcing the resistance by the same people who wish to reduce it, because their programmes do not attack in the correct direction the beliefs about this innovation which the population maintains.

Learning styles

Each culture has learning styles which are highly correlated with the didactic procedures in the formal education system and with the general guidelines for social behaviour. Education in Latin America has reinforced styles of dependency in learning of induced discipline and not self-discipline and has emphasized other characteristics such as memorization.

An open system of learning requires an independent student with self-discipline, with a high capacity for analysis and synthesis. Many programmes have tried to reduce this gap between formal education and the independent studies through propaedeutic courses and introductory courses of short duration. However, the percentage of desertion has reached 90 per cent in some cases and it would appear that this is one of the most adverse factors to the possibilities for use of open or distance education in Latin America.

Student population

The recent survey which was done by the National Open University of Venezuela concerning characteristics of the student population and their potentials determined that around 82 per cent are working adults interested in this institution. At the same time the majority come from lower and middle classes where the environmental conditions are not the most desirable and the material resources for learning are limited.

If we consider the city of Caracas, for example, the typical student in the Open University will work eight hours every day, spend two hours travelling to and from work, two hours eating, and two hours resting, which brings us to 14 hours a day of occupation with the aggravating situation that the conditions of housing and family do not offer an environment which has the minimum requirements for independent learning. Also, the work and communicational effort make it difficult to be in a pyschological and physical condition appropriate to carry a demanding academic load of half time.

On the other hand there are few studies done in Latin America about learning styles of adults. The majority of materials designed for learning have been prepared for a young population whose only significant work has been that of studying.

In cases such as England we must not lose sight of the fact that the learning styles of the student typically are different from Latin styles and that the academic load which he has is a maximum of two courses per year in general education.

The rapidity with which it has been necessary to plan the innovation has been one of the factors that have been self-destructive of educational experiments. The majority of the projects on open education in Latin America have begun without an empirical study of the potential population and the general behavioural patterns.

Organizations and institutional structures

A considerable part of the open and distance education programmes were generated in traditional institutions whose goals, organization and structure have limited the expansion of the innovative experience. Many of them reproduce the same structure of the conventional institutions in the innovation.

Even when they have created universities destined only for open education, political factors and conservative decisions have transplanted the organizational schemas of the typical Latin American university, generating conflicts between the assignment of responsibilities and the execution of specific tasks of an organization unique in its objectives and processes.

Another factor relates to the development of work teams. An open university is an integrated system made up of subsystems of design, production, distribution and administration of the teaching/learning process and its evaluation. Each subsystem comprises a group of complex tasks which requires an interdependent coordination with the other subsystems. This is what we could call a system of academic management. If the teams are not completely beyond the differences and the convergences of their members, this can create an institutional collapse when any one of the subsystems fails for some reason because of the cycle of decision and the interrelatedness of the subsystems.

Finally the logistic and administrative capacity of an open or distance system is the cornerstone where the success or failure of the system lies. The management of large quantities of material, its production, storage and distribution to the local learning centres, are businesslike tasks and are precisely those kind of tasks where educators have not shown themselves to be very good.

153

Human resources

The open university and the modality of instruction which it requires are something that have recently been developed. Even in highly industrialized countries, the human resources for this type of education are limited. Even though the in-service training of such resources is a solution, lack of personnel remains a grave problem, not only for the development of creativity in the courses, but for the production of these courses and for the execution of the academic tutoring process.

Communication media

The communication systems in Latin America do not have the experience and the service available in the developed countries. It is precisely this characteristic which is one of the indicators differentiating between countries that are developed or 'developing'. On the other hand communication media not only transmit ideological content but also develop conditioning through vocabulary, conceptual categories and attitudes. These media generate norms, values, ideologies that are explicit or implicit, which tend to relate to the dominant cultural model of participation in a social power structure, although of course they can generate changes in the actual cultural model.

In this manner the skills in the competition of radio and television programmes are much more highly favourable for media which are external to open universities. They probably will compete in the same time schedule as the educational programmes, but cannot displace the programmes which are more desirable and which at the same time are reinforcing for the population. The ideal period of transmission for a student who works is the time period after his working day and this is the period during which his family will select programmes which are more interesting and reinforcing for them. Even in England, which possesses one of the best systems of communication, this has been a factor which has required that 90 per cent of the materials use written media as the strategy of instruction.

Conclusion

Higher education in Latin America should renovate itself and should look for audacious strategies for improving its qualities. However in this search one must experiment with new forms of learning which are consistent with the environment and the permanent values of the culture, and not fall into improvisation which, besides generating irreparable damage in the target population, can also make future educational innovations more difficult.

Research, transfer and reproduction of educational models should be backed by scientific investigation as the only tool in the generalization of the processes and the proof of educational hypotheses. While it is true that in this article we have only mentioned adverse factors for open education, that does not mean we do not believe that, empirically controlling the various factors and with the appropriate doses of audacity and imagination which are necessary to combat adversity, it would be possible to develop a revolutionary strategy that could generate an authentic equality of educational opportunities.

References

Díaz-Guerrero,R., Bianchi,R., and Ahumada,R. (1975) Investigación Formativa de Plaza Sésamo, Trillas, Mexico

Dressel,P. (ed) (1971) The New Colleges: Toward an Appraisal. American College Testing Program, Iowa City

Escotet,M.A. (1972) The Measurement of Student Problems: A Cross Cultural Study in Five Nations. Doctoral dissertation, University of Nebraska.

Escotet,M.A. (1976a) Criterios de Evaluación Institucional en la Educación Superior, Ministerio de Educación, Caracas

Escotet,M.A. (1976b) Nuevas Formas de Aprendizaje: Reto para el Futuro. Trabajo presentado a la Reunión Latinoamericana y del Caribe sobre Nuevas Formas de Educación Post-Secundaria, Caracas

Escotet,M.A. (1977) Metodologia de la investigación transcultural. Revista Latinoamericana de Psicología, 2, 159-76

Escotet,M.A. (1978) Universidad Abierta y Pautas para su Evaluación. Annual convention of the Comparative and International Education Society. Marzo, Mexico

Escotet,M.A. (1980) Tendencias de la Educación Superior a Distancia. OAS, Washington,DC

Fishbein,M. and Ajzen,I. (1975) Belief, Attitude, Intention and Behavior. Addison-Wesley, Reading, Mass.

Garibay,L. (1976) Las Innovaciones de la Educación Post-Secundaria en Mexico. Reunion Latinoamericana y del Caribe sobre Nuevas Formas de Educacion Post-Secundaria, Caracas

Holtzman,W., Díaz-Guerrero,R. and Swartz,J. (1975) Desarrollo de la Personalidad en dos Culturas: Mexico y Estados Unidos. Trillas, Mexico

Latapí,P. (1978) Universidad y sociedad: un enfoque basado en las experiencias Latinoamericanas. Universitas 2000, 3, 1, 45-82

Perry,W. (1976) Open University. The Open University Press, Milton Keynes

Sears,S. (1961) Transcultural variables and conceptual equivalence. In Kaplan,B. (ed.) Studying Personality Cross-Culturally. Peterson and Company, Evanston

Serna,H. (1976) La Educación a Distancia: Una Nueva Forma de Educación Post-Secundaria, en el Area Andina. Reunión Latinoamericana y del Caribe sobre Nuevas Formas de Educación Post-Secundaria, Caracas

Tunnerman,C. (1976) Diagnostico y Tendencias Innovativas de la Educación Post-Secundaria en Latinoamerica y el Caribe. Trabajo presentado en la Reunión Latinoamericana y del Caribe sobre Nuevas Formas de Educación Post-Secundaria, Caracas

Universidad Nacional Abierta (1977a) Comisión Organizadora. <u>Proyecto</u>.
Caracas UNA

Universidad Nacional Abierta (1977b) Comisión Organizadora. <u>UNA Folleto
Informativo</u>. Caracas, UNA

Universidad Nacional Abierta (1978) Vice-Recorado Academico. <u>El Modelo
Curricular e Instruccional</u>. Caracas

WHAT ADVANTAGES CAN CONVENTIONAL EDUCATION DERIVE FROM CORRESPONDENCE EDUCATION ?
Bernard Pagney

The first exponents of distance teaching would hardly have been able to imagine how this particular discipline was to develop. This rather banal observation has been made of many an innovation: how could those pioneers have foreseen the new roads their discovery was to open up? Despite the faith driving them on, they were in no position to realize that, once the initial objective had been attained, distance teaching would increase its province by gaining new ground for an ever growing public service, and would thus inevitably be led to develop new ideas of communication.

Now, if this rich potentiality of distance teaching was barely conceived of in the beginning, we can hardly say that it is any more understood nowadays, even among those involved in education. There is a great temptation to continue to see distance education as retaining it original form and functions, essentially, that is to say, as a kind of palliative, and if by chance, some people have come to recognise its importance, they tend to see it in terms of the competition it represents to formal teaching. But one need only look closely at the present educational situation, and to realize how great the expectations or demands are in the field of education, to see that distance teaching should not be viewed as competitive with, but rather complementary to, formal teaching. Were it to be accepted as a full partner in the educational system, distance teaching could offer a great deal to formal teaching, both in covering certain aspects hitherto neglected, in rendering back-up service in specific areas, and in offering the benefit of those techniques developed with specific regard to the individual learner. Quite frankly, though, education would be all the richer if distance teaching could shed its marginal image once and for all, and be accepted as an integral part of the educational system.

At first sight, it would seem hazardous to suggest that formal teaching has its shortcomings. Over the last decades, in most countries so much has been done to give as many people as possible access to the diverse levels of further education available that it may seem presumptuous to assert that distance teaching has a role to play in this field.

Naturally, we all think of those students whom circumstances beyond their control keep, for a time or definitively, from attending regular educational institutes; but are not these the very students who have somehow justified the creation and development of distance teaching? And why speak of shortcomings, when we are dealing essentially with special circumstances concerning a relatively limited body of people? No one has ever doubted the importance of the service given these students by distance teaching, but most people have great difficulty in conceiving that it could move beyond this role of substitute.

Why, you ask? Because in seeking to simplify everything we cling obstinately to the idea that there is one teaching mode, often, revealingly, called normal teaching, which has been conceived to serve the greatest number and that for the others, the minority or the exception, if you like, there exists fortunately a substitute. How can we not notice that, in the domain of education, the exception rears its head much more frequently than we like to believe? But that is a different story, which we shall return to later on.

Suffice to say, for the moment, that the task of democratising education will not be fully achieved without recourse to distance teaching under conditions which, to be sure, still relate it to a makeshift solution; but this is of little importance, for it is already, in certain areas, an integral part of the system and can extend its field ever further. As a matter of fact, even if important and effective steps have been taken in formal education to open secondary teaching to everyone, we have not reached the stage where everyone without exception can actually choose freely from the whole range of educational programmes. Besides, who could reasonably blame the responsible authorities for this? We know full well that outside a common core of fundamental subjects and certain popular options, it is not materially possible to implement the same teaching programmes in a rural college as in its urban equivalent. To be serious, let us not talk of inequality, but rather recognise nevertheless that, in these conditions, students are probably driven to abandoning many courses which correspond to their aptitudes and tastes for the simple reason that it is impossible to reserve a teacher for their needs alone. Now, distance teaching is in a position to offer the service of a specialized teacher. We need not press the point: in such a case, the solution is quite obviously no longer provided by a formula of substitution, apologetically regarded as better than nothing; distance teaching is in fact the only appropriate means at our disposal to complete and enrich the range of the educational programmes of formal teaching, in other words to meet these requirements while keeping within the inevitable budgetary limits.

It is in this respect alone, in a positive way as it were, that it is appropriate to look at the economic considerations to highlight the advantages presented by distance teaching, when it is called upon to intervene in the general system of education. The argument should be clear on this point above all: distance teaching allows us to remedy the disadvantages resulting from the inevitable economic restraints, but it does not automatically allow us to economize. Indeed it is necessary to combat this misguided interpretation, according to which the proponents of distance teaching are motivated by pecuniary considerations, aiming at a greater rentability of the educational system.

Certainly, unless we are totally naive, we would never claim that such considerations are purely imaginary: everyday experience would soon prove the contrary to be true. They do exist, but they are the concerns of people who, for some reason or other, are ignorant of, or have no desire to understand the most fundamental principle of all education, which is to know how to help each and every person to become aware of his or her capabilities and limits, to determine his or her personal objectives accordingly, and then to ensure the provision of the means to attain them, and not to lead the greatest possible number from the same arbitrary starting line, along the same route, within the same time, to a pre-set educational 'finishing post' estimated as being the best placed for everyone, the best adapted to all situations. Such is also the mistake made by these same people in their evaluation of distance teaching, since they see it as a mere standardized educational instrument which makes it possible to provide for hundreds if not thousands of students at a relatively small cost. As a matter of fact, this way of conceiving of and carrying out distance teaching is not necessarily, on every occasion, a result of ill intention. We well know that, in certain cases, we have had to resort to just these means to deal with special situations and meet urgent needs. Such cases still arise here and there: but it is nevertheless not to this end alone that distance teaching has come into existence and that we should envisage its further development.

Thus, when one takes the trouble to examine its main characteristics, distance teaching does not strike us as a method of teaching whose essential virtue is that of being cheaper than all the others. The reason is simple: it is an educational and communication operation which brings people into contact with each other, and we are all aware what this implies in terms of investments of all kinds for launching, keeping up and rendering this activity effective, and in constantly attempting to compensate for the handicaps of isolation and distance. Of course, it would be quite a different story if it were a question of developing, once and for all, courses which could be printed by the thousand to last as long as possible at the lowest possible cost, without taking account of either the evolution of the students' needs or personal expectations. But if this were the case, who would have the effrontery to maintain that distance teaching is entitled to a place of its own alongside formal teaching?

Enriching the educational process

Now, however it may appear, this claim is not excessive, for, if ever we were to concentrate our thoughts on the conditions in which formal teaching is normally put into practice, we would quickly discern the place marked for distance teaching. If it enters into the picture now, it is not to fill any gap, or to make an educational programme complete, it is really to enrich the educational process and permit it to reach its full potential.

We are all well aware that formal teaching, in most cases, is subject to what might be called the dictates of standardization. How could it be otherwise? The way in which a class, or a group, is formed always depends highly on contingencies; nevertheless circumstances impose on it the same curriculum, at the same level, pursued at the same rhythm, and submit it to the same standards of control, at various pre-determined stages. No doubt each organization should have its rules, but these are inevitably based on a hypothetical 'average' case and we all know the rest of the story perfectly well. In this race, very little time elapses before a straggling column develops, becoming increasingly strung out: at the head, naturally, are those able to keep up with the pace without exerting themselves; others, unable to catch or maintain this rhythm, watch in envy as the fast ones draw away from them, and fall further back to the point where they simply abandon the race. There are those, nevertheless, who grit their teeth, persevere and who somehow manage to complete the first leg of the race; but how many of them will be fit to embark on the next leg? But I see no point in continuing with this allegory: the problems we are talking about are much more serious. We are no longer dealing with a sports competition where, all things considered, the individual freely undertakes the risks involved: in the case of formal education, it is the system which has to a great extent arbitrarily decided the level of ability which the competitor should have on starting by setting standards which are appropriate to only a few of the competitors.

This is no unfair criticism of formal education: that would be most unwise indeed, for petty internal feuding has no place in a debate which concerns the whole of the educational community. Neither are we here to delude ourselves in imagining that distance teaching, which after being perceived only as a palliative, has suddenly become the panacea for all the ills of education. We think, more modestly, that for certain educational programmes, for some subjects, under specific circumstances and for individual cases, it is capable of constituting the 'back up wing' of formal education.

The curricula offered to students in this type of teaching are generally conceived with the presence of the teacher in mind. Now there is so much to do, in so little time, that the teacher's vigilance is strained to the limits, and if he manages to perceive a student's difficulties and to give him at the right moment that encouragement that sets him back on his feet again, who is to say that this occasional aid will help the student sufficiently to enable him to overcome the next obstacle by himself? It should be possible to take him aside and provide him with the means to assess his own capability, and practise certain exercises adapted to his particular needs. But since school is open to everyone, at every level, should it not be able to take into account the special situations of these children or young people, of whom it is far too facile to say that they are not gifted in a particular subject or that they lack the persistence necessary to follow a particular course? Our purpose here is not to deny the evidence; of course, everyone knows that family and social background has a considerable role to play; but it is no less certain that one of the missions of the educational system is to restore equality of opportunity as much as possible in the interests of the individuals and the community as a whole.

This is another instance where distance teaching can intervene, as a reserve force of formal teaching, whenever one is faced with particular situations. For proof of this we need only refer to what makes distance teaching a specific type of education: the taking into account of the constraints imposed by distance and studying in isolation which has naturally led to the creation of courses whose content structure, presentation, development and even pace have been conceived not only to guide the individual's activity, but also to encourage and, where necessary, to instigate it. Why do we think that a correspondence course can never be the written replica of an oral course? A basic tenet of the profession, you say; but these tenets are also founded on the necessity of furnishing an answer appropriate to the expectations of a public placed in a situation which makes certain modes of communication inevitable. Now, if we look at the situation more closely, we see that, due to circumstances, there is fairly often little difference, in terms of pedagogical assistance, between the pupil as a member of a class who has been, or at least feels, left out, and the student who is engaged in a correspondence course.

It would be relatively easy for specialists to determine the subjects, or more exactly the notions, and to pinpoint the stages of educational programmes where the intervention of distance teaching can be justified. Let us take the example of foreign languages, not out of any taste for paradox, but because it is revealing in that it is in this field that the uninformed see distance teaching at its weakest. And yet, if we offer him a complete and coherent course, training all the necessary skills, is not the distance education student called upon, indeed obliged, to express himself in the language taught much more than his counterpart in formal education, with the added advantage of being heard and helped on a personal basis? In the final analysis, everything is there: if distance teaching represents an arm of support for formal teaching, it is simply because it has acquired a certain experience in the field of individual tuition, and it would perhaps be a pity not to make good and full use of it.

Towards educational autonomy

In these conditions, our purpose is clear, and our intentions should also be clearly stated: in no way do we mean to extol the virtues of distance teaching or to argue for its promotion as a competitor of formal teaching. To present it as a supporting arm moreover excludes any suggestion of encroachment or eventual replacement. We know very well that nothing can replace the benefits brought by direct teaching institutions to children or young people, besides and beyond the strict acquisition of knowledge, and if we are particularly aware of this, it is precisely because a large part of our task consists in serving students who cannot participate in classroom activities, and because, at times, we realize only too well all that the best of correspondence courses will never be able to offer them.

If competition has no place in our deeper considerations, it is also because we share an opinion which is beginning to be held, if not rather commonly accepted: if teaching can only really exist through establishing relationships between people, communication, in its sustaining and animating function, cannot be restricted to a single mode of expression; it must have recourse to several modes and be able to make use of them simultaneously or successively, as needs be.

However, let us be careful here: these variations are not being explored for the fun of it. They form part of the educational programme whose prime objective should not be lost sight of: it is vital not only to teach and import knowledge or know-how, but to help the individual concerned to acquire gradually an educational autonomy and to retain the desire to exercise it.

It is here, undoubtedly, that formal teaching and distance teaching find themselves on common ground, fighting the same fight, in the cause of 'life-long' education. Indeed if we do not consider that the initial stages of education constitute a completed whole to which may or may not eventually be added what we call continuing education, in other words if we want to be serious in speaking of 'permanent' education, we must admit that its foundations lie in the very first school years. Certainly, we find ourselves again in a period of transition where we have to apply distinctions based on institutions which are getting out-moded. This is why when earlier we were alluding to a possible integration of distance teaching, we were still short of the mark, in many respects. In reality, if we situate our case in the perspective of permanent education, the contribution of distance teaching is no longer simply interesting or even enriching, it becomes quite indispensable.

Indeed, since it is also engaged in the direction leading to what we have called educational autonomy, formal education should help an individual to take charge of himself gradually, which can be achieved through training to independent studies. In other words, it is necessary to make intelligent use of the most favorable opportunity so as to enable the students to familiarize themselves with the techniques of individual teaching and that entails, in certain study situations, the use of distance teaching material. At this stage, the question no longer arises as to whether formal teaching has anything to gain from this initial level of integration with distance teaching. The problem has to be posed in different terms and situated at another level entirely: it is necessary now to take cognizance of the significance of permanent education and all its implications. The first consists, we feel, in watching carefully over each stage in the educational programme. At present in most cases there is, properly speaking, no organized syllabus and, to speak again in terms of races, if the baton is safely seized at the change over, we know very well that it is often due to sheer luck.

A solution must be sought not only in active collaboration in the various stages of the race, which would already be a real improvement, but also in a pooling of experience leading to a concerted organization of all the various aspects of the competition. This idea is not original for those practicians of distance teaching who are already engaged in this type of experiment. Perhaps it would be worth stopping here for a moment, before concluding, on this simple observation, offered to the undecided or sceptical who do not make it a point of honour to remain entrenched in their position; the initiatives taken here and there toward the association of various forms of teaching are not laboratory experiments, conducted as a mental exercise without ever seeing the light of day as a practical, viable operation; and they do not lead either to the construction of educational prototypes whose control is reserved for specialists operating in a cloistered milieu focusing only on a carefully selected public. The results noted show, in fact, that we have come to the first stage of a new direction in education, accessible to all who resolve to cast their eyes to the future.

Conclusion

Thus the time has come when distance teaching will be forced to leave its restricted field behind to become involved almost entirely within the cause of permanent education. This is a coming-of-age which we have sought for a long time, because we are convinced that this new partner will bring a great deal to society as long as it is no longer assigned the role of a mere substitute or 'understudy'.

This change of role invites certain consequences; there is no hiding the fact that one cannot live in isolation for years without paying the price for it, and even if we complain of being viewed as outsiders, we end up by being true to the character, and dread a little the return to society. Having for so long been kept in the background and having nevertheless done not too badly in the limited field conceded to it, distance teaching would all the same be ill-advised to enter the main stream of education too sure of itself: specialized though it is in the field of individual tuition, it should engage upon a modest self-evaluation on getting access to the general system of education. Faced with a public now no longer exclusively its own charge, it will be necessary, among other things, to re-examine its techniques, create new communication means, adapt to new forms of dialogue: in a word be prepared to play its part correctly.

That this imposes a constraint is fairly obvious; what is less obvious perhaps, but nevertheless true, is that this constraint contains the germs of a regeneration of distance education. Seen in this light, there is every chance that it will soon cease to be regarded purely as a palliative or as a last resort. Let us hope, at any rate, that distance education will not be led to disown those origins which gave it its character, and sometimes compelled it to become what it is to-day. The outsider would gain nothing but the trappings by turning 'bourgeois', neither would society which in the field of education has a great need of adventurers of this stamp. This is only a wish of course, but it is a most ardent one.

164

SECTION 4: STUDENTS AND THEIR PROGRESS

INTRODUCTION

Educational services of the traditional kind are now such an integral part of modern society that we rarely pause to reflect upon their constituent parts. In particular the student body in our traditional framework of education is normally prescribed by central government or state legislation, at least at primary and secondary level. At tertiary level too there is a traditional age group with traditional objectives relating to initial employment. For distance education, however, there is no such tradition. The students are not a homogeneous body. They are studying through distance education because they do not fit into, cannot be brought into, or choose not to enter the conventional educational framework. Thus the basic yardstick for the design of courses, namely the target population is for distance educators so much more intangible. In all education the content of the course is constrained by the level of the students on entry and the level which should be achieved on completion. The latter is reasonably easy to attain since custom has established widely agreed yardsticks but the former is almost impossible for the distance education course designers. Even if they are able to establish a more or less coherent academic standard on entry, the variation in the personal circumstances of the students, their domestic, social and work situation, as well as their individual objectives and motivation cannot be computed. If in addition a policy of open entry is established, the problem becomes so much the more complex.

If the students who learn at a distance cannot be regarded as a homogeneous group, there are however certain common factors which are normally identifiable and here the last decade has shown enormous advances both in the collection and dissemination of information. From its earliest days, the Open University's Survey Research Department has systematically collected and collated a mass of valuable data concerning students, their successes and failures, their hopes and expectations.[1] Naomi McIntosh the former head of that unit, whose research output can only be briefly represented here, has created totally new standards in this area such that some of the old gut feelings have been substantiated for the first time in a rigorous academic manner, others have been refuted and, in addition, new sets of principles have been established.

Although there are large numbers of younger students in certain specific distance education systems, it is generally the case that the students of distance education systems are adults for whom education must take second or third place behind domestic and work commitments. These people are engaged in distance education for the most part either because the conventional system cannot cope with the numbers seeking educational qualifications, a factor often prominent in setting up distance education institutions in developing countries, or because their needs were or are not satisfied by the conventional system. In the case of the latter group, the majority will be seeking training or better training in relation to present day manpower requirements although there will also be perhaps a significant group who are taking courses purely out of interest.

The single factor which would appear to be common to all successful distance learning students is motivation. In his personal account of the Open University, Walter Perry remarked "Ours is the most difficult way of getting a degree yet invented by the wit of man".[2] This motivation is all the more remarkable when we consider some of the characteristics which regularly appear. The great majority of adults learning at a distance are in the 20-40 age range and are studying on a part-time basis from their homes.[3] Because of their work commitments distance education is the only form of education which provides reasonable openings for them and it is hardly surprising, therefore, that they offer as reasons for choosing it the fact that distance education allows them to plan their own study programme, assess their progress and establish their own pace of work.[4]

Any analysis of the students in distance education must be concerned also with their progress. All would agree that the successful students must have motivation but motivation is not in itself susceptible of simple analysis and in the end is seen as peculiar to individual students and their work, domestic and general social situation. Are there other factors which are more easily isolated?

An initial problem has arisen in attempting to define withdrawal or failure. The latter is most certainly a perjorative term; the former might also be. The popular conception of distance education at the beginning of the 70s was that it success rates were extremely low.[5] It is in the last decade that we have seen a major revision of this viewpoint, occasioned by the great leaps forward in the content and presentation of distance study materials and the student support services which have evolved. Considerable progress has also been made on a definition of drop-out. It is now accepted that some students do not enter distance education programmes with the intention of completing the whole programme, whether this be defined as a degree or a diploma or merely as credit certificate. They embark upon programmes because they see within these programmes certain elements which they wish to obtain for a specific purpose. It may be, of course, that their initial objectives are widened during their studying but this need not necessarily occur and the students may achieve success and complete satisfaction in relation to their own objectives without appearing to do more than register from the point of view of the distance education institution. Such students, and there would seem to be many, must still be counted as drop-outs by the institution.

The articles in this section relate to very different systems of distance education. Kevin Smith is concerned with a University which in its charter has an explicit responsibility for provision for external students while at the same time fulfilling the role of a conventional university in Australia. It is an institution which has not relegated its off-campus students to second class status but rather has accepted in its student/staff ratio and in many other ways that the needs of the off-campus students are different but certainly no less when compared to the traditional on-campus students. The University of New England now has some 25 years of experience in this area and, therefore, a widely recognised role and reputation in Australia.

NKI is a very different institution which offers a variety of teaching services to students in Norway and overseas. Torstein Rekkedal has carried out an analysis of student progress relating this to certain student characteristics including age and geographical location but also to the turn-round time for tutor marked assignments. At NKI students send in assignments which are then forwarded by the institution to particular part-time tutors. After grading and commenting, the tutor returns them to the school where the results are registered. The school then returns the assignments to the students. Other institutions arrange for the student to mail the assignment directly to the tutor thus cutting out the first of these steps and the importance of the "immediacy" of assignments for students is seen in Rekkedal's experiment to cut down on this time factor.[6]

The importance of a speedy return of assignments by the tutor has always been recognised by the Open University but there is no research study available directly comparable to that of Rekkedal. In the third of these articles McIntosh, Woodley and Morrison cover in relatively short compass many of the areas which either together or as individuals they have covered in great detail in more specialist papers and reports. From its foundation, the Open University has kept detailed records of its students' progress and their individual personal details, including age, previous qualifications, occupation etc. It would appear to have, therefore, an unparalleled source of data on students learning at a distance and a success rate for its finally registered students now approaching 60%. It is not surprising, therefore, that it has aroused interest in scholars and politicians alike.

Yet it is necessary to see all these details in the context of earlier remarks. Each distance teaching institution attracts a unique clientele of which almost nothing can be said in general terms. Consequently results are hardly ever directly comparable. Each of the student bodies represented in these articles comes from a different part of the world. If two of them teach to degree level, their starting points are nevertheless different. In the final analysis, we are left with the conclusions that neither age nor distance nor domestic environment nor any other quantifiable term stands out as a salient feature. It is motivation above all else which, despite physical and general social and environmental problems, brings success. But motivation is an all embracing term. The support services of the institution play no small part in motivation as does the whole presentation of the institution and its prestige. The study of students and student progress in distance education becomes more complex and inter-related as each element is researched but without the basic data exemplified in these articles, further progress would be impossible.

David Sewart

Notes

1 The Open University produces each year a Digest of Statistics providing a cumulative information base on its applicants, students and a number of other aspects.

2 Walter Perry (1976) Open University, Milton Keynes, p.167.

3 This statistic is widely reported in relation to institutions engaged in further or higher education, see for example, Flinck, R. (1979), "The research project on two-way communication in distance education: A review". EHSC Workshop paper, pp. 7-9.

4 Research in the last decade has confirmed the findings of Glatter, R. and Wedell, E.G. (1971), Study by correspondence. An enquiry into correspondence study for examinations for degrees and other advanced qualifications, London.

5 In commenting on the appointment of the Open University's first Vice-Chancellor, The Times, 7th June 1968, quoted an example from Chicago in which 0.2% of some 53,000 students gained a degree and only 2% gained

any form of credit.

6 For further details see Rekkedal, T. (1973), _Innsendingsoppgavene i brevundervisningen_, Oslo.

STUDENT DEMAND AND PROGRESS AT THE OPEN UNIVERSITY - THE
FIRST EIGHT YEARS
Naomi E. McIntosh, Alan Woodley and Val Morrison

1 Introduction

> But what would happen in a university of the air? The
> numbers attracted to it would certainly be out of all
> proportion to the numbers that stayed in the course.
> Can we really afford the fantastic cost that this would
> entail? The government give no estimate. It is just as
> well. This is one of those grandiose schemes that does
> not bear inspection while so much else that is already
> begun remains half done. We shall need to be very sure
> that it is necessary before we commit ourselves to the
> expense. (The Times Educational Supplement, 1966).

This quotation taken from a leader in The Times Educational
Supplement under the heading 'Pipe Dream' was typical of the
scepticism that greeted the original proposals for a 'University of the Air' or an 'Open University' as it later became.
This scepticism was shared by a wide range of educationalists, politicians of both parties and informed commentators.
Among many, the scepticism was accompanied by hostility,
clearly documented by Perry in his account of the University's first years (Perry, 1976). Demand was not proven,
students would not stay the course, degree-level work could
not be taught in such a way, there was a vast array of
existing educational opportunities - the criticisms were
numerous, and strongly argued. Now, ten years after the
granting of the University's charter and eight years after
the first students commenced their studies, it is possible
to start to make some assessment of how far the University
has confirmed the prophecies of its early critics and how
far it has confounded them.

Early attempts to study the progress of Open University
students and to make comparisons with the graduation rates
of other relevant groups have been limited and fragmentary.
The problems stemmed both from the difficulties of making
comparisons (Calder and McIntosh, 1974) and from the fact

that the majority of students were going to need several years to complete their studies (McIntosh and Morrison, 1974). In this paper we propose to look at the pattern of demand as it has built up over the years, and then to concentrate on the progress and graduation patterns of the early intakes, as it is only for these that we are able to display a nearly but still not complete picture. Inevitably this paper will cover much of the same ground as an earlier one on the same topic (McIntosh and Morrison, 1974). However, we propose to repeat the data where appropriate, thereby providing a more complete picture of the University's first years.

Before commencing our discussion, it is worth reminding those unfamiliar with the detail of the Open University's structure what its key characteristics are, and how it differs both from other conventional and other distance learning institutions. It was set up specifically as a distance learning institution, and

1   it is designed for adults of all ages who are normally working, and study is expected to be part-time

2   its educational opportunities, initially, were provided at degree level only

3   its study is designed to be mainly home-based

4   it uses open-network BBC television and radio in addition to written and other materials

5   it requires no formal educational qualifications for entry.

Unlike other institutions providing degree studies in the United Kingdom at that time, the Open University decided to use a credit structure, allowing the students to study at their own pace and take years off from their studies if they so wished. Six credits are required for a BA Ordinary degree and eight for an Honours degree. Additionally students who have previously successfully completed other 'higher' education courses are allowed to claim exemption from one to three credits. Originally it was anticipated that each credit would require an average of ten hours study a week for thirty-six weeks of the year. In practice it is now generally agreed that most courses require, and most students spend, twelve to fourteen hours a week on each full-credit course, and many other courses now run for thirty-two to thirty-four weeks. The University currently offers around 120 different courses. They range in difficulty from foundation to fourth level and many have been designed as half credits.

Although the University is now extending its range of courses into the area of continuing education, this paper confines itself to a discussion of the undergraduate programme, the University's first mission. For a more detailed account of this programme readers are referred to the Open University's BA Degree Handbook (Open University, 1979a) and Courses Handbook (Open University, 1979b).

2 The Level of Demand

At the time of its inception there was little *firm* evidence of demand which could be drawn upon to back the case for setting up the Open University. The Planning Committee quoted estimates of the potential pool of adults who had been born too soon to reap the benefits of increasing educational opportunity (Open University Planning Committee, 1969). They suggested that applying Robbins' targets retrospectively indicated a pool of such people of at least one million, of whom 10% (at least 100,000) might apply. Similarly they estimated that some 10% (i.e. 25,000) of the pool of 255,000 non-graduate teachers in the UK might be interested in up-grading their qualifications. They also commissioned a study of the adult population which asked people about their degree of possible interest in such an institution. About 5% indicated that they would be 'very interested'; and 0.9% said that they 'would certainly be one of the first students'. Inevitably these survey figures were subject to wide limits of error. Applied to the country as a whole the 0.9% yielded a figure of total possible students ranging from 34,000 to 150,000. However what nobody could foretell was exactly what the demand would be and whether or not it would be a continuing demand. In a very real sense then, 'supply' preceded 'demand' rather than the other way round.

In the event, applications in the first year were high enough to satisfy the hopes of the planners; and although the characteristics of those who applied were not necessarily what everyone had expected, there were far too many applicants for the places available. Consequently admission procedures had to be devised to choose the first 24,000 students. The basic procedure adopted was one of 'first come, first served' with early applicants being favoured over late applicants. However, there were also course and regional quota restrictions to ensure that there were viable numbers of students taking each foundation course in each geographical area.

Figure 1 shows the absolute number of applicants for each application year since the University started. After the high number in the first year, the number of applicants dropped in the second and third years. The figures for 1973 showed a slight rise but the largest increase came in 1974. Applications reached a peak in 1975 with large numbers of potential students having to be turned away, and since then there has been a gradual decline. However, there is still no sign of the pool of applicants drying up and in fact the provisional figures for 1979 show an increase of four thou-

Figure 1 Open University applicants 1970-78 - overall
numbers, men and women

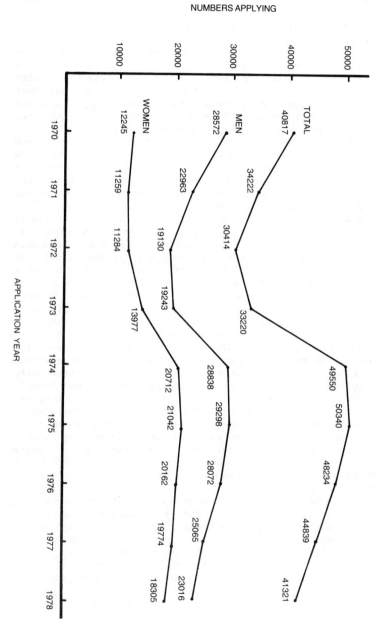

NUMBERS APPLYING

sand from the previous year.

We can offer no conclusive explanation for the pattern of applications in the early years. We assume that the first year represented a build-up of demand among people who had been waiting for the OU to be set up. However, it was still a new and untried institution from which no students had graduated and few courses were yet available to display its academic quality. The end of 1972 saw the first small number of students graduating and it does seem that the media coverage of their success in early 1973 added to the credibility of the University and stimulated demand.

The gradual decline in applications in later years may be due to one of a number of factors. The cost of OU studies is known to deter a large number of potential applicants (Woodley and McIntosh, 1975) and therefore the increases in student fees may have reduced demand. What is of interest is that the number of 'fresh' applicants has remained fairly constant in the later years. Although many unsuccessful applicants re-apply in subsequent years there has been a decline in the proportion who do so.

Table 1 shows the pattern of enquiries, applications, places available and places accepted over the years. Each year many thousands of people enquire about the OU but then decide not to apply for admission. Their reasons for taking such a decision have been reported elsewhere (Woodley and McIntosh, 1977). Here we merely note the general increase over the years in the ratio of applications to enquiries. The situation is complicated by re-applicants who will not usually count as 'enquirers', but it does seem that the proportion of 'serious' enquiries is increasing.

The OU has to take into account two factors when deciding how many places are *offered* in a given year, namely, the number of places available and the rate at which applicants decline the offer of a place. The number of places the University has been able to offer from year to year has varied according to the resources made available by the Department of Education and Science, who have usually indicated both the number of students they expect to see admitted in any one year and the total number overall within the University. From 1975 the DES have approved an increased intake at a level of approximately 20,000 which has gone some way towards reducing the backlog of applicants waiting for a place. In 1976 the University reached the permitted plateau of student numbers and had to limit that year's intake. However the intake was raised in 1977 and again in 1978 and this together with the slight decrease in the number of applicants meant that the chance of being offered a place improved during this period. In fact the OU offers many more places than there are available, because over a quarter of the places offered in a given year are declined by applicants. The acceptance rates vary from occupation to occupation and region to region and these rates together with the reasons for non-acceptance are documented elsewhere (Woodley, 1978). This over-offering of places meant that only one in three applicants in 1978 was not offered a place at all.

TABLE 1 Enquiries, applications, places available and acceptances (1971-78)

For study year*	1971	1972	1973	1974	1975	1976	1977	1978
Enquiries**	123 556	77 722	71 757	81 392	109 858	86 433	75 541	87 335
Total applications	43 444	35 182	32 046	35 011	52 537	52 916	49 956	45 293
Applications transferred to computer file	40 817	34 222	30 414	33 220	49 550	50 340	48 234	44 839
Places available	25 000	20 500	17 000	15 000	20 000	17 000	20 000	21 000
Provisionally registered (new) students	24 220	20 501	16 895	14 976	19 823	16 311	19 886	20 882

*Enquiries and applications occur in the year prior to the year of study.

**This line represents the number of formal written enquiries received in the Admissions Office and does not include contacts made with other University offices nor with Open University students or staff. The figures contain an unquantifiable but not very large number of those who enquire more than once.

To improve our knowledge about demand we have commissioned year by year a study of the awareness of the Open University among the adult population in the United Kingdom. It is clear that people cannot be expected to apply to an institution if they have not heard of it. Not surprisingly, the level of knowledge in the country as the OU started was quite low among the general population, although higher among the better educated and middle class groups. Over the years the numbers who know of the OU have increased from one in three to over two in three of the population, and in some social class groups it is obvious that saturation point has been reached in 'advertising awareness' terms. The phenomenon that marked the early years of applications - the fact that the middle class and particularly teachers applied earlier and therefore were earlier in the 'first come, first served' queue (McIntosh, Calder and Swift, 1976) - still occurs, but is now less marked, as more people have learnt about the OU and how its admissions system works. Table 2 shows how awareness has increased over the years.

175

TABLE 2 The percentage of the population who had heard of the Open University (1971-79)

Year	Total	Sex Male	Female	AB	Social class C_1	C_2	DE
1971	31	33	29	66	50	21	12
1972	40	43	37	78	58	30	22
1973	44	47	42	78	61	38	26
1974	54	58	51	82	71	49	37
1975	55	60	50	86	70	53	32
*——							
1976	45	49	42	68	57	42	29
1977	67	71	63	90	81	63	51
1978	72	76	68	93	85	69	57
1979	70	74	66	92	79	69	54

*The break in the trend between 1975 and 1976 was due to a change in research agency. The research was carried out by Louis Harris Research from 1971-1975 and by Social Surveys (Gallup Poll) Limited from 1976 onwards.

3 The Nature of the Demand

We turn now to the types of people who were attracted to the Open University and the courses they wished to take. While our basic concern here is with applicants to the OU, some of the relevant information is not available for the early years and we have therefore had to use student data. This does not present great problems as the OU's admissions policy ensures that the student profile is very similar to the applicant profile. However there are slight differences which should be borne in mind. For instance, those with low educational qualifications are more likely to decline the offer of a place and therefore form a smaller proportion of students than of applicants. There has also been a decline in the proportion of women at this stage in some years. This has been because women apply predominantly to take Arts or Social Science and they have therefore been less likely to be offered a place due to course quotas which restrict admission to the most popular courses.

(a) *The occupation of applicants*

In Table 3 we show the occupation and sex of those who applied to the Open University in 1971, 1974 and 1978. The figures for 1970 have not been included as unfortunately no sex breakdown is available. However, in that first year 36% of all applicants were teachers. This fell to 30% in 1971 and continued to fall so that by 1978 only one in five applicants was in this occupational category. With the national decision to make teaching a graduate profession, and given the large

176

TABLE 3 Occupational analysis of applicants in 1971, 1974 and 1978

Application year	1971			1974			1978		
No of applicants – 100%	34 222			49 550			41 321		
	Total %	Male %	Female %	Total %	Male %	Female %	Total %	Male %	Female %
Housewives	11.0	0.1	10.9	14.3	0.1	14.2	14.4	0.0	14.4
Armed Forces	1.6	1.6	0.0	2.5	2.4	0.1	2.5	2.4	0.1
Administrators & managers	4.6	4.3	0.3	4.3	3.8	0.5	4.6	3.8	0.8
Teachers & lecturers	30.2	19.8	10.4	24.0	13.0	11.0	21.3	11.1	10.2
The professions & the arts	12.6	8.0	4.6	11.1	5.9	5.2	11.9	6.1	5.8
Qualifed scientists & engineers	4.4	4.3	0.1	3.1	3.0	0.1	2.9	2.8	0.1
Technical Personnel: inc. data processing, draughtsmen & technicians	11.9	11.1	0.8	10.0	9.0	1.0	10.2	9.1	1.1
Elect., electronic, metal & machines, engineering & allied trades	3.0	3.0	0.1	4.0	3.9	0.1	3.7	3.6	0.1
Farming, mining, construction & other manufacturing	2.3	2.2	0.1	3.4	3.2	0.2	2.9	2.7	0.2
Communications & transport: air, sea, road and rail	1.3	1.2	0.1	2.1	1.8	0.1	2.0	1.7	0.3
Clerical & office staff	9.4	5.3	4.1	11.7	4.9	6.8	11.6	4.1	7.5
Shopkeepers, sales, services, sport & recreation workers	4.4	3.8	0.6	5.4	4.5	0.9	5.0	3.9	1.1
Retired, independ-ent means, not work-ing (other than housewives),students	3.1	2.2	0.9	3.9	2.5	1.4	6.9	4.3	2.6
In institutions, e.g. prison, chronic sick	0.1	0.1	0.1	0.2	0.2	0.0	0.1	0.1	0.0
Total	100.0	67.1	32.9	100.0	58.2	41.8	100.0	55.7	44.3

pool of non-graduate teachers remaining in the country, it looks as if teachers will continue to form an important though declining group for many years to come. With the exception of an increase in the retired and unemployed, the rest of the occupational groups show very little change.

The OU has attracted relatively few applicants from 'working class' occupations. Between 1970 and 1975 manual workers increased their share of the applications from 5% to 10% but since then the figures have levelled off and may even be declining. It has to be remembered that the educational opportunities being applied for are at degree-level, opportunities in the UK which are normally only available to a highly selected 10% of school leavers. The barriers to access - educational, financial and cultural - are formidable and unlikely to be overcome by many other than the most able and motivated of people from such disadvantaged backgrounds. These questions have been discussed at greater length elsewhere (McIntosh and Woodley, 1974, McIntosh and Woodley, 1975).

As is clear from Figure 1 the number of women who applied to the OU in the first years was quite low and certainly lower than many people had expected (McIntosh, 1975). However, Table 3 shows that the proportion of women has continued to increase steadily over the years. By no means all of this increase has been in the expected category of 'housewives'. There has been an important increase in the clerical and office group and female teachers continue to form 10% of all applicants whereas the proportion of male teachers has declined. However, the OU has continued to fail to attract female manual workers.

(b) *Previous educational qualifications*

In Table 4 we show the educational qualifications held by new students at the time they entered the Open University. Students in recent intakes have tended to have lower qualifications than those in earlier years. For instance, 34% of those who entered in 1978 held no qualifications higher than GCE O-levels compared with only 25% of the 1971 intake. Over the same time period the proportion of students with qualifications which would entitle them to credit exemptions declined from 52% to 44%. However, most of these changes occurred in the first few years and the patterns have been relatively stable for the last four years.

On the face of it, over one-half of new OU students have the qualifications necessary for admission to a

full-time degree course. However, it should be remembered that many of these students were 'unqualified' at
the time of leaving school. A great number of the
teachers, for instance, gained admission to a College
of Education on the basis of their GCE O-levels.

TABLE 4 The highest educational qualifications held by entering students (1971-78)

Year of entry	1971	1972	1973	1974	1975	1976	1977	1978
No of students = 100%	24 220	20 501	16 895	14 976	19 823	16 311	19 886	20 882
	%	%	%	%	%	%	%	%
No formal educational qualifications	6.8	8.6	9.1	8.5	11.2	10.7	9.3	9.8
CSE,RSA, or school leaving cert. in 1 or more subjects	1.8	3.8	3.8	2.9	3.6	3.3	3.4	3.5
GCE 'O' level, SCE 'O'grade,school cert. or equivalent in 1-4 subjects	5.9	7.6	8.1	8.0	10.2	9.9	9.8	10.2
GCE 'O' level, SCE 'O'grade,school cert. or equivalent in 5 or more subjects	10.8	12.8	12.3	10.8	12.9	12.3	11.5	11.4
GCE 'A' level,SCE 'H' grade,higher school cert. or equivalent in 1 subject	3.5	4.2	4.1	4.3	4.7	4.8	5.0	4.9
GCE 'A' level,SCE 'H' grade, higher school cert. or equivalent in 2 or more subjects	9.5	9.3	9.4	10.2	10.8	11.4	11.7	11.2
ONC/OND	3.8	5.1	4.4	3.8	3.8	4.0	4.2	4.2
HNC/HND	10.7	10.6	9.2	7.7	6.7	8.0	7.7	7.6
Teachers cert. or equivalent	28.9	24.0	25.8	27.7	24.6	24.6	25.0	24.9
University dip. or equivalent based on at least one year's full-time study	8.6	7.4	7.1	7.8	7.6	8.1	8.2	7.6
University first degree	4.1	5.3	5.8	6.3	2.7	2.8	3.6	4.1
No information	5.5	1.1	0.9	2.1	1.1	0.3	0.6	0.6

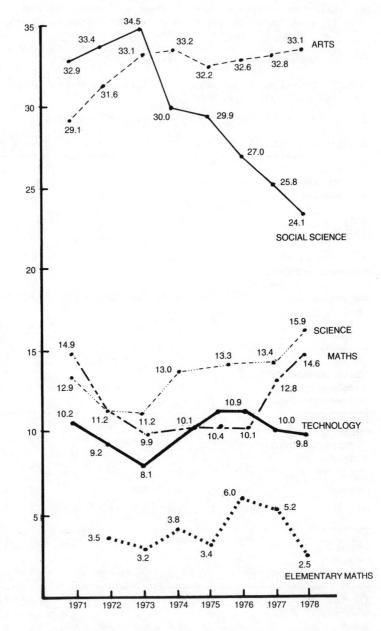

APPLICATION YEAR

Fig 2 Course applications 1971–78; percentages

(c) *Course choice*

Every new Open University student begins by taking one of the foundation courses in Arts, Social Science, Maths, Science or Technology. Students with little or no previous experience of higher education must study two foundation courses before they can graduate, while those with two or more credit exemptions are only permitted to study one. Students can take two foundation courses in their first year or one foundation course plus a half-credit course in elementary maths, but the great majority settle for one foundation course. The actual pattern of course applications over the years is shown in Figure 2. (The figures for 1970 have not been included as the Technology foundation course was not available then.)

TABLE 5 The foundation courses taken by men and women (1971-79 intakes)

	1971	1972*	1973*	1974	1975	1976	1977	1978	1979
	%	%	%	%	%	%	%	%	%
Base - all students = 100%	6274	5477	5176	4301	6187	4916	6004	6024	6080
Arts									
Male	55	48	49	42	38	35	36	32	33
Female	45	52	51	58	62	64	64	68	67
Base - all students = 100%	6188	6689	6156	4886	6395	4801	5747	5846	5728
Social Science									
Male	66	59	57	55	52	52	50	48	49
Female	34	41	43	45	48	47	50	52	51
Base - all students = 100%	4778	3827	2701	2099	2960	2475	3039	3613	3559
Maths									
Male	89	88	87	82	80	78	79	75	74
Female	11	12	13	17	20	21	21	25	26
Base - all students = 100%	5087	3629	2904	2355	3005	2423	3029	3449	3421
Science									
Male	87	81	77	70	72	67	69	67	68
Female	13	19	23	30	28	32	31	33	32
Base - all students = 100%		3319	2663	2238	2202	2632	3071	2837	2905
Technology									
Male	**	95	93	92	89	88	90	90	89
Female		5	7	8	11	11	10	10	11

*New and continuing students are included in these figures
**Course not available

The dominant trend has been the decline in applications for the Social Science foundation course. Though the rate of this decline was arrested somewhat in 1975 by the introduction of the new Social Science foundation course, D101, this was only temporary. The explanation is not, however, that it is a poor or unattractive course, but the more mechanistic one that it is the course predominantly chosen on entry by teachers and the fall in numbers is very closely correlated with the decline in the number of teachers. The numbers applying for Arts increased initially and is now fairly stable. Many who have no qualifications at all choose the Arts course as their point of entry. The most encouraging sign is the increase in applications both for Science and Maths which appear to have been helped rather than hindered by the introduction of the new Science and Maths foundation courses in the application year 1978.

We do not have information available which separates out course choice by sex, at application stage, but it is clear from the student figures that the early reluctance of women to apply for Science and Maths courses is being gradually overcome, and the increase in Science and Maths applications is likely in some part to have been helped by the increase in the proportion of women applicants to the University. However, Arts is still the most popular course for women and they now outnumber men by two to one on this foundation course.

4 First Year Progress

Applicants who accept the offer of a place at the Open University pay a provisional registration fee. After three months study during the 'Provisional Registration' period the new students decide whether to pay the final registration fee which will entitle them to receive teaching materials for the rest of the first year. This decision is made entirely by the student and none are debarred from continuing on academic grounds.

In 1971 some 81% of the first intake proceeded to final registration (Table 6). This proportion declined somewhat in the next two years but has since remained remarkably constant at around 75%. These later figures are particularly encouraging given the changes in the student population over this period which were noted earlier.

Table 6 also shows the progress made by students on each of the five foundation courses and here there have been interesting changes over the years. In recent years the final registration rates for Maths, Science and Technology have all improved and in 1978 it was the Social Science foundation course that lost the most students.

TABLE 6 The proportions of new students who finally registered for each foundation course (1971-1978 intakes)

	1971	1972	1973	1974	1975	1976	1977	1978
	%	%	%	%	%	%	%	%
Total students	80.8	76.7	75.1	75.7	74.8	75.0	75.3	75.0
Arts	80.9	76.5	77.2	77.1	75.5	78.7	78.6	76.2
Social Science	77.6	72.4	76.1	75.5	74.5	71.3	74.0	69.2
Maths	69.2	66.6	62.0	62.4	65.9	68.0	69.7	72.5
Science	74.9	69.2	69.1	73.7	70.1	72.1	70.8	76.3
Technology	-	69.3	69.0	71.9	68.1	72.7	71.3	78.2

The great majority of finally registered new students proceed to gain some course credit at the end of the first year. The actual proportions have varied between 75% and 81% but there have been no clear trends over the years. Those who have taken two courses in their first year have generally passed both or neither of them.

5 Student Performance in Second and Subsequent Years

In Table 7 we show the percentage of students registered in a given year who successfully obtained some course credit. The patterns for each intake were found to be very similar. Performance drops slightly in the second year of study, rises again in the third year and then steadily declines in subsequent years. The greatest proportion of each intake graduates at the end of the third year and this is a possible explanation for the peak in performance at that time. The decline in performance in later years would suggest that the remaining students find it increasingly difficult to cope with their OU studies.

TABLE 7 The percentage of registered students gaining some course credit in each year of study (1971-74 intakes)

	Year of study							
	1st	2nd	3rd	4th	5th	6th	7th	8th
	%	%	%	%	%	%	%	%
Intake								
1971	80.0	74.0	79.5	73.5	67.0	64.3	57.7	54.0
1972	75.1	74.8	75.2	70.4	68.2	64.1	57.0	
1973	79.6	71.9	74.0	72.0	69.2	64.9		
1974	80.0	72.4	75.4	71.5	67.5			

Percentages based on the number of finally registered students in each year for each intake.

6 Graduation Rates

From the early days the Open University has attracted large numbers of visitors from overseas who want to find out more about this new distance-teaching system. Their questions have varied according to their special interests but few left without asking 'What proportion of your students graduate?' It was pointed out to them that no satisfactory answer could be given as the OU's credit system allowed students to take as many years as they wanted to obtain a degree. Ultimately everybody might graduate, it was too soon to say. However, the OU is now in its ninth teaching year and graduation patterns have begun to emerge. We are now in a position to make realistic estimates of eventual graduation rates.

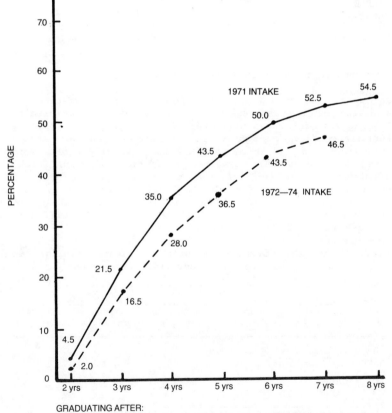

GRADUATING AFTER:
BASE = ALL STUDENTS WHO FINALLY REGISTERED IN THEIR FIRST YEAR

Fig. 3 The cumulative proportions of Open University students graduating over time

In Table 8 we show the cumulative graduation rates for each of the first six student intakes. By the end of 1978 54% of those who had finally registered as new students in 1971 had obtained an Ordinary degree from the OU. For those students who were awarded two or three credit exemptions it was possible to graduate after two years of study and almost nine hundred managed to do so. The third year marked the peak with 3318 obtaining a degree. Students continued to graduate in subsequent years but in decreasing numbers. When the cumulative graduation rates are plotted as a graph in Figure 3 it can be seen that the curve is beginning to flatten out and although extrapolations are always dangerous, it appears that the final graduation rate for the first intake of students will be slightly over 55%.

TABLE 8 The cumulative proportions of Open University students graduating over time

	Year of entry to the Open University					
	1971	1972	1973	1974	1975	1976
Base - all finally registered students = 100%	19581	15719	12680	11336	14830	12227
	%	%	%	%	%	%
Graduated by:						
1972	4.6					
1973	21.5	2.0				
1974	35.0	16.6	2.0			
1975	43.4	27.7	16.6	1.9		
1976	49.8	36.3	28.4	16.8	1.5	
1977	52.7	43.4	36.8	27.9	13.8	1.4
1978	54.3	46.8	43.5	35.0	22.5	12.8

The graduation rates for the second and subsequent intakes have been very similar to each other but somewhat lower than those for the first intake. This is shown graphically in Figure 3 where we have plotted the cumulative graduation rates for the second, third and fourth intakes.

From the evidence presented earlier in this paper, the slowing down of graduation rates was only to be expected. Changes in the student population, such as the declining numbers of teachers, have meant that fewer people enter the OU with credit exemptions and we also know that, on average, students are attempting fewer course credits per year. This results in a slower 'through-put' of students and hopefully the final graduation rates for later intakes will be at least as high as those for earlier ones. At the moment we can only say that it seems that at least 50% of each intake will eventually graduate.

While the factors outlined above may account for a general slowing down of graduation rates, they are unlikely to explain the markedly superior performance of the first intake. In the absence of other evidence one is tempted to suggest that here was a group with a particularly high motivation to succeed. They were the ones at the head of the queue to join the new institution and they were very much in the public eye as the 'experiment' was observed with great interest by the media.

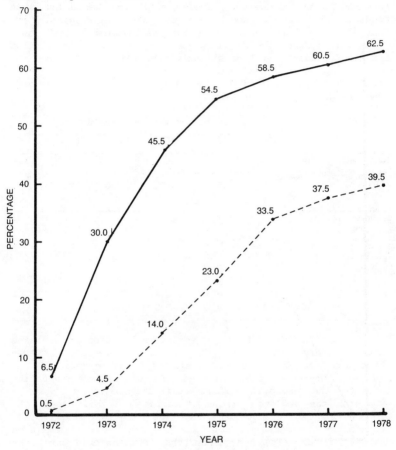

A 'QUALIFIED' STUDENT IS ONE WHO HOLDS TWO GCE A-LEVELS OR THEIR EQUIVALENT, OR SOME HIGHER QUALIFICATION.
BASE=ALL FINALLY REGISTERED STUDENTS IN 1971.

Fig. 4 The cumulative proportions of 'qualified' and 'unqualified' Open University students from the 1971 intake graduating over time*

We can now look at graduation rates among certain sub-groups of the student population. As the OU operates an open admission policy one obvious area of interest is that of prior education qualifications. Did the OU provide a real opportunity for those students who did not possess the entry requirements for a conventional degree course? In Figure 4 we have plotted the cumulative graduation rates for students from the 1971 intake both with and without the normal degree entry requirements. Those in the 'qualified' group graduated more quickly in the first few years but then the rates began to level off. By the end of 1978 62% of them had graduated.

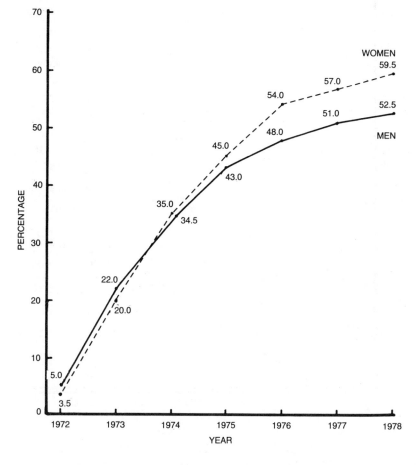

BASE = ALL FINALLY REGISTERED STUDENTS IN 1971

Fig. 5 The cumulative proportions of men and women from the 1971 intake graduating over time

187

Among the 'unqualified' group graduation rates picked up in later years and by 1978 40% had obtained a degree. As the 'unqualified' students were unlikely to have any credit exemptions, this pattern was to be expected. However, as the two curves are now almost parallel it seems unlikely that the 'unqualified' will catch up with the 'qualified' group. Nevertheless four out of ten of those students who, judging by the educational qualifications, were not 'university material' had obtained a degree.

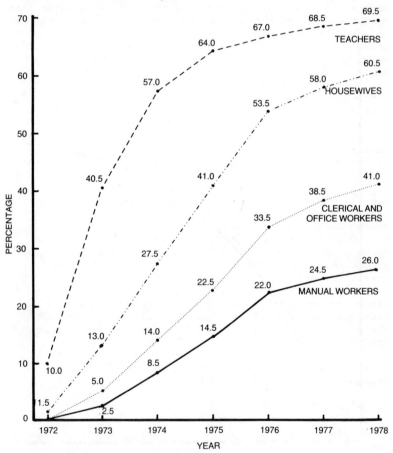

BASE = ALL FINALLY REGISTERED STUDENTS IN 1971

Fig. 6 The cumulative proportions of Open University students from the 1971 intake in selected occupational categories graduating over time

In Figure 5 we compare the progress of men and women from the 1971 intake. In the early years men graduated slightly more quickly than women. However, by the end of 1978 women had overtaken the men with 59% having graduated compared with 52%. This pattern seems to be repeating itself among later intakes.

There is great variation in graduation rates between the fourteen occupational categories used by the OU. In Figure 6 we show the cumulative graduation rates for students from the 1971 intake in just four of these categories. The teachers fared best and around seven out of ten are likely to graduate. Housewives graduated at a slower rate in the early years but the proportion who eventually graduate is unlikely to be far below the figure achieved by teachers. Among the clerical and office workers, slightly over four out of ten are likely to graduate. The picture is least encouraging for manual workers. Although small numbers of them continue to graduate it is unlikely that more than three out of ten will eventually gain a degree.

The Open University has now produced almost thirty-three thousand graduates with ordinary degrees. Over six thousand of this group did not possess the entry qualifications for a conventional degree course at the time they began their OU studies. Each year between five and a half and six thousand new graduates are added to the total. This means that of all the first degrees awarded each year in the United Kingdom, around one in twelve is from the OU.

Many of the OU graduates have proceeded to study for an Honours degree with the OU. To obtain an Honours degree a student has to gain eight credits, two of which must be at third or fourth level. By the end of 1978 one in ten of the 1971 intake had gained such a degree but the final figure is likely to be much higher than this as the numbers awarded each year are still rising. All we can say at the moment is that the OU has already produced over four thousand Honours graduates in total.

7 Patterns of 'Dormancy' and 'Re-entry' Among Open University Students

Students who have finally registered with the OU in their first year of study are entitled to re-enter in any subsequent year without negotiating the normal admissions procedure. Thus while there were 58,788 students registered in courses in May 1978 there were also over 40,000 'dormant' students who were not currently studying with the OU. A small proportion of these students were Honours graduates but the great majority were people who in theory might resume their OU studies in some future years. For planning purposes it is important to know what proportion of this group is likely to re-enter the OU. We approach this problem by looking at the registration patterns of 1971 entrants up to 1977.

For some 84% of the 1971 entrants their study with the OU could be described as 'continuous'. That is, at no stage did they resume their studies after one or more rest years. The actual number of years of continuous study undertaken by this group are shown in Table 9. We turn now to the 16% who studied 'discontinuously' and Table 9 also shows rest periods taken at some point between 1971 and 1977. Among this group, the most common pattern was to have one study-free year. Some students did return after a gap of four or five years but they were comparatively few in number.

TABLE 9 Patterns of continuous and discontinuous study among the first intake of Open University students (1971-77)

Finally registered students in 1971 who studied:			
Continuously		Discontinuously	
16,402		3179	
%		%	
Period of continuous study		Rest year patterns	
First year only	27	Single rest period of 1 year	66
2 years	9	Single rest period of 2 years	16
3 years	12	Single rest period of 3 years	8
4 years	13	Single rest period of 4 years	3
5 years	11	Single rest period of 5 years	1
6 years	11	Two or more rest periods of	
7 years	16	at least one year	6

The present evidence would therefore suggest that the great majority of students do not take rest years but study continuously until they have obtained their Ordinary degree or until they have studied as many courses as they want. Some students do take rest years, often before proceeding from an Ordinary to an Honours degree, but they are unlikely to take more than two years off from their studies. However, just as successive intakes are attempting fewer credits each year, it may prove to be the case that a higher proportion will elect to take rest years. Even if the proportion remains the same, it does mean that the number of students who are returning to OU studies after a gap of one year or more will continue to increase at least for a number of years.

8 Student Workload

Each course offered by the Open University represents one full credit or one half credit. Students can take up to a maximum of two credits per year through any combination of full and half credit courses. In their first year students must register for one full credit foundation course but in subsequent years the minimum requirement is one half credit course. In Table 10 we show the number of credits attempted by students from 1973 to 1978.

It is clear that students are now attempting fewer courses than in earlier years. In 1971 only 4% were attempting a single half credit course but by 1978 this had risen to 15%. Conversely the proportion taking the equivalent of two full credits declined from 10% to 3% over the same period.

TABLE 10 The number of course credits attempted by Open University students (1973-1978)

	1973	1974	1975	1976	1977	1978
Base - all registered* students = 100%	38424	42636	49358	51035	55127	58788
	%	%	%	%	%	%
Number of course credits attempted						
Half	4.0	8.3	11.1	13.6	14.6	15.4
One	74.0	73.0	73.4	72.4	73.1	73.6
One and a half	11.5	11.3	9.4	8.8	8.3	7.5
Two	10.5	7.5	6.1	5.2	4.0	3.4

*In the case of new students this means finally registered

This decline in the number of credits attempted, coupled with the fact that students are now slightly less likely to successfully complete a given course, means that students are accumulating credits at a slower rate. As we see in the next section, student survival rates do not seem to have been affected but what has happened is that students are moving more slowly through the system. In part the OU has become the victim of its own success in attracting more students with low educational qualifications. As they have no credit exemptions these students have to study for more course credits to graduate and at the same time they seem less willing or able to take on a high workload in any one year.

9 Student Survival

As a final indicator of student progress we look at 'student survival' patterns as measured by the percentage of finally registered new students who registered for OU courses in subsequent years. In Figure 7 we have plotted the 'survival curve' for the 1971-1975 intakes up until registration in 1978. (This method does not allow for discontinuous study patterns but, as we have seen, these were relatively in-frequent.) The survival rates for the five intakes were almost identical. Slightly over one-half of the students registered for courses in their fourth year and less than one in five was still studying by the eighth year.

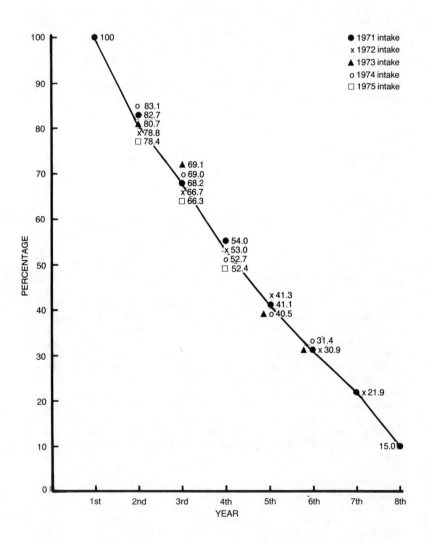

Fig. 7 Survival curve for the 1971-75 intakes up until 1978

For a complete picture we need to couple 'survival' rates with graduation data. We therefore conclude this section by summarizing the progress up until 1979 registration of those who finally registered in 1971 (Table 11). Some 12% were still taking courses in 1979 of whom over one-half had already obtained an Ordinary degree and were aiming for an Honours degree. The majority of those who were not studying had already graduated and 10% of all students had gained an Honours degree. Only 41% of the first intake appear to have given up any plans to graduate, at least for the present.

TABLE 11 The status of students from the 1971 intake as at February 1979

	Finally registered students in 1971
Base − all students = 100%	19 581
	%
Still Studying: Ordinary graduate	7
Non-graduate	5
Not Studying: Honours graduate	10
Ordinary graduate	37
Non-graduate	41

10 Conclusions

We have shown in this paper that the basic beliefs held by the Open University's founders have proved to be true. There was a great demand for degree-level studies among working adults and this demand has continued as evidenced by the application figures over the years. The information on student performance has also demonstrated that great numbers of people can study successfully at a distance. Every year three out of four admitted students proceed to final registration and over eight out of ten who do so gain some course credit. Approximately, one half of all finally registered students will eventually graduate.

Now that the Open University has established its credentials it must concentrate its efforts on becoming more 'open'. While its early years saw some increase in the proportions of students with low educational qualifications and in the manual trades, little progress has been made since then. Also those students from 'disadvantaged' groups who were attracted have found it more difficult to cope with the demands of OU study. There are no easy solutions to these problems but the tasks which face the OU over the second eight years are clear. We hope to return to these topics in a later paper.

References

Calder, J. & McIntosh, N.E (1974) Student drop-out, wastage and withdrawal - some problems of comparison between the Open University and other educational institutions. Higher Education Review, Autumn, 61-68

McIntosh, N.E. (1975) Women and the Open University in Women in higher education, University of London Teaching Methods Unit

McIntosh, N.E., Calder, J. & Swift, B. (1976) A degree of difference - a study of the first year's intake to the Open University of the United Kingdom. London: Society for Research into Higher Education; (1977) New York: Praeger

McIntosh, N.E. & Morrison, V. (1974) Student demand, progress and withdrawal - the Open University's first four years. Higher Education Review, Autumn, 37-60

McIntosh, N.E. & Woodley, A. (1974) The Open University and second chance education - an analysis of the social and educational background of Open University students. Paedagogica Europaea, 10, October, 85-100

McIntosh, N.E. & Woodley, A. (1975) Excellence, equality and the Open University. Paper presented at 3rd International Conference on Higher Education, University of Lancaster

The Open University BA Degree Handbook (1979a) Milton Keynes: The Open University Press

The Open University Courses Handbook (1979b) Milton Keynes: The Open University Press

The Open University Planning Committee (1969) The Open University: report of the planning committee to the Secretary of State for Education and Science. London: HMSO

Perry, W. (1976) The Open University - a personal account. Milton Keynes: The Open University Press

Times Educational Supplement (1966) Leader, 4 March

Woodley, A. (1978) Applicants who decline the offer of a place at the Open University. The Open University, mimeograph

Woodley, A. & McIntosh, N.E. (1977) People who decide not to apply to The Open University. Teaching at a Distance, 9, 18-26

EXTERNAL STUDIES AT NEW ENGLAND
A SILVER JUBILEE REVIEW, 1955-1979   (Extracts)
Kevin C. Smith

Introduction: external studies in perspective

An expanding system

External studies, as we define the term in Australia to
refer to teaching off-campus students in courses leading to
a formal qualification at the tertiary level, is an expanding
learning system.

In an obvious way, expansion can be measured in terms
of the growth of external enrolments in universities and
colleges of advanced education especially over the last six
or seven years, the wider selection of courses and qualifications now available externally, the more representative cross-
-section of students now enrolled as externals, the greater
variety of teaching methodologies and organisational models
that have been developed and more venturesome admission
criteria adopted for the benefit of mature age students.

Until the 1970s external courses were offered at the
tertiary level only by three universities and two institutes
of technology, the Royal Melbourne Institute of Technology
and the Western Australian Institute of Technology. Multi-pur-
pose colleges of advanced education had still to make a mark.

The first significant attempt at offering external
courses at the university level was made in 1911 by the
University of Queensland. Australian residents living outside
metropolitan areas in other states had no alternative but to
attempt a London University external degree which was completed only by the most highly motivated and persistent students who managed to survive working in complete isolation.
It was not until 1955 that country residents of New South
Wales had an opportunity to study, similar to Queenslanders,
when the University of New England as a new autonomous
university stepped into the breach, basically to serve the
needs of high school teachers in country areas seeking to
upgrade professional qualifications. Macquarie University
followed in 1967, offering external courses essentially in
science-oriented subjects, an area that was not being served

except in the field of Biology, by New England. Two other universities have since embarked on external programs - Murdoch University (Perth) in 1975 and Deakin (Geelong) in 1978.

External enrolments in the five universities now stand as follows:

University of New England	4998
University of Queensland	2733
Deakin University	2120
Macquarie University	1125
Murdoch University	785
TOTAL	11761

At the Advanced Education level, expansion has been quite rapid. Only a few colleges of advanced education have major commitments to external teaching but this position is changing as in-service education assumes greater significance and traditional full-time pre-service education for teachers diminishes, especially in single purpose colleges. In New South Wales, Mitchell and Riverina Colleges share 3000 external enrolments out of a total of 4800 for all of eleven colleges in that state. Eight Victorian colleges have a total of 3800 external students. Gippsland Institute of Advanced Education and the Royal Melbourne Institute of Technology (RMIT) account for 2200 of these. A similar picture is to be seen in Queensland and South Australia where almost half of the state's external enrolment is in one institution, in these cases, Darling Downs Institute of Advanced Education and Adelaide College of Arts and Education respectively. But a more rational arrangement seems to exist in Western Australia where the Western Australian Institute of Technology (WAIT) with 1250 external shares a total of 2000 students with one other college, Mt. Lawley. Altogether the Advanced Education sector has an anticipated total enrolment of 15300 this year, broken down by state as follows:

N.S.W.	4867
Victoria	3866
Queensland	2912
South Australia	1383
Western Australia	1942
Tasmania	341
TOTAL	15311

If Technical and Further Education (TAFE) is also considered, another 60,000 external students can be added. This is half as many again as there are full-time TAFE students. The vast majority are, of course, part-time students attending day-release or evening programs.

It must be recorded that external students represent only about 6% of the total post-secondary student population for Australia. But on the other hand numbers are almost certain to increase as institutions mount more attractive external programs to compensate for dwindling full-time student numbers. In any event, the figure of 6% gives a somewhat distorted view of the scope and significance of external studies in this country. Leaving aside the TAFE area, there are now 39 institutions (5 universities and 34 colleges) strategically situated in all states to form a national network of external studies opportunities, a goal that was espoused by the 'Open Tertiary Education Report' of the Universities Commission. In fact, only a few years ago external studies became such an attractive alternative for the college sector, especially in Victoria, that the Universities Commission, in its 'Recommendations for 1978' had to veto further expansion in the following terms:

> The Commission is aware that certain colleges of advanced education in Victoria have offered external courses for some time. It is also evident that there is a tendency for some institutions to undertake this work in order to maintain their enrolments. The Commission believes that there is merit in the concentration of external studies work in a limited number of institutions. Accordingly, it proposes to investigate the whole question of the provision of external studies and to report in Volume I of its Report for 1979-81 Triennium... *Meanwhile, institutions not already active in this field should not move into it.*

The communication challenge

Apart from numerical growth, development is also taking place in a qualitative way as well. Indeed, the increasingly effective teaching methods being employed in external courses, a belated recognition of the potential of mature students and a growing conviction in the philosophy of providing recurrent education as life-long education rather than 'education for life' have combined to give external studies programs validity and status that they have not enjoyed in the past.

One of the reasons for the growing acceptance of external studies as a learning mode is the progress being made in conquering the pedagogical and logistic problems of teaching at a distance. This progress is not just the result of improved technology in the sense of developments in hardware but rather the outcome of a more systematic approach to creating effective learning systems. The challenge of teaching at a distance has in many ways led to a greater emphasis on the learner learning rather than the teacher teaching. The process must be student-oriented, individualised and flexible, but these very qualities pose something of an educational dilemma for those planning external courses. The dilemma lies in the fact that external studies depend essentially on an independent learning situation and must be designed so that the motivated mature age student can plot his own path through a particular course with a minimum of outside assistance. On the other hand, systems which rely solely upon the stamina, perseverance and intellectual capabilities of its students to survive the rigours of external studies deserve to be deemed second-rate and perhaps even irresponsible. The compromise, it seems to me, is to provide a core of independent learning material but add other elements that provide incentives to study and ensure that there are opportunities for staff/student contacts and regular student group activities. Underlying the teaching/learning process there must also be efficient administration and an effective counselling and advisory service if real communication is to take place.

Man is essentially a conversational animal. The learning theory for distance education suggests that external teaching should really be an attempt to conduct a form of didactic conversation with students and effectiveness should be measured in terms of achieving two-way communication between tutor and learner. Since there is such great diversity amongst any group of external students in terms of motivation, maturity, educational backgrounds, confidence and intellectual capacity, not to mention lifestyle, occupational commitments and domestic responsibilities, it is fairly certain that the responses to any one teaching strategy or even an element in the system will be variable. Consequently, there is a case for providing a number of learning options: a student can shape a total learning strategy most suited to his individual needs and talents. A learning system can be devised which contains real conversational situations, such as face-to-face contact and residential and weekend schools or in visits to students at study centres or by telephone conversations. In a sense we provide a form of guided didactic conversation in a simulated way through our course materials both print and non-print. And then there is the internalised form of conversation where the student reflects upon the material that he has absorbed, thinks through or reaches conclusions in the form of written assignments. But the system overall must allow for and indeed encourage two-way communication between the teacher and the student as regularly as possible so that ambiguities, misconceptions and frustrations are minimised.

One of the most important tasks that any external studies system must face from the outset is to devise a way of giving reassurance as soon as possible in the academic careers of our new students. Externals are almost notorious for underrating themselves in academic terms and often feel inadequate for the task ahead, especially if they have had no previous tertiary education experience or such experiences happened some years ago. We must do more to hold our students through the first crucial semester or year. Each institution must build its own distinctive brand of educational mousetrap to suit the local situation. It is proper that such 'mouse-traps' should differ in detail but share at least two features in common: the entrance should be obvious and easily accessible for all inquisitive 'mice' and once inside, the educational 'bait' ought to be so palatable as to remove any desire to escape.

The story which follows is the tory of one institution's attempt to meet such design criteria without a satisfactory blueprint or precedent to follow. A unique model evolved. This review attempts to describe how it developed in its special way and why it succeeded to the extent that it has.

In the mainstream

Because the New England model of external studies (where full-time academic staff are involved in teaching both internal and external students) is now commonplace in Australia, many readers could be forgiven for assuming that this is the way that most institutions around the world set about providing educational opportunities to off-campus students. In fact, as a rule, they do not, and because they adopt other approaches, the status of distance education in other countries is variable in the extreme.

Compared with most distance education systems overseas, the New England model has certain cohesiveness and underlying strength that appears to be lacking elsewhere. These qualities are derived mainly from the fact that academic staff are responsible for the total teaching/learning process of writing courses, teaching them through a combination of independent study materials and face-to-face tuition and assessing the students by way of assignments and formal examinations. In almost all other contexts, in Britain, North America and Europe, 'teaching at a distance' is a shared responsibility. Courses are generally written by authors on a contractual basis, teaching in tutorial session and grading of assignments is delegated to part-time or adjunct staff recruited for the purpose and assessment often falls between these part-time recruits and the full-time staff of the institution concerned. Consequently there is a distinct tendency for the quality of the product to be regarded with suspicion. In other cases where 'open learning' institutions have been set up to cater exclusively for off-campus students, there seems to be a certain self-consciousness about operating on the periphery of the educational mainstream. In the United States, in particular, some educators are seeking ways of gaining wider acceptance for 'non-traditional' experimental approaches by having their programs and techniques integrated into the more traditional residential type institution.

Dr. D.B. Varner, President of the University of Mid-America (UMA), put his finger on the essential difference between open learning experiments in the United States and external studies as we know it here, in the following frank statement:

> We're working on paydirt but had better watch out. The dangers of poor quality are very real, and the regular academic faculties could hang us on this issue. There's a high degree of fragmentation in this field - everybody's doing something but the diversity has its dangers. *And we are much too separated from the mainstream of higher education which we'd better figure out how to rejoin.*

But convincing traditional universities to accept the additional responsibility of teaching externally is something that is difficult to effect. The Australian experience is proof enough of this. Of the five universities teaching externally Queensland (1911), New England (1955), Macquarie (1967), Murdoch (1975) and Deakin (1978), all began with charters expressing, in explicit terms, a responsibility for providing for external students. Despite heavy pressure from state and federal governments over the years and, at one stage, the enticement of more generous resource allocations for those who would accept the additional challenge, none of the older traditional universities has been prepared to enter the field.

The newly autonomous University of New England appeared at first to be somewhat uncertain about fully integrating external teaching into the mainstream teaching activities of academic departments. The ultimate decision to require all academic staff in the faculties concerned to teach and assess both internal and external students to ensure parity of standards and equal commitment to these dual responsibilities was a critical one, and with hindsight, we believe, has proven to be a correct one.

The integration of external studies with internal on-campus activities at New England has been facilitated by the fact that, not only does an enrolment of 5,000 externals constitute the largest operation of its kind in Australian universities and colleges, but it also represents a large proportion of the total student enrolment - in 1979, about 60%. From the beginning in 1955, external enrolments have always represented more than half of the University's enrolments, and in the first decade or so, were closer to two-thirds. This has assured external studies of a very visible place in the overall scheme of things: not only in the involvement of teaching departments but also in resource allocation, representation on faculties, boards, committees and other decision making bodies, the use of general campus facilities such as library services, the printery and audio visual services and the development of an adequately staffed co-ordinating administrative unit, headed by a Director with senior status.

But the success of integration cannot simply be explained in terms of numbers. Policy determinations and the development of good working relationships between and among various sectors of the total organisation are also essential. The sectors include the academic staff, the Department of External Studies, the Academic Secretary, service departments such as the Library, Printery, Audio Visual Services and the Colleges.

Academic staff

As Howard Sheath explains in his account of the early years of external studies developments, the decision to limit external enrolments on the basis of a staff-student ratio similar to that already existing in the traditional classroom situation, was a vital one, once it was resolved that staff members would bear responsibility for teaching both student groups as part of their normal duties. Although the original formula has undergone subtle changes over the years, the general principle of staffing external studies on the same basis as for internal teaching still applies. Consequently enrolments for each of 30 departments teaching externally are carefully controlled by the imposition of quotas; and although this means that every year several hundred applicants cannot be accepted, those that are enrolled can expect to be effectively taught by staff who are not overburdened by sheer numbers.

In the academic departments involved in external teaching there are 172 course co-ordinators who are responsible for the design and presentation of written courses, the marking of assignments, the conduct of residential and weekend schools, final student assessment and course evaluation. In general courses are taught internally before being adapted to the external studies mode. In this way, most external courses undergo a certain kind of 'developmental testing', with internal students acting as a pilot group. In turn, internal students benefit when the external course, which requires careful initial preparation and continuous refinement, is made available to them in whole or in part. Even if the printed material is not passed on to them directly, it is reasonable to assume that internal presentation has also undergone improvement in the light of experiences in teaching the course to another student group in a different mode. The beneficial effect of external teaching on the general quality of teaching in a university is all too often underestimated or overlooked altogether.

The positive attitude of academic staff to external studies in the University is basically a tribute to the attitudes and qualities of the external students whom they have taught. But without the Department of External Studies to co-ordinate departmental teaching activities and provide organisational support on a wide front, the present system would certainly not have developed in the way it has.

If academic staff are to be heavily committed to a dual
system of teaching, it is essential that they are not
diverted from this demanding role by administrative and
organisational responsibilities that are rapidly generated
in an educational system where students are widely scattered
across a continent. External studies will not operate effectively just by offering carefully prepared courses and marking
assignments. All too many systems at home and abroad bear
testimony to this with catastrophic withdrawal and failure
rates.

The functions of the Department of External Studies are
wide ranging as Figure 1 shows. They require the Director
and his staff to service needs of teaching departments in
maintaining effective communication with their students and,
at the same time, do all that is possible to facilitate
student progress through prompt, efficient and sympathetic
responses to inquiries or calls for assistance whether they
be by telephone, letter or personal visit.

The multi-faceted role of the Department can best be
explained under four main headings: Course production, Student services, Staff-student contact and Other functions.

Course production At the University of New England the
responsibility for teaching, both internal and external,
rests with the heads of the academic departments concerned.
In practice, course co-ordinators have a great deal of
freedom to decide the most suitable forms of course presentation for themselves, provided that the various elements of
the course such as printed material, audio-visual media,
weekend schools, residential schools and so on take into
account budgetary and other constraints especially those of
postal services, library facilities, and the University's
production-line capabilities. Such freedom might be regarded
as a weakness. Certainly there are some courses which are
less satisfactorily presented than others. But I believe
that on balance, this variety adds strength to the system,
for it exposes our students to a wide band of approaches to
particular disciplines and avoids the pitfalls of stereo-type
presentation into which tightly edited material might fall.
In this sense, our external students interact with individual
members of staff just as our internal students do.

Although academic staff enjoy freedom to determine their
individual methods of presentation relating to such matters
as number, size and frequency of batches of material to be
posted, the proportion of course material that one medium or
another should occupy and the extent of face-to- face contact
arranged at weekend and/or residential schools, it is necessary to ensure that staff members, especially new appointees
unfamiliar with external teaching, are fully aware of the

organisational framework in which they have to operate. It must also be made clear to students from the outset what they will have to do to meet course requirements and what teaching methods will be employed. To this end, the Department of External Studies has collaborated with academic staff to publish a booklet entitled Teaching Externally which is issued to all members of staff on appointment.

Once the teaching material is submitted to the Department of External Studies and the schedule for the despatch decided upon, the typing, printing, collating and despatch of the material become the responsibility of the Director of External Studies. If there are tapes or cassettes or other audio-visual media to be included in this material he must also ensure that Audio-Visual Services is aware of recording and production requirements well in advance so that the tapes, films or slides can be delivered to External Studies on schedule for incorporation with printed materials.

Student services Considerable emphasis is given to caring for our external students as individuals despite the growing numbers which have just reached 5,000. Indeed, we are sometimes accused of being too 'paternal', but in many ways this criticism reassures us that we have still managed to retain our original philosophy of making the student feel that his progress and problems are of concern to both academic and administrative staff of the University. Perhaps more than any other single factor, this attitude has contributed to the sense of identity with the University that most of our external students develop.

One of the central functions of the Department of External Studies is to monitor the progress of students in close collaboration with teaching departments and to provide advice and encouragement through correspondence on matters pertaining to their studies. Monitoring student progress involves the maintenance of accurate records of the receipt and despatch of assignments (about 40,000 per year) and tapes (20,000 per year). From these records regular reviews are made and defaulting students reminded of their overdue work. In cases of illness, accident or other unforeseen circumstances, extensions of time for the submission of work are given, according to policies determined by teaching departments. In serious cases of failure to meet course requirements, students can be withddrawn by the Faculty and deemed to have failed.

In matters of correspondence, students are urged to write to the Director of External Studies. The handling of correspondence in ,the first instance by the Department of External Studies has some important advantages:

203

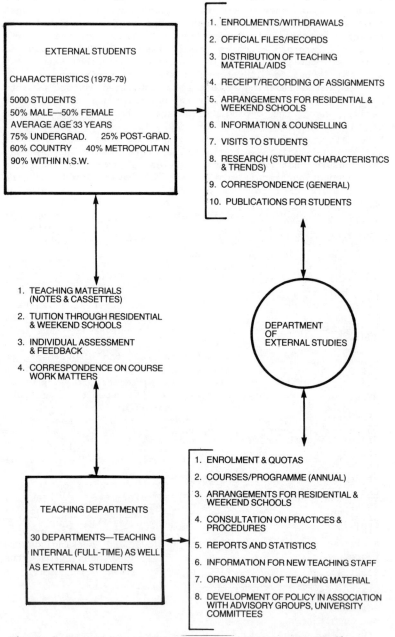

EXTERNAL STUDENTS

CHARACTERISTICS (1978-79)

5000 STUDENTS
50% MALE—50% FEMALE
AVERAGE AGE 33 YEARS
75% UNDERGRAD.   25% POST-GRAD.
60% COUNTRY   40% METROPOLITAN
90% WITHIN N.S.W.

1. ENROLMENTS/WITHDRAWALS
2. OFFICIAL FILES/RECORDS
3. DISTRIBUTION OF TEACHING MATERIAL/AIDS
4. RECEIPT/RECORDING OF ASSIGNMENTS
5. ARRANGEMENTS FOR RESIDENTIAL & WEEKEND SCHOOLS
6. INFORMATION & COUNSELLING
7. VISITS TO STUDENTS
8. RESEARCH (STUDENT CHARACTERISTICS & TRENDS)
9. CORRESPONDENCE (GENERAL)
10. PUBLICATIONS FOR STUDENTS

1. TEACHING MATERIALS (NOTES & CASSETTES)
2. TUITION THROUGH RESIDENTIAL & WEEKEND SCHOOLS
3. INDIVIDUAL ASSESSMENT & FEEDBACK
4. CORRESPONDENCE ON COURSE WORK MATTERS

DEPARTMENT OF EXTERNAL STUDIES

TEACHING DEPARTMENTS

30 DEPARTMENTS—TEACHING INTERNAL (FULL-TIME) AS WELL AS EXTERNAL STUDENTS

1. ENROLMENT & QUOTAS
2. COURSES/PROGRAMME (ANNUAL)
3. ARRANGEMENTS FOR RESIDENTIAL & WEEKEND SCHOOLS
4. CONSULTATION ON PRACTICES & PROCEDURES
5. REPORTS AND STATISTICS
6. INFORMATION FOR NEW TEACHING STAFF
7. ORGANISATION OF TEACHING MATERIAL
8. DEVELOPMENT OF POLICY IN ASSOCIATION WITH ADVISORY GROUPS, UNIVERSITY COMMITTEES

Figure 1: Functions of the Department of External Studies

a   Many enquiries are concerned with administration, policy interpretation and Faculty requirements which can be answered without reference to teaching departments.

b   Academic enquiries are referred to the appropriate course co-ordinator or tutor but if he is absent other members of staff can be approached for a reply.

c   Inconsistencies in treatment by various departments are minimised.

d   The burden of composing replies and having them suitably presented in typed form is carried by the Department of External Studies, rather than academic staff.

e   Urgent enquiries can be relayed to academic staff by phone, answers obtained and, if necessary, a telegram sent in reply to reduce delay.

This centralised process not only has worked very satisfactorily for both students and staff but provides a continuous overview of the system and allows for prompt remedial action wherever deficiencies are detected.

Individual attention to students has been possible to maintain through the retention of a comprehensive filing system in which a personal file is kept on every student. Each file includes every item of his correspondence from the first enquiry, our replies to him, his academic record, his photograph and signature and, of course, name and current address. Such a dossier can build up quite a clear profile of the student. Indeed, we often know a good deal more about some of our external students than we do about many of our internal students.

Other services are also provided by the Department. Class lists and geographical rolls are despatched to all students. These are used to form local discussion groups or to assist students in making contact with one another to discuss mutual problems or seek moral support. Early each year we also ask some of our graduates to call meetings of students in their local areas to assist in this process of student interaction. Throughout the year, per medium of the External Studies Gazette, students are kept informed of general University developments, proposed changes in course offerings, innovations in teaching methods and other matters likely to be of interest to them. The Gazette also provides a ready means of conducting surveys and seeking general responses to important issues. An enrolment prospectus, External Studies, is also prepared each year mainly for intending applicants. More detailed advice is given in a Guide for External Students issued to all students after enrolment.

Staff-student contact One of the most important co-ordinating functions of the Department of External Studies is the organisation of residential schools. These are compulsory for all but one or two first year courses and several later year courses where weekend schools are considered more suitable. The co-ordination of this exercise begins about June of the preceding year when the requirements of each department are collated and submitted for approval to the External Studies Committee and Professorial Board so that the respective dates of each school can be included in enrolment publications that are posted to applicants from early in October each year. This information is necessary to allow for course selection which has to avoid residential school clashes. Furthermore, applicants must have a clear idea of compulsory course requirements before accepting enrolment in a course since there is no point in their enrolling if their attendance at a residential school is not possible.

A second phase in residential school organisation begins early in the academic year in preparation for accommodating up to 4,000 students during the May vacation between first and second terms. Being a residential institution, the University of New England is able to provide college accommodation for externals on campus. This has the very real benefit of allowing externals to see their University and enjoy at least a brief period of traditional university life as a full-time student in residence. It is also desirable that university facilities are utilized all the year round, especially when rising operating costs are making it difficult for the colleges to balance their books as they are expected to do. They simply cannot afford to stand empty while internal students are on vacation.

In the third phase, several weeks prior to each school, the Department of External Studies obtains academic programs from each department involved in schools, allocates lecture rooms and arranges for teaching facilities to be made available in these rooms as required by individual lecturers.

Co-operation is also sought from the Students Union and Students Representative Council which organise receptions to facilitate informal staff-student interaction, film evenings, debates and other social and cultural functions. The Sports Union also provides full recreational facilities while external students are in residence and the Library extends its hours to cope with the sudden intensive use from hundreds of students anxious to make the most of their few days on campus.

During the schools, the Department of External Studies plays host by providing morning and afternoon teas to students who are encouraged to visit the Department and meet staff personally, acts as a clearing-house for incoming student mail, records arrival and departure times for every student and provides an advisory service for students who may wish to discuss a problem or plan future study programs. Once the schools are completed, the final administrative task is to write to absentees and invite them to show cause why they should not be withdrawn from the course concerned for failing to meet course requirements. These cases are then presented to the External Studies Committee for consideration. In instances of ill health, bereavement and other circumstances, exemption from attendance will be considered, but failure to attend generally results in withdrawal from the course.

The Department is also heavily involved throughout the year in organising over 150 weekend schools in various centres throughout the State as well as in Armidale. Although attendance at these schools is voluntary, they are important supplements to course material and residential schools. Teaching departments determine their own weekend school programs, venues for the schools and who will staff them, but the Department of External Studies is called upon to make the necessary arrangements with the host institution concerned. This is generally any one of the three universities and the Institute of Technology in Sydney with whom we have an excellent working relationship, but on occasions, high schools in country centres are used as well. Lecture rooms, audio-visual facilities and even laboratory space are provided for these weekend schools at no cost except occasionally a small charge for janitorial services. Notices are sent to all students in the course concerned in advance to allow them time to make travel and accommodation arrangements. Attendance is at students' expense but this does not deter them from travelling several hundred miles if necessary.

In addition to residential and weekend schools, visits to students in their home towns are made every year by the Director and his senior staff who cover most of the state of New South Wales in about six broad sweeps each of which involves from five to ten days on the road. Advance notice of the planned itinerary is given and meetings are held in the larger centres to discuss matters of general interest, as well as individual problems. We also take these opportunities to talk to prospective applicants about enrolment for the ensuing year. More isolated students are visited en route at their schools, in their shops or on their farms. This personal contact undoubtedly has value for both parties. Firstly it breaks down any reluctance on the part of students to seek help when things go wrong and secondly, it provides essential feedback on how the system is operating from 'the other end'. Recently academic staff have been making similar tours in order to conduct intensive tutorial sessions with small groups of students in various localities. This activity is to be encouraged but because a wide choice of courses is offered it is not always easy to find a cluster of students in one town studying the same course.

Other functions In many respects the Department is also an external registrar. The Director of External Studies enrols all external students at the beginning of each academic year in accordance with enrolment policies and quotas determined by the External Studies Committee. Selection, as such, is not on the basis of academic merit. Certain other variables, however, must be taken into account. Continuing students have first priority, then new applicants from country areas not served by other universities and finally new applicants from Sydney where there are some opportunities for part-time evening studies. Enrolments must relate to quotas which are set for every subject, residential school clashes have to be avoided and degree patterns carefully checked to ensure that they comply with faculty regulations. It is a rather more complex exercise than for internal students and it is made more difficult by the fact that applicants are spread all over Australia and many are moving about on holidays during the height of the enrolment period.

Academic-administrative relationships

Although the Department does not have responsibility for teaching but is regarded as a facilitator of the learning process through its supporting administrative functions, it enjoys a very central place in the decision-making processes underlying academic developments that immediately affect internal and external students alike.

The organisational chart (Figure 2) illustrates the formal connections that exist through the Director of External Studies to the External Studies Committee, a sub-committee of the Professorial Board. The Board is the ultimate policy making body on academic matters, answerable directly to Council on behalf of academic staff of several faculties. The Director is the Executive Officer for the External Studies Committee. As such he has opportunities to initiate proposals, submit reports to the Committee and implement policy decisions approved by the Committee.

The Director is a member of all four faculties teaching externally and a member of the Professorial Board (soon to become known as the Academic Board). He is also a member of the Admissions and Matriculation Committee, the Residence Committee, the Board of Continuing Education, and numerous ad hoc committees set up from time to time to deal with specific problems of policy issues. All in all, the Director or his nominees are able to represent the interests of external students within the mainstream of decision-making at almost all levels of government in the University. External students also have more direct forms of representation in departments, on faculties and in Council through their own elected representatives.

Despite this comprehensive organisational structure, the present Director, soon after taking office in 1973, recommended the creation of an academic group with a special interest in external teaching practices to complement the broader role of the External Studies Committee. This body,

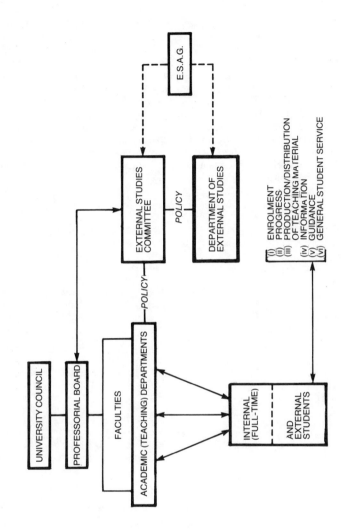

Figure 2: Teaching Externally - Organisational Structure

known as the External Studies Advisory Group (ESAG) consists
of a representative from all departments teaching externally.
Its chairperson and deputy are automatically members of
the External Studies Committee to whom ESAG reports. In
recent years it has held workshops and seminars on various
facets of teaching externally, conducted surveys on its
own behalf and at the request of the External Studies
Committee, developed essay style guides for students,

orientation booklets for new members of staff, produced a series of reports on teaching practices entitled 'Experiences in External Teaching', and in general, acted as a sounding board for new ideas aimed at improving both teaching practices and administrative services.

In the absence of a Teaching Practices Unit serving the University as a whole, the burden on this volunteer group of enthusiasts has been heavy and yet, one suspects, not fully appreciated. ESAG, for obvious reasons, would like to see such a Unit placed high in the priorities for funding in the immediate future. Submissions have been made in the hope that some of the scarce resources available might be diverted for this purpose.

RESEARCH AND DEVELOPMENT ACTIVITIES IN THE FIELD
OF DISTANCE STUDY AT NKI-SKOLEN, NORWAY
Torstein Rekkedal

NKI is a Norwegian educational institute offering various teaching services nationally and internationally. We shall here try to describe the research activities carried out at NKI in the field of correspondence or distance study during the 70s. Parts of this article have earlier been published in the ICCE Newsletter [1].

The research activities started in 1970, at which time research in correspondence education in Norway was indeed negligible. Administrators felt the need of more research in this area to provide systematic knowledge and guidelines for this means of instruction.

1 Survey of recruitment, achievements and discontinuation

Our first project was designed as a pilot survey in which we wished to throw some light upon the following four areas, which we considered to be of interest:

1   Recruitment to the correspondence courses at the NKI.

2   Persistence.

3   The students' own reasons for discontinuation.

4   Correlations between important background variables and specific criterion variables.

Furthermore, the survey was planned to constitute a starting point for subsequent experimental research on different aspects of methods and means applied in correspondence education.
Results gathered from this survey were reported some time ago in Epistolodidaktika [2]. Thus, I shall here only try to present a short account.
For practical reasons we chose to sample all students enrolled for one of the course combinations during one academic year. This sample consisted of 1,417 students who ex post facto were followed for two and a half years from

the date of their enrolment, after which time their academic status was examined.

The pilot survey showed that the institute attracts most of its students from towns and industrial areas. Rural areas characterized by high employment figures in the primary occupations were under-represented among the students. The student body consisted practically of men only: 2% being women. The students were relatively young: about 80% under 30 years of age. With respect to previous education received, approximately half of the students had not reached O-level, and the other half had attained about that level of education or more. Most of the students had allowed a very short period of time to elapse between their last school experience and their enrolment for the correspondence courses.

The status of the NKI students two and a half years after enrolment was as follows:

1,085 (76.6%) had discontinued, 283 (20.0%) were still active, while 49 (3.4%) had completed their courses. We observe a high drop-out rate. Consequently the drop-out problem has been considered to be the most important one during our subsequent research activities. However, in this survey we used a rather strict measure of discontinuation. All individuals who had ceased submitting assignments without completing the number of study units for which they origin-ally enrolled were included in the 'discontinued' category.

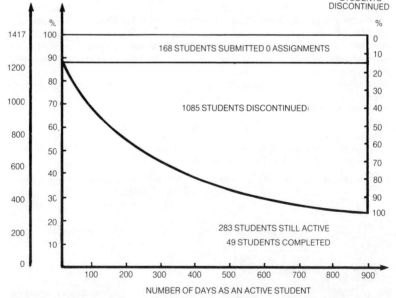

Figure 1: Curve showing the negative cumulative frequencies for the number of days as an active student.

The drop-out tendencies in the sample can be described by Figure 1.

Figure 1 shows the number of days as active students. We see that 168 individuals (11.9%) did not even submit one single assignment. These individuals constitute 15.5% of those who discontinued. Half of the students who dropped out had submitted their last lesson before their 150th day of study, while 75% had submitted their last work before the elapse of one year.

This variable is hardly a good measure of what the students really had accomplished. The total variation on the variable 'lessons submitted' by those 1,085 students who discontinued extended from 0 to 165 study units, the median being 8.3 study units, i.e. one half of the drop-outs submitted less than 9 assignments.

The course combinations consist of various complete and independent single courses. We found that among students who really started their studies, 74% completed at least one single course; among the drop-outs the figure was 55%.

We made a few additional interesting findings on the drop-out problem. Firstly, we found no relation between discontinuation and geographical background, students from all the different municipalities showing the same tendencies; ·about 75% discontinued. Among seamen students, however, the percentage was 91. Thus it seems difficult to adapt the correspondence study method to the situation prevailing on board ships in the merchant marine. Secondly, the seasons of the year appeared to bear an influence in that it seems more difficult to start a correspondence study during the Spring months and in December (non-start rates varying from 17% to 22% compared with about 12% in the complete sample).

Furthermore, discontinuation among the students who actually started reached its peak rates during the months April to July. These findings have obvious consequences for the school's follow-up efforts.

We have so far described some of the findings from the enrolment and discontinuation survey. In a third section of the inquiry we examined the relations between the different variables by using a measure of correlation. When examining the relation between two variables we were very careful in controlling the influence by other variables.

Here, we shall only summarize some of the conclusions. We found that age was positively correlated with status (not dropping out), number of days as an active student and number of lessons completed, i.e. the older students per-formed better than the younger ones. We found, however, no correlations between age and achievement (grades) or rate of submissions.

The level of previous education was positively correl-ated with all the criteria measured, while the number of years since last school experience was negatively correlated with status, number of days as an active student and number of lessons completed. The variable of number of years since last school experience did not correlate with achievement and rate of submissions.

2 Experimental studies

During the years following this pilot study we carried out some experiments on the methods of correspondence education, follow-up of students and administrative arrangements, the goal being primarily to reduce the number of students discontinuing their studies without at least some success, and to increase study efforts and rate of study among active students.

2.1 Follow-up of students

In the first of these experiments we tried to measure the effect of postcards and letters to encourage submission of assignments [3]. The follow-up material consisted of a sequence of one postcard and two letters, sent to inactive students at an interval of one month. The sequence was started automatically when a student had failed to submit assignments for one whole calendar month, and stopped when the student resumed his studies or made other contacts to the school's administration or counsellors. The system was tried out on an experimental group and a control group, each consisting of about 240 students. Differences in study activities were examined every month and statistical significances calculated by the chi-square method. Large and highly statistical, significant differences between the groups were found after the three months, e.g. during the third month 46% of the experimental group had submitted lessons or made other contacts, while this was the case for only 31% of the control group students.

The results derived from this first systematic study of the effects of following up students initiated another experiment comprising three experimental groups and one control group. Here we tried to measure the effect of an introductory course in study technique and different schemes of encouraging letters on recently enrolled correspondence students [4].

The four groups selected at random received different treatment during the first one and a half months after enrolment. The experimental variable was designed as follows:

x_1 A course in study technique was sent to the student immediately after receiving his/her enrolment form: the study material was posted one week later. Letters were sent on enrolment and 14, 28, and 42 days afterwards.

x_2 Both the course in study technique and the study material were sent immediately after enrolment. The same system of encouraging letters was used.

x_3 Study material sent immediately after enrolment, but the students received no course in study technique. The same system of encouraging letters was applied.

The letters were typed on an automatic typewriter, personally addressed and signed by hand by the student's personal counsellor. They were designed differently for each one of three cases, i.e. whether the student had received the course in study technique, whether he had submitted this course for correction and comments, or whether he had submitted ordinary lesson assignments. The final letter (42 days after the ordinary study material was sent) was not posted if the student had started on his ordinary studies. About one and a half months after enrolment the students in all groups were given the treatment described in the first experiment.

Summary of results: We found that the students who received the follow-up letters started their studies earlier than those not receiving these letters. Correlations between the time taken by the student in preparing his first assignment and the rate of completion and number of assignments totally completed have been shown in other studies[5]. We found small and not very significant differences between the groups on the number of lessons submitted within two and four months after enrolment. All experimental groups showed better results than did the control group. With respect to discontinuation rates the data made us conclude that the course in study technique and follow-up letters together may have helped to decrease the discontinuation rate. We may further note that the students in the three experimental groups expressed a much more favourable attitude towards the institute's counselling services, and in fact did, to a larger extent, make formal arrangements when they wanted to make temporal breaks in their studies or cancel their courses.

2.2 Administrative arrangements

We would also like to mention two small experimental studies where different aspects of the two-way communication process in correspondence education were examined.

Turn-round (circuit) time for written assignments   One of the big problems which occur when using part-time tutors is that the turn-round time - i.e. the lapse of time from the point when the student sends in his answer until he gets it back from the school with the tutor's comments on it - will tend to be relatively long. This problem was dealt with in a questionnaire that was distributed by CEC. [6]

The results showed that the average length of time from the date on which the school received student answers until they were returned to the student was 7 days. From this we may infer that the turn-round period would be about 10 days. The turn-round time may be illustrated as in Fig. 2 .

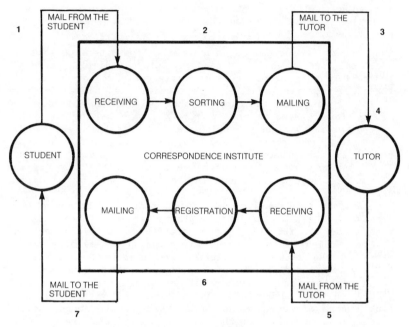

Figure 2: Factors making up turn round time

The illustration shows that the circulation of student papers normally includes four postal operations plus a number of internal handlings.

At the NKI the normal routine for handling written assignments is:

1   The student sends his assignments by post.

2   Assignments are allotted to the respective teachers at the NKI,

3   and are mailed to the teacher

4   who corrects them and comments on them, and

5   returns them to the school,

6   where results are registered on the student files,

7   and the assignments are returned to the student by post.

In an experiment on the written assignments we tried to measure the effects of reducing turn-round time[7].

We found that, normally, it took 4 to 5 days between the mailing of assignments for the course chosen to the teacher and receiving them again at the school. By engaging a teacher who was able to collect the assignments personally every day and deliver them the next, we were able to reduce the time element for points 3 to 5 above to only 1 day.

127 students who enrolled in a 4-unit course in arithmetics during about one calendar year were divided at random into two experimental groups. The teacher received no information about which of the students belonged to either of the groups, and the students did not even know that they were taking part in an experiment.

The project leader saw that assignments belonging to one of the experimental groups were returned to the students at once, while the rest of the assignments were kept back for 3 days. Consequently, for this first group the turn-round time was reduced by 3 days in relation to the second group of students. It may be important to observe that even the delayed assignments were returned a little quicker than was the normal situation before the experiment was started.

We found that at the time of data collection, the percentage of completions in the two groups were 91 and 69 respectively. The difference was found to be highly significant statistically. Consequently, we may conclude that quicker handling of the students' assignments seems to result in higher completion rates, which were, as mentioned earlier, considered to be the most important criterion variable. We also examined whether turn-round time influenced other aspects of student performance.

With respect to length of time taken to complete the course, and to final marks received, we found no significant differences between the two groups. However, the single course examined was the first course in a sequence constituting a larger course combination, and we found that altogether the students in the first group submitted a larger number of study units during the first three months of study.

Through a minor questionnaire we found that the first group normally got their assignments back less than a week after they were mailed, while most students in the second group experienced a turn-round time of more than one week. Most students in the first group seemed to be quite satisfied with the turn-round time experienced in this course, while a high percentage of the students in the other group reported that the handling of the assignments was too slow.

Irrespective of which group they belonged to, the students seemed to be quite satisfied with a turn-round time of one week or less; more than one week seemed to result in a large portion of the students becoming dissatisfied. This is why at NKI we have made great efforts to reduce the turn-round period as much as possible. As well as rationalizing internal routines, one has to examine the position of the part-time tutor in the system.

Different measures may be introduced aiming at reducing

turn-round time:

1 Rationalizing internal routines.

2 Establishing one's own distribution system, e.g. by using special cars bringing the papers to and from the tutors. This necessitates the tutors being recruited from the geographical neighbourhood of the institute.

3 Requesting tutors to return the student papers within one day.

4 Engaging full- and part-time tutors to work inside the school premises.

5 Decentralizing tutoring.

2.3 Preproduced tutor's comments

Initiated by the Council on Correspondence Education in Norway, NKS (Norsk Korrespondanseskole) and NKI, two parallel experiments were carried out on the effects of introducing printed preproduced tutor's comments in addition to the tutor's handwritten comments and corrections[8]. Students at both institutes were divided at random into an experimental and a control group. The students were enrolled for courses in mathematics consisting of 4 (NKI) and 6 (NKS) study units.

Results from such experiments are not easily generalized, because courses, comments and teachers' behaviour differ and may affect which system or combination of means is functioning most satisfactorily. The results derived from these two experiments were not directly comparable, e.g. among the NKI students the experimental group showed a completion rate of 80%, while the completion rate in the control group was 61%. At NKS the experimental control groups did not differ significantly on this criterion variable.

However, attitudes towards preproduced tutor's comments were examined among both groups of students in both institutes. At both institutes the students who had received the preproduced comments reacted very favourably towards this practice. In fact, each student in both experimental groups who answered this questionnaire responded that he would prefer to receive such preproduced material in every course or some courses. The majority of the students in the control groups, who had not experienced this preproduced material, were very sceptical about it, even though it was explained to be an additional service.

We think that general feedback, advice on study techniques and motivation concerning all students, should preferably be taken care of by means of preproduced material. The tutor might then allocate more time and educational resources to individual help to the students.

However, as generalizations are difficult to make,

this hypothesis should be further examined.

3 Other surveys

Parallel to the experimental studies, we have carried out two other surveys to control findings from the first survey and to extend the number of variables to examine.

3.1 Three years' enrolments of correspondence students [9]

In this survey we examined three years of enrolments to see if enrolment and discontinuation trends differ significantly from year to year, and if results from our pilot survey were generally applicable to other samples of students. We concluded that enrolment trends differed very little from one year to another, so, other conditions being equal, results might to some extent be true of other samples of NKI students. Further, we found a systematic trend towards better results concerning students' endurance in correspondence study and completion rates. This fact was assumed partly to be an effect of measures described in connection with the experimental studies above.

3.2 Comparative and longitudinal study of correspondence and classroom students

Because NKI offers both correspondence and classroom teaching for the training of enginering students, we are in a good position to examine differences in recruitment and discontinuation trends among students choosing the different methods of study. In 1972 we started a comparative and longitudinal study of the two groups of students enrolled. The survey has partly been financed by the Ministry of Education. Two reports have so far been published. [10]

The purpose was to collect information about factors which affect study success in the two study methods, why the students started to study, and reasons for the choice of method. We were also interested in information about the students' general attitudes and expectations as to different aspects of the system of correspondence education, and how these attitudes change as a result of study experiences. Both groups of students were examined by means of two questionnaires and information from study records.

Our conclusion from the enrolment survey, supported by other findings in this and other surveys, was that correspondence education in Norway was primarily chosen as a means of study by individuals who, because of family situation, vocational engagements or other obligations, were not able to take advantage of educational offers which demand regular class attendance. Correspondence students often came from urban areas where traditional educational opportunities were offered. In fact, students who enrolled for class instruction more often lived in rural areas.

Therefore, geographical reasons do not seem to be of

major importance for recruitment to correspondence education. Only 9% of the correspondence students mentioned 'no other possibilities in the neighbourhood' as the most important reason for choosing correspondence studies.

The main hypothesis in the follow-up study of the correspondence students was that during this study a selective drop-out takes place, which reinforces the selective recruitment. Thus individuals who are well established in family, social and vocational life achieve more than younger individuals who are not married, living with their parents and often coming directly from other traditional schools and having only minor vocational experience.

This hypothesis was to a large extent supported by the findings. However, as this study is not yet finished, reports have been published only in Norwegian. We hope to be able to finish an English report on the whole project in the near future.

Notes

1 Rekkedal, T., Research in the field of correspondence education at NKI, Norway. ICCE Newsletter, 7, No.1, March 1977.

2 Rekkedal, T., Correspondence studies. Recruitment, achievement and discontinuation. Epistolodidaktika, 1972-2, pp.3-38.

3 Rekkedal, T., Systematisk elevoppfolging, NKI-skolen, 1972. (Results from this study were summarized in Epistolodidaktika, 1973-2, pp.57-63.).

4 Rekkedal, T. & Hallem, S.A., Follow-up of correspondence students. The effects of an introductory course in study techniques and encouraging letters to new enrollees. English summary in Begynneroppfolging av brevskole elever. NKI-skolen, 1975.

5 Donehower, G., Variables Associated with Correspondence Study: A Study to Test Twelve Hypotheses. 1968.

6 Saxe, B., Graff, K. & Østlyngen, E., Correspondence Education in Europe Today. CEC Yearbook, 1968.

7 Rekkedal, T., The written assignments in Correspondence Education. Effects of reducing turn round time. English summary in Innsendingsoppgavene i brevundervisningen, NKI-skolen, 1973.

8 Rekkedal, T. & Ljoså E., Preproduserte laererkommentarer i brevundervisningen, Oslo 1974. (Not available in English).

9 Rekkedal, T., Three Years' Enrolment to NKI-skolen's Correspondence Courses. Recruitment and Discontinuation Trends. English summary in Tre årskull brevskoleelever. NKI-skolen, 1973.

10 Rekkedal, T., Tekniske studier, Korrespondanseundervisning og klasseundervisning. En komparativ og longitudinell undersøkelse. Delrapport 1: Rekruttering, Delrapport 2: Brevskoleelevene (Not yet available in English).

SECTION 5: CHOICE OF MEDIUM: THE NEW COMMUNICATIONS TECHNOLOGY

INTRODUCTION

Few areas of the literature of distance education have received more attention during the period 1971-1981 than choice of medium. The financial implication of the decision of an institution to select one medium against another can be immense and the range of questions which remain to be answered is extensive.

The reader's attention is drawn to a selection of these questions as a point of focus while studying this section and the related literature:

- Is print inherently superior?

- If print is inherently superior should non-print media be used?

- Which media are suitable for carrying course content and which for student support services?

- Should broadcasting be abandoned in favour of home-based technologies?

- Are media taxomonies productive or even possible?

- Who chooses the medium: the author or the educational technologist?

Basic to the development of every distance education course is the question: 'what medium or media shall we choose to replace the interpersonal communication, usually supported by printed documentation, that is the characteristic way that course content is transmitted in the conventional classroom or lecture theatre?' This is an immediate problem for each course author or for each course team. There is another question that is a corollary to the preceding one: 'once the learning materials have been developed and dispatched to the students, what media will be used to support distance learning?'

Attitudes to the question of the choice of medium in distance education characterise the three major comparative

221

studies of distance systems that were published in the 1970s: Peters' (1971) <u>Texte zum Hochschulfernstudium</u>, McKenzie, Postgate and Scupham's (1975) <u>Open Learning</u> and the Swedish <u>TRU Report</u> (1975).

Peters identified two fundamental typologies of distance systems *both* of which were print-based: Western systems based on a combination of printed materials plus postal correspondence and Eastern systems based on a combination of printed materials plus, often compulsory, face-to-face sessions.

In both the McKenzie, Postgate and Scupham and the Swedish study the Western/Eastern split is not recognised and the role of broadcast television in distance systems is underlined. The article by Bates in this section will enable the reader to evaluate these positions.

Of the major Western systems the Open University of the United Kingdom (OUUK) has been unique in its reliance on broadcast radio and television - even then its teaching package can be analysed as 80% correspondence materials, 10% face-to-face instruction in compulsory summer schools and voluntary evening seminars and 10% broadcasting. The Open University in the Federal Republic of Germany (Fernuniversität) is one of the institutions that seems to consider that the extensive research on educational technnology in the late 1960s and the early 1970s has shown that print is inherently superior. Fernuniversität course materials are expressly print-based with no broadcast elements and rare use of audiocassettes or videotapes.

A simple presentation of the choice of media available for carrying the content of a distance education course might be represented schematically thus:

```
                    ┌─────────────────┐
                    │ AVAILABLE MEDIA │
                    └─────────────────┘
   ┌─────────┐    ┌─────────┐    ┌─────────┐    ┌──────────┐
   │ PRINT   │    │ AUDIO   │    │ VIDEO   │    │ COMPUTER │
   │ BASED   │    │ BASED   │    │ BASED   │    │ BASED    │
   └─────────┘    └─────────┘    └─────────┘    └──────────┘
```

<u>Print-based</u>. Most of the distance education systems throughout the world, both Western and Eastern, are print-based and likely to remain so. A theoretical basis for the choice of print as the medium of distance systems is given by Peters (1978). To this the reader is referred.

Great advances were made in the use of print-based media in the 1970s. There was a rediscovery of the flexibility of print; introduction of text-processing and typesetting by computer; harnessing of instructional design to course material development and better understanding of the use of layout, illustration and colour. A whole science of the use of advance organizers, guidelines, overviews, pretests, objectives and questioning techniques has developed (Marland and Store, 1982). The Canadian scholars Daniel and

222

Stroud claim that the 1970s were 'the decade of print'.

Besides these developments in distance teaching materials other forms of print-based distance education emerged, the most interesting being Courses by Newspaper in which the learning materials are not dispatched to the students but syndicated out for publication in a range of newspapers in a defined area.

Audio-based. The literature shows that broadcast radio has distinct advantages, especially in developing countries. Young et al. (1980) report extensive use of radio in French and English-speaking Africa and in Latin America.

The advantages of radio are its almost complete availability and its ability to reach isolated audiences quickly and relatively inexpensively. It has four strategic functions: accessing students; publicity and recruitment; variety, enrichment and motivation; pacing. Its disadvantages are well presented by Bates (page 229).To these may be added the necessity of requiring students to listen at fixed and often awkward broadcast times and the judgement that it is more successfully used as a motivator than as a carrier of course content.

A decade of research at the Open University of the United Kingdom on the use of non-print media in distance education by Bates and his associates has led to the finding - which may come as a surprise to many - that the 'greatest media development during the Open University's 12 years of existence has been the humble audiocassette' (page 233).

Audiocassettes are inexpensive, simple to operate, durable and portable; studies carried out in a number of distance institutions in developed countries show that every student with few exceptions in the 1980s, either possesses or has access to an audiocassette recorder. Individuals can control the time and place (a car in a traffic jam) at which learning from audiocassettes occurs, they can be reviewed and replayed as often as needed and provide a confidential setting for two-way communication between teacher and student.

Institutions like the Centre National d'Enseignement par Correspondance in France, which have extensive ranges of courses in modern languages and music, have always been extensive users of audio-cassettes and the C.N.E.C. has shown how audio-cassettes of exceptional didactic quality can be produced with relatively cheap equipment.

Video-based. The prominence given to broadcast television in distance systems by two major comparative studies, both of which were closely associated with educational television networks, has already been mentioned. In the same way the Open University of the United Kingdom was publicised as the 'new university of the air' rather than as a user of the century-old correspondence tuition mode. The relationship between the OUUK and the BBC is well known and has done much to change the image and status of distance education in the last decade.

Under the heading video-based distance education one needs to consider a selection of the following in addition to broadcast television: telecourses; cable systems; slow scan television; videotaping; teleconferencing; videodiscs; education by satellite; videotex and teletex. A comprehensive introduction to all these possibilities is given by Ruggles et al. (1982) and the articles by both Bates and Sparkes in this reader will enable the reader to commence an evaluation of their value in education at a distance.

Much work was done in the 1970s to identify those didactic problems that are better presented on videotape or television than by face-to-face lecturing or print: the illustration of principles involving dynamic change or movement; the illustration of principles involving two, three or n-dimensional space; the presentation of geographic features, famous people, famous buildings that are in danger of being destroyed or already dead; the demonstration of social reactions (mother-child), decision making processes (by observation, dramatisation or simulation), and of attitudinal change. (For a complete list see Bates (1982)).

It is likely that distance systems will seek to select media that are homebased and not broadcast and therefore the penetration of the videocassette recorder and of videotex systems (Antiope, Telidon, Prestel, Captain) to the homes of individual students will be of vital importance.

<u>Computer-based</u>. A number of distinctions need to be made with regard to the introduction of microcomputers: (i) between the use of microcomputers in classrooms and in distance education, (ii) between the use of microcomputers to deliver courseware in *any* subject as opposed to courses about microcomputers and programming, (iii) between computer-assisted instruction (CAI), a teaching process directly involving a computer in the presentation of instructional materials in an interactive mode, and computer-managed instruction (CMI) which adds features like monitoring and evaluating student progress to CAI.

The costs of developing a valid computer-based distance learning course are high and will remain so for many years to come. Courses presently available on major systems tend to concentrate on elementary presentations of accounting and mathematics, though a number of private institutions have bought time on these systems and developed more complex materials in their own specialist areas. Some distance universities (the Fernuniversität is an example) doubt if a computer can carry the complexities of the higher level university courses and plan for all courses, even in computing, to be print-based with the use of the computer restricted to practical applications.

Bates, Sparkes and Beare, in the articles chosen for this section, give an introduction to the literature on choice of medium. This choice is a significant one for educational administrators and managers of distance institutions as it appreciably affects the costs of each distance system, as Rumble (1982:119) points out:

> Broadly speaking, very significant costs are incurred in the preparation of materials *irrespective* of student numbers. The level of cost incurred will vary depending on the choice of media. In conventional educational systems teaching costs are traditionally held to be a recurrent cost that is variable with the number of students in the system. In contrast, in distance learning systems the cost of developing the materials can be regarded as a fixed cost that can be written off over the life of the course of which they form part. Hence at some point, and this depends on the choice of media, a distance system should become cheaper per unit of output than a traditional system.

Bates' article chosen for this reader gives an overview of the success and failure of non-print media in distance education over the last decade. In addition, it evaluates the role of certain media in the 1980s: video cassettes and videodiscs; cable and satellite TV; audiocassettes; telephone teaching; viewdata and teletext; domestic computers.

Sparkes puts forward the view that it is the experienced university teacher who will best be able to choose media for distance education because research is no replacement for experience. He writes so that 'the knowhow of experienced teachers, rather than the results of academic research, can be passed on to others' and rejects the isolation of scientific research in order to preserve the natural complexity of the educational process.

It did not prove possible to provide for this reader an article on each of the major non-print media that can be chosen for distance education. A succinct presentation from Australia on experiences with education by satellite has been selected to point the way to the future.

Desmond Keegan

References

Bates, A.W. (1982) Roles and characteristics of television and some implications for distance teaching. Distance Education, 3,1,28-50

Daniel, J.S. and Stroud, M.A. (1981) Distance education: a reassessment for the 1980s. Distance Education, 2,2,146-163

Marland, P.W. and Store, R.E. (1982) Some instructional strategies for improved learning from distance teaching materials. Distance Education, 3,1,72-106

McKenzie, N., Postgate, R. and Scupham, J. (1975) Open learning. Paris: UNESCO

Peters, O. (1971) Texte zum Hochschulfernstudium. Weinheim: Beltz

Peters, O. (1979) Some comments on the function of print material in multi-media systems. Epistolodidaktika, 1,10-21

Ruggles, R.H. et al. (1982) Learning at a distance and the new technology. Vancouver: ERIBC

Rumble, G. (1982) The cost analysis of learning at a distance: Venezuela's Universidad Nacional Abierta. Distance Education, 3,1,116-140

Swedish Commission for Radio and Television in Education (1975) A programme for sound and pictures in education (TRU Report). Stockholm:SOU

Young, M. et al. (1981) Distance teaching for the third world. The lion and the clockwork mouse. London: Routledge and Kegan Paul

**TRENDS IN THE USE OF AUDIO-VISUAL MEDIA IN
DISTANCE EDUCATION SYSTEMS**
Tony Bates

The main trends

It is easier to set out what I think are the main trends
than it is to justify my views, so let me start with what
normally might be considered conclusions:

- There is a clear movement away from using broadcasting
  by distance learning systems.

- The range of audio-visual media suitable for distance
  education is rapidly increasing.

- The educational potential of audio-visual media still
  tends to be under-exploited by distance learning systems.

The evidence

It is impossible for one person to be familiar with
trends in every distance learning system. However, in 1980 I
was commissioned by the International Institute of Educational Planning in Paris to carry out a survey of the use of
audio-visual media in 12 distance learning systems, deliberately chosen to provide a variety of distance learning
institutions known to use audio-visual media (see Table 1).
In other words, the sample was deliberately biased towards
those already using audio-visual media, as the survey was
part of a study designed to identify the main planning and
management needs of distance learning institutions using
audio-visual media (Bates,1981).

My evidence is based primarily on the data provided by
the 12 institutions through a specially designed postal
questionnaire, and from discussions at a workshop in Paris
attended by representatives of each of the 12 institutions.
This evidence is also supplemented by my experience of
working on distance projects in Norway, Thailand, Iran, and
the Philippines.

TABLE 1

The 12 distance learning institutions in the survey

Institution	Country	Type of Distance Learning Institution*
		(see Bates, 1981 for full discussion)*
1 Educational Television Foundation of Maranhão	Brazil	Media-based formal school system
2 College of the Air	Mauritius	Independent d.l.i. teaching to external formal qualifications
3 Distance Learning Centre	Lesotho	or syllabuses
4 Allama Iqbal Open University	Pakistan	
5 Athabasca University	Canada	
6 Everyman's University	Israel	
7 National Radio and Television University for Teachers	Poland	Autonomous credit-giving multi-media system established solely for distance learners
8 Open University	United Kingdom	
9 Sri Lankan Institute of Distance Education	Sri Lanka	
10 Universidad Estatal a Distancia	Costa Rica	
11 Norwegian Institute of Distance Education	Norway	Cooperative multi-media systems,involving several autonomous organizations
12 Institute of Adult Education	Tanzania	Autonomous multi-media systems,non-credit giving

The move from broadcasting

The move from broadcasting is not recent, but goes back
to the original shift from "A University of the Air" to
the creation of "An Open University". The original Planning
Committee of the Open University soon realised that the
amount of learning materials required to meet the needs
of a full range of degree courses would be too great to
cover by broadcasting alone. However, I was surprised
to find that while 9 of the 12 institutions used broadcast
television, and 10 used radio, apart from the Open University
and ETV Maranhão (which is a schools system) only one
broadcast more than 10 hours a week of television, and

none broadcast more than five hours a week of radio. The Open University in the UK with 35 hours a week of television, and 24 hours a week of radio, was clearly very different from the other 11 institutions. In only 3 of the 12 institutions (ETV Maranhão; NURT, Poland; and Mauritius College of the Air) was television the main medium. In all the others, print was the main medium.

Why is it that broadcast television and radio services, with their glamour and appeal, their ability to reach mass audiences, their many years of experience in educational broadcasting, and their often formidable political influence, appear to be playing so small a role in the development of distance learning systems? The survey provided some suggestions, none of which is likely to come as a surprise.

Firstly, in most countries, the broadcasting service is provided by an organization - a national broadcasting organization, commercial stations, or a government department - separate from the distance learning system. Eleven of the 12 institutions were dependent on a separate broadcast organization for the production and distribution of at least some of their broadcast material. Despite the high costs, the problems of recruitment, and the difficulty of fully using expensive facilities, most institutions wanted their own television production facilities. The main reason was their perceived lack of control over production material. Satisfactory cooperation between broadcast organizations and educational institutions seems difficult to achieve in most countries. It has obviously proved hard for others to find a model equivalent to the unique cooperative partnership between the Open University and the BBC.

The second major problem was getting adequate transmission facilities. Most institutions were dissatisfied with the *quality* of the times available, particularly for broadcasts aimed at adults. However, I have some sympathy for the broadcasting organizations here. Since none of the institutions had more than 10,000 students following any single course, this was the maximum target audience for what were often national transmissions. Many transmissions - especially at the Open University - are aimed at fewer than 500 students. It is not surprising that broadcasting organizations are unwilling to make available peak viewing or listening times to such small, specialist audiences. *Serious* teaching, even in distance education systems, is rarely aimed at *mass* audiences, in broadcasting terms.

Perhaps more surprising was the difficulty in several countries of *accessing* the target audience through broadcasting. While it is perhaps to be expected that in Tanzania, radio can reach only about 45% of the population, I was surprised to find that Athabasca University had real problems in getting television programs to students because of the complexities and limitations of the cable TV system in the province.

Cost, however, did *not* seem to be a major reason why broadcasting was not heavily used. Many institutions in any case do not have to pay the "real" cost of broadcasting, and when they do, it is sometimes separately paid for by their governments. None of the 7 institutions that provided cost information used more than 20% of its total budget on broadcasting.

I believe that the *main* reason why broadcasting is not used more by distance learning institutions is because of academic distrust. Those responsible for the academic content of courses in 12 institutions rarely had received any training in the use of audio-visual media. Few of the institutions were able to specify why television, for instance, should be used instead of print. There is a lack of an educational theory that can provide clear guidelines as to the unique advantages of television or radio over print or face-to-face teaching. I shall be returning to this issue later, but most teachers and educators are unable or unwilling to see the *educational* (as distinct from the *distributional*) advantages of television and radio. Little has been done in the last 10 years to remove this distrust. Indeed, in some institutions, closer exposure to broadcasting and broadcasters has increased this distrust.

A wider range of media

There are two distinct trends emerging here. The *number* of different audio-visual media suitable for distance education is increasing rapidly, offering more choice, and more difficult decisions regarding the selection and integration of media. Secondly, the *boundaries* between different media are breaking down, again causing difficulties for distance learning systems, this time regarding management and production. I will discuss below some of the new developments in audio-visual media that are affecting - or will very soon affect - distance education systems.

Video cassettes and videodiscs

Six of the 9 systems in the IIEP survey using television now offer a video cassette service to students. In all cases, this is mainly a back up to transmitted programs - in other words, each program is broadcast at least once, and some programs are also available on cassette for use at local centres. Currently, though, market penetration is not yet sufficient, even in the more prosperous countries, for distance education systems to be able to assume that a majority of potential students will have video cassette machines in their own homes. Indeed, it is likely to be several more years before this situation occurs - if ever - although for certain specialist courses, like post-graduate training for doctors, or in-service training for teachers, availability

230

of cassette machines is already high in North America, Japan, and Western Europe.

Video cassettes are used in most courses to back up transmission, rather than as the main system of distribution, because broadcasting (or cable) penetration is generally more extensive. However, the use of cassettes merely to distribute programs made as broadcasts means that the full educational potential of video cassettes is not yet being fully exploited. This potential will become clearer when I discuss audio cassettes, but video material produced right from the beginning for use only on cassette (or disc, for that matter) requires a very different style of production and can serve a different range of teaching functions from broadcast television. Where distance education systems depend heavily on students attending local centres, video cassettes can more easily be used specifically as video cassettes. Group use of video cassettes enables students to draw out much more from the programs than if they are watching in isolation; programs used individually by students on cassettes lend themselves much more to the teaching of skills.

Video cassette use is certain to increase. Costs will continue to drop, particularly with the availability now of a ¼" video cassette system. More importantly, production for distribution on cassette will free distance education systems from their dependence on broadcast organizations for television production. In-house production or the use of small video production companies becomes feasible. While this will give more flexibility on costs, and perhaps more control over program material for distance education systems, there could be a loss of range and quality in programming that would reduce the range of educational functions that can be met by television.

Therefore the judgement of whether to use video cassettes *instead* of broadcasting will remain a difficult decision for several more years for some institutions. For distance education systems, like the Open University, with large numbers of programs and students, transmission costs can still be lower than video cassette distribution costs. The main advantage of broadcasting is its ability to reach into every home, and cassettes will not be able to do that for a long time, if ever.

The difficulty of writing a paper a year before publication is nowhere better illustrated than when discussing videodiscs. In Britain, at the time of writing, we are still awaiting the launch of any videodisc system. In terms of hardware, discs appear to have advantages over cassettes: freeze-frame, a rapid and accurate search, large single frame storage capacity, slow and speeded-up motion, and lower machine cost. The value, however, of videodiscs for distance education will depend crucially on three factors: the speed and extent of domestic market penetration of any

231

single system compared with video cassettes; the unit cost of producing discs in relatively small production runs per program; and further developments in cassette and television distribution technologies. There is evidence for instance that the next range of cassette machines will incorporate several of the technical features currently unique to discs, such as freeze-frame and fast search. The high cost of copying discs currently makes them economical only for very large runs. Many institutions, however, want small runs, perhaps 1000 to 5000 copies at the most for home use, even less for local centre use. Cassette use also makes it possible to despatch video material through *transmission* (perhaps at night) using automatic recording devices activated by coding signals. Thus a single student requires only one or two cassettes for all his programming, instead of several discs. In a system with 50,000 students and perhaps 1000 programs, this could give significant cost advantages to cassettes over discs.

All this, however, is speculation. I do not expect discs to be in widespread use in distance education within the next five years. I do expect video cassette use to expand substanially over the next five years. Anyone wanting to speculate on these two media beyond that time scale is either very brave or very foolish.

Cable and satellite TV

Satellite and cable TV should provide more channels and hence more and better transmission times for the minority broadcasting required by distance teaching systems. However, satellites are not significantly different in structure or function from terrestrially transmitted broadcasts, unlike programs made for use on cassettes or discs. Moreover, terrestrial transmissions may still be better at reaching the kind of target audiences often given priority by distance education systems. Rural communities are often not well served by cable.

Athabasca University shows how difficult it is to provide systematic and comprehensive coverage for its students via cable. Memorial University, Newfoundland, provides general education programming via cable for the population of St. John's, but its distance education courses have to use video cassettes for the outreach centres in the rest of the province.

Satellite TV will give better rural coverage, and a uniform national or at least regional service, but, like cable systems, commercial and financial structuring could well result in satellite TV being received by only the more wealthy sectors of society. Furthermore, it is likely in Western Europe that the maximum number of television channels available to any single country via satellite will be five, so increased access to peak times for distance education systems is by no means certain via satellites. Government regulations will be crucial, and distance education systems will need a strong lobby to ensure their interests are protected if they wish to use cable or satellite.

Audio cassettes

Video cassettes, videodiscs, and satellite TV are "exciting" technologies and arouse great interest in educational circles, but in my own institution, the greatest media development during its 12 years of existence has been the humble audio cassette. In 1981, there will be 68 courses using 184 audio cassette productions, equivalent in playing time to 588 radio programs. In 1977, hardly any OU course used program material created specially for cassette use.

In the production year 1981/82, 164 radio programs and 234 cassette programs will be made, so the OU is now already making more material for use on cassettes than on radio. Furthermore, over a third (38%) of the students who listen to radio programs hear them on recordings. I was therefore surprised to see that only 5 of the 12 institutions in the IIEP survey used audio cassettes. The main difficulty for developing countries was the lack of cassette machines in student homes and the difficulty of physically distributing cassettes. At the OU, over 87% of students had access to audio cassette machines, and it is no more expensive for the OU to purchase and copy cassettes, and to mail them to students with their other materials, than it is to pay for radio transmission times for courses with fewer than 500 students.

There are several reasons why audio cassettes are so popular now at the Open University. The academics like them, because they feel they have more control over their use, and can integrate cassettes more tightly into course design. Cassettes can be used in a variety of ways - for mastery learning, for commenting on diagrams, charts, tables or text, for backing up or commenting on other media (cassettes have been found extremely useful for analysis of linked television programs), as resource material (bringing record-ings of real-life situations, conversations, interviews, etc., which are then analysed), or for specialist lectures that explore the wider significance of the course subject. The use of two channels - sound and vision - in a controlled and integrated way, through the combined use of cassette and print or "media", is a very powerful teaching medium.

Students like audio cassettes. In a majority of courses, they are ranked as the most useful component after the correspondence texts. In a few courses, they have been ranked as the *most* useful component of the course. The features that appeal to students are their convenience (they can use cassettes whenever they wish to study), the control students have over them (they can play parts of the cassette

233

as many or as few times as they need), and their informality. Students frequently comment that cassettes are like having a personal tutorial with the course author in the student's own room, a quality that appears to be lacking in radio programs, however skilfully they are made. Cassettes have a production style and process very different from that of radio programs.

I therefore see audio cassettes integrated with correspondence material as a major area for development in distance education: they are cheap, easy to control and make, convenient for students, and above all, educationally effective. (For further discussion see Durbridge, 1981).

Telephone teaching

Telephone teaching is used extensively in 4 of the 12 institutions and is proving to be popular with both tutors and students. There are, nevertheless, still many problems. Several institutions did not have a telephone system widespread enough or reliable enough to be useful (e.g. Tanzania). Even where there is good national coverage, line quality is often a problem. In some countries (e.g. Norway), telephone teaching is prohibitively expensive because of problems of distance. It is also clear that special skills from tutors, and discipline from students, are required, particularly for teleconferencing. This again is an area where careful costing is necessary, particularly since telephone charges can easily be "lost" in other budgets, but nevertheless contribute a real cost to the institution.

However, if distance education systems wish to provide a wide range of courses to students who are often scattered or isolated, telephone tuition is the only practical way of providing two-way, interactive tutorials. For instance, at the Open University, in one region covering a population of around 4 million, there are over 100 courses with fewer than 50 students. The most that such a region can afford to provide in the way of face-to-face tuition is one or two day schools on a Saturday. Even then, many of the students will have to travel over 100 miles to attend. Telephone tuition in such circumstances is not a poor alternative to face-to-face teaching; the alternative is no direct tuition at all.

There is still great resistance to telephone teaching. At the Open University, each region is responsible for its own tutorial arrangements. In 1981, one region scheduled over 200 hours of telephone tuition. Several other regions scheduled none. Such differences cannot be explained solely in terms of geography. There seem to be four main problems: technical problems; lack of visuals; costs; user resistance.

Line quality and connection is still a problem in many countries. Lines from rural locations in particular (ironically, the areas that benefit most from telephone tuition) can be poor. Poor operator performance can wreck group telephone tutorials via conference call systems. Distance learning systems can overcome this by installing conference bridging equipment in area offices, providing their own operators and renting dedicated lines from local centres to the headquarters (as at Wisconsin). However, the latter solution does not help the home-based student. Nevertheless, despite the technical difficulties, there are enough examples of successful tuition by telephone to suggest that well prepared, well trained tutors supported by committed administrators, will usually succeed. But it is still very hard work. (See Robinson, 1979).

The lack of visual support can be overcome by use of systems such as CYCLOPS, developed at the Open University. This allows tutors and students to use a light-pen to write or draw on an ordinary TV screen. The picture is converted digitally to a second signal and sent down a standard telephone line, where it is decoded and appears on the TV screen at the other end of the line. Pre-prepared visual material (stored on audio cassettes) can also be sent down the line. This low-cost system is being used in 1981 and 1982 on 20 courses in 15 centres in one of the OU's regions. Again, while the system works well technically, it requires tutors, students, and telephone operators to be carefully trained. (See McConnell and Sharples, 1981).

While costs depend very much on geographical factors and phone company pricing policies, a general problem arises from the fact that students usually pay their own costs of travel to face-to-face tuition, while distance education systems tend to pay the telephone charges for telephone tuition. Thus telephone teaching tends to *reduce* student costs, but *increase* institutional costs.

The main problem, however, still seems to be human factors. Telephone teaching requires administrative and financial procedures that are not always understood by administrators who are geared to providing face-to-face support. Tutors need to change their tutorial methods if telephone tuition is to be successful. More structure and preparation are required. Some students, particularly the more elderly, at least in Britain, often regard the telephone as an instrument to be used only in emergencies. They even worry about the cost to the University - it is considered (quite often wrongly) to be much more expensive than face-to-face tuition. Training of administrators, tutors and students, is crucial for successful use.

I think, therefore, that more and more distance education systems will, use telephone teaching, but it will spread slowly, and will meet considerable resistance.

Viewdata and teletext

Developments using the standard television screen for the display of textual and graphical information will also have

235

important implications for distance education systems. There are two different kinds of system: those that use spare transmission capacity to broadcast textual information (such as Ceefax and Oracle in Britain), which I shall describe as "teletext"; and those that connect the television set with the telephone system (Prestel, Telidon, Optel, etc.), which I shall call "viewdata systems".

The main use of teletext is for instant news-type services: stockmarket prices; weather forecasts; news summaries. Teletext services are currently limited by the number of pages available (at the moment about 800). Capacity is determined by the memory store of the microprocessor in the TV receiver, which decodes the signal. Linking of independent but compatible, larger-capacity microprocessors, in the form of domestic computers, to standard television sets will allow for greater capacity in the future, but even then it is unlikely that teletext will be of great use to distance learning systems. The main limitation of teletext, apart from capacity, is the lack of interaction. There is little the user can do but search for material that is being transmitted. Publicity and advertising seems to be the most likely function of teletext for distance education systems.

Viewdata systems appear to have more educational potential. By combining the telephone with the television set, the user has access to a potentially limitless source of information and computing power. Quite apart from the powerful central computer system provided by national telecommunications systems for viewdata, it is in theory possible to access other powerful mainframe computers, provided the owners of such systems are willing to be accessed and have compatible software. Furthermore, organizations can set up their own viewdata computer systems, so that all the telephone company is providing is the line for carriage. Thus the Open University is experimenting with its own viewdata system, called Optel. The aim eventually is to enable staff, students, and tutors, to communicate from anywhere in Britain. While such developments must be compatible with the "national" viewdata system in terms of connections and display of material on the screen, variations on methods of accessing or of searching for information can be independently developed. Thus, because of the limitations of the current branching system used by Prestel, the Open University is experimenting with a keyword system for accessing information. (See Bacsich, 1981).

Viewdata is clearly a major new technology, which is still in a very early stage, so it is difficult to predict its potential for distance education systems. Much will depend on the speed and extent of the domestic market penetration, and above all on costs, particularly of telephone charges and the preparation of software. However, viewdata systems do have the potential for rapid updating of information (particularly useful for professional training and development) and for computer-aided instruction. My own belief, though, is that it will eventually be more useful for administrative purposes, providing students or potential students with information about courses and course regulations, tutors with student records, and for providing changes or alterations in supplementary materials for courses.

Domestic computers

The rapid development of microprocessors will make powerful but cheap computing facilities a realistic possibility for many homes in the more prosperous countries. Already some Open University courses provide students with a cheap microprocessor as a home experiment kit. Quite apart from the value of using computers for students to learn about computing, microcomputer systems can be linked to a standard TV set and aid instruction, using cassettes or discs mailed to students.

The major problem is not hardware costs, but the costs of preparing and writing computer programs, and the problems of compatibility between different domestic computer systems. Because of the special skills and the time required to develop effective computer-aided instruction, the target number of students must be large. There is a danger then of centralizing learning through the eventual domination of two or three major systems (such as PLATO); in the event, it will be cheaper for many distance education systems to buy programs.

For this reason, I suggest that the greater flexibility of systems such as CYCLOPS and telephone teaching where no computing skills are required of tutors or course designers, where direct interaction between tutor and student is still possible, and where individual teachers or institutions feel they still have control over teaching content and methods, may eventually be more important for distance education than home-based computer-aided instruction. I suspect that many of the educational functions of computer-aided learning can be done more easily, conveniently, and cheaply through a combination of audio cassettes and print.

Looking to the future

Only a few years ago most distance education systems relied almost entirely on correspondence teaching backed up by face-to-face tuition in groups, or they relied on broadcast series backed up by a textbook and possibly some face-to-face tuition. Now the range and combination of media available is suddenly bewildering. Nevertheless, it is possible to pick out some features that enable us to estimate what will be most useful over the next five years, accepting that varying socioeconomic and geographic factors will result in differences in what will be more important to one system rather than another.

The first feature is accessibility. What media are likely to be available - or can be provided economically - in most students' homes over the next few years? Accessibility will also be influenced by the extent to which a distance education system is dependent on the use of local centres - more expensive equipment can be provided in local centres, where shared use is possible - but I am more concerned here with home-based learning. The second is convenience. Can the student use the medium when and where it suits him, and without extra training? The third is academic control. How easy is it for the teacher to design and prepare the material himself? How much training will be required? The fourth feature is the extent to which the medium provides a "human" touch - to what extent can the learner relate to the tutor or teacher through the medium? And lastly, what is available *now* that can be used?

Using these criteria, print materials, audio cassettes and possibly telephone teaching still look the best immediate bets. Within five to ten years, the next most promising developments appear to me to be video cassettes and viewdata systems. But it would be wrong to suggest that one should look to just *one* medium. Choice is clearly increasing, but even existing audio-visual media are under-exploited. New media will not be adopted unless we look a little more closely at the reasons for the third trend - the under-exploitation of audio-visual media - and what needs to be done to improve their use.

The under-exploitation of audio-visual media

It was clear from the IIEP survey that existing audio-visual media were not being used as much as they could, and that when used, they were not always successful. The reasons for this cannot be understood without first answering a more fundamental question: do distance education systems *need* audio-visual media? Just because the technology is there, do we *have* to use it?

In some ways, it is hard not to use it. Teaching takes place in the wider context of people's lives. They use television and the telephone for reasons other than learning, and often distance education systems need to use technology to access their students in the first place. But the main reason why I believe it is important to use a wide range of media, including audio-visual media, is that different media serve different educational functions. Thus using a media broadens the range and effectiveness of distance education.

There is clearly no satisfactory single "theory" that tells educators which media to use in which situations. Nevertheless, the increasing range of media does make it a little easier to see what are the main educational differences between media in distance learning situations, and hence to spot some of the unique educational characteristics associated with each medium. Here I can only briefly give examples of what I mean (see Bates, 1981a for a fuller treatment).

Broadcast television (including cable and satellite) or radio is still the easiest way of reaching adult learners or potential learners at a distance. Its main advantage is its accessibility - it reaches every home - and it can be entertaining and attractive. It is therefore important for recruitment and motivation. It can also make available to the learner educational resources that would be difficult to provide in any other way - such as film of overseas countries, ingenious and expensive graphics, access to world leaders in politics and education, etc. Broadcast programs can provide an overview of subject matter dealt with in more detail in texts. Because of the high costs of such activities, they can be justified only if the target audience is large, and follow-up is generally required. Perhaps broadcasting's greatest value then is as part of "campaigns": adult literacy, raising awareness of social issues, etc.

Print material is more useful for providing content where a good deal of ground needs to be covered or where the subject matter needs to be dealt with in depth, or where certain skills (analytical, mathematical, conceptual) need to be developed. Like broadcasting, print can reach into every home if there is a decent postal service.

Video cassettes can assist the application of the more abstract and analytical ideas covered in print to the more concrete and complex real world. Students can be asked to understand how these abstract concepts explain real-world situations and the limitations of such concepts through video. Video can provide models or bridges to understanding by giving concrete examples or visual models of abstract ideas. Broadcast television can also do this, but video is more suitable because of the increased control and repetition available to the student.

Audio cassettes allow for mastery learning, explanation and discussion of graphical, tabular, and printed conceptual material, practice in problem-solving, and exercises in mathematical processes. Audio cassettes can be used for providing resource material, such as discussions, interviews, case-study material, language use, for analysis by students, and for step-by-step analysis and discussions by the unit author.

Telephone tuition (and CYCLOPS) enable individual problems to be dealt with directly by a tutor, and can provide seminars and tutorials where the interpersonal and interactive communications can take place between students and tutor, and students and students. Telephone tutorials can provide guidance on assessment, feedback on progress, diagnostic analysis of problems, and a broadening or a linking up of core teaching materials.

239

Viewdata provides the opportunity for computer-assisted or programmed learning and enables material to be corrected or updated quickly and cheaply. It can also cut down on administrative mailings and provide easier access to administrative information and student records.

There is no super-medium. Each can serve different functions. Thus media do not differ as much in their suitability for dealing with different *content* but do differ in their suitability for dealing with different *learning skills* or *teaching approaches*. Each medium therefore *enriches* or *adds* to the educational process. The logical consequence of this is not to select but one or two "super-media", but to use a range of media in a planned and integrated manner so that a variety of educational functions and approaches can be offered.

It is perhaps easier now to see why audio-visual media in particular still tend to be under-exploited in distance education systems. Conventional education - the route through which most teachers in distance education systems have progressed - is dominated by face-to-face tuition and print. Few teachers fully understand the unique characteristics and limitations of audio-visual media. In Britain and many other countries, university academic staff receive no training in teaching methods. School teachers rarely, if ever, receive training in the use of the kind of audio-visual media available to distance education systems. Perhaps more surprisingly, none of the 12 distance education systems in the IIEP survey provided any systematic in-house training for its academic staff. Furthermore, understanding of media is little helped by the professionalization of media production - television is left to the producers to get on with; selection of media is the job of the educational technologist.

However, new developments in media are making nonsense of these professional boundaries. Some media - telephone tuition, for instance - do not need a specialist producer, although the teacher does need to develop additional skills; others, like CYCLOPS and viewdata, would be helped by specialist graphic designers or computer programmers, but are not dependent on such help (and the same would apply to production help for audio cassettes - useful but not essential). However, teachers do need *training* to make the most of these media, first to raise their awareness of their potential, and secondly to make sure that the media are used effectively and competently.

It therefore seems to me essential that, given the rapid developments in media, each distance education system now needs a unit to monitor and develop appropriate media and train academic staff.

There seems also to be a major implication for broadcasting organizations. I have seen a trend in recent years towards more cooperative projects between broadcasting organi-

zations and other agencies concerned with continuing and
adult education (correspondence schools, workers' educational
associations, etc.). However, broadcasters, even in these
cooperative projects, have often been reluctant to give up
their autonomy. Programs tend to be proposed on a "take-it-
or-leave-it" basis, and other agencies are often invited to
participate only when a program series has been decided. The
development of new media, particularly video cassettes, could
lead to two quite opposite developments. Distance education
systems will become less dependent on broadcasting organizations and will therefore be less willing to be treated as
minor partners. This could result in broadcasting organizations becoming *more* isolated and running their *own* series
with little use of other media, or (as I would hope)
broadcasters could get down to a more equal partnership as
one of several agencies working together to provide integrated, multi-media courses.

Lastly, I see the possibility of a move *away* from
large, national distance education systems and projects towards more local initiatives based on local, conventional
education institutions. The new media provide local institutions with the opportunity to develop their own off-campus
programs at reasonable costs, and with enrolments of full-
time students steadily dropping in a number of countries,
this may be an important life-line for a number of institutions. However, if training is still inadequate in national
distance education systems, at least they are deliberately
structured and organized for distance education. I have my
doubts about whether conventional educational institutions,
particularly at a higher education level, will be able to
make the structural and career development changes that
would be necessary for successful distance teaching.

References

Bacsich, P. (1981) The Open University Viewdata System. Milton Keynes:
   Open University (mimeo)
Bates, A.W. (1981) The Planning and Management of Audio-Visual Media
   in Distance Learning Institutions. Paris: Unesco
Bates, A.W. (1981a) The unique educational characteristics of television
   and some consequences for teaching and learning. Submitted to
   Journal of Educational Television and Other Media
Durbridge, N. (1981) Audio-Cassettes in Higher Education. Milton Keynes:
   Open University (mimeo)
McConnell, D. and Sharples, M. (1981) Distance Teaching by CYCLOPS:
   Tutor Handbook. Nottingham: Open University
Robinson, B. (1979) Telephone Teaching: A Handbook for Tutors. Nottingham:
   Open University

EDUCATION BY SATELLITE:
AUSTRALIAN POSSIBILITIES
H. Beare

This paper begins like a cautionary tale. The claims for schooling by satellite can be grandiose, unrealistic, and over-ambitious. In her assessment of SITE, the Indian experiment in rural education by means of satellite, Mody warned about "the glamorous media" and the expectation that it could "shoulder... onerous responsibilities alone as if it were a magic wand".[2] Indeed, the same extravagance of expectations is evident even in the tag-phrases used to describe such satellite experiments. In a review of the literature, I came across the following:

"Education's rising star"

"The orbital antenna farm"

"Communication in seven league boots"

"Teacher in the sky"

"Education in the space age"

"Satellite TV : new learning era"

"Highway in the sky"

"Education on the beam"

By now, however, there have been sufficient examples of how satellite transmission can affect educational programming to enable at least the idea to be brought down to earth. By now, the early extravagant claims can be tempered with a realism based upon experience.

The Australian satellite is obviously not the first. The celebrated pioneer ventures, from which we can profit, are listed below.

SITE, the Indian satellite instructional TV experiment, was trialled during 1975-76. This was "probably the largest communications experiment of modern times", according to Mody who was involved in both its design and its evaluation[3] The programs provided non-formal education to the subcontinent of India in agriculture and health aimed largely at rural or village dwellers, many of them illiterate. It also provided formal programs for both children and teachers, usually at primary school levels. The programs were viewed by people in cities as well as in country locations. Four hours of programs were transmitted daily.

PEACESAT (Pan-Pacific Education and Communication Experiment by Satellite): This project, based on the Pacific Basin during June/July of 1971, showed that it was possible to coordinate instruction between the two campuses of the University of Hawaii.[4] It thereafter expanded to involve twelve countries in the Pacific, using the American satellite ATS-1.[5]

Project SACI was begun in 1969 as an 8 year project to introduce satellite transmission into Brazil's educational system. It aimed to reach 500 primary (Years 1-4) schools, some 3,000 teachers and 25,000 students across an area of 100,000 sq.kms. Teachers were trained up to 1974 with the satellite launching due in 1976. [6]

ATS-6. In May 1974, the Applied Technology Satellite Number 6 was launched in USA. Among the jobs it was expected to make possible were three education projects based on Appalachia, the Rocky Mountains and Alaska. [7]

ESCD: The Alaskan Education Satellite Communications Demonstration was set up for policy makers in education and technology in 1974-75.

S.T.D. The Federation of Rocky Mountains States used the Satellite Technology Demonstration to test the feasibility of programming for isolated communities. Broadcast topics covered education, consumer affairs, health, and the environment. There were 12 programs of 40 minutes each with a 19-minute question-and-answer segment; and aimed at an evening adult audience; the S.T.D. receivers were placed in local junior high schools.[8]

AESP. The Appalachian Education Satellite Program was established in 1971 to deliver graduate and undergraduate courses to nearly 600 educators in the Appalachian region.[9] There were 15 classroom sites scattered between New York and Alabama; as well as the ATS-6 equipment, each was equipped to receive and transmit by two-way radio via ATS-3. The activities included

pre-taped televised programs, including lectures, interviews and demonstration lessons;

audio reviews of the TV materials;

live seminars with experts, on site;

on-site resource libraries.[10]

The program was expanded in 1977 to cover a much wider audience.

C.T.S. The Communications Technology Satellite, Hermes,

was made in Canada and launched by the United States in January 1976, as a joint venture between the countries. Twenty-five projects were approved for its use.[11]

Not surprisingly, then, there is now an extensive literature reviewing the outcomes of these projects. They warn us not to be too starry-eyed about satellite technology. For example, from the ESCD (Alaska) experience, a survey revealed that the demonstration was *not* worthwhile, that the satellite was only one of several methodologies available and that greater value would be derived from investing in normal secondary education facilities and in using tapes rather than real-time video broadcasting.[12]

It is not merely cost which gives rise for concern. It is how the costs are parcelled up. The impact of TV comes not so much from the hardware (the technology) but from the software (the program). There is quite clearly a temptation to build a costly machine and then have no money left over with which to drive it.

It is salutary to note Mody's comment about where the money was spent on the Indian experiment. Eighty-two percent of the money went on hardware, only 9 per cent was spent on software production and 3 per cent on evaluation. In this context, Mody comments, "it is a major miracle that there were four hours of programmes ready for transmission every day..."[13]

In his article on communication satellites, Bransford comments,[14]

> The key to effective utilisation of such a resource... is not hardware but meaningful and entertaining mediated software.

Thus, for educators it is not the existence of the satellite which should be our concern but rather whether the means are available to make use of it. In particular, the production of the programs should be our major concern. In short, the satellite simply expands the possibility of using TV as an education medium. TV programs, not the satellite, should be the focus of the educator's attention. For this reason, the satellite projects have already made possible a range of educational offerings, many surprisingly repetitive.

Some of the programs beamed from the satellites were as follows:

Program Offerings	Satellite Experiment
Health education programs	India
	Appalachia
Instruction about career options and vocational training	Rocky Mountains
Education to nomadic people and people in tribal settings	Canada

Occupational skills	India
Family planning	India
Food producation	India
Hygiene	India
Teacher training	India
Drug education	Rocky Mountains
English as a second language	Alaska
The arts and aging	Appalachia
Resource conservation	Appalachia
Health planning and administration	Appalachia
Teacher values and disciplines	Appalachia
Developing a healthy self-concept	Appalachia
An overview on teaching the young handicapped child (3-8 years old)	Appalachia
Diagnostic reading instruction	Appalachia
Teacher training on using TV in the classroom	Appalachia
Instruction to teachers on curriculum, and administration, and decentralization	Alaska

Why these, I wonder? Why not literature? Why nothing on mathematical skills? Why so little on the mainstream subjects? Why the absence of science lessons? Or multiculturalism? The experiments, it seems, were seen as *ancillary* rather than middle-of-the-road, enrichment rather than mainstream curriculum. The satellite, which expanded the reach of TV educational programs, nevertheless seemed to sidestep the most important question posed by the new medium of TV. It *is* educational, negatively or positively: it *does* compete with normal schooling, and has done for years. Yet we apparently perpetuate the myth that educational TV does not replace education-in-schools. Do the realities support this notion?

The literature on TV-satellite transmissions throws up the following possibilities for its use, based on the experiences people have already gained with the satellite to date.

A School by Satellite. Could it be done? Apparently yes. Writing in 1971, Barnett and Denzau argued that instructional television (ITV) could produce an inexpensive form of schooling. Videotape recorders (VTR), tapes, and cameras are now relatively cheaper than they were. A package of ten mobile VTRs and television sets, a tape library and several TV cameras per school of 50 classrooms could cost little, per pupil. An active head-end at the school would transmit the programs to each classroom. The costs would be lowered by a cable to each school, and especially if the school system owned or leased a dedicated educational channel.[15]

The *Open University* format is of course an obvious use for the satellite project, especially in bringing continuing professional development to people in localities remote from the university from which the courses originate. The satellite may help to minimize duplication of courses and a national rationlization of course offerings. It could lead to a university and CAE network of courses, a mixed blessing which could run foul of institutional rivalry and autonomy. *Six community colleges in USA formed in 1970 a consortium* called ACCESS to develop six courses to be generally available to educational institutions.[16]

University program networks

John S.Daniel[17] proposed for Canadian universities a system which would transmit audio and video courses from about 10 universities to about 20 locations. The classrooms from which the programs would be transmitted would be equipped with

> monochrome cameras
>
> microphones
>
> loud-speaker system

The receiving stations would need a TV monitor and loud speakers. He linked with the project another based upon a telephone system. Both projects would have a network control centre.

16mm films have been used for many years in school lessons, but purchasing them is now costly and distributing them requires organisation - usually a film distribution centre in a school system. In the STD (Rocky Mountains) experiment, 300 programs were leased from Encyclopedia Britannica Educational Corporation and 100 programs from Great Plains National Instructional Television and these were telecast to schools; the films could be videotaped and used by the STD schools at times convenient to them during the 1974-75 school year.[18]

Career education

Career education is an area of the curriculum neglected by teachers through ignorance. It is not that they do not consider the subject important; rather they do not have training and exposure in the subject. Not surprisingly, then, several of the experiments have focussed on career education, and especially for secondary school teachers. Thus:

A career education program was beamed to 56 rural

junior high schools and 12 broadcasting stations in 8 Rocky Mountain States.

A 16 - session course for secondary teachers was given at 15 sites in Appalachia.

An 8-session series was provided at 15 sites for 234 elementary school teachers in Appalachia.

"Time out" was a course for junior high school students provided in the Rocky Mountains; and the parallel program "Careers and the classroom: a new perspective for the teacher" was an inservice program for teachers. There was high audience response and substantial gains in student knowledge reported .[19]

This experience shows that the TV medium allows new subjects or new priorities to be promulgated, popularized, and their introduction technique learnt.

Professional inter-actions can be heightened by satellite technology. The Appalachian experiment linked hospital administrators and field tested the following devices

video seminars between doctors

teleconsultations

"grand rounds" of the hospitals

out-patient clinics

"computer-mediated events"

The ten hospitals in the experiment, all geographically removed from each other, all reported significantly heightened morale.[20]

In one *live inter-active seminar*, run in 1977 in the Appalachian project, and involving educators dealing with handicapped children, the course linked 270 participants at 34 different sites.[21] The five components of the course used

videotaped programs

live on-air seminars

activities in class

a practicum

and printed materials

It is unlikely, therefore, that TV, or methods of TV transmission, will provide us with a new educational panacea, as one gets the impression from the projects in India and Brazil. Rather the gains will be piece-meal, more messy than one would like, but new nevertheless. Bransford, in his 1978 article, endeavours to summarize what techniques TV and satellite transmission make possible.[22]

A perusal of the literature relating to satellite applications would include one or more of the following as specific samples:

Telecommunications in lieu of transportation

Delivery of continuing education

Teleconferencing for planning, instruction, advisory and administrative functions

Mechanism for introducing new and advanced training techniques

Alternatives to workshops, conferences, seminars

Access to diagnostic specialists not in proximity to schools

Mechanism for management information acquisition, storage, and dissemination

Access to data banks, clearinghouses, and cataloguing services

Distribution of instructional programs and materials

Provisions for interinstitutional communication and cooperation

Access to mediated courses of study

Paradoxically, it may be schooling rather than TV which is at fault. W.M. Gordon put it this way:[23]

> Television has had at best a minimal impact upon the formal education of children. Commercïal development has been extraordinary, with millions of children watching thousands of hours of programming and then dutifully demanding the cereals and toys they see advertised. Considering these extremely divergent success records within the same basic population, educators must look to the utilization of the media and not to the technology.

Thus, Gordon concludes,

> If satellite technology is utilized for primary level education, without any change in the structure, role, functions, and subject matter of today's elementary school, it will have the same impact that regional television had - i.e., none! The very paradox of something as twenty-first century as a satellite supporting something as nineteenth century as today's elementary school system strikes at the very core of educational change. Satellite technology must be a support technology for education, but it must support an educational enterprise that is fundamentally diff-

erent from that which exists in today's schools.

Are we creative enough, then, to conceive what those changes should be, not to educational TV, but to education itself?

Notes

1 I gratefully acknowledge the expert assistance of Mr. Michael O'Brien and Mr. Page Dixon in the research for this paper.

2 Mody, B., (1978), Lessons from the Indian satellite experiment, Educational Broadcasting International, Sept., p.117.

3 Mody, op.cit., p.118.

4 Byers, B.H., (1973), Classroom interaction, satellite-imposed. Audio-visual Instruction 18 (10), Dec., pp.20-23.

5 PEACESAT, Project early experience: the design and early years of the first educational communication satellite experiment, Report No.1 (Honolulu: University of Hawaii, 1975).

6 Cusack, M.A., Space technology for rural education; Brazil experiment, Project SACI, Sao Jose dos Campos, Brazil: Instituto de Pesquisas Espacias, 1973.

7 Bramble, William J. et al., A follow-up report on the Appalachian Education Satellite Project, Journal of Educational Technology Systems 5 (2), pp. 81-94, 76-77.

8 Darby, K., (1975), Programming as an instrument for community development, Satellite technology demonstration technical report No.503. (Denver, Colorado: Federation of Rocky Mountain States Inc.).

9 Perritt, L.J. and Mertens, D.M. (eds) (1978) Appalachian education Satellite Project. (Washington, D.C.: National Institute of Education).

10 Bramble, W.J. et al. (1975) Education on the beam: a progress report on the Appalachian Education Satellite Project. (Lexington, Kentucky: A.E.S.P., April).

11 Richmond, J.M. and Daniel, J.S., (1979) Evaluation of the educational experiments on the Hermes satellite 1976-1978, Final Report. (Ottawa, Canada: Dept. of Communications).

12 National Institute of Education, (1975), Implications of the Alaska Education Satellite Communications Demonstration for technological and educational policy-makers. First annual report. Volume 1: Analysis for the demonstration. (Washington, D.C.: Practical Concepts Inc.).

13 Mody, op.cit., p.120.

14 Bransford, L., (1978), Communication satellites: applications for the hearing impaired, American annals of the Deaf. Oct., p.673.

15 Barnett, H.J. and Denzau, A.T., (1971), Future development of instructional television. (St. Louis, Missouri: Washington University).

16 Goldmark, P., (1977), Proposed planning study for nationwide delivery of learning programs, paper presented at the Conference on Educational Applications of Satellites, Arlington, Virginia, Feb 2-3.

17 Daniel J.S. et al., (1977), The use of satellite delivery systems in Canada: the costing of two networks and a preliminary needs survey. (Ottawa, Canada: Dept. of Communications).

18 Lonsdale, H.C., The development of a materials distribution service for a satellite-based educational telecommunications experiment. STD Technical Report No. 0501. (Denver, Colorado: Federation of Rocky Mountain

States, Inc. 1975).

19 Satellite technology demonstration: executive report. (Denver, Colo.: Federation of Rocky Mountain States Inc., 15 Sept. 1976).

20 Caldwell, K.S. The Veterans Administration experiments in health communications on the Applications Technology Satellite ATS-6, (Final Report). Los Angeles: Foundation for Applied Communications Technology 1976).

21 Daugherty, D., (1978), Summative evaluation of teaching the young handicapped child, AESP, Lexington, Kentucky (Washington, D.C., N.I.E.).

22 Bransford, op.cit., p676.

23 Gordon, W.M., Communication satellites and the future of elementary education, World Future Society Bulletin 12 (3), May-June, 1978 p13.

24 ibid.

ON CHOOSING TEACHING METHODS
TO MATCH EDUCATIONAL AIMS
J. J. Sparkes

1 Introduction

Within the fields of teaching and learning it is necessary
to make distinctions between different aims and methods,
since not all educational aims can be achieved by one style
of teaching, and equally, learning by students can take a
variety of forms. So the main aim of the following discussion
is to present a description of the teaching and learning
processes and to draw from it some guide lines on how to
enhance the effectiveness of either or both. This can hardly
be regarded as a novel aim, since teacher training courses
and psychological research have been directed towards it for
many years. The complexity of the learning process in human
beings has, however, made it necessary for thorough scientific research to be confined to a number of rather special-
ised topics, with the result that making use of the results
of such research in practical teaching situations is not an
easy matter.

At the same time, however, it has always been possible
for gifted or experienced teachers to bring about successful
learning in the class-room even though it is rarely possible
to be explicit about how success has been achieved. It has
also always been possible for such a teacher to help teacher
trainees by example and by coaching. Indeed most complex
skills have to be taught mainly in this way, even though
verbal or practical instruction play a key part. With the
recent growth of methods of teaching-at-a-distance, however,
it has become clear that new teaching abilities are called
for and that there are few experts to call upon. Furthermore,
the normal process of coaching by which trial-and-error can
become trial-and- 'success with the help of an expert, does
not work well with these methods since it occupies so much
time. A teaching text, for example, may take weeks to write
and more weeks to rewrite. The learning strategy of "practice
makes perfect" which may well work with tennis or golf, with
piano playing or even with class-room teaching, or lecturing,

is very difficult to adopt with such a teaching method. The same difficulty arises with educational television or with computer-aided instruction. So the development of expertise in the distance teaching environment must be based as much on understanding the capabilities and limitations of each teaching medium - including face-to- face methods - as upon acquired skills.

But if research has not yet reached the stage of prescribing successful methods, the only way to bring about the necessary understanding is to encapsulate and present the knowledge that experience brings in such a way that it can be studied by others. This is the basis of the approach adopted in this paper.

Unlike the results of normal scientific research, the knowledge of experience cannot always be tested in controlled experiments. Its sole test may be that it is shared by those with the appropriate experience. Accordingly the distinctions between, say, different educational aims that are made in this paper should be non-controversial in the sense that they should appeal to the "common sense" of teachers, even if scientific evidence is not yet available to confirm them. Hopefully teachers will be inclined to remark that they are well known or even obvious! However, being obvious is not a sufficient condition for acceptability in the present study; it is also necessary that the models and categories discussed clarify courses of action, as to the choice of teaching methods, which could otherwise remain confused. For example, I think it is "obvious" that *knowledge* (of facts), for any individual, is not the same as *understanding* but the distinction would not be worth making in the present context if it did not lead directly to differences in teaching techniques when one or other (or both) are the educational aims being pursued.

Thus the aim of this paper is to describe the teaching and learning activities in common sense terms, using models and categories which are reasonably straightforward but which also map in a fairly clear manner onto the special capabilities of different teaching methods. If this strategy is successful it should lead directly to criteria by which appropriate educational techniques can be chosen to satisfy particular educational aims.

2 Two Aspects of Teaching and Learning

Of the many factors which contribute to successful learning this paper concentrates on only two. It is, of course, important to ensure that both teachers and students feel at home with the methods being used, and that the students are in reasonably congenial surroundings. It is also the case that different subjects demand different approaches to teaching. But none of these factors is discussed here. The aspects of the teaching and learning activities which are discussed are those that are characteristic of all subjects to a greater or lesser extent. It is assumed that the teaching and learning environments are satisfactory for those involved.

The two aspects discussed are:

(a) a feedback model of the teaching and learning processes; following, but simplifying Pask [1] ;

(b) a classification of educational aims; following, but simplifying and modifying Bloom [2]

The reason for selecting these two aspects is that they may also map well on to characteristics and limitations of different teaching techniques.

2.1 *Education as a feedback process*

It is a common experience, of teacher and student alike, that both teaching and learning are improved when errors and inadequacies are pointed out and, preferably, dealt with in some way. Equally, both processes benefit when good performance is encouraged. So the imnportance of such feedback processes in education can hardly be a matter of argument. The following remarks merely encapsulate this idea in a formal model.

Figure 1 illustrates a feedback model of the educational process. It exemplifies Pask's "conversational" theory since it illustrates that learning is achieved by a continuous iteration between absorbing new information, trying to use it and checking whether it was correctly used. In other words, concepts are recycled through the learning regions of the brain and gradually acquire sufficient richness of meaning for them in the end to be used with confidence to express the learner's own ideas. Such a process applies to learning a language and the meaning of words, to acquiring skills as well as to learning concepts and ideas.

Referring to figure 1, the output of the system is (intended to be) educated students. If the forward path were faultless, and if all students could learn immediately, the output could be achieved without feedback playing a part. In practice, however, the forward path (e.g. written teaching texts, lectures, T.V. programmes, etc.) is rarely wholly successful educationally, and in addition, students do not all live up to expectation. So it is necessary to include feedback in the system in order to correct any errors that occur, both in the students' and teachers' performance and to provide "conversational" recycling of ideas.

Several kinds of feedback are possible; they have different characteristics and serve different functions. In descending order of response time these are:

(a) The statistical feedback (shown dashed), obtained from large surveys of student response, indicates whether the forward path is appropriate for the chosen target student populaltion. The time period within which changes to the forward path can be made in response to this kind of feedback is so long that it can normally only affect the next, or next-but-one, cohort of students. It does not, therefore, play any part in the conversational learning process. It is useful only as a means of correcting gross errors in the forward path (e.g. books, lectures, T.V. programmes, etc.). It does not, of course, usually specify what was wrong (or right) about the forward path, it merely indicates whether it was good or bad. How to improve matters remains a problem.

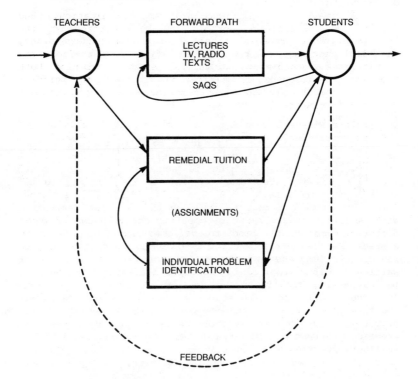

Fig. 1 A feedback model of the teaching process

(b) Assignments have a response time of a few days and provide specific help to each individual student. Computer-marked assignments (CMAs) linked to preprogrammed wordprocessors can provide similar help with certain kinds of topics. To obtain the best educational effects from assignments tutors should give helpful comments on scripts. Assignments can fulfil three different roles: (i) assess a students' performance (and award marks), (ii) correct errors by giving correct or model answers and (iii) encourage further work on the problem so that students will arrive at better performances by their own efforts. As far as effective learning is concerned the last role is generally the most successful.

(c) Tutorials, telephone conferencing and self-help groups provide immediate feedback and true "conversational" learning. A useful distinction can however be drawn between "individual-problem-identification" and "remedial tuition" as shown in the diagram. In tutorials both functions are combined. Computer methods, however, can be used for individual-problem-identification, and various alternative methods can be specified for the provision of remedial teaching (e.g. computer exercises, dial access, telephones, specified face-to-face tutorials, audio-vision, Cyclops, etc.). Combining both aspects (problem identification as well as remedial tuition) in face-to-face tutorials is rarely as successful as one would wish.

(d) Self-assessment questions are the simplest stimulant to conversational learning and redirect the student to further study. They also provide a useful check on the effectiveness of the forward path. With the forward path comprising printed or recorded material further study of it is possible. Otherwise students have to seek out alternative educational material.

With small groups a good teacher can provide the several different components of a good conversational education system. In distance teaching, however, it is necessary to pay particular regard to the whole system as well as to particular elements of it; for even a feedback loop tends to be only as effective as its weakest link.

The main purpose of this analysis and of the feedback model is to clarify the roles each teaching component can play, so that where necessary, the continuous conversational process can be kept active and not inadvertently broken by failing to provide a key part to it.

2.2 *A classification of educational achievements*

It is, of course, well known that there are different kinds of learning. For example, the learning of skills is a very different activity from acquiring knowledge or from embracing a belief in, say, religion or Marxism or apartheid. Yet it is not always apparent that the teaching and learning methods used to achieve these different educational aims take full account of such differences. The purpose of this section, therefore, is to list a range of relatively easily distinguished educational aims (following Bloom in some respects but with much less detail) with a view to arriving at appropriate educational strategies for each kind of educational aim. We shall find, for example, that different educational aims will stress different aspects of the feedback model of education, and will also lay particular emphasis on different teaching techniques.

It should perhaps be stressed that these distinctions are not related directly to subject matter (e.g. athletics, aesthetics, mathematics or engineering) but are concerned more with the *kinds* of learning that form a part, to varying degrees, of all such topics. There are *also* differences between academic subjects, and these also have to be taken into account, but these do not form the subject of the present study.

The most useful classes of educational aims, that are both relatively independent of each other and capable of being matched to existing educational techniques, appear to be as follows:

(i)　learning in the affective domain;
　　　(a)　attitudes, values, etc.
　　　(b)　affective skills (communication, adaptability, etc)

(ii)　learning in the <u>cognitive</u> domain;
　　　(a)　of facts
　　　(b)　of understanding

(iii)　learning of intellectual skills;
　　　(a)　of particular techniques
　　　(b)　of analysis (e.g. logical, systemic, historical)
　　　(c)　of synthesis (e.g. problem solving, design, invention)

(iv)　learning of manual skills.

These eight categories can be further explained and illustrated as follows:

(i)　<u>The affective domain</u>

　　The affective domain is concerned with values, beliefs, attitudes, predispositions, prejudices, etc. Most people have fundamental beliefs which they are prepared to cling to even if certain items of evidence seem tc contradict them. Such evidence can usually be "explained away". To paraphrase Lakatos: [3] "core" theories can be "protected" by layers of auxiliary theories. Thus it is possible to believe in an omnipotent God of love despite the prevalence of evil and hate in the world; or to believe in evolution or creationism despite the contrary evidence about both. Equally "affective skills" such as attention to detail, reliability, flexibility are deepseated and habitual and one is usually more concerned to explain or justify one's own behaviour than to change it.

Because such core beliefs and habits are so deep-seated and so vehemently and effectively protected, *affective* education is the most difficult to achieve. Perhaps the most effective external influences are a charismatic teacher, a moving novel or an unforgettable T.V. programme or film. Social pressures are, however, usually more effective than any formal teaching technique.

(ii) The cognitive domain (a & b)

A simple fact for one person may be very abstruse for another. The facts of a Balance Sheet may be immediately grasped and remembered by an accountant, but may be quite incomprehensible and unmemorable for someone with no understanding of numbers or of the terminology and conventions that accountants use. Thus, understanding at some level - even if it is of the meanings of everyday words, let alone jargon - must precede the learning of facts.

This distinction is particularly important in continuing education. A long undergraduate education in medical understanding is an essential pre-requisite for a factual course in professional medical updating. Undergraduate courses in general are concerned primarily with teaching understanding - supported, of course, with a good deal of information. Understanding usually takes a long time to teach well, but, given the understanding, factual knowledge can be rapidly and easily learnt by interested students. Indeed the verb "to teach" is often reserved for the development of understanding and skills rather than the sharing of facts or opinions.

(iii) Intellectual skills

Intellectual skills are concerned with techniques and methods. Methods tend to require more insight than techniques. Thus it is possible, for example, for someone to have mathematical skills (addition, equation solving, differentiation) with no understanding. Such a person would be said to have been *trained* in mathematical *techniques*. On the other hand using mathematical methods to solve a problem requires more than mere technique. Learning to do so effectively is both an education and a training. It is possible to gain understanding without developing intellectual skills (indeed such is a common enough complaint about some graduates) but in general the two have to be intermixed to be of use.

257

Two particular kinds of intellectual skills are those of *analysis* (the breaking down of a complex problem into manageable parts) and *synthesis* (the putting together of manageable parts in order to achieve a new complex whole). Universities are mainly concerned with analytical skills (as well as with knowledge and understanding, of course). Synthesis skills are taught and practiced to a much lesser extent than analytical ones, even in such fields as engineering, in which creative design is a key skill. Also in the Arts criticism, rather than creative skills, is given pride of place.

(iv) <u>Manual skills</u>

Manual skills, even typing for computer keyboard operation, are taught very little in universities, though perhaps they should be given more attention. They usually call for relatively little knowledge, understanding or intellectual skills.

3 Choosing between different teaching methods and techniques

Different teaching methods and techniques have differing capabilities and constraints, as regards -

(a) their place in the educational feedback loop of figure 1

(b) their suitability for different educational aims

(c) their suitability to different kinds of subject matter

(d) their suitability for different kinds of students

(e) their suitability for different kinds of teachers

(f) their cost (e.g. per student-hour of effective study).

This paper only considers the first two and the last of these factors.

3.1 *Teaching media and methods*

The following is a list of different teaching media (or methods) that are at present available or likely soon to be so. All methods require some technology to support them (even if it is just paper and pencil or a blackboard). The level of technology, however, varies very much -

1 <u>Face-to-face</u> (including audio-visual aids)

(a) lectures

(b) classes (as in schools)

(c) small group discussions, usually for remedial purposes

(d) tutorials (i.e. a teacher with no more than 3 students)

(e) self-help groups (i.e. small groups without a teacher)

(f) laboratory or practical work (see 7 below)

(g) the telephone and telephone conferencing

Note: Films, tapes, T.V. programmes, etc., intended for use in face-to-face teaching situations (e.g. in support of a teacher's instruction) are very different from those intended to stand alone, or be supported by other material such as a printed text.

2 Printed texts

(a) text books

(b) structured tutor-texts (as used in the Open University)

3 Films or T.V. programmes

(a) for broadcasting (i.e. *not* for repeated replay)

(b) films for T.V. tapes (for repeated replay)

Note: The replay facility which at present is expensive because of the cost of the replay device, should strongly affect the content of such films or tapes, for *some* educational purposes.

4 Audio

(a) for radio broadcasting

(b) audio tapes

(c) audio-vision (i.e. audio tapes supported by printed illustrations, diagrams, calculations, etc)

(d) telephone conferencing

5 Audio-graphic systems such as Cyclops (i.e. the recording on audio tape of both spoken commentary and of graphic or alphanumeric data for display on a T.V. screen).

6 Computer-aided learning (CAL)

(a) using teletype terminals

(b) using Visual Display units. Such methods include Prestel, Optel and similar systems

(c) using the mail (for distance teaching) and a word-processor for preparing the communication from the computer

7 Laboratory or practical work

(a) in purpose built teaching laboratories

(b) based on practical apparatus for use in the home or at work

(c) projects

8 Assignments

These can be associated with any of the above, but except in the case of CAL or tutoring they require the use of a further channel of communication.

3.2 *Relating teaching methods to educational aims*

As pointed out at the beginning of this section the choice between teaching methods is a multi-dimensional one. Too often in the past a technique such as programmed learning, T.V., or lecturing have been used or commended when one or more of the many factors which make for educational success have been lacking. Consider for example the two forms of face-to-face teaching that are most widely used in universities: the lecture and the small group remedial tutorial.

The lecture is often criticised because it does not *teach* well [4] ; it does not compare, for example, with the small group teaching that is normal in sixth forms in schools. But we can now see why this is; lecturing is not a complete teaching method. It is very deficient in the scope it offers for feedback from students to teacher. As a consequence its pace is normally so fast that it leaves little time for more than note-taking, and teacher and students have little opportunity to get to know each other. Conversational learning of the concepts being taught is reduced to a minimum. Indeed no experienced lecturer expects many of his students to have *learnt* any of the difficult concepts or skills his lecture has dealt with by the end of the lecture; private study, discussion and further reading are normally necessary to complete the learning process.

This does not mean that the lecture should play no part in the teaching process since it can fulfil several roles very effectively. Its primary function in most universities is to present to students an explanatory statement of what should be learnt, and to pace the students' rate of studying. Referring to figure 1, it provides the first forward path (through the student's head) of the concepts to be learned, but it plays little part in ensuring that the concepts will circulate round the learning loop. As a popular and convenient forward path it can be well used to achieve those aims that require little feedback. Thus it is effective as a means of presenting facts (especially recent developments) and practical demonstrations (for example, of calculations, skills or of experiments). A good lecturer can also motivate and enthuse students and so influence their attitudes and values in a variety of ways. Indeed it is often this quality in a lecturer, when it is present, that students appreciate most.

Similar, though different, comments can be made about the use of small group classes or tutorials. Such classes provide what is probably the most effective form of teaching

260

available to us, yet it is common practice not to use it for this purpose [4] . It is widely used as a means of providing occasional remedial tuition on a particular course, or even on a set of courses; and it is widely regarded as being difficult to manage well if used solely for this purpose. Again, it is clear that in *not* being used to provide the primary forward path in the teaching process it has been deprived of a key part in the learning process. Indeed, using a group to provide both the "individual problem-identification" and the "remedial tuition" components of the model in figure 1 is bound to be somewhat unsatisfactory since each individual is likely to have a different problem and so to require different remedial help. There are good reasons, therefore, for using different techniques for individual problem identification, such as diagnostic tests, assignments, etc., and for providing individualised remedial help, such as recommended texts, audio tapes on particular topics, encouragement (!), individual classes, either face-to-face or on the telephone or small group classes on particular, specified topics where a need has been identified. But small group teaching is a complete teaching system so it should be reserved for dealing with selected difficult conceptual subjects or skills, the extent to which teachers' time is available.

In the same way it is possible to relate each of the teaching methods listed above to the feedback model and to the set of educational aims listed earlier.

However, there is not sufficient space in an article of this kind to fully explore each possible technique, though it is not difficult to arrive at useful distinctions and guidelines for oneself. Table 1 is a much simplified mapping of educational aims onto educational methods, using different symbols to indicate the part played in the learning feedback process of each method. Circles indicate methods in which the teacher plays the dominant active part and crosses those in which student activity tends to dominate. Where both play a significant role both symbols are used. The number of symbols, on a scale of 0 to 6, indicates the degree to which a particular method can be expected to contribute to each particular aim. In arriving at the indicated assessment of each method an estimate of costs is also included. That is the relatively expensive methods are regarded as less cost-effective than those of comparable effectiveness but less cost.

The entry under television, for example, indicates that it is, of course, a "forward path" component of the learning loop, in which the teacher is active and the students are passive. The various entries show that its strengths lie in the affective domain and in presenting knowledge. Its weakness in teaching skills lies in the fact that it can only "instruct", it cannot exercise student skills or correct errors. Its weakness in conceptual development stems from

TABLE 1

Method \ Aim	1(a) Attitudes	1(b) Skills	2(a) Knowledge	2(b) Understanding	3(a) Techniques	3(b) Analysis	3(c) Synthesis	4 Manual
Lectures	OOO		OOO	OO	O	O		
Small Group Classes	⊕	⊕⊕⊕	⊕⊕⊕	⊕⊕⊕	⊕⊕⊕	⊕⊕⊕	⊕⊕	
Laboratory or Workshop	⊕⊕⊕		‡	‡	‡			OOO
Teaching Text			OOO OOO	OO OO	OO OO	OOO	O	
Video Tape	O	OOO	OOO OOO	OO OO	O	O	O	OO
Audio Vision			OOO	OOO	OO OO	OO		
Broadcast, T.V. and Radio	OOO OOO		OO OO	OO		O	O	OO
CAL		‡		‡ ‡	‡ ‡	+	‡‡	
Teleconferencing	⊕⊕⊕	⊕⊕	⊕⊕⊕	⊕⊕⊕	⊕	⊕⊕ ⊕⊕	⊕	
Home Kit	‡	‡	‡	‡ ‡		‡		+
Dial Access			OOO	OO OOO				
Projects	‡ ‡		‡	‡	+	‡+	‡‡ ⊕⊕	‡
Assignments		⊕ ⊕⊕⊕	⊕⊕⊕	⊕⊕⊕ ⊕⊕⊕	⊕⊕ ⊕⊕	⊕⊕ ⊕⊕	⊕⊕⊕ ⊕⊕⊕	
Self-help Group	‡ ‡	‡						

Domain groupings (from the brackets beneath the table):
- affective domain: 1(a) Attitudes, 1(b) Skills
- cognitive domain: 2(a) Knowledge, 2(b) Understanding, 3(a) Techniques, 3(b) Analysis
- skills: 3(c) Synthesis, 4 Manual

O in which the primary activity is one of teaching by the tutor
+ in which the primary activity is learning as a result of the students' own initiative

262

the fact that concepts are abstract and so cannot be photo-graphed! However, since television is so rich and flexible, it can make use of both verbal description and visual symbols (as in mathematics) or of visual analogies and simulations even more effectively than a lecturer. The more it uses such techniques for conceptual development, however, the more costly it tends to become and so is regarded as less cost effective for this purpose than, say, for affective teaching.

Similar reasoning lies behind each entry but, of course, they are only indications of cost-effectiveness and give no more than guidelines as to practical use. They are also subject to modifications according to the subject matter being taught or learnt.

The costs of each teaching method vary greatly both in time and money. A useful measure of the cost in human terms (which can be related quite easily to the cost in monetary terms) is the number of man-hours of teacher time required to produce one student-hour of study. The following are some approximate figures intended only as a guide -

classes in school	1.5	tutor-text (as in O.U.)	50.0
lectures	2.0	full O.U. multi-media course	70.0
radio or audio tapes	6.0		
		CAL	200.0
T.V.	50.0		

These figures indicate the degree of motivation required of an experienced teacher (once the novelty has worn off) if he is to embark on the use of each method.

The actual cost per student of each method depends upon other factors too:

(a)   the number of students that are taught as a result of the investment of teacher-time

(b)   the proportion of a teacher's time spent on teaching (e.g. in most universities only about 10% of a lecturer's full time appointment (including vacations) is spent on teaching, whereas in schools or in the Open University this figure is nearer 60% though for different reasons)

(c)   the number of man-hours of support staff needed per man-hour of teacher-time

(d)   the cost of the technology (including the buildings) of each method.

Table II shows some typical approximate, estimated comparative costs - excluding hardware (i.e. (d) above whose costs are too variable to estimate).

TABLE 11

	teacher-hours per student hour (A)	portion of teacher time spent on teaching (B)	number of students per teacher time invested (C)	multiplier to give all staff active per teacher (D)	cost per student A D B C (staff per student hour)
Classes (school)	1.5	0.6	30	1.1	0.09
Lectures	2.0	0.1	50	1.5	0.6
Full O.U. course	70.0	0.6*	5000	10.0*	0.23
CAL	200.0	0.5	1000	2.0	0.8

*Open University estimate for a 2nd level course which runs for 8 years. (Includes estimates for administrative and other staff in the University needed to operate the system).

These figures are again very approximate but they indicate a method of comparing costs between very different teaching systems.

However, costs are only one factor to be considered. Even the cheapest method wastes money if it is educationally ineffective - for whatever reason. A method can be ineffective because students don't like it, because teachers find it too demanding, because of its inherent limitations for the kind of educational aims it is being used for, etc. Thus, although these data give some guidance, they are not the only factors. Indeed there are times when costs are not important and effectiveness is paramount, in which case the data of table II are irrelevant.

Conclusion

The aim of this paper has been to bring together very simple and commonsensical ideas about teaching and learning, so that the know-how of experienced teachers, rather than the results of academic research, can be passed on to others. Even the reason for adopting this strategy is based more on experience than research. That is, it can readily be seen that in all complex fields such as economics and other social sciences, management, human relations as well as education, the methodology of scientific research has its drawbacks. Yet it would be difficult to establish through a programme of scientific research that some other methodology would be preferable. The methodology adopted in this paper, therefore, has more in common with "illuminative" methodology of Parlett and Hamilton [5] than with the scientific methods of Popper or Kuhn [6]. So the conclusions cannot be said to be well tested or corroborated, though they should be helpful and practical.

One of the main techniques used in scientific research is analysis and isolation, leading to reductionism and to research programmes on isolated elements of an overall system. A key aim of this paper has been to avoid this kind of analysis and to preserve as far as possible the natural complexity of the educational process. Inevitably, however, some analysis has been necessary. But the elements have been kept as simple as possible, consistent with their being useful and discriminatory. The choice of models and categories has been predicated by two main considerations.

1   Whilst it is certainly true that there will never be clear boundaries between the elements of a complex system, since this is one of the factors which justify the adjective "complex", it is also true that broad, readily perceived categories can usually be identified by experienced people. (Many illustrations of this premiss are to be found; for example, the continuous spectrum of light is readily perceived as distinct colours even though there are no demarcation points; and the more or less continuous and audible signal that we call speech is readily segmented into discrete words, even though the many tiny pauses in the signal do not coincide with the spaces between words; they occur before plosives such as p, d, k, etc.)

2   That the purpose of the analysis is to enable the mapping of the categories and the models on to the characteristics of the many teaching methods that are available. For this reason, for example, the categories of subject (e.g. history, biology, mathematics, etc.) have not been used since such a mapping does not seem to be very successful as a primary means of choosing between techniques. It can be brought in later to provide finer distinctions if they are needed.

The paper, then, is offered as an attempt to make headway with this methodology. Its success should, I think, be judged in the light of the illumination it brings to teachers and students rather than by the results of any research programmes it may stimulate.

References

1 Pask, G. Conversation, Cognition and Learning. Elsevier, Amsterdam, 1975
2 Bloom, B.S. and others. Taxonomy of Educational Objectives Handbook I, the Cognitive Domain. David McKay, New York, 1936
3 Lakatos, I. The Methodology of Scientific Research Programmes. Philosophical Research Papers, Volume 1. Cambridge University Press, Cambridge, 1978

4 Bligh, D. Methods and Techniques in Post-secondary Education. UNESCO, Paris, 1980

5 Parlett, M. and Hamilton, D. "Illuminative Evaluation: A New Approach to the Study of Innovatory Programmes". University of Edinburgh, Centre for Research in the Educational Sciences; Occasional paper No. 9. Reprinted in: Tawney, D. Curriculum Evaluation Today: Trends and Implications. Macmillan, London, 1975

6 See, for example, Chalmers, A.F. What is this thing called Science. Open University Press, Milton Keynes, 1978

SECTION 6: COURSE DEVELOPMENT

INTRODUCTION

Research on the development of instructional material in general is largely relevant to the development of courses for distance study. This above all applies to printed courses.

Readability and effectiveness

The importance of simple grammar for readability and understanding has been shown to be great. The active form of verbs facilitates reading compared with the passive form, although practice in the reading of passive sentences seems to eliminate this difficulty, which may be an important fact for presentations in German, for instance. Short clauses, many finite verbs, many pronouns, short and well-known words are advantageous from the points of view of readability and understanding (Coleman 1965; Groeben 1972, pp. 18-23).

Readability formulae using word length, word frequency, sentence length and similar measures to predict reading difficulty have been used with success in various kinds of instructional text. Macdonald-Ross, who has thoroughly studied the use of language in texts, claims that a 'readability "filter" is ...more reliable than the exercise of unaided human judgement' and refers to a study by Klare & Smart 1973, in which a rank-order correlation of 0.87 was found between the readability level of correspondence material and the probability that students would send in all their lessons (with length held constant) (Macdonald-Ross 1979, pp. 4-5).

Course developers usually try to avoid on the one hand extreme concentration leading to high information density, on the other hand long windedness. However, some scepticism has been expressed against making course texts too easily readable and too perfect from an educational point of view. Thus Groeben 1972 and Rowntree 1973 reject the most readable texts as patterns to be followed:

Do not accept the principle that you must be entirely intelligible to the student... (Groeben 1972, p.148)

267

> The more explanatory and 'clear' the exposition, the less
> there is for the student to do. Some texts are so
> 'perfect' as to stifle all real thinking activity. (Rown-
> tree 1973, p.2)

It is probable that a text that seems too simple and is full
of platitudes makes readers inattentive, but in that case
that is because the text is unattractive and uninteresting.
The fault with the type of texts criticised by Rowntree and
Sanders is not their readability and clarity, but lies
elsewhere, i.e. in the presentation of learning matter as a
ready-made system instead of as something to be looked into
and considered. The texts described do not require of the
students that they should ask themselves questions, try
possible solutions or search on their own, which is what a
distance-study course should do.

Specific concerns of distance education

While the general principles and practices referred to above
are highly relevant to distance education, there are specific
problems of course development for distance education which
are equally important.

Among these the question how best to divide the study
material into course units is a very tricky one. The generally accepted idea behind the division of the material into
study units is that students should be offered a suitable
quantity of learning matter at a time so that they can
regard the study of each unit as a separate task and can
always survey the material to be learnt. The theory is that
in this way it is possible to prevent the bulk of possibly
difficult study material from being intimidating. With each
finished unit and with the tasks in it completed, the
students see a result of their work.

The size of study units varies considerably with the
schools and universities that develop them. Units from eight
small pages to more than 100 large-size pages exist. Some
attempts have been made to define criteria for the decision
as to what is a suitable size (and the frequency of communication desirable), but so far nothing conclusive can be said
(Rosberg 1966, Bååth 1980).

The size of study units is evidently related to the
comprehensiveness of the total course presentation. Extreme
differences are to be found between self-contained courses
and mere sheets listing what books, chapters or papers
should be read and containing tasks for submission assignments. This reflects two basically different approaches to
course development resulting on the one hand in self-
contained courses, on the other hand in study-guide courses.

A self-contained course in principle provides all
the learning matter that is necessary. It has proved partic-

ularly valuable when the course content is fairly elementary and does not call for a study of different sources. Such courses are complete in themselves and are particularly common in proficiency subjects like foreign languages and mathematics.

Sometimes, however, students must be made to see a complicated picture of a subject with conflicting theories and views, or they have to learn how to trace facts and arguments from different presentations and to study various sources critically. In such cases the study-guide approach is evidently more suitable in that the study guide causes students to read and/or listen to presentations of various kinds, to compare and criticize them and to try to come to conclusions of their own. This study-guide approach is generally practical when the learning is to include part or the whole of the content of various books, papers and other sources of knowledge (cf. Holmberg 1977, Ljoså 1975).

Most distance-education courses with their various components aim at leading their students straight to specific goals. The course developers then tend to regard each study unit as an integral part and as a compulsory course component.

This all-embracing course structure is often considered too rigid. Many educators feel that the students should be offered a choice of what units of a course are to be regarded as relevant in each individual case. Such an approach leads to each unit or each small set of units being separate and providing a sufficient treatment of a limited, and strictly defined, part of the subject. When that is the case, students can build their own curricula from units or sets of units belonging to different courses.

There is evidently a danger that a very effective course may become autocratic in the sense that the course tells students what they ought to do. Ljoså refers to the danger that in this way distance education tends to become 'teacher-centred education' (Ljoså 1977, p.79). Both the study-guide approach and the modular principle can be used to make distance education learner-centred. It is, in fact, possible for a distance-study course to offer and suggest choices of study material and approaches as well as as of work to be done instead of prescribing what must be done (Lehner & Weingartz 1981, p.10).

Another advantage of this principle is that each study unit or set of units can be used in different contexts, which is economical and can contribute to widening the offer of educational opportunities. Further, it makes provision for requirements to study one little part of a subject only (cf. Ljoså & Sandvold 1976).

There is a dichotomy between ready-made and individualised distance education, i.e. 'off-the-peg' vs. tailor-made study programmes, that is relevant in this context. Weingartz has, on the basis of a consistent view of learning as understanding and problem-solving, provided an in-depth analysis of some distance-study courses from different parts of the world illustrating the two approaches, and Lehner has developed a learning theory bearing on this. He describes all learning as problem-solving in the sense that it is composed of making assumptions (i.e. developing hypotheses) and modifying these as the learning progresses. This leads to what he terms a 'genetic learning approach'. Starting out from problems instead of from the comprehensive systems that the knowledge amassed through the centuries constitute (for instance, when studying gravitation asking the questions of Arisotle and Galileo as Einstein & Infeld do, instead of starting by learning the solutions found) favours genetic learning. Weingartz's theoretical approach is linked with Lehner's and has led her to study current practice in distance education. To judge from her study, much remains to be done to improve problem-solving learning in distance-study. (Lehner 1979, Weingartz 1981).

The following texts look into the practicability of some of the principles discussed above and contribute ideas which should be profitable to anyone active in distance education.

Börje Holmberg

References

Bääth, J.A. (1980) Postal two-way communication in correspondence education. Lund: Gleerup

Coleman, E.B. (1965) Learning of prose written in four grammatical transformations. Journal of Applied Psychology, 49, 332-341

Einstein, A. & Infeld, L. (1950) Die Evolution der Physik. Hamburg: Zsolnay

Groeben, N. (1972) Die Verständlichkeit von Unterrichtstexten. Dimensionen und Kriterien rezeptiver Lernstadien. Münster: Aschendorff

Holmberg, B. (1977) Das Leitprogramm zur Fernstudium. ZIFF Papiere 17. Hagen: Fernuniversität

Klare, G.R. & Smart, K. (1973) Analysis of the readability level of selected USAFI instructional materials. Journal of Educational Research 67, 176

Lehner, H. (1979) Erkenntnis durch Irrtum als Lehrmethode. Bochum: Kamp

Lehner, H. & Weingartz, M. (1981) Ready-made and individualised distance study. ICCE-Newsletter 11, 1, 7-10

Ljoså, E. (1975) Why do we make commentary courses? In Ljoså, E. (ed.) The system of distance education, 1, ICCE, 112-118. Malmö: Hermods

Ljoså, E. (1977) Course design and media selection - some implications on co-operation between broadcasting, publishing and distance-education organizations. Epistolodidaktika 1977:1, 75-84

Ljosá, E. & Sandvold, K.E. (1976) The student's freedom of choice within the didactical structure of a correspondence course. Paris: EHSC

Macdonald-Ross, M. (1979) Language in texts: a review of research relevant to the design of curricular materials. In Shulman, L.S. (ed.), Review of Research in Education, 6. Itasca, lll.: Peacock

Rosberg, U. (1966) How should the most efficient correspondence course be designed? The Home Study Review 7, 4, 17-19

Rowntree, D. (1973) Student exercises in correspondence texts. IET internal memorandum. Milton Keynes: The Open University

Weingartz, M. (1981) Lernen mit Texten. Bochum: Kamp

A LIST OF IDEAS FOR THE CONSTRUCTION OF DISTANCE EDUCATION COURSES
John A. Bååth

Some possibilities of attempting to fulfil instructional functions

The prototype of the kind of distance education programmes dealt with here is a correspondence course which may or may not include other media than the written word or combinations with oral instruction or group work.

The following lists of factors and ideas are the result of a series of seminars held at Hermods in connection with a study of pedagogical functions associated with Gagné's instructional model.[1]

1 Factors to be considered

When making use of the list you should from the start have a clear conception of some basic characteristics of the course you propose to use the list for. Five important factors are

1 The budget situation with regard to the project

2 Type of course (purpose: qualifications - hobby)

3 Type of distance education (distance education only - various forms of combinations with oral instruction)

4 Nature of the subject

5 Target group.

Every one of these factors is of importance for the kind of measures that may be possible or suitable in connection with the construction of a course. Let us consider these factors for a moment, one by one in the first place.

1.1 *The budget situation with regard to the project*

In the case of a low budget project there is little point in devoting thought to AV accessories, imaginative typography and layout, etc. Instead we should try to fulfil the pedagogical-functional requirements as well as possible in the simplest and cheapest possible outward form.

1.2 Type of course

Courses leading to qualifications probably differ in certain essential respects from courses of hobby character (etc.) For example, the motivation is not really of the same kind in the two cases. The aims of qualification courses must be presented in the first instance as course objectives (What are the requirements for a pass? What questions shall I have to answer in the examination? etc.), whereas in hobby courses it may be possible to content ourselves with the demands of 'practical life'.

1.3 Type of distance education: 'pure' or combined with other forms of instruction

If distance education is not to be the sole medium and some element of tutoring involving direct contact is to be included, the first thing to do is to work out a distribution of pedagogical functions. It might tentatively be a good idea to let the direct instructor/tutor assist in the majority of the other pedagogical functions but *not* to use him to act as the medium for the instructional material itself.

When making use of the list of ideas you should, of course, bear in mind the possibilities afforded by any direct contact between student and teacher/tutor. If possible, you should 'think in' these contacts in the construction of the material.

On the other hand, in the construction of 'pure' distance education courses you should make every effort to fulfil as many as possible of the pedagogical functions with the aid of material alone. In practice we are often compelled to use the same course material for individual correspondence students, members of study circles or students attending schools in which supervised correspondence study is applied. Certain compromises may then become necessary. We should, however, remember that they *are* compromises and form them as close to the ideal as possible. You can pay some regard to the study and instructional situation for which the material is to be used by drawing up one or more appendices or supplements to the course. For example, you produce one appendix for the 'oral' tutor/teacher in combined instruction. Furthermore, you can set partly separate series of exercises and assignments for submission to suit individual students and participants in combined instruction. And in the combined version the students' material need not, perhaps, have to include answers to the exercises.

1.4 *Nature of the subject*

A very rough but essential division may be made into 'proficiency subjects' and 'orientation subjects'. The important distinction here is that in the main the proficiency subjects have a more strictly sequential structure than the orientation subjects. Proficiency at a certain level must often be trained until almost perfect command is attained so that, based on the acquired proficiency, a further advance may be made to the next level.

This implies consequences above all for

the definition of objectives (which must often be more exact in the case of proficiency subjects)

the link with previous knowledge (which must be meticulously worked out in the case of proficiency subjects)

the structure (where nothing may be left to chance in the proficiency subjects) and

the activation-feedback-transfer-retention functions (since the exercises may be supposed to be of special importance in the proficiency subjects).

Mathematics and languages are naturally proficiency subjects in this sense, but also the majority of technical and some economical subjects belong to the same category, as does also logic in the subject of philosophy.

1.5 *Target groups*

Two vital factors are *age* and *educational level*.
1.5.1 Age Maturity as a rule means wider experience and in many cases increased self-control. But adults often have less time at their disposal for the purpose of studying and therefore greater need for the studies to be felt as immediately meaningful. For this reason courses for adults ought not to be constructed in the same way as courses for young students.

It is probable that this distinction will be expressed, for example, in

suitable methods for arousing interest and motivating

selection of teaching objectives and their presentation

possibilities of linking up with previous knowledge and experience

choice of material and

manner of activation.

Here, too, compromises may be necessary in practice as the same basic material must sometimes be used for both young students and adults. The solution in this case also

274

may be one or more differentiated appendices (cf. 1.3 above).

1.5.2 Educational level The previous knowledge and habits of study of people with little education differ from those of people with a more advanced educational background. Function 3 - the actualization of and linking up with relevant previous knowledge - is thus of special importance in courses for people with little educational background. This is probably also true of Function 5 - guidance and structure - and Function 6 - activation.

1.5.3 Other target group factors Naturally other distinctive features of the target group may also be of importance, in so far as we know anything about these factors. Examples: intelligence, motivation, practical experience and attitudes.

1.6 The factors in combination

Each one of the factors is of importance for the choice of measures. Naturally you should make a compilation of them in order to find out how they might conceivably act in combination. Take, for example, a qualifying pure distance education course of low budget type in mathematics for adults. How do the factors interplay in this case? What pedagogical functions should probably be given extra emphasis? What means can we/can we not use?

For the more systematic-minded course designer/planner/-editor some form of schedule can conceivably prove useful. The schedule should include factors which have been taken into consideration and show possible combinations. It is advisable to construct such a schedule yourself. (It is unlikely that you would have any use of a ready-made standardized schedule of a type we could show here - the best thing is to devise one to suit your own needs.)

2 List of ideas

We have now arrived at the list of ideas. This is an adaptation of the modified version of Gagné's instructional functions used during a series of seminars for Hermods editorial staff in the spring term of 1973.

N.B. The list makes no claim to be either complete or as clear as crystal. Use it in the way that suits you best. All being well, it may *assist you to hatch your own ideas* for your own project after you have considered the factors we have now dealt with.

The main headings (functions) on the list of ideas are (with Gagné's partially corresponding functions in brackets):

1 Arouse attention and motivate ('Gaining and controlling attention')

2 Present objectives of the instruction ('Informing the

learner of expected outcomes')

3 Link up with previous knowledge and interests etc. ('Stimulating recall of relevant prerequisite capabilities')

4 Present the material to be learned ('Presenting the stimuli inherent to the learning task')

5 Guide and structure ('Offering guidance for learning')

6 Activate (without correspondence in Gagné's model)

7 Provide feedback ('Providing feedback')

8 Promote transfer ('Making provisions for transferability')

9 Facilitate retention ('Insuring retention')

If you are already acquainted with Gagné's instructional model you may miss one function, viz. *'Appraising performance'*. In distance education this function is normally performed by the correspondence tutor/instructor, not by the instructional material. Since the following list of ideas is concerned with the design of instructional material in correspondence courses, the function of appraising performance is omitted here.

2.1 Function 1: Arouse attention and motivate

Sub-dividing the proposals into those calculated to arouse attention and those calculated to stimulate motivation has been attempted but does not seem to work very well, since in many cases it is difficult to distinguish between these aims. For this reason we shall try another form of sub-division: structural and functional factors. (The *structural* measures are of an 'external' nature, making use of colour, designs and other factors in the field of perception. The *functional* factors are directed rather to inner aspects of the personality - to needs, experience, attitudes, etc.)

It may be the case that the structural factors are mainly biased towards arousing attention, whereas the functional factors lean more towards the side of motivation.

2.1.1 Measures with regard to structural factors

1 Cover: striking and at the same time attractive

2 Format: attractive, possibly unusual. (For reasons of economy - wastage of paper, packaging, postage - a standard size is normally to be recommended.)

3 Handy material

4 Layout: carefully planned, attractive

5 Colours: striking and/or attractive

6 Typography: attractive, easy to read

7 Typography: arousing interest by means of contrasting effects (e.g. use of capitals, italics, panels, headings in heavy print)

8 Illustrations: diagrams, drawings, photographs - aesthetically composed and/or striking *(but* as far as possible instructive, explanatory, concretizing: not *only* inserted for the purpose of arousing attention/-stimulating motivation)

9 AV accessories:

9a Diafilm strips with small viewers (conceivable for most types of courses, particularly suitable for pure distance education: available also in - more expensive - three-dimensional form)

9b Recording tape (conceivable not only for language courses but, e.g., in combination with diafilm strips or illustrated booklets, in most subjects)

9c Diapositive series, TV cassettes, films, overhead material etc. (at present conceivable only for high budget courses of combined type)

10 Smells (really creative!)

11 Presents (really creative!)

2.1.2 Measures with regard to both structural and functional factors.

12 Design the course by making use of advertising methods (thus e.g. in the same style as an advertising brochure: layout, language etc.)

13 Variety: vary both appearance and manner of presentation, method of working, etc. (valuable above all for young students - difficult to achieve for low budget courses)

14 Surprises: try to make it somewhat exciting to read a distance education course

15 Panels for facts

2.1.3 Measures with regard to functional factors

16 Motivating presentation of objectives: e.g. what the student can conceivably achieve and derive pleasure from in life after he/she has passed the course

17 Appeal to the student's needs, e.g. (partly dependent on target group) curiosity, aesthetic needs, need to manage better in contact with other people, to succeed, to achieve security, to take care of children, to gain knowledge for its own sake, to attain intellectual enlightenment, to realise himself/herself

18 Paint a stimulating background to the subject to be taught: link up with current developments

19 Time standards, timetable: state a mean value for the length of time required for the course and outline a couple of study timetables

20 Division of the material into suitable portions (e.g. suitable for dealing with during a single evening devoted to study)

21 Inform the student regularly about the state of his progress towards the objective (e.g. by showing how far he has progressed in a hierarchy of objectives or more informally by giving him revision assignments and then pointing out in this context that he has now dealt with that part of the course and that only so much remains to be done)

22 Make the presentation concrete in character with interesting examples which stimulate the imagination

23 Cultivate an encouraging and personal style. (Avoid officialese, abstract and insipid phrases, long and involved sentences, foreign and incomprehensible words.)

24 Make use of controversial statements, mild provocations. (Begin, e.g., your presentation with a controversial statement or an apparently staggering question.)

25 Appeals, directly addressed *(not* as in a conventional text-book)

26 Encouraging exclamations, praise/consolation

27 Enjoyable exercises and assignments, possibly on the lines of games

28 Assignments classified in order of difficulty

29 The tutor who does the corrections: explain about the part he plays - a living person to keep in touch with (alternatively, in connection with computer-assisted distance education: the studies consultant or equivalent contact person)

30 Measures for rapid feedback (a problem arising with students' solutions; nothing can be done at the time of the construction of the material, but regard must be taken to this problem even at the planning stage of the course). Ensure that as a rule it should not take more than a week *at the most* from the date of submission before the student has received his solutions back with corrections and comments.

31 Measures for effective correction of students' solutions. (Sensible assignments, expert correction, friendly, encouraging, well formulated comments and reasonable marking are probably of the greatest importance for most students ' motivation to study.)

32 Course evaluation forms (not only give us the opportunity of obtaining points of view about the course but also give the student greater possibilities of feeling his involvement)

2.2 *Function 2*

It is important that we help students to understand the purpose of the instruction and studies, to grasp what they ought to be able to achieve after taking one part of the course or the course in its entirety - and also the point of the course in the long run.

Behaviour or product catalogues ('objectives in behavioural terms') may be desirable in psychomotoric subjects, with which we are not so often concerned in distance education, and in proficiency subjects such as mathematics and foreign languages. In aesthetic and purely orientation subjects of humanistic type definitions of objectives of this kind are more open to discussion, since they can result in an undesirable inflexibility of the studies. But since, as a rule, we must award marks even in subjects of this type, we must also in some way inform the students of the requirements they have to meet. Most subjects that are taught, e.g. commercial and technical subjects, lie somewhere between these two extreme types.

Here are some ideas as to how to present objectives in a distance education course:

1 Panels containing objectives, placed in various possible positions:

a at the beginning of every section of the course or
b a the end of every section of the course or
c in the text of every section of the course

2 Differently defined objectives:

Present, e.g., (A) the objectives defined in the syllabus (if any) at the beginning of the course, (B) a more popularly defined variant:
the principal objectives of the course, and (C) the objectives of every chapter or section of the course.

3 Simply formulated definitions of objectives at the beginning and more specialized definitions at the end:

At *the beginning* of a section we can define objectives in more general terms calculated to *arouse interest* (cf. Function 1!). The form may be a leisurely written summary (similar to that of preambles in the daily papers) or a presentation of a problem, its solution exemplifying the most important subordinate objective, or an attempt quite simply to define 'the demands of life' (What is the point of this section?), or an invitation to the student to 'guess' the objectives (on the basis of certain given conditions) - with the right answer. The most important thing here is thus to direct the students the way that they should go - and at the same time give them the necessary motivation to keep them moving in the right direction.

A more detailed definition of subordinate objectives can be given at *the end* of the study unit or section. With the aid of this definition the students, once they have become familiar with the terminology and other matter, should be able to check whether they have mastered the necessary knowledge and skills included in the objective of the study unit/section.

4 Students' assignments for submission as exemplifications of subordinate objectives:

If students' assignments are effectively drawn up and cover all essential objectives (this degree of congruence is most surely attained if they are constructed *before* the rest of the course material), they can very easily be made to serve as subordinate objectives. In that case the students could possibly be instructed to study the assignments at the beginning of their work on a study unit.

5 Self-tests as exemplifications of subordinate objectives:

Self-test questions can often be provided in larger numbers than assignments for submission. If the self-test is in close congruence with the objective and can be furnished with clear answers (even for questions on high taxonomic levels), such series of questions can take the place of definitions of subordinate objectives.

6 Objectives on various taxonomic levels:

Do not state 'knowledge of specifics' objectives *only!* Try to include comprehension and application objectives also, possibly even objectives of types analysis, synthesis and evaluation (Bloom's terminology) - if these should suit the purpose of the course.

7 Diagrams:

Present - in subjects where this suits the purpose - a total hierarchy of objectives at the beginning (including previous knowledge) and afterwards focus on the relevant parts of the hierarchy as the course proceeds. (Cf. Idea 21, Function 1: Always keep the student regularly informed as to how far he has proceeded towards the objective.)

8   Different definitions of objectives for different 'consumers':

The formulations of objectives intended for the students cannot always be identical with those used by the course construction team for their own internal communication and for possible marketing to authorities, clients, etc. The students' version must be written in a manner attractive to the students and given as concrete and clear a formulation as possible.

9   Examples:

Objectives can be concretized with the aid of examples of test question type.

10   Illustrations:

Sometimes an objective can be concretized with the aid of an illustration.

11   Situations in practical life:

What the student can conceivably achieve and derive pleasure from in life after he/she has passed the course/section of course. (Cf. Function 1, Idea 16: Motivating presentation of objectives.) Possibly not only the carrot but a touch of the stick: if the student does not learn this, things may not turn out well for him/her (= the demands of life point the moral).

12   Check lists for attainment of the objective

a possibly modelled on airline pilots' check lists
b possibly in the form of questionnaires linked to assignments for submission, in which the student himself states whether he considers he has attained the objective of the study unit.

13   Variation:

Do not use *exactly* the same form for definitions of objectives in all courses or even for the same course. AVOID MONOTONY! Variety is a principle of teaching which is often neglected. Students must, it is true, feel the security associated with a relatively stable form. But within that framework we are free to vary, to give scope to the imagination. E.g. we can - when using panels - vary their size, the length of formulations of objectives, the type of definitions and the choice of words.

2.3 *Function 3: Link up with previous knowledge, interests etc.*

'If I had to reduce all of educational psychology to just one principle, I would say this: The most important single factor influencing learning is what the learner already knows. Ascertain this and teach him accordingly'. (Ausubel[2])

By previous knowledge here we do not mean only knowledge, skills, experience, habits, etc., possessed (or not possessed) by the student at the beginning of the course, but also the knowledge etc. required at the beginning of every new study unit or new chapter and which should have been learned in part during previous sections of the course.

The greatest difficulty in distance education is, however, to forge a link with the student's knowledge at the start of the course, since - as authors and editors - we often know so little about it, certainly very little indeed as to the way previous knowledge can vary between individual students. And even if we did, what could we do about it?

In spite of these difficulties, here are some suggestions:

1 Previous knowledge test or placing test - distinct from the course material, but constructed in such a way that students achieving a certain minimum result may be assumed to have a certain level of previous knowledge in common, making it possible for them to participate in the course.

2 Diagnostic test at the beginning of the course or before the start of every study unit containing questions on necessary previous knowledge. Students failing to give satisfactory answers to one or more assignments must in such a case receive extra instruction within the framework of the course. The test/tests can be given either as self-tests or assignments for submission. In the latter case the tutor (or computer) responsible for correction will also be responsible for giving the extra instruction.

Before the commencement of a new study unit it could be possible to make use of the preceding study unit's 'Self-test as exemplification of subordinate objectives' (Function 2, Idea 5) - provided that the preceding study unit contains all the knowledge necessary for studying the new unit. (The same argument can be applied to 'Students' assignments for submission as exemplifications of subordinate objectives', Function 2, Idea 4.)

3 Make a 'gentle' start - with revision of knowledge necessary or suitable to bring up if the fresh material is to be learned in a purposeful manner. This

applies at the beginning of a course and at the beginning of a new study unit and often also of a new chapter.

4 Link up with experience and interests:
a with everyday matters and situations
b with nature, natural phenomena
c with familiar material from mass media, etc.
d with the interests and experience of the group of students (if it is a case of a special group of students who may be assumed to have special interests and experience)
e with tales, games, common experiences in childhood
f with proverbs and sayings
g with experiences as adult students

5 Forge the link with the aid of phrases such as 'You may have wondered about ....'

6 Individualize with the aid of
a assignments arranged in order of difficulty
b assignments individualized in respect of interests

7 Make helpful suggestions on the subject of study technique: students often have very different experience of study. Refer, therefore, to booklets issued to all students and give additional helpful advice and suggestions, suitable for the specific subject and course, on how to acquire knowledge and proficiency.

2.4 Function 4: Present the material to be learned

Here we are concerned with the actual serving of facts, principles, etc., to some extent isolated from other instructional functions. In courses based on text-books the text book should in principle fulfil this function and the commentary (study notes, in the USA often called study guide) be concentrated on other pedagogical functions. The following short list of ideas thus refers to 'independent' distance education courses (or the basis text-book in a course with commentary).

1 Intellectual clarity
Logic, orderliness, continuity, consistency in presentation - a necessary (but not by any means all-sufficient) precondition for good results.

2 Linguistic simplicity and clarity
A simple and easily flowing, exact but relaxed style without unnecessary complications, adapted to the students' probable vocabulary and reading habits, helps the students more than we often suppose.

3 Write in a personal style, encouragingly, by all means with a touch of humour! (Cf. Function 1, Idea 23) *How* personal, exciting and amusing may our presentation be? As on other counts, we must pay regard to what we know or may assume about the student group's previous knowledge, previous experience, attitudes, and object of their studies. For example it is a reasonable assumption that an exaggeratedly simple, extremely varied and comic presentation would counteract its intention if addressed to a highly motivated and relatively highly educated group of adult students.

4 Concretize, illustrate with the aid of
a interesting, stimulating - and of course at the same time elucidatory - examples. (Cf. Function 1, Idea 22)
b pictures of various kinds: diagrams, drawings, photographs - instructive, explanatory, concrete in tendency. Note that a picture does not always by any means say more than a thousand words! Moreover, most pictures have to be explained before they can be understood. (Cf. Function 1, Idea 8)

5 Lexivision: Pictures and words fused into an integrated unit. As a rule a complete lexivision system is very expensive. Nevertheless lexivision may be the star we should aim at to reach the tree-tops.

6 Variable media (cf. Function 1, Idea 9a, b, c). Special attention should be paid to:
a *Wholly taped* courses (e.g. for car drivers, people with defective sight)
b Courses in which *the major part* of the information is presented on *magnetic tape*, supplemented by a thin booklet containing pictures, summaries and assignments. For courses with small editions this may prove a cheaper alternative than presenting all the material in written form. In other cases the combination of magnetic tape + picture text booklet may offer decided instructional advantages.

2.5 *Function 5: Guide and structure*

One of the most important duties of a teacher is to explain, elucidate, make comprehensible - without putting too much strain on the truth. This applies as much to the distance education teacher embodied in the course material as it does to an oral teacher.

The problem for the designer of a distance education course in this respect is much the same as that implicit in Function 3, 'Link up with previous knowledge...':How can we cater for individual students' individual needs for guidance and help with the material? A large number of elucidatory measures may be necessary to help all or at least most students.

In this respect a course with commentary can have certain advantages over an 'independent' distance education course. In a course of the latter type it can be difficult to provide a large number of explanations etc. in the body of the text if the general survey and context are not to suffer as a result. In a course with commentary, on the other hand, the majority of the explanations etc. can be left to the study notes, while the basic text is retained in a 'purer' and more surveyable form.

Some suggestions:

1 Typographical and logical arrangement for constructive purposes
   - e.g.

   Margin headlines, section headlines

   Division into paragraphs

   Italics/<u>underlining</u>

   CAPITALS

   Panels/frames, dotted screens

   Varying sizes of type for sections of varying importance

   Indention of entire paragraphs (e.g case studies, lengthy quotations*)*

   Figures or letters (1,2,3 etc.; a, b, c etc.)

   Compressed presentation in the form of lists of items.

   Note that such arrangements must be logically worked out. (Even if the structuring aim is not the most important in a given case, the main object being to arouse attention, the logical factor must at the same time be observed.)

2 Introductions of various kinds:
   a Panels describing the objectives can serve for guidance
   b Links with the students' experience of different kinds (cf. Function 3, Ideas 3-6)
   c Indication of the arrangement in the following section
   d *'Advance organizers'*: short, introductory texts facilitating the student's structuring of the material. According to Ausubel, this takes place, among other things, by bringing to the fore necessary previous knowledge in the form of *overriding principles*, to which the fresh material can be made subject as special cases. But it can also take place by means of

285

pointing out *similarities and contrasts* between material previously mastered and the fresh material - thereby reviewing desirable previous knowledge and relating it in a purposeful way to the fresh material.

3 Exercises can function as a kind of organizer
In exercises students can be encouraged to assist with the structuring of the material themselves, e.g. by identifying differences or similarities between new material and something of importance presented earlier, or by themselves drawing conclusions from material hitherto received. Adequate explanations must, of course, accompany the solutions to the exercises.

4 Verbal explanations in the body of the text (or in the study notes) - including definitions and other verbal explanations and also concrete examples - are perhaps the most common and important forms of guidance. Do not be grudging with explanations, in as much as they are important and really can be considered helpful to the students - but at the same time see to it that the overall view of the subject is not lost!

5 Dealing with possible questions by students: If one can foresee that some students are going to have problems with a certain section, one should naturally consider amending it - simplify, elucidate, exemplify. But if this course is impossible (e.g. if the section is included in the basic text and this has already been printed), it is still possible in the notes either to elucidate in the usual manner *or* introduce an explanation in this way, for example: 'You may possibly have been wondering about...'
  Note: Do not waste too much space on inessentials! Explain in detail only that which is really important according to the (implicit or written) course objectives.

6 Skeleton drawings and other explanatory illustrations can sometimes provide the key to an entire section of text.

7 Summaries of various kinds
a Entirely ready-to-serve or
b Summaries in the form of answers to a (hard structured) self-test or
c Summaries which the students are required to draw up entirely by themselves - some form of key being provided, however.

2.6 Function 6: Activate

Learning is always something that happens within the student himself. Strictly speaking, teaching does not mean that one person teaches something to another person, but that the person who teaches helps the student to learn something himself. A pre-condition for the student learning something is that he - in one way or another - is active.

In distance education material we can attempt to activate the students, e.g. as follows:

1 Exercises - many and of many different kinds, e.g. in the form of

    conclusions to be drawn (cf. Function 5, Idea 3)

    diagrams to be drawn

    games and crosswords

Possibly the questions can sometimes be recorded on tape or a record (or transferred to another medium) e.g. if we wish to present a case history with 'local colour' and wish to ask questions in connection with this.

2 Assignments for submission - also varied wherever possible

3 Tests covering the entire course (in sealed envelope)

4 Practical applications (or at least suggestions as to how knowledge can be applied practically as soon as possible)

5 References to helpful supplementary material, e.g.

    information concerning special literature of current interest (also journals on the subject)

    comparisons with fiction, films, etc.

    references to examinations set by central authorities, etc., if such exist

    suggestions for suitable study visits

6 Possibly make the students themselves construct part of their instructional material, e.g.,

    certain figures

    parts of the panels describing the objectives

    summaries

7 Express positive criticism (e.g. in model answers to exercises or self-tests):
As a rule encouragement strengthens self-confidence and liberates constructive powers within the individual

8 Time standards: Indicate a mean value for the time

required for the course and/or every study unit, so that the student can coordinate his resources in accordance with this. (Cf. Function 1, Idea 19.)

9 Encourage the students to take a break after subsections of suitable length (in order to be able to work all the harder afterwards).

2.7 Function 7: Provide feedback

Activity - training, exercises - do not take us very far unless we receive some form of feedback, that is to say are informed as to how we are progressing, whether we are doing the right thing or the wrong thing.

In particular the individual distance education student - who cannot make comparisons with his fellow students or ask a teacher or tutor through direct contact - must be given a great deal of help as regards feedback. Naturally, in this respect the assignments for submission and the tutor (alternatively the computer) responsible for correction play a vital part. But in addition to that the students must receive help as regards feedback in the study material itself. Here are some suggestions:

1 Answers or explanatory solutions to *all* exercises, self-test questions, etc. (Only for participants in combined education courses - distance education + oral instruction - can exceptions to this rule be permitted. Cf. Idea 3 below, however!)

2 Step-by-step construction: exercise - feedback - exercise - feedback

3 Feedback in the text following an exercise or question. The ensuing text can sometimes be written so as to provide answers to questions or show the student that he is on the right path.

4 Summaries

In addition the tutor responsible for correction should be provided with

5 Directions for model solutions, preproduced comments, etc.

2.8 Function 8: Promote transfer

Positive transfer arises when new learning is facilitated by something one has learned previously. *Negative* transfer takes place when new learning is made more difficult in consequence of something previously learned.

As a rule we wish to use our knowledge in other situations than just that in which it was acquired. This means in fact that we aspire to positive transfer.

1 *Vary* examples to illustrate a concept/a principle

2 Point out parallels (e.g. in other subjects)

3 Point out dissimilarities (in order to avoid *negative* transfer in languages, for example)

4 Refer forwards and backwards in the material

5 Suggest how knowledge can be practically applied (cf. Function 6, Idea 4)

6 Vary application exercises, e.g. of a principle

7 Use overlapping application assignments requiring knowledge and/or skills from different parts of the course (e.g. of the type construction analysis, fault analysis)

2.9 Function 9: Facilitate retention

Unless special steps are taken, we very soon lose part - in some cases most - of what we have recently learned. Here are some possible measures to facilitate the retention of knowledge on a long term basis:

1 Try to make the students *understand* the material (cf. Functions 3, 4, 5) - what has been learned then 'sticks' better in the memory.

2 Encourage *revisions* and a sensible study technique (e.g. with the aid of a simple argument on the retention and forgetfulness graph).

3 Provide immanent ('built-in') revisions in the material itself, e.g. by making the students in later sections bring up what they have learned previously and apply the knowledge.

4 Summaries

5 Self-test questions, exercises, assignments for submission

6 Special sections dealing with the basic course material from fresh angles

7 Suggestions as to how knowledge can be practically applied - 'not for the school, but for Life'. (Cf. Function 6, Idea 4, and Function 8, Idea 5.)

Notes

1 Gagné, R.M. The Conditions of Learning, 2nd edition. London: Holt, Rinehart & Winston, 1970, p. 304. - A more thorough-going analysis of distance education didactics in terms of a revised version of Gagné's model (The Conditions of Learning, 3rd edition. N.Y.: Holt, Rinehart & Winston 1977) is provided in Bååth, J.A., Correspondence Education in the Light of a Number of Contemporary Teaching Models. Malmö: Liber Hermods 1979, pp.94-108

2 Ausubel, D.P. Educational Psychology. A Cognitive View. N.Y.: Holt, Richart & Winston 1968.

THE STUDENT'S FREEDOM OF CHOICE WITHIN THE DIDACTICAL STRUCTURE OF A CORRESPONDENCE COURSE

Erling Ljoså and Karl Erik Sandvold

1 Background

In Norway two reform bills which revive the question of the freedom of choice for the student have recently been passed. The first of these concerns a new framing of the general secondary school for the age group 16-19. The curriculum that has been worked out for this school level sets up:

1   a common core of compulsory study material that all students are required to work on,
2   certain frames for the optional study material from which the class or the individual student can choose. This choice can be made according to special interests, qualifications or needs or according to special conditions in the local milieu of the school.

The other reform comprises a new Adult Education Act which decides that an organization or institution, in order to fulfill the conditions for public support, must be

> required to have an educational practice which secures the influence of the course participants, both as regards the form and the contents of the course.

These are only two examples of the introduction of a new principle in the theory of education - both in the ordinary school system and in adult education. The principle means that the student himself/herself to a larger degree than earlier takes over the control of the learning process, such as to become the actual subject of the learning process. The learning will then happen in an interchange between the student and the tutor/school. And this is not a specifically Norwegian development. Document upon document from national and international institutions and organizations show that this is a common thought. There is good reason, then, to take this principle seriously, and discuss to what extent it ought to influence the didactical structure of the correspondence courses we develop. What freedom of choice can we, and should we, give the correspondence students? And how will the freedom of choice influence the course design and the roles of the students, the tutors, and the school's administration? These are some of the questions about which we want to start a discussion.

The principle is not, however, completely new to correspondence education. Correspondence education is generally assumed to demand a certain autonomy on the part of the student, and various people have discussed what this autonomy can and should involve. Michael G. Moore contributed to this discussion in a paper to the ICCE Conference in 1972, "Learning autonomy: The Second Dimension of Independent learning" [1]. Börje Holmberg took up the subject in the ICCE Newsletter in 1975 [2]. He describes an autonomous student like this, based on Moore's paper:

> An autonomous student decides on his/her own goals and objectives, acquires the information he/she wants, collects ideas, practises skills while working to solve problems and to obtain his/her objectives; further he/she judges if and to what extent the study matter and what has been learnt is relevant.

This differs more or less significantly from the types of study usually practised in distance education, says Holmberg, and he asks how this ideal can be realized:

> But the problem how this is to be done remains. Within what frames in a specific field of study can a student select his/her own objectives, study methods and learning media? Can a system that provides a battery of voluntary and alternative tasks for submission, among which the student makes his/her choice on the basis of an individual definition of objectives, constitute one step on the way? What apparatus for counselling and providing background data for the student's decisions will be required?

R.M. Delling sides completely with the students and requires the school to be a "helping organization":

> The function of the "helping organization" is to take over, upon the wish of the learner, everything he cannot (yet) do for himself, with the tendency that the learner eventually becomes autonomous. Finally, the only function left for the helping organization is that of an information and documentation center (as, for example, a good library). The helping organization should not at any time pursue aims of its own making... [3].

John A. Bååth has presented a fuller discussion on various views on correspondence education and autonomous learning in a recently published research report [4].

2 The student's possibilities of choice today

We shall first give a short summary of the possibilities of

choice that correspondence students traditionally have had, based on the practice at NKS - Norsk Korrespondanseskole.

- The students can choose at what point in life they want to start the course, and also at what time of the year they wish to start.

- Once having decided to start a course, they normally have a choice between two or more correspondence schools.

- The students will often have the possibility to decide on which level they want to start.

- The students can choose their own study plan. They can also choose when and where to study.

- In the larger courses containing different interchangeable components, the students can usually choose which component they want to start with.

- The students can sometimes choose the mode of study they want to participate in. Some will prefer to work on their own, others may choose to work together with other students in groups. Others again may choose to participate in regular classroom teaching arranged as a support to correspondence teaching in some courses. In a few cases multi-media courses are offered.

The mode of study chosen by the student will necessarily influence the possibilities of choice mentioned above. However, this kind of choice is of little further interest in the following discussion, and we shall therefore, in the following, think about the student as working on his/her own with his/her correspondence course(s).

The choices we have mentioned are in a way outside the course material. In a traditional correspondence course the course material itself is supposed to be studied by all the students. The courses are rarely organized in such a way that the students are encouraged and practised in making personal choices based on e.g. their own qualifications, interests, or their own local milieu. Very few students are able, themselves, to emphasize certain parts, and work less seriously with - or completely skip - other parts of the study material. In practice, this means that few students make personal choices within the course material. Most of them accept that the course developer has chosen *for* them, and go through the material without letting their own background consciously influence their work.

A student's work with such a traditional course can be schematically illustrated as in figure 1 (see following page). The core material and the correspondence tutor are placed respectively on two "lines" in the diagram. The student's way through the course is marked with a thick line. The symbol ━O━ signifies submission of assignment to the

293

Figure 1

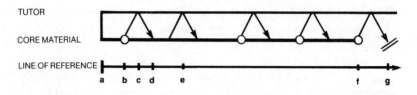

correspondence school. The tutor contact is marked with ⟨symbol⟩ and the symbol ⟨symbol⟩ all the way to the right in the figure signifies the end of the course. Referring to the points marked with letters at the bottom line of the figure, we can explain the figure like this:

a   The student starts working with the course.

b   The student submits his/her first assignment.

c   The tutor comments and evaluates the assignment.

d   The student gets his/her assignment back.

e   The student asks a question about the course material which is answered by the tutor.

f   The student submits the last assignment of the course.

g   The student gets his/her last assignment back together with a certificate for having completed the course.

Looking at the diagram of a traditional correspondence course we notice that the student always works within the frames of the core material where there are few options. We also notice that the tutor contact to a large extent is connected with the submissions. (Further, we notice the "empty space" from f to g. Should the correspondence schools give their students something to fill in this empty space?)

3 Approach

The preceding section summarized the choices a student has in connection with a traditional correspondence course. The following sections will look into the possibilities the students may have:

-    to choose material on different levels

-    to choose material in accordance with personal interests.

These two kinds of choice are not, of course, totally separate, but we shall, nevertheless, consider them separately. It may seem natural to offer the students a course material which makes such choices possible. In addition,

294

we shall consider two other types of choice where the student must look for material outside the course material. This concerns the student's possibility to

- select material from supplementary reading etc.

- find material and working projects in her/his local milieu.

These two kinds of choice are no more separate from each other than the two previous ones. They also cover partly the same field as the two previous ones.

The rest of the paper will describe these types of choices more fully, and we will mainly emphasize the opportunity for the student's personal choice. In particular, we shall discuss the possibilities for organizing the courses in such a way that the student is able to make these choices.

4 Four main types of choice

We can guide the student in his/her choice in several ways within the course material. It may be done by suggesting alternatives of objective, study method and aspects of the material. Further, we can inform the students about the consequences of each alternative. The symbol ▬□▬ on the line for the core material (see figure 1) signifies that such information has been given before a specific choice is made. The choice made by the student based on this preparation, is called a *structured* choice. Without such preparation, it is called an *unstructured* choice.

Many of the choices made in everyday life are more or less unstructured. One of the objectives for a correspondence course could be to prepare the students for these everyday choices. Even though it would be desirable in many cases to make the choices structured, the correspondence course should also offer unstructured choices. In the case of an unstructured choice, we think that the student must be prepared for it through a gradual reduction of the structuring of the previous choices.

In many cases the course material will indicate at what point in the course the student is to make a choice. This will be marked in our diagram with the symbol ▬■.We say that the choice is *placed*. If the point of choice is not indicated in the course, we say that the choice is *unplaced*. This is marked with the symbol ▬■.

In order to illustrate the four main types of choice, we shall take a passage from the syllabus in Norwegian as our starting point, where it says:

The students are to read a Norwegian translation of a non-Nordic work of fiction.

A possible Norwegian course would then have several possibilities. Example:

> We can choose to give the student background material for a selection of works of fiction by non-Nordic writers. Further, we can refer to reference books or survey articles in case the student doesn't catch any interest for any of the works of fiction suggested in the course material. In addition to this guidance, we can suggest when, during the course, the student should study this work.

If the course is organized as in this example, the student is guided in his/her choice, and he/she is also instructed *when* such a choice is advisable to make. The choice is structured and placed, and we can illustrate it as in figure 2:

 STRUCTURED AND PLACED CHOICE

Figure 2

Example:

> We can choose to give guidance in the same way as in the previous example only without suggesting when during the course the work of fiction ought to be read.

Organized like this, the choice becomes structured, but unplaced. We illustrate this in figure 3:

 STRUCTURED AND UNPLACED CHOICE

Figure 3

Example:

> There is also a possibility that the course material gives no particular guidance how to choose a work of fiction, but the choice is nevertheless placed at a certain point in the course.

In this case the choice becomes unstructured, but placed, see figure 4:

 UNSTRUCTURED AND PLACED CHOICE

Figure 4

296

Example:

> Finally, we must consider perhaps the most common possib-
> ility today. The students get the reading list, and have
> to choose both the work of fiction and the point of time
> for reading it without any further guidance in the course
> material.

This is an unstructured and unplaced choice as we have
illustrated in figure 5:

UNSTRUCTURED AND UNPLACED CHOICE

Figure 5

5 Organized and unorganized material

Any subject material that is presented as learning material,
is *organized* by the author in a special way so as to ease
the learning. In a correspondence course this organization
is often carried further than what we find in a regular text
book. Correspondence school people sometimes talk about a
"built-in-teacher", and what they mean is that the learning
material is not only presented with a logically clear organization, but also that the student's way through the course is
pointed out and all necessary guidance given on his/her way
through the course.

   In contrast to this we may think of a material which is
not specifically organized with a view to learning. Such
material can also be used by a student in a learning
process. In many cases this kind of material may be gathered
for use in a teaching situation, but still be left in its
original form. When it is not specially organized with a
view to learning, we will call it *unorganized* material. (In
some cases we should perhaps say "less organized", because
in reality there is a question of degrees of organization).
Example:

> An official report, a collection of factual prose arti-
> cles, a statistical yearbook, material from a local trade
> or business.

We will symbolize these two kinds of material in the following way (figure 6):

ORGANIZED MATERIAL

UNORGANIZED MATERIAL

Figure 6

In a correspondence course it may be desirable to let the students work with unorganized units of material within a course which in the main is organized. It may also be that the student, on his/her own initiative, wishes to include such unorganized material in his/her work with the course.

In this section we talk about unorganized material without any connection with choices, to point out some general aspects of the handling of such material. The reason why we have included it, is because some of the choices we are going to discuss later, are precisely choice of unorganized material.

Working with unorganized material demands more of the student if he/she is to profit from it. If the correspondence school plans the use of unorganized units of material, it is important to give the student sufficient guidance, of a general kind as well as specific for the various units. The student may nevertheless wish to contact the tutor in order to get help in his/her work with the unorganized material. Also, it is an advantage if the student gets a gradual training in his/her work with this kind of material. Example:

> If one wants a student in a mother tongue course to work independently with a selection of texts (factual prose), one should start with a short text, and give a reasonably thorough guidance. Later, one can increase the length and difficulty of the texts and reduce the guidance. This is illustrated in figure 7:

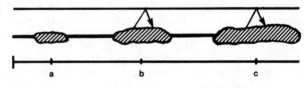

Figure 7

a The guidance is good and the material easy, so the student needs no tutor contact.

b,c The student contacts the tutor about problems arising from the work with the unorganized material.

The time lag in connection with tutor contact is a special problem in such cases, and one should therefore find special "express-routines" for this kind of student communications. The telephone is one possibility, and in any case the communications should go directly from student to tutor and back, not through the school for registration as is the case with ordinary submissions.

6 Choice of material and exercises within the course material

In previous discussions about the students' possibilities
for choice within the course material, the main emphasis has
often been put on the way the tutor, through exercises and
assignments of various kinds, can *direct* the student through
the route which "suits him/her best". The student's own
participation in the choice was in the background. This will
be changed with the new thoughts which place the students in
the centre of the learning process. Instead of letting the
course material choose for him/her, the student himself/her-
self will be the active part, taking the initiative in the
choices that have to be made. Through a long series of
personal, conscious choices the student will make his/her
own course from the basis material that the correspondence
course offers.

We shall particularly discuss choice of level and choice
based on special interest.

6.1 *Choice of level*

Students enrolling for a course have different previous
knowledge and qualifications in the subject. Also, their
objectives for choosing a course are different. Some take
the course for the sake of general orientation, others
prepare for an exam. Besides, there is a differene in how
the students intend to use the knowledge they get through
the course. All this leads many students to demand possibilities for a personal choice of level. A simple way of
choice of level is letting the student choose between assignments that are grouped according to level. Example:

> As an assignment in a course in the history of philosophy,
> the students can choose between:

a giving a summary of the basic thoughts of three given
   philosophers .

b comparing the three philosophers, pointing out similarities and differences.

c sorting three given texts unknown to the students,
   under the three respective philosophers.

In order that the choice does not lead to unforeseen consequences for the students later in the course, it must be
structured. In this case it is perhaps natural to place the
structuring in direct contact with the assignments for submission. The choice is structured and placed, see **Figure 8** below:

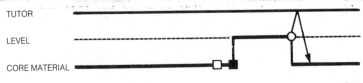

There is also a possibility to place the structuring of this choice earlier in the course. In this way the student gets a possibility to go through the material about three philosophers with the specific view-point which his/her choice of assignment demands. In such a case it is hardly necessary to ask the student to choose immediately, but let him/her choose at some point between the guidance and the submission of the assignment, see figure 9:

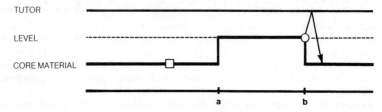

Figure 9

Here the choice is unplaced. We have moved the student's work between a and b to the level line in order to indicate that he/she now reads the core material with his/her own choice of level constantly in mind.

Another possibility for choice of level is when the course material gives a definite/concrete offer about different types of material. Example:

At a certain point in a natural science course the student can choose between:

a   doing exercises that give extra practice.

b   going through material that gives deeper knowledge of the subject.

c   going through simple material which supports the core material.

This case as well needs structuring. Since possibilities for such a choice of material are placed at specific points in the course, the choice is placed, see figure 10:

```
TUTOR         ━━━━━━━━━━━━━━━━━━━━━━━━━━━━━━━━━━

LEVEL         ------------------┏━━━━━━━━━━┓-------------

CORE MATERIAL ━━━━━━━━━━━□━■━━━━━━━━━━━━━┛━━━━━━
```

Figure 10

In such cases the students may often wish to ask the tutor for advice. Since it takes time before the student receives the answer from the tutor, one must consider whether the structuring should be placed slightly earlier in the course material, see figure 11:

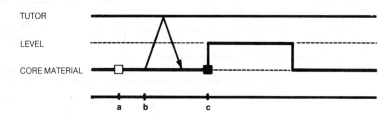

Figure 11

We see here that the student has enough time between the structuring, (a), and the point of choice, (c). The tutor needs certain information about the student in order to guide him/her in such choices. When we plan such structural, placed choices with the possibility for tutor contact, the structuring must also inform the student what sort of background information must accompany the communication to the tutor.

Within all types of choice of level the tutor will have a central position as study guide and source of information. There will also be cases where the tutor personally takes the initiative to suggest a choice of level for his/her student. But since we are concentrating on the student's personal choice, we shall not discuss any further the choice of level which is directed by the tutor.

6.2 Choice based on interest

With the type of curriculum mentioned in the introduction, comprising both compulsory core material and optional material, the student's choice will often be made based on personal interests. A correspondence course which aims at covering the intentions of such a curriculum, must offer certain options, that is, contain certain alternative units.

In some subjects it will be natural to choose to read one's optional material after having gone through all the compulsory core material, simply because all the optional units make use of knowledge acquired from the core material. Example:

A mathematics course contains a core material of algebra and functions. Having worked through this, the student can choose two of the following subjects: formulae, trigonometry, vectors, derivation, statistics.

The choice in this case is placed (at the end of the course) and it must also be more or less structured, see figure 12:

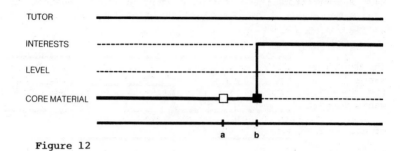

Figure 12

The structuring, (a), may be placed slightly before the point of choice itself, (b). If the choice is made purely based on interest, there will hardly be any need for tutor contact. It is quite another matter, however, if the choice has consequences for what possibilities the student will have in his/her studies, for example if certain subjects are prerequisites for certain other courses on a higher school level.

It is also possible that the optional subjects do not require specific knowledge from the core material, but are more detached. In this case, one may let the student choose the time when he/she wants to read the optional material, figure 13:

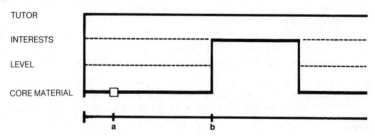

Figure 13

The student, then, may decide himself/herself when he/she wants to leave the core material (b). The guidance ought to be placed early in the course (a).

It is an in-between case when the optional subjects offer material for intensive study of certain units within the core material, so that certain parts of the core material must be read before the student studies the optional material. Example:

In a course about living religions the syllabus consists of:

302

1   a general survey of the geography of religion (core material),

2   an intensive study of one of the religions which is studied in the core material.

In this case the student is free to choose whether he/she wants to read the intensive study material immediately after the respective unit of the core material, or whether he/she wants to wait.

An intensive depth study may also occur with the help of unorganized material. Example:

In the course Living Religions one may use a text anthology and possibly recorded tape material in order to throw light on, and give a deeper understanding of the various religions, figure 14:

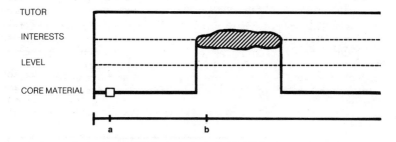

Figure 14

a   General guidance for the choice of intensive study material and the work on the unorganized material.

b   Here the student may get special advice about the intensive study material he/she has chosen, questions to answer in connection with this, etc.

Especially when there already exists suitable unorganized material, the above organization of a course may make it economically possible for the correspondence schools to increase the possibilities of choice for the student, beyond what the correspondence schools would otherwise find justifiable.

One of the simplest forms of choice based on interest is letting the students choose between *different assignments for submission* from the core material. This is already found in several correspondence courses, and can be illustrated as in figure 15: (see following page).

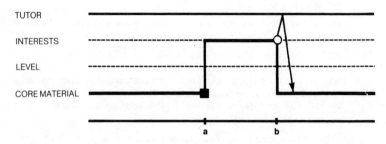

Figure 15

a   The student chooses an assignment.

b   The assignment is submitted.

The student may perhaps attain a more conscious attitude for his/her choice if we make the choice of assignments more structured, i.e., try to adjust the various assignments to different ways of working with the material, different objectives, different interests, etc. See figure 16 (Compare also with Holmberg, quoted in the introduction to this paper):

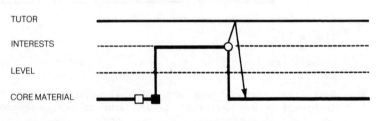

Figure 16

Example:

A course for leaders of study groups may contain optional assignments which offer the opportunity to take up problems connected with the respective subjects that the group leaders will be working with (languages, social sciences, etc.) or with the kind of students that the leaders are likely to get (participants from a trade, from a political organization or from a more heterogeneous group).

Maybe the student ought to inform the tutor about the reasons for his/her choice, in order that the tutor can consider these in his/her evaluation and guidance.

Finally we must also consider the possibility that the student himself/herself formulates his/her assignments,

304

giving the reasons for the choice. The tutor's task then, will be to give comments and to guide the student in accordance with his/her special choice. One condition, perhaps, is that the course is not exam oriented.

7 Choice of material and assignments outside the course material

The principle of making the student the subject of the learning process, leads naturally to a practice of basing the learning on the student's *total situation*. As developers of course material we tend to think of the student solely as a student, so that the student's environment consists of nothing but the course.

For an independent student it is of main concern to place the contents of the course in connection with the rest of his/her environment. Often it is his/her immediate surroundings which make it worthwhile to spend some time on one specific course. And even if "pure" interest is the motivating force, it is a positive experience if the contents of the course are relevant to one's own situation in life.

Also, the student has resources which can contribute considerably to the learning. The student's background should, e.g. not only be considered as a condition for the learning of certain material, a motivating force etc. - but also as the basis and background for various kinds of choices. Besides, the student may have access to types of resources other than those the course itself gives - for example a library, newspapers, radio and television, and local community which he/she lives in and knows (more or less well).

We shall here mainly discuss choice of material and assignments from the student's local milieu and from supplementary material of various types .[5]

7.1 *Choice of supplementary material*

All correspondence courses may be supplemented with material from outside the course material itself. When the student looks for such material, it is often motivated by special interest, by a need for additional support, or by the wish to include his/her local milieu. The students normally find that this material is not organized in advance for their specific needs. In this context we will therefore consider supplementary material as unorganized.

Usually, some sections in the course material have literature references. Example:

> Following each section of a course in child psychology, the course may refer to other specialist literature. It may also refer to novels which describe particularly well, aspects of child psychology discussed in the course.

We also have other possibilities to include various types of supplementary material: magazines, newspapers, and material from radio and television. Example:

> When the students in an English course have a large enough vocabulary, they may be referred to simple British newspapers and periodicals which they may find in libraries or buy themselves. In addition they can be made aware of suitable programmes on British radio.

The students themselves decide at what time during the course they want to use supplementary material. Any choice therefore, is unplaced. Since references of the type mentioned above will always be more or less structured, we get a choice like the one schematically shown in figure 17:

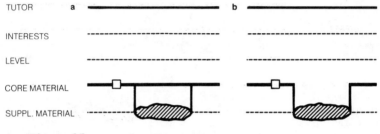

Figure 17

In figure 17a, the student uses the supplementary material parallel to the work with the correspondence course. Figure 17b shows that the student works intensively with the supplementary material first, and then continues with the core material.

TUTOR

INTERESTS

LEVEL

CORE MATERIAL

SUPPL. MATERIAL

Figure 18

Even if the course does not have any references to supplementary material, the student is able to find such material through the local libraries, the teachers at the local schools etc. Example:

306

A student of a history course wishes to study the local history of his/her own community parallel to the course. By applying to libraries and museums, he/she may be referred to books and papers on the history of the community. The choice is schematically illustrated in figure 18.

When the student looks for supplementary reading on his/her own, it is often desirable to ask the tutor for advice. Example:

A student of a mathematics course is interested in reading more about a subject than what is in the course. He/she asks the tutor for suggestions to further reading within the field, see figure 19:

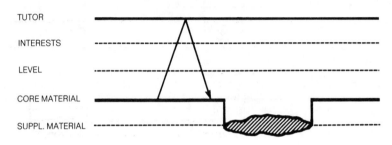

Figure 19

As a final note to this section, we mention that supplementary material may often be other correspondence courses at the same or other correspondence schools.

7.2 Choices from the student's local milieu

The student's local milieu will never be organized for learning, and therefore all material and all assignments chosen from the local milieu will be unorganized. This does not mean, however, that a course developer cannot plan such choices in relative detail. He/she may, for example ask the student to apply the material that one goes through in the course, on situations or circumstances that the student knows. Example:

A method for calculation, or for filing e.g. may be carried out on an example chosen from the student's own place of work.

Another possibility is that the student seeks out and analyses information from the local milieu, and makes all kinds of inquiries. Example:

In a course about environmental protection the student may be asked to study the local environment. The student may undertake similar studies of economic life, religious and cultural life etc. for other social science oriented courses. Such assignments (with or without submission) are illustrated schematically as in figure 20 a or b:

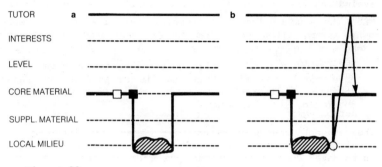

Figure 20

In this figure the choices are structured, but one may imagine unstructured choices of this type.

However, it is in the nature of the case that neither the course developer nor the tutor knows the student's local environment as well as the student does. Therefore it is much easier for the student to say when something from the course can be applied, or when information from the local milieu is likely to be of interest. Here the student's own interests are decisive for what he/she wants to work with. It seems obvious then, that choice of material and assignments from the local milieu should usually be unplaced, and in many cases also unstructured, see figure 21:

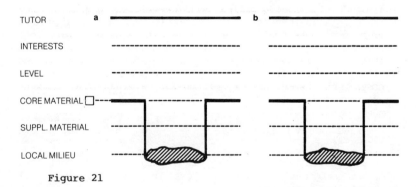

Figure 21

In order to encourage this type of choice, a certain structuring seems desirable, for example as a general introduction to the course with some examples of how the local environment can be of use.

It is the goal of many courses that the students shall be able to perform certain types of practical tasks. In some cases it is possible to carry out such tasks during the work with the course. Carrying out such tasks in practice and evaluating the result of them are excellent ways of learning. Examples:

In a Norwegian course the student can get good practice by writing (real) applications, letters to the editors of newspapers etc. Participants in a language course can go on holiday to the country in question, or find people around them whom they can talk with. In connection with socially oriented courses the student can try to take action against local authorities and organizations.

The student can profitably use his/her knowledge of the local milieu to *evaluate the contents of the course* : Is it up to date? Does it square with the facts? Example:

A course about office work or technical subjects can be evaluated from knowledge of one's place of work or one's trade.

The student can make such evaluations himself/herself, but it can also be useful to discuss them with the tutor.

Larger assignments from the local milieu will lead to needs for tutor contact, perhaps both at the stage of the planning, the carrying out and the evaluation. This may be a reason why it seems advantageous for the student to work simultaneously with such assignments and with the core material of the course, see figure 22:

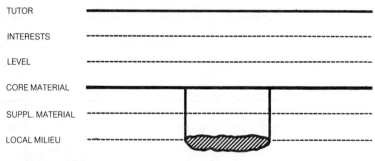

Figure 22

8 Combinations of choices

So far we have discussed each type of choice separately, while actually they occur consecutively and in a series of combinations. To conclude, we wish to give three examples of how a student's way through a course with an extensive freedom of choice, can be described with the symbols we have introduced.

We have chosen three different courses. Within each course there will be innumerable variations for each student, but these three examples are sufficient to illustrate our way of describing the choices.

Example 1: A course about living religions

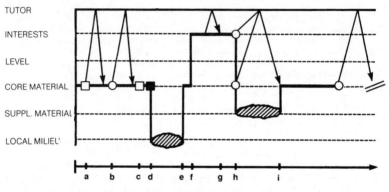

Figure 23

The student

a   gets general guidance about the choice of *one* religion for intensive study. He/she asks the tutor about unclear information in the guidance,

b   submits the first assignment,

c   gets the introduction to an assignment which he/she is to carry out: finds information about a freely chosen denomination or religion in the local milieu,

d   starts working on the assignment at a given time,

e   returns to the core material,

f   chooses to start the study in greater depth of the religion/denomination he/she worked on in d-e, and works with this in an optional intensive study unit of the course,

g   asks the tutor for advice and information in connection with this religion/denomination,

h   submits an assignment which is partly from the core material and partly from the religion he/she studied in

310

greater depth. Then he/she continues to read about his/her special religion in a book he/she finds at the local library,

i   continues with the rest of the core material (and completes the course).

Example 2: An introductory mathematics course about equations
(See figure 24 on following page)

The student

a   gets general guidance about the planned possibilities for the choices that are part of the course. At the same time the student is asked to contact his/her tutor and tell about his/her background and objective with the course. The student takes this opportunity to contact the tutor early in the course,

b   submits the first assignment,

c   is supposed later to choose one of these options:

- learning to discuss possible solutions of the equations with a parameter

- solving problems for extra practice without drawing in new factors/elements

- getting help with those parts of the basic theory of equations that have proved particularly difficult

and receives guidance in this. The student is uncertain which level to choose, and asks the tutor,

d   has chosen one of the three levels and starts the work with this material,

e   submits an assignment on the level he/she has chosen,

f   is interested in learning about systems of equations and asks the teacher for further reading in this field,

g-h works with the core material and reads about systems of equations at the same time,

i   submits the next to the last assignment,

j   is supposed, in this last study unit, to apply what he/she has learnt about equations, to work with formulae. He/she is offered to work with this in one of these fields:

- natural science,

- engineering,

- consumer economics,

and gets guidance about these three possibilities,

312

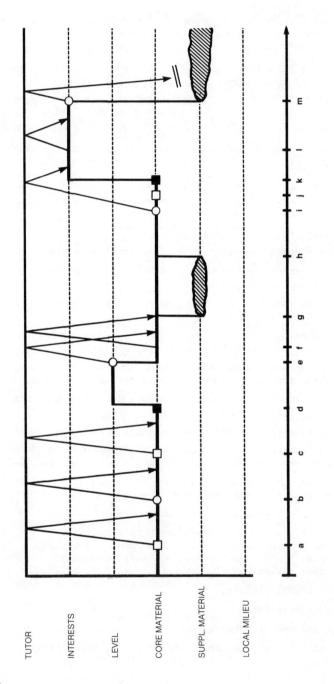

Figure 24

k   chooses the field of most interest,

l   has a problem with this subject and asks for help from the tutor,

m   submits the assignment from his/her special field of interest. At the same time he/she continues to read about systems of equations in the supplementary literature.

Example 3: A course in business administration
         (See figure 25 on the following page)

The student

a   receives general guidance about the course which builds largely on assignments relating to the student's own place of work,

b   gets the first assignment: to describe a problem from his/her own place of work in relation to the aim of the course,

c   submits this description of which the tutor keeps a copy,

d   is asked to choose a new assignment from his/her own place of work,

e   faces a problem, and seeks help from the tutor. While he/she is waiting for the answer, he/she reads on in the core material,

f   returns to the assignment after having got the answer from the tutor,

g   finishes the assignment and returns to the core material,

h   submits a new assignment,

i   gets guidance about the choice of a larger project. He/she sends the tutor a proposal for a project so that the tutor can give comments,

j   starts the project,

k   realises that he/she knows too little about a subject he/she needs in connection with the project and asks the tutor for help to find literature about the subject concerned,

l   gets a tip from the tutor about a relevant chapter in a textbook, gets hold of it and reads what he/she needs,

m   continues with the project,

n   works with the core material parallel to the project,

o   submits an obligatory report as conclusion to the project,

p   submits the last assignment.

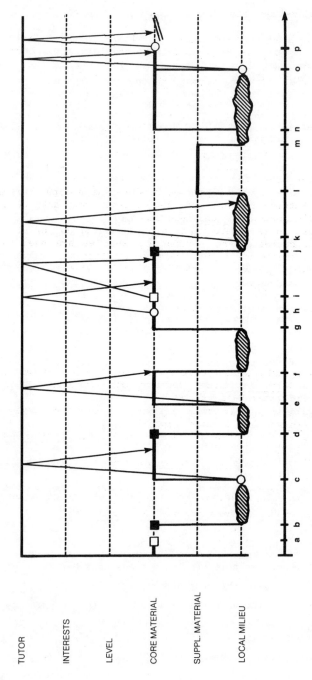

Figure 25

9 Conclusive comments

Considering the possibilities for choice we have discussed in this paper, the work with a course may have a rather complicated pattern, see figures 23-25. It is also clear that the work will vary from student to student.

In order to make this possible, the correspondence course must be organized, in advance, in such a way that the student can choose "his/her own course". This makes new demands on the developers of course material and on the administrative routines.

The role of the tutor is also beginning to change its character. The evaluation of the fixed assignments is not any longer the tutor's most important task. The tutor functions to a larger degree as study guide and partner in a dialogue between him/her and the student. This asks more of the tutor's imagination and understanding.

We are indeed aware that this "loosening up" of what we mean by a correspondence course and what we are used to as being the tutor's tasks, will necessarily face the correspondence schools with great problems. But we also believe that the correspondence schools are able to readjust and offer their students a type of education which is in tune with future views on adult education.

Notes

1 Moore, M.G., Learner Autonomy: The Second Dimension of Independent Learning, in Ninth International Conference on Correspondence Education. A Collection of Conference Papers, Vol.II.

2 Holmberg, B., Distance Education - Research and Development Work, ICCE Newsletter, Vol.5, Nos 2-3, pp. 9-10.

3 Delling, R.M., Telemathic Teaching? Distant Study! ICCE Newsletter, Vol.6, No.2, pp.19-20.

4 Bååth, J.A., Postal Contacts and some other Means of two-way Communication: Lund 1976, pp.2-9.

5 The possibility of using such resources ("open activities") is briefly discussed in Ljoså, E., "Why Do we Make Commentary Courses", in The System of Distance Education, Malmö 1975, pp.117-118.

TELL ME HOW TO WRITE

Janet Jenkins

Course writers today demand training. Gone are the days when the novice writer would confidently set about the task of writing with only minimal guidance. Gone are the days of experiment, when the enthusiastic writer would, unaided, become aware of the problems of teaching by correspondence and creatively adapt his or her classroom techniques to teaching at a distance. Gone are the days when the intervention of an editor or educational technologist was considered a wrongful intrusion into the preserve of the teacher.

Ten or more years ago, at least in my experience then at the National Extension College, writers did not expect to be trained. With better writers this was not a problem. They would produce good lesson drafts to start with, and tended to welcome discussion of their work. With weaker writers, the only acceptable form of training was tactful suggestion and quite often, such advice was not followed.

This experience was, I suspect, typical in any country where people were only just beginning to take distance teaching seriously. That time is now past. Today, distance teaching is an acceptable form of education. Those without experience do not attempt to struggle alone. They look to institutions or people with experience to provide advice and training.

How does a new writer feel?

First, there are the confident writers: "Just tell me all about the techniques I need and I'll have no trouble in applying them." They assume there are a few simple rules to be learned. They are shocked and surprised when they are presented with a challenge to their assumptions about teaching. They are forced to rethink how they should present their subject. This process contains an implicit questioning of the effectiveness of all their teaching. What they *want* is a quick guide to the theory and practice of distance teaching. What they *need* is to learn to think very carefully about what they teach and how they do it.

Any good teacher is, of course, prepared to do this. The shock to the course writer comes because a mystique has built up around the idea of distance teaching. Writers expect, and look for, a new kind of challenge. They discover instead that the major requirement is a familiar one, the hard slog of teaching to a high standard; and, worse, their teaching no longer takes place in the privacy of the classroom or lecture hall, but is open to the scrutiny of their peers and a variety of course development personnel. Their initial confidence is often severely shaken. Their training must, indeed, bring about this disruption, but it must also go on to restore confidence.

Second, there are writers who lack confidence: "I've never done any writing and I'm worried about it." The ones who admit to this worry are easy to help, with encouragement and constructive criticism. The difficult ones - and there are plenty of them - are those who don't like to acknowledge that they are worried. If a college provides only informal training, the problem may come to light when the deadline for submitting lessons arrives, and nothing has been written.

Third, there are those who resist training. There are still a few who believe it is quite unnecesary. If you've ever attended a writer's workshop, you may have met the sulky-faced person who sleeps ostentatiously in the back row. Others pay lip-service: "Give me the right books, I'll read them and get on with it." They are nevertheless determined to do things their own way. Sometimes, with patience and luck, they become more receptive; in other cases, the production of a course becomes a stormy and unpleasant experience for all involved.

There are, of course, other attitudes, but these three are typical and each presents training difficulties. The problem for the trainer is to build on the writer's initial receptivity; and to do so without destroying enthusiasm. In those cases where the writer has a negative attitude, the trainer has to attempt to break through the barrier.

What kind of training?

I have dwelt on the question of attitudes because I believe it crucially affects the content and conduct of training. Institutions can only provide limited training, and a training programme should therefore be designed to train writers in essentials. Opportunities for training may be limited for many practical reasons; a course may be needed in a hurry, money may be short, or trainers may be unavailable. But perhaps the most serious constraint is the one imposed by the writers themselves: they are seldom prepared to devote much time to training.

However, we must accept that, particularly for part-time writers, time is important. People want to get on with the job. This implies that a training programme should be efficient and selective. Our objective should be pragmatic rather than perfectionist: that is, to train writers to be competent. And the training needs to be built round the writers' experience and to take into account their attitudes.

A minimum curriculum for training

A typical new course writer has considerable experience of teaching in class but will know little about distance education, and have little or no experience of writing. For such people, a minimum curriculum should cover the following 6 topics:

1   What it is like to learn at a distance. In particular, the writer must consider the study environment, motivation and the needs of the group of students he is to teach.

2   Planning and writing by objectives. Most teachers have only a vague notion of objectives and their use. They need to clarify their ideas and, in particular, learn to write precise objectives.

3   Relating activities to objectives. The next step after writing objectives is to provide activities to test that they have been achieved. This is not obvious to those who are unfamiliar with teaching by objectives.

4   Providing constant feedback. Teachers need to learn to translate into print the normal classroom interaction. They need to be shown why frequent self-assessment questions are necessary, and need guidance on devising a variety of such questions.

5   Writing clearly. First attempts at writing are often unnecessarily heavy and complex. Writers need to learn to write simply and clearly. They also need to learn to write thorough but clear instructions.

6   How the course will work. Writers, particularly external ones, cannot be expected to understand the administration of a course. They need to know exactly what kind of support services are available to students, and how they operate. In particular, they need to understand how best to use a tutor's assessment skills, if a tutor is provided.

In addition to these six essentials, training should include some writing, either part of the writer's actual course or a lesson written as an exercise. The temptation to cover more topics must be resisted, if as a result writing is postponed. Any delay in starting to write increases the fears of writers with little confidence. Others immediately see the relevance of their subsequent training, as they can apply what they learn directly to their own drafts. They learn, too, that a writer must be prepared to redraft his work several times. The International Extension College has produced a training manual, <u>Writing for Distance Education</u> (1979), which starts by asking people to use some given information to write a few pages. Only then does it begin to look at techniques. We have used the manual in several workshops and find it is effective in helping all writers, even reluctant ones, develop their competence.

There is also the problem of time. Writers need to feel they are achieving something, and doing so quickly. It is tempting to introduce more topics into a training programme, but if time is limited, training should be kept to the basics and to helping writers get started.

How can we train writers?

A number of training methods can be used to suit different circumstances.

Training by correspondence

Some years ago the International Extension College produced a correspondence course for correspondence course writers. It consisted of nine units, some of which were related to teaching particular subjects at a distance. It proved less than satisfactory. The problem was time. Although people began to write their courses as they worked through the units, they wanted to proceed faster than the course allowed. The delay while assignments were marked and returned was, for most, a severe handicap. This method of training has its uses, and other institutions may have found it more satisfactory; but I prefer other methods.

Self-tuition

There are now a number of training manuals available. It is difficult to assess their effectiveness, as feedback from users is lacking. My impression is that they are much better than nothing, but are more efective if used with some tutorial support, such as occasional seminars or a trainer who will answer queries. One institution, which asked its writers to use the International Extension College manual on their own, found that the trainees needed an opportunity to discuss their work.

Workshops

In my experience, intensive training and writing workshops are the best form of training. In a workshop of 2 or 3 weeks, trainee writers both learn the job and produce some finished lessons. Training manuals come into their own, forming the basis for seminars. Writers get feedback from trainers and other writers, which builds their confidence. Even a workshop of 1 week can be satisfactory, especially if it is followed by support from an editor.

In-service training

This is the best term to describe training which involves an editor and a writer working closely together. Such training can be individualised, and can take place face-to- face and by correspondence. Training manuals can be used, on the advice of the editor. This method has many advantages: in particular, the problems of teaching specific subjects at a distance can be closely examined. However, there is a risk that it will not be systematic enough, and writers will lack the benefits gained from group work in a workshop.

Given the choice, I would prefer to train writers in workshops. But, clearly, different methods are appropriate in different cases. Whatever the method, it is important to give writers the satisfaction of achieving results soon. And this means that a writer needs to get at least one lesson written quite quickly. Once a writer has written a lesson or section and revised it, or knows how to do so, he should be able to continue with confidence. Formal training can stop here, to be supplemented with informal advice.

Conclusions

This paper has looked at the sort of training writers require, what that training should include, and different training methods. I've suggested that, since training must be selective, training programmes should be designed to take into account writers' attitudes. Dominant attitudes today are largely due to the mystique that has grown round the concept of distance teaching. Writers are misled into thinking either that the whole business is very difficult, or that there is a simple system which will provide them with infallible guidance. I've suggested that, to overcome these difficulties, actual writing of lessons should form part of a training programme.

References

International Extension College (1979) <u>Writing for Distance Education</u>. Cambridge: International Extension College

SECTION 7: STUDENT SUPPORT SERVICES

INTRODUCTION

Among distance educators there are two basically different approaches to student support, one relying exclusively or almost exclusively on non-contiguous communication, i.e. communication by media like the written, recorded or tele-transmitted word, the other including face-to-face contacts as more or less self-evident elements of distance education. This difference is related to - although it does not completely coincide with - two other dichotomies: there are two distinct types of students, those taking odd courses to supplement their education and those who study at a distance to acquire a degree or a similar formal competence. Furthermore, there are large-scale and small- scale approaches to distance education.

The large-scale approach implies developing courses for very large numbers of students, which means printing or producing in other forms hundreds or thousands of copies of each individual course, while at the same time providing individual tuition through the tutors' marking and commenting on individual students' work as well as - in some cases - offering face-to-face tutorials. The British Open University is a typical example of this. The small-scale approach usually expects of a course author that he or she should also teach his students at a distance and face-to-face. Whereas the large-scale approach in most cases consciously benefits from the economies of scale, it is considered acceptable - and in some cases advantageous - to keep the same tutor-student ratio for distance study as for on-campus study (Sheath 1972, pp.228- 289; cf. also Smith 1975, p.163).

It is evident that the differences indicated result in different views of how student support should be provided and on actual practice. This applies to counselling as well as to teaching. A common denominator in most systems where responsibility is taken for student support is what David Sewart has called a continuity of concern (1978).

Non-contiguous tutorial two-way communication

A survey of the problems related to non-contiguous two-way communication has been produced by the present author (Holmberg 1981a (Chapter 4) and 1981b). The situation of distant tutors is the subject of studies by Harris 1975, Gibbs & Durbridge 1976 and Fritsch 1980 and 1981. Other, mainly somewhat earlier investigations into tutors' status, qualifications, tasks, attitudes and influence on students' work have been summarised by Bååth 1980, pp.36-40. Empirical studies have shown conclusively that there is a distinct correlation between turn-round time - i.e. the time elapsing between students' dispatch of assignments completed and their return - and course completion (Rekkedal 1973; cf. Bååth & Månsson 1977). Quick handling with proper tutor comments on students' papers has proved essential for students' success.

A very thorough empirical investigation of postal two-way communication as applied in the distance study of some 1800 students has been made and published by John Bååth (1980). High submission density, i.e. frequent postal contacts (due to short study units), was found to correlate with a stronger inclination to start the submission of assignments. No other substantial and unequivocal finding resulted from the experiments on submission density. It was found that half and even three quarters of the assignments for submission could be replaced by self-checking exercises, with practically no appreciable effects either on study perseverance or on attitudes, final test results or study time. A third result was that computerised postal tuition was experienced as more positive by the students than traditional tution. Moreover, students getting computer- assisted correspondence tuition started submitting assignments to a greater extent than students receiving traditional tutoring by mail. In one experimental course, they also completed their studies to a greater extent, and did so within a shorter time.

A study by Flinck (1978) on correspondence education combined with systematic telephone tutoring showed that telephone tutoring had a positive effect on the achievements of students of a foreign language but not on the achievements of students taking economics. Whereas students reported that they were given valuable encouragement by telephone tutoring, no difference in study time between students tutored by telephone and those doing without telephone tutoring was found. The study indicates that telephone tutoring led to increased interest in the subject studied. Further studies on the use of the telephone for individual tuition and for teleconferencing have been made by Ahlm 1972, Turok 1977 a and b, Holloway & Hammond 1975 and others.

The use of the computer 'off-line' in distance education has been studied in various contexts. Both systems based on multiple-choice questions and a system which allows the free rendering of replies in the form of numbers (CMA, Fernuniversität) have proved successful. (cf. Bååth & Månsson 1977, Graff 1977, Möllers 1981).

This positive view of off-line computer-assisted distance tution can hardly be interpreted as a general recommendation to do without tutor-marked assignments or personal non- contiguous communication generally. A number of subjects, themes within subjects and general types of learning, e.g. free problem-oriented learning, make it imperative that live tutors communicate with students.

On-line use of computers in distance study occurs where students can be offered the possibility to work at computer terminals in study centres. The experiences are very favourable (cf. Lockwood & Cooper 1980). As a new development should be mentioned a configuration developed to make it possible for blind students to work at computer terminals. A blind student types into the computer a question to which it replies in an artificial voice. This is brought about by means of a micro computer combined with a 'voice synthesizer' which has 62 phonemes at its disposal. The result is an artificial but easily intelligible English. Experiments have also been made with oral instructions received ('understood') by the computer (Vincent 1981).

Face-to-face sessions

A number of studies indicate that cognitive objectives in general and psychomotor objectives aimed at skills in the field of written achievement (in languages and mathematics, for instance) are attained at least as well by distance study based on the written word as by conventional classes (Granholm 1971). It is difficult to generalise the relevance of such statements, however, as some comparative studies do not seem clearly to have kept all independent variables under control.

On the one hand this knowledge about the effectiveness of distance study and on the other hand research indicating that many psychomotor objectives and objectives in the affective domain are more effectively attained by personal contacts lead many distance-study institutions and their students to use face-to-face sessions mainly for the purposes of practising psychomotor skills in laboratories and under similar conditions (also verbal skills through personal communication); encouraging attitudes and habits of relevance for the study; mutual inspiration and stimulation of fellow students, and training in co-operation.

A question that is under debate is to what extent face-to-face sessions should also, more or less as a matter of routine, be used for the purpose of securing cognitive learning by discussion and application of the knowledge acquired to themes brought up in direct contact with tutors and fellow students. Whereas one school of thinking finds face-to-face sessions essential, another finds them unnecessary and even, in some cases, harmful. In cases where course completion within a pre-determined period of time is a target, students using supplementary face-to-face sessions have often been found to be particularly successful. For a discussion of the advantages and dangers of different types of face-to-face sessions supplementing distance education see Holmberg 1977 and Müller 1981.

Counselling and general student support

It is perfectly possible to leave the whole of the responsibility for the study success with the students, to offer them facilities but to make no attempt to make sure that they make use of these facilities. This is an approach that is not unknown among distance educators. It may, in fact, reflect a recognition of the students' independence and it may - or may not - support the development of student autonomy. All those institutions, however, which feel that they should prevent interruptions and drop-out as far as this is humanly possible, make all kinds of efforts to support students. This is done by encouraging letters and encouraging telephone conversations as well as by counselling face-to-face. Allocating each student to a particular tutor or counsellor (tutor-counsellor in the Open University practice) has proved a successful framework for this kind of support.

At least three major studies on counselling distant learners have been made during the last few years: an analysis of the thinking behind and the practice of the Open University counselling and tutoring (Sewart 1978), a survey of trends and literature in the field by Thornton & Mitchell 1978 and a case study by Roger Lewis 1980. Thornton & Mitchell illuminate institutional practices mainly in Australia but also with overseas references. They discuss correspondence counselling, audio cassette counselling, telephone counselling and face-to-face counselling.

Attempts have also been made to make use of the computer for counselling purposes. An application of this kind is to be found in a pre-study advisory system developed at the Fernuniversität in West Germany. In connection with an informative booklet a number of questions are asked. The foreseen replies to these, in their various configurations, are commented on by computer through the automatic selection and use of pre-programmed text modules (Fritsch, Küffner & Schuch 1979).

The following papers selected for this section illuminate both practice, principles and problems concerned with important aspects of student support.

Börje Holmberg

References

Ahlm, M. (1972) Telephone instruction in correspondence education. Epistolodidaktika 1972:2, 49-64

Bååth, J.A. (1980) Postal two-way communication in correspondence education. Lund: Gleerup

Flinck, R. (1978) Correspondence education combined with systematic telephone tutoring. Kristianstad: Hermods

Fritsch, H. (1980) Zwischen den Stühlen. Untersuchung zur Situation der Korrektoren an der Fernuniversität 1980. ZIFF Papiere 34. Hagen: Fernuniversität

Fritsch, H. (1981) In between the chairs. ICCE-Newsletter 11, 1, 11-12

Fritsch, H., Küffner, H. & Schuch, A. (1979) Entwicklung einer Studieneingangsberatung für Fernstudenten. Hagen: Fernuniversität

Gibbs, G. & Durbridge, N. (1976) Characteristics of OU tutors. Teaching at a Distance 6, 96-102 and 7, 7-22

Graff, K. (1977) Vorschläge für ein Projekt EDV-Buchhaltungsprogramm im Rahmen des CMA-Projekts. In: Wilmersdoerfer, H. et al., Zwischenbericht Projekt Standardisierte Testverfahren, 39-42. Hagen: Fernuniversität (ZIFF)

Granholm, G. (1971) Classroom teaching or home study - a summary of research on relative efficiency. Epistolodidaktika 1971:2, 9-14

Harris, W.J.A. (1975) The distance tutor. Manchester Monographs 3, Bournemouth: Direct Design

Holloway, S. & Hammond, S. (1975) Tutoring by telephone: a case study in the Open University. London: University College (Communication Studies Group)

Holmberg, B. (1977) Die Ergänzung des Fernstudiums durch Nahstudium. ZIFF Papiere 15. Hagen: Fernuniversität

Holmberg, B. (1981a) Status and trends of distance education. A survey and bibliography. London: Kogan Page

Holmberg, B. (1981b) Zur medienvermittelten Zweiweg-Kommunikation im Fernstudium. ZIFF Papiere 38. Hagen: Fernuniversität

Lewis, R. (1980) Counselling in open learning: a case study. National Extension College Reports 2, 6 Cambridge: National Extension College

Lockwood, F. & Cooper, A. (1980) CICERO: computer-assisted learning within an Open University course. Teaching at a Distance, 17, 66-72

Möllers, P. (1981) Computergestützte Lehre zum betrieblichen Rechnungswesen. Ein integriertes Modell. Hagen: Fernuniversität, ZIFF

Müller, K. (1981) Einzellernen und Gruppenarbeit im Fernstudium: Wofür eignet sich welche Lernform? In: Müller, K. & Delling, R.M. (eds.), Kleiner Fernstudien-Almanach 1981. Hildegard Focke zum Abschied. 21-30 Tübingen: private publication

Rekkedal, T. (1973) Innsendingsoppgavene i brevundervisningen. Hvilken betydelse har det å reducere omløpstiden? With an English summary: The written assignments in correspondence education. Effects of

325

reducing turn-round time. Oslo: NKI

Sheath, H. (1972) Integrating correspondence study with residence study. In: Bern, H.A. & Kulla, F. (eds.), Ninth International Conference on Correspondence Education. A collection of conference papers, 290-294

Smith, K. (1975) External studies at the University of New England. An exercise in integration. In: Ljosá, E. (ed.), The System of Distance Education, 161-169. ICCE. Malmö: Hermods

Sewart, D. (1978) Continuity of concern for students in a system of learning at a distance. ZIFF Papiere 22. Hagen: Fernuniversität

Thornton, R. & McD. Mitchell, I. (1978) Counselling the Distance Learner. A Survey of Trends and Literature Adelaide: Adelaide College of the Arts and Education

Turok, B. (1977a) Group tutoring by telephone. Epistolodidaktika 1977:2, 63-67

Turok, B. (1977b) Telephony: a passing lunacy or a genuine innovation? Teaching at a Distance 8, 25-33

Vincent, A.T. (1981) Computer-assisted support for blind students - the use of a microcomputer linked Voice Synthesizer. Paper presented at CAL 81. Computers & Education 6, 1, (1982), 55-60

TEACHING FOR THE OPEN UNIVERSITY
(Extracts)
S. Clennell, J. Peters & D. Sewart

The Teaching Package

The Open University student's tuition takes many forms. The major element is the series of correspondence units, despatched at regular intervals to the student's home. Much of the working material is designed to help him to learn for himself. The correspondence units are closely related to radio and television broadcasts and the whole teaching package of written and broadcast material is produced by a course team which is composed of central and regional academic staff, members of the BBC and educational technologists. The student must respond to this teaching material in an active way, by carrying out experiments, writing essays, working through problems, projects, etc., and while some of this work may be used for self-assessment, the majority is assessed in written form either by a tutor (tutor-marked assignments) or by the computer (computer-marked assignments). Ultimately the best of the student's assignments together with the final examination determine the award and standard of a credit.

Study Centres

Although the Open University student works mainly at home, the University has established, usually in other educational institutions, some 260 study centres sited throughout the country in areas of high population or where transport links are good. Attendance at the study centre is voluntary. They offer students a range of facilities which can supplement some of those available at home but above all they enable students to meet each other and to learn from each other in discussion groups. The study centre is also the focal point for the undergraduate students' meetings with tutor-counsellors. These meetings are an important element of the programme at foundation level where numbers normally allow provision for local contact.

The main purpose of this contact is to remedy in tutorial sessions any academic weaknesses or deficiencies of understanding and to support in counselling sessions the individual student's overall progress.

The range of correspondence units and broadcasts provides the student with information and guidance in a standard package. It is through the tuition and counselling system, however, that this standard package is interpreted according to the student's individual needs and ability.

Local Support

When they begin their studies undergraduate students are assigned to a tutor-counsellor at their local study centre. The tutor-counsellor will normally be responsible for all tuition and counselling in the foundation year, although in some instances, e.g. for the science foundation course, specialists may be brought in for particular tuition and assessment. The tutor-counsellor is available on a fairly regular basis at the study centre and may discuss strictly academic matters associated with the course or may deal with study skills on a much wider basis as well as reviewing and assisting with his students' progress in the University's unique and complex teaching system. As a supplement to these meetings, and as a substitute in cases where students cannot or choose not to attend the study centre, contact between the tutor-counsellor and student is maintained by other means, including correspondence and telephone. In addition the tutor-counsellor is responsible for marking and commenting on scripts sent to him by individual students. When the undergraduate student advances to post-foundation level courses the correspondence tuition is provided by a specialist course tutor who may in addition meet his students for tutorials or, increasingly, contact his students by other more flexible means. However, the tutor-counsellor continues to provide an element of stability and continuity in the life of the Open University student since he retains his broad role as a general educational adviser at a local level throughout the student's educational career.

Correspondence Tuition

Correspondence tuition is the central and continuing teaching process in the Open University system. The techniques and approach of the correspondence tutor are not always immediately grasped by those who have successfully taught students in conventional full-time and part-time teaching. In the same way learning through correspondence does not always come easily to the adult student to whom such a system is generally new. At foundation level the tutor-counsellor has the responsibility for training and preparing undergraduate

328

students for this novel method of learning. The student is asked to make a response from time to time to correspondence texts, broadcasts and other course material. This response is given in the form of an assignment. The assignment is graded and commented on by the tutor and these comments constitute the main part of the student's personal tuition. Even at foundation level, the assignment may be the only opportunity for regular communication between the student and the tutor.

It would be difficult to overstate the importance of the correspondence teaching function in the Open University context. In writing assignments students are reconstituting their newly received knowledge in terms of their previous experience and knowledge. The way in which they do this will depend to no small extent on the ways in which they perceive their relationship with their tutor. If they perceive the relationship as one of strict authority on the part of the tutor, their attempts to explore and to present ideas will be minimised and the educational value of the tutor-marked assignment will tend to become subservient to its role as a grading instrument. The students' initial estimation of the role of the tutor marked assignment is likely to be an enduring one. It is therefore of considerable importance that as foundation level students they should be directed to use assignments as a means of exploring knowledge within a particular framework and of receiving specific guidance which will help to improve their work.

Teaching by Correspondence

A university which aims to teach students who have homes and families, and perhaps a full-time job as well, and who may be relatively remote from centres of population, cannot expect to rely on the traditional lecture and tutorial method of teaching. Thus, in the Open University correspondence teaching is central and over-riding in importance. The main source of individual advice, guidance and constructive criticism for an Open University student on a particular course is his course tutor, who bases his teaching primarily on the student's written work in his 'tutor-marked assignments', and his advice is primarily written advice. This implies that a tutor new to correspondence teaching may need to make a conscious adjustment to his new role: marking a script that is to be returned to a student by post, if it is to be a helpful and constructive process, is not at all the same as marking an examination paper or making notes on an essay that will be discussed in a conventional tutorial.

General principles

What, then is it like to teach at a distance, by correspondence? It is perhaps surprising, though gratifying, at first to realise the depth of involvement that can develop and the sense one has of getting to know the student, at a personal level, through his written work, even when one never sees the student at all. Much depends on previous teaching experience. After that, an ability to put oneself in the student's position and thus assess the relevance and clarity of one's own comments made on the script is the single most important factor. Naturally, the work varies between levels and between faculties. However, what follows will attempt to discuss, with examples, the common features underlying all correspondence teaching work.

In commenting on assignments the tutor (or tutor-counsellor - we shall not distinguish between the two in the correspondence teaching role) must seek to adapt the course material to individual needs as best he may. By evaluating the work and offering criticism, he may suggest to his student ways in which he might improve. This requires two things from the tutor: the ability to convey, through his comments, advice for further study and the ability to perceive his student's present state of knowledge and conceptual framework so that the advice may be relevant. How this works out in practice may be seen in the following example. A social science tutor had to award an 'F' grade on assignment 1. He wrote the following explanation on the PT3 form (the form accompanying each written assignment, copies of which are kept for reference by the tutor, the student and the University), in the space provided for overall assessment:

> I am sorry that the mark is so disappointing, and I hope I do not seem over-critical. The essay was not a catastrophic fail, but I do not feel that it merits higher than 'F' for the following reasons:
>
> 1   The wording of the question means the main focus must be on the contemporary situation - major portions of your essay were essentially historical.
>
> 2   The concepts I have just outlined need to be matched with relevant evidence - too often your discussion was at too general a level - you could, e.g. have drawn on Sec. 62 and 63 of Unit 3, TV 2 on Ibadan, or several authors in Breese. It is early days yet, and this block and questions were difficult - don't let the failure to hit the target this time worry you unduly.

The key features of this comment are that it is humane, and not destructive of the student's self-esteem, and that it is both constructive and supportive. It also underlines an important restriction placed on tutors by the framework of the Open University. Part-time staff must use, in some manner, the package of written material and broadcasts. upon which the University centres its tuition, and in relation to it the responsible tutor must be at once critical and independent, yet knowledgeable and constructive. As in the example quoted, references to Open University course material in a tutor's actual correspondence comments seem an obvious means of helping the student to achieve a similar relationship. This is not, of course, to imply any kind of slavish dependence on the course material any more than on any other book (or on any other experience that one learns from). But specific references to particular passages in the texts should be a valuable and economical way of expanding adivce - the student can then follow up the suggestions independently.

In some courses, assignment rubrics and tutor notes have been carefully 'escalated' to suggest a teaching strategy over the year's work - moving from the exercise of minor or basic skills to more sophisticated assignments requiring a more searching analysis and a more comprehensive synthesis of ideas by the student. The conscientious tutor will try to work within any such overall strategy, aiming to develop the individual student's distinctive abilities methodically and cumulatively. There is a tendency towards over-simplification among adult students (and tutors) working under pressure - each assignment or section may be seen in isolation so that the course becomes a mere succession of disconnected 'blocks' lacking any cumulative rhythm or dynamic. Such a danger may be especially real in inter-disciplinary courses and certainly in multi-disciplinary ones. Careful attention to assignment rubrics and tutor notes is likely to be especially important at foundation level when good habits need to be established. The assignment questions and rubrics are the University's main means of helping to develop powers of disciplined thought in its students. Accordingly Open University students have to be led to interpret assignment rubrics with scrupulous fidelity to the intentions behind them. Adult students have ideas of their own which they wish simply to substitute for those they are asked to consider, but while freshness or independence of mind is vital and not to be discouraged, discipline is also necessary.

A further point that we have already noted in the example of the social science tutor's comment was the manner in which criticism was offered. Much tutorial discussion at university level inevitably involves taking issue with a student's opinions, at times even in a robustly sharp manner. Open University correspondence work, however, may require a rather more circumspect or 'remedial' tutorial tone - 'nursing' the student (good nurses being cheerfully stimulating and sensibly practical rather than 'sympathic' in the sentimental sense). Written comments need to be very carefully phrased and considerate - the opportunity for a hasty aside or added explanation is not available when the student opens the envelope. More important, though, at foundation level a tutor-counsellor may need to be especially concerned not just to strike out errors or to debate with the student but to assist him to develop basic skills and form views that are worthy of debate. At higher levels, the balance may change, though in a multi-disciplinary context one cannot depend upon that.

Course tutors in the Open University system may find it helpful to remember that students taking the course that they tutor may have come from a very different kind of course, or even from a different faculty. Students are sometimes taken aback when the abilities expected of them, and painfully acquired, in one course seem to count for little in a subsequent one. If a student had done well beforehand, a sudden barrage of low grades, however well warranted, may upset him considerably. Indeed, all students given low grades - and certainly all given 'R' and 'F' grades - should be given careful, specific advice by Open University tutors. The temptation to comfort a student with higher grades than are strictly deserved must be denied. In such cases, a telephone call might be invited or a meeting at a tutorial or, at foundation level, a special session for remedial tuition might well be arranged.

It is essential to do everything to forestall demoralization and consequent 'drop out' in a 'distance teaching' system. To illustrate some of these matters, here is a PT3 comment (accompanying a 'D' grade) that may seem to be on the right lines, though the actual advice could, with advantage, be more specific.

It's clear that you have spent a lot of time on this, and there are aspects in which it is good, but on the whole I felt that there were one or two areas needing attention. You have not, perhaps made the fullest use of Unit 6. Have another look especially, at Sections 20.4 and 20.5: this was where the crucial material for this assignment was covered.

You write clearly, but not always in complete sentences. It is important to do this: as I've commented on the script, it is not advisable to write in note-form unless specifically asked to do so. Again, your answers, even though brief, needed rather more careful planning. You tend to set down your ideas rather as they occur to you, I think. Your answer to question 5, unfortunately, contained a great deal of material that wasn't really relevant, and you omitted to consider the second part of the question. But don't be disheartened: there's a lot to commend here too.

Thus tutors might take pains to avoid anything like an abrupt or curt style. It is not easy to write short comments that do not seem 'short' in the adverse sense. This is not to advocate unction, but a correspondence tutor has to study how to raise the issues with a largely unknown student on paper while conveying the air of companionable co-operation that is usually shown in a live tutorial by 'non-verbal gesture'. A correspondence tutor therefore has to acquire the knack of friendly 'verbal gesture'.

Even the new tutor-counsellor (perhaps especially the new tutor-counsellor) should not (and, indeed, cannot) depend on meeting the students to establish good relations. He ought to excel as a correspondence tutor first and foremost.

Admittedly, considered comment takes time to produce and part-time staff do not have excessive time at their disposal, but 'not too little, not too much' is a sensible rule of thumb in correspondence tuition as in other matters. A half dozen points of constructive criticism or positive advice on the PT3 form, related to half a dozen specific comments in the margins of the script itself (together with correction of factual errors) should normally suffice. There is a law of diminishing returns here, in that students may respond more to a few well directed comments than to a large number of miscellaneous suggestions. This may be particularly true of weak students, who, faced with an overdose of criticism and correction, may pursue the less important at the expense of the more important, or even give up altogether in the face of so big a task. Certainly many students at foundation level seem to need to learn how to learn from written comment and may need some coaching in how to do so. But the hard-pressed tutor would also do well to remember that the *good* student deserves stimulus as much as the weaker one needs 'remedial' advice.

Not only should comments be specific to be effective, they must be clearly self-explanatory, even to the point of giving examples of what is meant. The PT3 comment should contain specific references making it concrete and comprehensible. If some of these can refer to points also commented on within the body of the script, so much the better (e.g. 'see your second paragraph, page 3' directs the student firmly and encourages him to follow up advice).

An example of phraseology on a foundation level social science script which reads well and which invites a student to pursue his argument further is:

> Yes . . . though this in turn might reduce productivity, by keeping workers in low productivity jobs. This in turn would reduce wages which in turn . . .?

Or, from a mathematics script:

> It is easier, and more elegant, to start by adding x to both sides of $y > x$. Try it!

Then too, comments should be clear. For example, if a tutor criticises a student on the PT3 form for being 'repetitious', then the repetitive passages should be clearly marked on the script.

Tutorial Teaching

We have seen that correspondence marking is the chief method
by which a tutor teaches his students. But most courses
offer a limited number of face-to-face tutorials which course
tutors have to plan and give. It must be realised that
face-to-face tuition within the Open University does not try
to assume the function it has in most colleges, polytechnics
and universities, where it is of prime importance. In the
conventional teaching system, face-to-face tuition embraces
both lecture (formal dissemination of information) and tutorials (opportunities for educative dialogue). In the Open University the former is executed through the medium of course
units and broadcasts, and the latter for the most part
through correspondence tuition.

The class tutorial in the Open University does have an
important, if restricted part to play in the teaching system.
Its original intention was that it should be remedial and
supportive in nature. The main role of the tutor here is not
to develop new themes and ideas, but to ensure that students
understand the ideas and arguments in the course units and
broadcasts, and to remedy students' academic weaknesses.
This sounds a very narrow brief: many tutors and students
believe strongly in the value of tutorials and one of the
commonly heard questions is: why doesn't the Open University
provide more opportunities for face-to-face contact? But
there are some general points which the Open University
tutor must bear in mind. Many students have so little spare
time that they cannot afford to travel to a study centre
even for a 'good' tutorial, because they feel the time spent
on travelling and on the tutorial itself is better spent on
the course materials. Some students are deterred by expense
while others are kept at home by family responsibilities or
physical handicaps. This is summed up by a D101 student :

> It was a waste of time coming - it took an hour to get
> in and an hour to get back, I spent two hours there,
> turned to page x, looked for answers to these questions.
> Honestly, I'd rather put in four hours' serious study
> at home . . . I wanted it really to be just a correspond-
> ence course. I'd find it binding to *have* to go every
> week.

So it is clear that one cannot expect even the majority of
one's group to attend tutorials. Moreover, it is clear that
while class tutorials need not be narrowly 'remedial', they
are most likely to fill a definite need if they are dis-
tinctly different from a lecture, which could after all be
broadcast or read. The essential feature of a face-to-face
meeting is that the students can participate; perhaps it is

334

not too much to say that if students are not active in the class, the tutor should ask himself what is the point of the meeting.

Of course, students may expect to be allowed to sit and listen while the tutor does the work, and they may even say that they expect to be 'taught'. Even arts students, at day schools, have been known to clamour for lectures, and to dismiss any idea of 'hearing each other talk'. Once a class has begun to think in this way (because only the more passive students are still attending?) it can be tempting to take the line of least resistance, but observations of class tutorials suggest that this is not the best solution. The alternative of stimulating the class to think in a new way about a few topics related to the units is likely to be much more profitable, and perhaps more true to the ideal of university education.

Use of Broadcasts

The broadcasts form a vital component of the teaching materials provided for Open University students. Increasingly, as the pattern of student performance becomes clearer, they are being more effectively integrated into the rest of the materials, and on some courses, such as the new mathematics foundation course, M101, they provide the only place where a particular topic is taught. To assist students to make effective use of broadcasts, tutors might consider arranging for their group as a whole to listen or watch, at home or at the study centre, and then to compare notes. (For some courses audio visual cassettes are available, and all radio broadcasts can be provided, on loan, recorded on tape cassettes.) This note-taking can of itself be a useful skill for students to acquire, and the notes can be used as a point of departure for tutorial classes.

It may be that students do not obtain the maximum benefit from broadcasts at present. Research[1] tends to show that the more successful students watch broadcasts more consistently, though there is no clear pattern of cause and effect. It seems very probable that some students on each course value broadcasts highly, while others do not. (In the same way, perhaps, some students value tutorials, while others do not). This may reflect a genuine difference between the preferred learning pattern of students, but it is also possible, or even probable, that more students could benefit from broadcasts if they were given more help to do so. It may be the case that broadcasts encountered resistance, from both students and tutors, because of the tendency to judge them solely on aesthetic criteria. If so, tutors can play a very useful part in encouraging the use of different criteria in judging programmes and in developing more positive attitudes to the broadcasts by making more use of them in their tutorials.

We shall not discuss regional day schools at length here, although some course teams lay down a programme of day schools. In some cases, when held at a major population centre, they offer a better use of restricted tutorial time for groups of students who live some distance from their tutor. Such day schools may offer a most fertile 'mix' of lectures, seminars, films and special exercises where the effect of the whole is more than the sum of its parts. For courses without summer schools, well planned and integrated day schools may be invaluable, and tutors should plan them carefully in consultation with their regional staff tutor.

Finally, what may one say about classroom manner? At the risk of labouring the obvious, it is important to point out that the tutor must avoid embarrassing the shy or less able student, some of whom hesitate to expose their (real or imaginary) weaknesses to their fellow students' scrutiny. It is easy for a tutor to appear very discouraging when a student makes a contribution that is not relevant or wrong; but ignoring contributions or dismissing them abruptly soon reduces the number of good contributions as well as the bad! Indeed, this aspect of tutoring needs careful cultivation: if one catches oneself being dismissive of a student's suggestion, it is often a good idea to apologise, to try to let him down lightly. According to Gibbs and Durbridge[2], the characteristics most often mentioned by staff tutors in discussion of Open University tutor's work were warmth and understanding. One assumes that competence in the subject was taken for granted, but even so it is a telling comment on the importance of a tutor's personality.

The framework for study

Continuity of concern

By linking each undergraduate student at foundation level to a tutor-counsellor and by continuing this association beyond foundation level wherever possible the Open University has sought to meet a discerned need. It seeks to provide a continuous educational support which cuts across disciplines and across faculties. The frequent contact, whether by face-to-face or other methods, the subject link which is reinforced through the correspondence element and the provision of sympathetic help in planning a beneficial work pattern, all these generate a sound basis of mutual understanding between students and tutor-counsellors at foundation level which students may rely on throughout their later studies. It is this relationship which breaks down the isolation of the home-based student and begins to encourage and shape the effective dialogue which is the basis of education. There has always been a perspective which regards education as personal development rather than helping people to memorise information. The continuity of contact and concern which is the basis of the relationship between a tutor-counsellor and a student facilitates this personal development.

Support for associate students

The system of continuity of concern on the part of a tutor-counsellor for individual students from foundation level to course completion is, of course, particularly important for undergraduate students. Associate students enter the University for a period of study which is of shorter duration than a degree. Often, however, such students remain with the University for longer than a year taking two or more courses which may or may not be recognised in themselves as a specific qualification. For them the same principles hold good, namely local support of a general academic nature and normally more distant support from a course tutor relating to the specific academic content of the course. However, because their registration as students is normally of a more transient nature, it is not always possible to establish the same relationship at a local level as for undergraduates. The University's response to the varying needs of associate students is to tailor support systems to the particular needs of associate students. Equality of consideration rather than equality of provision is the aim here.

Complexity and flexibility

The Open University student probably has more freedom and more choice in his degree profile than any other student. This freedom, however, in turn demands of the individual student a number of important decisions. It is an interesting and sometimes infuriating paradox that this provision of fexibility to cater for individual needs tends to result in complicated administrative procedures which may in themselves present the student with problems. The tutor-counsellor must be able to help each student administratively, academically and vocationally. He must interpret and resolve with the student any divergence between the objectives of the course and any preconceptions with which the student might approach his work. But he must not merely deal with the various problems as they arise. He is not the deus ex machina of the crisis but rather a supportive and knowledgeable adviser who is closely involved with every aspect of his students' studies.

Personal relationship

As we have seen the students in any one tutor-counsellor's group can be and are likely to be diverse in their backgrounds; but they all have in common the fact that, as part-time students they can suffer from feeling isolated and are working within a very complex organisation which might tend to increase that isolation. The tutor-counsellor can best make his advice, knowledge and support available, if he develops a personal relationship with each one of them. Early individual contact with new students is clearly important for the establishment of this personal relationship. It is, however, difficult to say much about this in a general way, as so much depends on an individual's approach[3], but aspects are discussed throughout this booklet and in the Handbook for Part-Time Tutorial and Counselling Staff. Certainly a trusting and friendly relationship can be established only if the tutor-counsellor is in regular contact with his students. With many students particularly in their foundation year, this contact occurs at meetings at the local study centre ; but such meetings are not an essential requisite for success ; much counselling work may be carried out by correspondence and telephone, especially in the case of higher level students. Tutor-counsellors, like - course tutors, can develop a good relationship with students whom they seldom or perhaps never see.

Notes

1 Bates, A. Survey of student use of broadcasting, Teaching at a Distance No. 5, 1976.

2 Gibbs, G. and Durbridge, N. (1976) 'Characteristics of Open University Tutors, Part 1', Teaching at a Distance No. 6; (1976) Part 2, Teaching at a Distance No. 7.

3 See in particular Thomas, A.B. (1974) 'Success and failure in Open University counselling', Teaching at a Distance No. 1, and Cook, R. (1977) 'Counselling continuity and the committed tutor-counsellor', Teaching at a Distance No. 9.

INTERACTION AND INDEPENDENCE:
GETTING THE MIXTURE RIGHT
John S. Daniel and Clément Marquis

Introduction

A major educational development over the last decade has
been the creation and growth of remote learning systems in
many countries of the world. This article is primarily
concerned with multi-media distance study systems at the
university level.

The conceptual and historical bases for this new mode
of higher education have been discussed elsewhere.[1][2][3]
They can be summarized by observing that the long tradition
of independent study has, with the aid of modern developments
in the technology of education, been married to the more
recent ideological trend of open learning to produce new
types of educational enterprises which fulfil economic and
political needs in both industrial and developing countries.

We wish to examine in particular the difficult synthesis
which distance learning systems have to effect between those
activities in which the student works alone and those which
bring him into contact with other people. It is in this
sense that the terms *interaction* and *independence* in the
title of this paper are to be understood. However, since
these words are used widely elsewhere with a variety of
meanings, further clarification of their connotation in this
context will be useful.

Interaction

In what is probably the most general theory of human learning
to appear to date, Pask[4][5] holds that all learning is based
on conversations. However, these conversations are often
internalized as when a solitary and silent student mulls
over the 'knowables' in a text he is reading. Clearly in
this sense all learning involves interaction.

In this article we shall use the term interaction in a
more restricted manner to cover only those activities where
the student is 'in two-way contact with another person (or
persons) in such a way as to elicit from him reactions and

responses which are specific to his own requests or contributions. Such contact need not imply face-to-face meetings, indeed we shall examine the role of interaction by telephone, nor do the reactions have to be immediate (e.g. the mail delay in correspondence tutoring). The modes of interaction we shall be studying are:
- counselling students before entry into the system and during their studies;
- tutoring students involved in courses and projects;
- contact about projects with tutors or *animateurs**
- teaching over interactive telecommunications systems;
- bringing students together into discussion groups;
- residential gatherings of the 'summer school' type.

Independence

The term independence will be used broadly to denote those learning activities where there is no interaction as we have defined it. These include:
- study of written material;
- watching/listening to broadcasts (or audio-visual materials that can be played back at home);
- writing essays and assignments;
- working alone at a computer terminal;
- laboratory experiments at home;
- surveys and project work.

Placing essay writing and computing in the 'independent' category requires a word of justification. Clearly most essays or assignments are done with a view to later interaction with a tutor about their content. However, we shall consider that the interactive phase begins with the tutor's reply. We also class interactive computing as an independent activity, except where an electronic mail system is employed, because the replies which a student elicits, however appropriate they may be to his needs, are standard and pre-programmed.

Having divided students' activities in remote learning into these two categories, we shall now explain why we regard the balance which is maintained between them as the crucial issue facing distance study systems.

The problems of distance education

Distance education already embraces a variety of approaches. In systems such as Britain's Open University centrally produced multi-media courses are taken by large numbers of students whereas in most US open learning projects the emphasis is placed on allowing students to define their own curricula. Naturally systems pursuing different aims will encounter different problems although all face the problem of apportioning resources between interactive and independent activities. In this article, we shall place greater emphasis on the problems encountered at the multi-media course end of the distance education spectrum, simply because this has been the approach espoused most commonly in Canada (e.g. Quebec's Télé-université, [6] Athabasca University, and the off-campus offerings of many other Canadian universities). For this reason, we shall refer frequently to articles in the excellent journal Teaching at a Distance published by the Open University.

Problem 1 - Choice of content: authority vs autonomy

Multi-media courses centrally produced for large student enrolments have an authoritarian flavour.[7] Kirk[8] talks of the creation of 'a large teaching proletariat and a small academic ruling class', and Harrison[9] says that 'part-time tutors and the students face similar problems as fellow travellers on the outside rim of the Open University wheel.'

Particularly among the part-time tutors at the Open University one detects a certain jealousy at the role of the central course teams which not only decide the content of the course but by all accounts have great fun doing it. In a sense the traditional university, in which a course is conceived in solitude in the lecturer's study and delivered interactively in the classroom, has been stood on its head in the Open University approach where the course is conceived in interaction and studied (largely) in solitude.

In a sensitive article Perraton[10] argues that the problem of who chooses the content is not a simple one. He suggests that the Americans are wrong in looking to greater individual-ization of content choice as a cure for dissatisfaction with universities, for this may exacerbate the bittiness of curricula which he sees as the major fault of the existing system. Quoting Mao Tse Tung to the effect that the role of the educator is to 'teach the masses clearly what we have received from them confusedly', Perraton suggests that the local tutor or animateur, who is present at the interface between the student and the centrally produced course, is best placed to ensure a happy medium between irrelevancies imposed by authority and bittiness chosen individually. Mentioning with approval Quebec's Tévec project, he insists that learning is a social activity and that local animateurs should provide a supportive artificial network which will enable the content to be gradually adapted to the existing natural network in which people are living. The animateur's task is thus to discover local needs and relate course materials to them so that knowledge can play its key role as an agent of change in society. Harrison[9] concurs with this function of the tutor as the meeting point between 'popular culture' (the real and local life patterns of particular students) and 'educated knowledge' (the course texts, audio-visual materials, the tutor's academic background).

Problem 2 - Economies of scale

Among ten characteristics of open learning systems Wedemeyer2 includes the following:

> As an operating principle, the system is capable, after reaching a critical minimum of aggregation, of accommodating increased numbers of learners without a *commensurate* increase in the unit cost of the basic learning experiences: i.e. costs must not be directly and rigidly volume sensitive. After reaching the necessary level of aggregation, unit costs should show a diminishing relationship to total system costs.

This criterion is, for the most remote learning systems, the crucial issue in determining the blend of interaction and independence. Coming on the scene at the dusk of the golden era of university expansion of the 1960s, remote learning systems are expected to be more cost effective than tradition-al approaches. Broadly speaking, independent activities have great possiblities of economies of scale since the marginal costs of printing extra copies of texts or broadcasting to more students are low. However, the costs of interactive activities tend to increase in direct proportion to the number of students.

The choices forced upon remote learning systems by these simple facts are extremely painful. Most educators want high quality and a healthy degree of redundancy (so as to accommodate differences in learning styles) throughout the system. In the early days choices can be made conscious-ly, but as the system grows and different departments are created to handle the various components of the learning experience, competition for resources can become severe, political and acrimonious. In our own institution, the Télé-université, there is a particularly lively debate between the protagonists of more interactive support in the regions and those who would like the graphic presentation of the course texts to be immediately attractive.

Thus the economic problem requires choices to be made - but other problems have to be taken into account as well.

Problem 3 - Does the activity suit the student?

Most remote learning systems recruit their students among working adults. Although such students are usually highly motivated, family and professional obligations compete with their studies for the little spare time they have available. Not surprisingly our students at the Télé-université tell us that the flexibility in planning study time which our courses permit is one of the main reasons why they chose to enrol. This constraint of student availability is of such fundamen-tal importance for a remote-learning system that it is worth

342

discussing its impact on each of the activities listed earlier. We shall take the independent activities first.

Written texts Media buffs often criticize remote learning systems for what they see as their retrograde emphasis on the written word. Leaving aside claims, such as that of Turok,[11] that correspondence is the best vehicle for degree-level distance study, we feel that such critics underestimate the remarkable flexibility of print. No other medium at present available can be carried around and consulted with the same ease.

Broadcasts/Audio visual materials Broadcasting has tremendous possibilities for economies of scale. However, the very detailed studies that have been conducted at the Open University by Bates,[12] and which are probably applicable to most systems, show that only by broadcasting programmes twice a week at different times is it even theoretically possible for more than 90 per cent of students to view or hear them. Audio-visual materials (e.g. cassettes) which can be played back at home circumvent this problem to some extent, but with the penalty of losing economies of scale.

Essays and assignments Since students can plan essay and assignment writing to fit their own schedules this type of activity is inherently flexible. However, the value of assignments depends greatly on the quality of the later (interactive) marking phase. It is important to match the style of assignment to the student's background. The academic essay, for example, is not a natural form of expression to most entrants to a distant study system and some training is needed to attain the high level of written exchange between student and tutor reported, with examples, by Harrison.[9] Similarly many of our students at the Télé-université claim that our objective tests require unfamiliarly lucid and careful reasoning on their part.

Computing Remote learning systems working to less densely populated areas than Europe will have some difficulty placing 'interactive' computing facilities within the reach of all students in a cost-effective manner. Furthermore few students are accomplished typists and operation of even the simplest and most foolproof terminal can pose problems for the adult who may have to work with it alone in the evening at his local centre.

Laboratory experiments The Open University home experiment kits are the object of worldwide admiration and provide a rich source of photogenic material for films on distance study. Since such kits are greatly appreciated by most students, it is a pity that only the largest institutions such as the Open University have large enough enrolments in science and technology courses to achieve economies of scale on the enormous costs of designing simple, safe and telling experiments and the equipment to go with them. Buying kits from the big institutions is probably the only way for smaller systems to incorporate this element of remote learning.

Surveys and project work   These are usually a form of assignment and once again there can easily be mismatch between the student's preparedness and the tacit assumptions of the course planners. Students almost invariably bite off more than they can chew and grossly underestimate the time a project will take. Henry[13] argues that projects are best considered in the category of interactive activities because of the guidance needed at the three major stages of choosing the topic, collecting information, and writing up the results.

When we consider the interactive aspects of remote learning the difficulties we have enumerated for independent activities pale into insignificance, for interactive experiences, to the extent that they require the bringing together of people, submit the remote student to just those constraints of geography and time that he enrolled in the system to escape. Crucial to all remote learning systems is the scatter problem described by Turok[11] and we shall return later in this article to the important role of telecommunications in overcoming the geographical difficulties.

The interactive pièce de résistance is clearly the summer school type of gathering. The Open University planners incorporated summer schools into their programme after visiting Australian correspondence operations and their role has been a subject of heart searching ever since.

Woodley and McIntosh[14] report that a quarter of those who decide not to apply to the Open University desist because they could not have attended summer school. In another article McIntosh[15] examines the whole question of summer schools and highlights the essential problem: although summer schools are a hugely appreciated experience for most students their very existence prevents some students enrolling. However, were attendance made voluntary there is a fear that, in common with all optional extras, their 'mainline' role in the system would disappear.

Moreover, even the much more minor disturbance in the schedule of an adult student which is caused by the opportunity to meet tutors and counsellors or to attend discussion groups at other times during the course must not be underestimated. Since such interactive activities tend to be inconvenient for the student and expensive for the institution, all remote learning systems have a strong incentive to

344

use them efficiently. This article includes a guide to good practice which we hope will be useful in this regard.

Problem 4 - To pace or not to pace?

Pacing is a question fraught with ideological issues and pregnant with practical administrative problems. Upon the decision of a remote learning system with regard to pacing will largely depend the sort of mixture it can achieve between interaction and independence.

The ideological issue is simply stated: if a system has, as its chief priority, respect for the freedom and autonomy of the individual students, it will allow him to begin a course of study whenever he chooses and to finish it at his convenience. The student paces himself and there are no external constraints although the good correspondence school, whose model this is, will have a system of written reminders, encouraging phone calls and even financial incentives to incite him to keep at it. Nevertheless the drop out, or non-completion rate, with such a free approach is usually horrendous (over 50 per cent) if the students are humans rather than angels. In the nineteenth century, when correspondence schools began, the idea of the survival of the fittest was more acceptable than it is today and most modern remote learning systems, knowing that many of their students join them with feelings of educational inadequacy, are concerned to do everything in their power to prevent the student dropping out with his sense of failure reinforced.

The usual way to encourage students to continue with a course is to provide some form of pacing, i.e. to introduce into the system a series of events taking place at fixed times which become deadlines for the students to meet. Several remarks about pacing can be made with reference to our two categories of activity.

> *Independent activities* Of the independent activities identified in an earlier paragraph, broadcasts and assignments are the most obvious means for pacing. The Open University has always regarded this as a major function of its television and radio programmes and practically all institutions which adopt pacing use assignments in this way by fixing 'cut-off' dates for each.

> *Interactive activities* Whilst individual contacts between a student and his counsellor or tutor are not a mechanism for pacing, and indeed should provide a safety net for the student who is having difficulty keeping pace, group interactions are usually impossible without pacing, simply because they are based on bringing together students who are at the same point in a course. Admittedly there are interesting exceptions; Athabasca University holds group meetings for students who have

reached widely different points in a course and the Open University, in response to the problems of residential gatherings already mentioned, now holds joint summer schools for several courses within the same discipline.

However, homogeneous group meetings remain more common and at the Télé-université, where we do not have access to broadcasting for most of our courses, the local meetings with an animateur, held at approximately three-week intervals, are our key pacing mechanism. We are sure that these meetings keep many students up to the mark and that without them our drop out rate would be higher.

Finally mention should be made of completely paced systems such as the Wisconsin Education Telephone Network where weekly interactive teleconferences are the major element of the courses.

To conclude this discussion of pacing it may be helpful to give a concrete example of how different mechanisms can be used. The Télé-université offers to the adult population of Quebec, without academic prerequisites, a series of credit courses in a programme entitled *Connaissance de l'homme et du milieu* Table I indicates the pacing mechanism in each of the thirteen courses available to date.

The Télé-université claims to run a paced system where courses are offered in periods corresponding roughly to regular university terms. Whilst we feel that some sort of pacing is essential and would not contemplate changing to the correspondence model, our present problems with pacing may be of interest. These are two; the start and the finish.

How do you administer a staggered start? Although we hopefully indicate starting dates, and even enrolment deadlines, in our publicity, the majority of students enrol after the deadlines, sometimes several weeks after. Admittedly we are in a phase of rapid growth (enrolments doubling every term) so that the ripples of our publicity reach potential students later, but we also have the impression that students like, and take advantage of, our image as an open university unconstipated by the usual bureaucratic rules about enrolment.

Although the Open University has the luxury of refusing applicants, the Télé-université (in common with most North American remote learning systems working to the relatively small populations of individual states or provinces in an era when higher education is no longer the favourite of government) has good political and financial reasons for accepting as many applicants as possible.

Naturally late applicants pose problems for the pacing mechanism. In the case of broadcasts the obstacle

346

is almost insuperable and even in the case of group meetings postponing the first course meeting in a particular region may displease and discourage the students who enrolled in good time.

Bringing in the stragglers   Other problems occur at the end of courses. Once the broadcasts and meetings are finished and the deadline date for the last assignment is past there usually remain a significant number of students who have not completed the course but who do not consider themselves to have dropped out. They intend to finish the assignments/exams at a later date. In the Université du Québec network such students receive an 'I' (incomplete) grade which, if not converted within one term into a letter grade, results in failure. We are under pressure from our course teams to change this procedure and will probably do so. However, it is unlikely that simply extending from one term to one year the period of grace before the guillotine falls and puts a 'fail' on the student's record is going to cause many stragglers to complete - unless a mechanism is set up to help them do so. Remote learning systems must beware of the illusion of solving problems with flexible rules which make the staff feel liberal and warm inside but which do not of themselves help the student attain his goals.

Analyzing these four live issues in distance education has shown us why it is important for remote learning systems to achieve a good mix between indpendent and interactive activities. Interaction with others can temper the otherwise authoritarian style of a course and motivate the student to persevere by providing psychological support and a degree of pacing. However, since interactive activities are expensive, expecially if they require the maintenance of a network of study centres, and usually inconvenience the student to some degree, the effectiveness of each must be examined regularly. In their study of seventeen open systems around the world, MacKenzie et al [16] recall that although the Open University allots nearly one third of its budget to ineractive student services a causal relationship between use of these services and success in gaining credits has yet to be established.

In the next section of this article, we shall try to provide a guide to good practice in the interactive components of remote learning. The functions of counselling, tutoring, and group meetings will be examined in turn.

TABLE I

Course title	Pacing mechanism
Initiation à la coopération	3-weekly meetings (5); assignments
Initiation à l'économie du Québec	3-weekly meetings (5); assignments
Histoire du Québec d'aujourd'hui 1 et 2	3-weekly meetings (5); assignments
La gestion: un art méconnu	Meetings (2) at beginning and end of course; assignments
L'informatique, c'est pas sorcier	3 group meetings; schedule for work at computer terminal
L'environnement: un bien collectif menacé	4 group meetings
Action-environnement (project)	None – except tutorial exhortation
L'individu, son affectivité, sa sexualité 1 et 2	6-7 group meetings; assignments
Français pour tous, français pour tout	Assignments only
La publicité au Québec	Weekly broadcast TV programmes (30); assignments
Vieillir, c'est quoi?	Weekly meetings

Interactive activities: a guide to good practice

Counselling

In this context we shall denote by counselling the advice, help and support given to an adult to facilitate his progress in the remote learning system. Excluded by this definition are the tutoring function with respect to a particular course, which will be considered in the next section, and the advice and help an individual may need to solve various personal (e.g. family and financial) problems which may impinge on his studies but are not directly related to them. Nicholson[17] distinguishes three stages in the relation between the adult student and the institution at which counselling is necessary: induction crisis, differential transit, and settled connection, a classification which we shall adopt.

Induction crisis The adult student approaches remote learning with some anxiety and in this first period of contact, when his investment of effort is still small, he will be more likely to withdraw from the system in the face of difficulties or unexpected demands. MacKenzie et al[16] insist on the importance of treating adults as adults, not simply in the design of course materials but also in the wording of forms and letters and in answering enquiries. These authors suggest that the counsellor has three tasks at this stage:

- instilling self confidence: the adult may have a sense of failure from his previous contact with formal education;
- helping the student cope with the freedom of open learning;
- helping the student improve his study habits.

In this context Redmond[18] reminds us that the adult student may not consider the learning role to be part of adult life in the same way as his occupation and family obligations. If this role can be accepted and internalized the student will be likely to do better in his studies. Furthermore the adult is used to controlling his environment - limiting the number and type of unexpected things that can happen to him - and will feel vulnerable in unpredictable situations. The sensitive counsellor will realize that the new student is having to accommodate himself to a specialized and formalized pattern of interaction which may be foreign to his everyday habits. Those with the least formal education probably need the most help and encouragement.

The development of good study habits has been discussed by Gibbs and Northedge[19] who suggest it is not enough simply to give the student a text on study skills. Since people change their existing habits and constructs on the basis of cautious negotiation, constantly relating the new to the old, these authors propose holding group sessions in which students are encouraged to develop a self-analytic attitude and to question their present study habits. We shall return later to the discussion technique used but a typical starting point would be for students to make notes on the same text, swap and criticize them in pairs, bring their conclusions on note-taking together in a group of four and so on. In a similar manner marking essays is urged as an excellent training for writing them. Experience with these techniques shows that a good counsellor can organize an intensive group session on study habits which leads students to continue to refine their study techniques independently thereafter.

Differential transit   Nicholson[17] suggests that rather different challenges face the counsellor once the student is fully integrated in the system, especially as the academic challenge increases on going from early general to later specialist courses. Family and colleagues may feel by then they have made enough

349

allowances for the adult's studies. Good counselling on the choice of advanced courses is especially important.

Settled connection   Even for those fortunate students who achieve a harmonious equilibrium between study and day-to-day life, the counsellor has a role to play. He should be ready to guide at the recurrent choice points and to help the student who finds job satisfaction decreasing or is faced by an unforeseen event which upsets his schedule. Simpson[20] has compared the views of both Open University students and counsellors on counselling at the 'settled connection' stage. Counsellors were generally uncertain about their role but divided fairly easily into *interventionists* who initiated contact with students and *consultants* who waited for students to contact them. Naturally interventionists have more contact with students although both types had some reluctance to invade a student's privacy by making contact. All felt that continuity and knowing the students were essential to good counselling.

Nearly all students expected their counsellor to take an interest in their progress and over three-quarters both wished to keep the same counsellor throughout their studies and wanted him to initiate contact at least every three months using the phone where possible.

What makes a good counsellor? This question has been addressed by Thomas,[21] Northedge[22] and Murgatroyd.[23] After a study based on the critical incident approach Thomas identified the following qualities and habits of good counsellors: enthusiasm, takes initiative, sympathetic, contacts students, helps with problems, uses the hierarchy, has a flexible programme, can manage group activities, competent academically, knows the system, liaises with others, shares management tasks. Northedge concentrates on the roles of counsellors and distinguishes the *caring supporter* and the *efficient manager* as the two key functions. Since caring and managing require different skills the counsellor must make a conscious effort to balance the two. Murgatroyd cites Carl Rogers' three conditions for personal development through face-to-face interactions, namely empathy, genuineness and an unconditional positive regard for the student.

In remote learning systems other than the Open University counselling is more often a case of guilty conscience than a help with problems since there are few systems where the function has been institutionalized. Although a counselling service is clearly desirable, the need for continuity in the counsellor-student relationship to make it effective is a refrain that runs through writings on the subject. Cook[24] has discussed the administrative and organizational aspects of ensuring continuity.

Young institutions such as the Télé-université which do

not have, nor feel the need for, a counselling service may be living in a fool's paradise. Experience elsewhere shows that remote learning systems begin with a 'cream-skimming' stage when they attract students who have both higher motivation and greater experience than those who will provide the steady state clientele some years later. This gradual change in student profiles, together with the greater complexity and bureaucracy which occurs as an institution grows may create a real need for counselling.

Tutoring, animating and facilitating

By tutors, animateurs and facilitators we shall understand those people whose interaction with the students is based on a particular course. Since the word facilitator still sounds to the present authors like the name of a new brand of prophylactic we shall use the more expressive 'animateur' to cover this function. The difference in meaning between tutor and animateur was evoked in the first paragraphs.

As the next section will deal with group discussions we shall postpone consideration of the tutor-animateur's role in group meetings and concentrate here on the one-to-one relationship.

We can agree with Perraton[10] that 'the thing which a live tutor can do which we can't mechanize and we can't mass-produce, is to enter into a dialogue with his students'. Beevers[25] has described how this function was made operational in the early days of the Open University and emphasizes how few of the University staff were experienced in what was to be the main mode of a dialogue, namely correspondence tuition. Official documents tell tutors that 'In this essentially home-based teaching system, where attendance at the occasional tutorial is voluntary, your relationship with students is formed mainly through the exchange of assignments'. In a revealing phrase Kirk,[8] herself a tutor, after quoting this directive states, 'Thus, the part-timer's teaching duties are regarded *merely* as the assessment of, and support for, a centrally designed programme...'(our italics).

Naturally there is a tendency for tutors unused to dialogue by correspondence to attempt to pull the system towards more of the face-to-face contact which they find more familiar and fulfilling. The Open University seems to have successfully resisted this move, which would have imposed inconvenient and costly constraints on both students and the University, and indeed has developed impressive expertise in correspondence tuition. Harrison[9] describes how essay marking should be an exercise in conversation rather than an issuing of directives. On the same theme MacKenzie[26] discusses how to combat 'an established tendency, quite foreign to the way thought really develops, to see assignments as a series of paper hoops to burst through and discard'. Both tutors and students need to pay more attention to the progressive nature of the learning process. Occasional reviews of a series of assignments by a given student might be useful here.[27]

Rhys[27] suggests that the tutor, when marking assignments, should be balancing three types of consideration against each other; organizational requirements, communication with the student, and attention to the content. The balance will vary from essay to essay since the whole point of the dialogue is to avoid a mechanical process in which the tutor merely decides to what extent the student has followed the recipe for a good Open University essay.

The characteristics of Open Unversity tutors have been studied by Gibbs and Durbridge.[28] There was a broad agreement across faculties that the personal style of the tutor (understanding, systematic, informal, flexible, interesting) was the most important quality, followed by his teaching competence. Academic qualifications, as opposed to knowledge and handling of the subject matter, rated very low.

There is a parallel here with the experience of institutions using non-academic animateurs for dialogue with students. At the Télé-université we are finding that animateurs are moving from one course to another in different subjects with greater versatility than we expected. Implicitly we are placing more emphasis on personal characteristics and less on academic respectability in selecting these staff. The animateur's own confidence in his ability to handle the subject matter is a sufficient guarantee in nearly all cases.

Since few other remote learning institutions place as much emphasis on written interaction as the Open University we would encourage them to examine the examples of student-tutor exchanges collected by Lewis and Tomlinson[29] which show impressive maturity and thoughtfulness. Indeed, the main conclusion of our discussion of the tutoring functions is that remote learning systems would do well to place greater emphasis on written interaction. Not only would this reduce both time and travel constraints on students and part-time staff compared to face-to-face encounters, but it would also be more cost-effective.

Such a move would pose problems of training for part-time staff who, as already mentioned, are normally inexperienced in this function. However, this is only one aspect of the general issue of training and briefing of part-time staff, and we shall devote the rest of this section to this question.

We know of no remote learning system which is proud of the way it trains part-time staff. Macintyre[30] has been one of few people to study needs in this area. He found that part-time staff most wanted training in grading** and with face-to-face sessions. Interestingly most respondents held that meetings with other part-time staff were the most effective form of training. In view of our previous remarks it is perhaps surprising that few tutors felt the need of help with correspondence tuition. Macintyre is unable to decide whether this reflects cool competence or misplaced confidence.

Since personal characteristics have been shown to be so important in good counsellors and tutors, their selection should be uncomplicated. The articles we have reviewed suggest that their training should include information on the structure, organization and methods of the remote learning system which is employing them and clear directives on their role in it - which may be counter-intuitive or at least very different to their regular job in another institution. Once the staff have been trained and are in the system, regular and loosely structured meetings with other part-timers may be a sufficient incentive to further development.

Group meetings

Group sessions have become the pons asinorum of our time and this fad has taken root in adult education with infectious rapidity. This is not to suggest that group meetings have no place in adult learning, simply to recall that bringing people together does not automatically create a useful educational experience. Since students in a remote-learning system will be sceptical about any gathering which implies travel and time constraints, institutions have a duty to make group meetings effective. We shall first discuss face-to-face meetings and then examine the increasingly frequent use of telecommunications.

> *Face-to-face* Lewis [32] reminds us that students dislike 'face-to-face aimlessness' and do not necessarily appreciate a sharp contrast between highly structured media packages and amorphous get-togethers. Watkins [33] and Northedge [34] have addressed themselves to the problem of making discussions useful to students. Both acknowledge their debt to Hill [35] but suggest that his techniques need some modification in remote-learning systems.
>
> Northedge has found that the pure Hill technique is too introspective and places too much emphasis on the mastering of psychological concepts and the analysis of interaction with others. He proposed maintaining Hill's emphasis on an agreed agenda and reports on a technique which includes the following steps:
>
> 1 individual work (note making) (5 minutes)
> 2 work in pairs (comparing and consolidating) (10-15 minutes)
> 3 small groups (4-6) (comparing and consolidating) (30-45 minutes)
> 4 report back to whole group (30-45 minutes)
>
> Use of this technique, which he claims is 'robust enough,

and simple enough to survive a wide range of condi-tions', produced greater student enjoyment and increased the participation of quieter students whilst improving the quality of the argument considerably. In contrast to Hill's method this technique does not require the group to cover all the content, thus respecting Watkins[33] claim that the students themselves should control the pace and orientation of the discussion. Both Watkins and Northedge emphasize the importance of starting the meeting with a short period when students write prepara-tory notes. This helps to delay subjective reactions to the content until it has been objectively analyzed.

So far we have implied that a part-time staffer is present to lead and guide discussions. However, remote-learning systems are finding, in response to the scatter problem, that discussion groups with no tutor present can be found very useful by students. Sewart[36] has reported on the formation of such study groups, of which there were over one thousand in the Open Univer-sity in 1974, and Whitlock,[37] writing later, warns against the danger of stereotyping these groups into set paradigms. It appears that about one-third of stu-dents, many of them taking only one course and finding the going fairly tough, attend student study groups regularly. The groups meet roughly every three weeks and often, particularly in mathematics, an informal network of telephone contact operates as a result. Whitlock urges that regional staff pay more attention to helping these groups get started and that courses suggest some group activities.

Telecommunications As lower enrolments in advanced courses scattered students further from each other and from potential tutors, the Open University turned to the teleconference to surmount the problem of maintain-ing group meetings. Short[38] reviewed available evidence to show that teaching by telephone is acceptable in many cases and L'Henry-Evans[39] has reported on how it feels to guide a group discussion by telephone. More recently Turok[11] has summarized Open University exper-ience with group telephony and concludes that it has an important future. Naturally similar developments are occurring in other remote-learning systems. The Télé-universite uses teleconferences to link animateurs to isolated students at their home phones in groups of five or six and has published guides[40] for those involved with this medium. In other places, notably Wisconsin, dedicated educational telephone networks are used as the main vehicle for a whole series of adult courses. Those interested in the role of the telephone in educa-tion should consult the proceedings of two conferences on the subject.[41] Telephony can make a very cost-effective contribution to remote learning and even in the densely populated UK it provides interaction at a lower cost than face-to-face meetings for advanced courses. Study groups without a tutor can of course meet by phone too although they will probably need help to set up the conference. Drop-out from telephone groups has been shown to be very small.

Conclusion: putting it all together

We must disappoint the reader who, having persevered thus far, is expecting a recipe for the ideally cost-effective and educationally efficient remote-learning system. Such a recipe is impossible, simply because a system can only be conceived in relation to the country and context in which it is set. Barker[42] reminds us that printing and publishing resources are rare in developing countries, let alone television and radio production facilities. MacKenzie et al[46] point out that not all postal systems combine universality, reliability, uniformity, speed and low cost sufficiently to make them the basis for remote-learning.

Although the political, cultural and technological context of a country will affect all components of a remote-learning system it will have greater impact on what we have called the independent activities. This is partly why we have devoted most of this article to interactive activities, the other reason being that the costs of interactive activities are more rigidly volume-sensitive and hence can eat dangerously into the cost-effectiveness of a system. It is no doubt possible to write a guide to good practice for text-writing and electronic media production in remote learning, although for such common activities it is surprising how few systematic guidelines exist, but we shall leave that to others.

In building a remote-learning system from the components we have examined, we stress first that the adult student is a vehicle that can run well on a variety of mixtures of instructional fuel. Dubin and Taveggia,[43] in their much quoted but little read comparative study on the effectiveness of various types of instruction, found no significant difference with dull regularity. This means that a remote-learning system has considerable room for manoeuvre with the purely instructional parts of its programme. However, the adult student is busy and pragmatic. His involvement with the remote-learning system is only a minor aspect of his life. Learning activities must be organized to provide maximum advantage for minimum inconvenience.

Within these limits there is great scope for diversity. Indeed, Baume and Hipwell,[44] in an article about courses for workers on offshore oil rigs written with engaging verve,

355

suggest the mixture should be changed constantly to maintain a permanent Hawthorne effect. At the Télé-université we seem to have observed this maxim - although more by serendipity than by design!

Although some remote-learning systems operate without any personal contact we hope to have shown that the inclusion of properly planned interaction can be a help to the student. As well as socializing his learning it can provide an element of pacing and round off the authoritarian edges of the courses. However, interaction need not always mean face-to-face contact and most remote-learning systems would benefit by exploiting more fully written exchanges and teleconferences.

A second guideline is that the maxim 'nothing succeeds like excess' does not hold true in remote learning. Perhaps the major defect of the team approach to course design is the tendency to overdo things. Partly because the team invariably underestimates the time an average student will take over a piece of work, and also because many 'nice to know' sections are given the benefit of the doubt when the team is faced with choices, the remote-learning course that requires less study time than advertised is a rare phenomenon. The adult student is usually very conscientious - over-conscientious perhaps - and it is only fair for the course designers to be equally thorough in ensuring that the credit given for a course is commensurate with the study time the student puts in.

Related to the question of workload is our third guideline, namely the need to combine complexity with clarity. The more complex the combination of activities in a course becomes, the more important is it for the student to have a map of the maze in the form of a well written study guide. The students are the only people who experience every aspect of a course and unless the designers realize this they may find that the course as a whole is greater only in confusion than the sum of the parts.

Oddly, for people whose profession is devoted to precise thought, many academics have great difficulty specifying exactly what they want a student to do. It seems to them childish to indicate the time a student should spend on an activity or the length his essay should be. In a rather similar way some feel that their profession requires them to include frequent bibliographies along with vague exhortations, even though they know the student has no means of consulting the references cited.

In conclusion then, the leader of a team putting together a course for a remote-learning system must first bring his people down to earth and then keep them there. He must ensure that the diversity of activities planned and the enthusiasm of his team does not lead to overkill and confusion. He must remember that he is working for a busy adult, who always has good reasons for putting study off until tomorrow, and whom he must motivate. Pacing and interaction can be useful but it helps if the course is fun. The somewhat technocratic approach to course design used in distance education should not mean that the product is laundered of that zest for life and learning so necessary to the human spirit.

* Various titles are used to denote the staff, usually part-timers, which most distance systems employ to ensure some human contact at the local level. In this article we shall use the terms tutor and animateur more or less interchangeably although as the article proceeds it will become apparent that these two titles imply a slight difference in approach.

** James [31] has shown, for example, that there is a clear correlation between the length of an essay and the grade awarded.

Notes

1 Wedemeyer, C.A. (1971) Independent Study, The Encyclopaedia of Education, Vol. 4, New York, Macmillan.

2 Wedemeyer, C.A. (1974) Characteristics of Open Learning Systems, in National Association of Educational Broadcasters, Open Learning Systems, Washington, D.C.

3 Daniel, J.S. (1977) The Open University Concept, Canadian Journal of Information Science, 2(1) pages 129–138.

4 Pask, G., Scott, B.C.E., and Kallikourdis, D. (1973) A theory of conversations and individuals Int. J. Man-Machine Studies, 5 pages 17–52.

5 Daniel, J.S. (1975) Learning styles and strategies: the work of Gordon Pask in How Students Learn, N. Entwhistle and D. Hounsell (Eds), Lancaster IPCE pages 83–92.

6 Daniel, J.S. and Umbriaco, M. (1974) Distant Study in French Canada: the Télé-université, Teaching at a Distance No.4 pages 8–13.

7 Farnes, N. (1975) Student-centred learning, ibid. No.3 pages 2–6.

8 Kirk, P. (1976) The loneliness of the long-distance tutor, ibid. No.7 pages 3–6.

9 Harrison, B. (1974) The teaching-learning relationship in correspondence tuition, ibid. No.1 pages 2–8.

10 Perraton, H. (1974) Is there a teacher in the system? ibid. No.1 pages 55–60.

11 Turok, B. (1977) Telephony: a passing lunacy or a genuine innovation? ibid. No.8 pages 25–33.

12 Bates, A.W. (1975) The use of broadcasting at the Open University, IET paper, Open University.

13 Henry, J. (1977) The course tutor and project work, Teaching at a Distance No.9 pages 1–12.

14 Woodley, A. and McIntosh, N. (1977) People who decide not to apply

to the Open University, ibid. No.9 pages 18-26.

15 McIntosh, N. (1975) The place of summer schools in the Open University, ibid. No.3 pages 48-60.

16 MacKenzie, N., Postgate, R., and Scupham, J. (1977) Extract from Open Learning, ibid. No.8 pages 77-82. (This article is Chapter 5 of Open Learning: Systems and Problems in Post-Secondary Education, UNESCO Press (1975).

17 Nicholson, N. (1977) Counselling the adult learner in the Open University, ibid. No.8 pages 62-69.

18 Redmond, M. (1977) Aspects of adult learning, ibid. No.8 pages70-76.

19 Gibbs, G. and Northedge, A. (1977) Learning to study: a student-centred approach, ibid. No.8 pages 3-9.

20 Simpson, O. (1977) Post-foundation counselling, ibid. No.9 pages60-67

21 Thomas, A. (1974) Success and failure in Open University counselling ibid. No.1 pages 9-34.

22 Northedge, A. (1975) How many counsellor characteristics? ibid. No.3 pages 70-72.

23 Murgatroyd, S. (1976) Counselling in Continuing Education (2), ibid. No.6 pages 40-45.

24 Cook, R. (1977) Counselling continuity and the committed tutor-counsellor, ibid. No.9 pages 54-59.

25 Beevers, R. (1975) The function of the part-time academic staff in the Open University teaching sytem, ibid. No.3 pages 11-15.

26 MacKenzie, K. (1974) Some thoughts on tutoring by correspondence in the Open University, ibid. No.1 pages 45-51.

27 Rhys, S.M. (1975) The process of marking assignments: the tutor in action, ibid. No.4 pages 52-56.

28 Gibbs, G. and Durbridge, N. (1976) Characteristics of Open University tutors, ibid. No.6 pages 96-102.

29 Lewis, R. and Tomlinson, N. (1977) Examples of tutor-student exchanges by correspondence, ibid. No.8 pages 39-47.

30 Macintyre, G. (1977) Briefing and training: what do the consumers want? ibid. No.9 pages 68-70.

31 James, A. (1976) Does the amount written on assignments bias the grades awarded? ibid. No.7 pages 49-54.

32 Lewis, R. (1975) The place of face-to-face tuition in the Open University system, ibid. No.3 pages 26-31.

33 Watkins, R. (1975) Cooperative learning in discussion groups, ibid. No.2 pages 7-9.

34 Northedge, A. (1975) Learning through discussion in the Open University, ibid. No.2 pages 10-19.

35 Hill, W.F. (1969) Learning thru discussion, California, Sage Publications Inc.

36 Sewart, D. (1975) Some observations on the formation of study groups, Teaching at a Distance No.2 pages 1-6.

37 Whitlock, K. (1975) Study groups: some follow up proposals, ibid. No.3 pages 44-47.

38 Short, J. (1974) Teaching by telephone: the problems of teaching without the visual channel, ibid. No.1 pages 61-67.

39 L'Henry-Evans, O. (1974) Teaching by telephone: some practical observations, ibid. No.1 pages 67-69.

40. Keating, C.A., Daniel, J.S., and Marchand, R. (1977) <u>Guide de</u> <u>l'animateur téléphonique; La Télé-université au téléphone</u>, Quebec, Télé-univ- ersité.

41 Parker, L., and Riccomini, B. (eds) (1976,1977) <u>The Status of the</u> <u>Telephone in Education</u> and <u>The Telephone in Education Book II</u>, Madison, University of Wisconsin.

42 Barker, J. (1977) A package approach to distance teaching for developing countries, <u>Teaching at a Distance</u>, No.9 pages 36-42.

43 Dubin, R, and Taveggia, T.C. (1968) <u>The teaching-learning paradox:</u> <u>a comparative analysis of college teaching methods</u>, Eugene, Oregon, CASEA.

44 Baume, D., and Hipwell, J. (1977) Adaptable correspondence studies for offshore engineers - a course that learns, <u>Teaching at a Distance</u> No.9 pages 27-35.

Acknowledgement

This work was partially supported by the Department of Communications (Canada) and this assistance is gratefully acknowledged.

THE CONSULTATION IN THE PROCESS OF DISTANCE EDUCATION

Rudolf Schwarz

In the German Democratic Republic distance education has become a specific form of studies which does not entail interruption to professional work and which can be started by working people who have reached university entrance standard and have obtained professional experience.

Because the students have regular jobs, it objectively follows that in most cases their place of work or their home is not in the same town as the university. Hence the studies have to be planned and carried out alongside their daily work. Besides their family obligations, many students are active in social functions, so that the conditions of their studies are essentially different from those of full-time students.

In the course of more than twenty five years of development of this form of studies, we in the German Democratic Republic have built a firm, legally-regulated interrelationship between professional work and studies. On this basis - e.g. in the economically important scientific branches of technical, agricultural and economic sciences - a didactic conception of teaching and learning alongside professional work could be developed which meets the specific requirements of this mode of study. I would like to sum up this conception in 3 points:

1   As the distance student does not live in the town where the college is situated, he is not able to attend lectures every day. The aim and the contents of the studies have to be communicated by the college teacher with the help of special media, i.e. in a non-direct way. This is nowadays mainly done using specially designed and didactically and methodically prepared materials (*Lehrbriefe*) and textbooks which can be used for private study.

2   The distance student has to acquire knowledge and abilities independently with the help of these study materials. Therefore, in addition to providing subject matter, the teaching and study material has to fulfil

teaching functions that will give the student guidelines for his independent studies as well as helping him in the reinforcement and self-assessment of the knowledge and abilities he has acquired.

3   To secure optimum results, the educational work must be supported regularly and systematically, especially at the beginning of the course, by specific lectures in which firm relations between the teacher and the distance student need to be developed in connection with the guidance of independent studies and the assessment of results. The course consists of two parts, the first of which is held in a conveniently situated 'consultation centre' and the second at the enrolling college.

As in full-time studies, the basis of this conception is strict planning. An important consideration in the first part of the course is to ensure by all possible means that a uniform educational level is reached before the transition to the enrolling college. The lessons which are held to consolidate the process of studies are called 'distance education consultations'. They cannot be compared to consultations in full-time education.

The aim of this article is to deduce the place and the function of this consultation in the study process determined by study materials and independent studies, and hence to find out the tasks that the teacher has to fulfil vis-a-vis the distance student. From experience we know that the teacher who gives the consultation is able to influence greatly the intensity and the effectiveness of the studies as well as the efficient completion of the distance education course. By means of his educational work and control measures, he exerts a strong influence on the students' readiness to learn and on the progress they make not at least by his willingness to give individual support during the studies, which helps many distance students to overcome certain difficulties that would otherwise lead to their dropping out of the course. Thus the consultation becomes an important part of the organization of the process of studies. Its place is determined by the primacy of independent studies. Because the consultation takes place every other week for a group of distance students working in the same basic field, e.g. mechanical, electrical and civil engineering, economic sciences, or agricultural engineering, it becomes a firm but not inflexible connection between the phases of independent studies at home, so that study materials and teacher complement each other in their functional work for the distance student. Moreover, the teacher organizes his work not only with the effectiveness of study materials in mind, but also with an eye to external factors that further or hinder the study process. This means that, for instance, insufficient independent studies because of professional stress, social activities, family reasons, or even illness can lead to a student falling behind in the course, in which case the teacher has to make efforts to further the process of studies. On the other hand, the close link between study and practical professional work and the distance student's experience of professional and social work can be used to great effect by the teacher to intensify his educational work. Thus a consultation can never be formal, and in his work with the distance students every teacher is grateful for any impulses he gets from the field of professional practice which can be useful in the shaping of the study process.

The functions of a consultation thus result:

- from the place of the consultation in the process of studies and its interaction with independent studies and study materials;

- from the relationship between professional work and education and,

- as the unity of instruction and education is one of our basic social concerns, from the general demands made on a socialist teacher in his educational work.

The didactic conception of the distance education consultation depends on the function of the given study materials. As a rule, the aim and the subject matter of independent studies, ways, and methods of acquiring knowledge as well as certain forms of self-assessment and exercises to consolidate knowledge and abilities have to be contained in the study materials. On the basis of a set plan and concrete teaching recommendations, the task of the teacher is, on the one hand, to exercise influence on the methodical and organizational shaping of the independent studies and, on the other hand, to guarantee the continuous and systematic repetition, consolidation and checking of the knowledge and abilities acquired in the course of private studies.

In practical terms, the role and importance of the distance education consultation as described here is as follows:

1   In the consultation, the teacher has to supervise independent study with the help of study materials. In an introduction he will emphasize the main points of the next part of the course, motivate the studies and point out special links between theory and practice. In connection with an explanation of the aims of the course he will also outline the results that are expected.

2   He has to guarantee an up-to-date, rational course of independent studies alongside the student's professional work by setting concrete tasks and indicating ways and methods of solving them. This furthers the development of the ability to think scientifically, to

acquire theoretical knowledge and to generalize acquired knowledge and apply it creatively.

This way of leading the consultation counteracts a formal accumulation of knowledge, because facts - as far as their acquisition is necessary for the course - can be learned systematically if the student is regularly set selected, purposeful tasks that always meet his requirements.

3   He will give the distance student advice on the techniques of intellectual work, and on the basis of his own experience he will point out to him ways and means of organizing private studies, including individual and collective self-assessment methods.

4   Last, but not least, he has to build up the consultation as an effective system of consolidating and checking knowledge and abilities. He guarantees optimum results by:

- continuously and systematically checking the student's knowledge,

- dealing with open questions and problems and completing, widening and deepening the student's knowledge,

- systemising acquired knowledge.

No teacher who realizes the complex tasks that must be tackled in a consultation will want to deal with just a few of them. He will not, for instance, consider that a consultation should always be devoted exclusively to the communication of knowledge (by lectures) or to repetition exercises or to question and answer sessions. In practice, this course of action often followed because the distance student has done insufficient private studies or has complained about lack of time and so on, or determined by inadequate consideration of the peculiarities of distance education, has a very bad effect. A consultation which always serves only one aim, does not reach its real goal.

Experience shows that a distance student who is not consistently confronted with tasks is inclined to concentrate in his study only on a review of the material provided in classes; he may be content with just the material given in the lectures, which are relatively few and far between in comparison to a full-time course and are unable to meet the student's needs alone. He then makes the mistake of thinking that he is prepared for all difficulties. In such cases, not only the effectiveness of distance education but also its very viability is thrown into doubt.

An essential educational function of the consultation is to teach distance students how to proceed systematically in their independent studies. The main method used in this respect consists of setting high standards appropriate to the aim of the course, being uncompromising with the distance student and consistently checking the results of his studies. It is obvious that the fulfilment of the task to make independent studies the most important component of distance education by means of regular assessment depends above all else on the pedagogical qualities of the teachers. In this connection the distance education teacher must also be trained to stick consistently to the principle of consultations - that is to say, that they should be built up on the basis of the results of independent studies. Furthermore, this task is closely linked to the fact that the entire educational work of the staff must be geared to training the distance student to acquire knowledge for himself and to go on and think and act independently. In the study process, the time must come when the distance student is able to meet all the challenges of private study on his own, without the aid of consultations. There is no doubt that this task is the main function of the consultation in distance education. It is a prerequisite of the transition to the second part of the course, where there are no longer regular consultations every other week.

In this second part, only four to five seminar courses lasting several days each take place every study year; additionally, the distance student carries out independent studies based on a set plan and prescribed literature.

If we consider the nature of the tasks enumerated above, we see that, didactically speaking, the consultation has the component parts, which, no matter what the area of study, must be dealt with in the given sequence if the consultation as a whole is to be effective.

```
Assessment ——— Consolidation ———Introduction to
    ¦               |              independent studies
    ¦               |                     ¦
    └ − − − − − Consultation − − − − − − − ┘
```

These parts connect a phase of independent studies preceding a consultation to a phase following it in a form which is appropriate as far as timing is concerned, but which is not inflexible. The obligatory nature of the consultation for the distance student is an important factor, and in any special field it is always carried out by one and the same teacher, because optimum educational results can only be achieved if the teacher knows the ability of each distance student in his group and systematically watches his progress.

The amount of time which is spent on each of the three didactic parts in a ninety minute consultation depends particularly

-    upon the didactic preparation of the study materials,

-    upon the specific features of the material (e.g. degree of abstraction), so that in a series of consultations on the same subject may take many different forms, and

- not at least upon the progress the distance students are making towards learning how to work independently.

For instance, if the didactic functions of independent studies are emphasized and the distance student is trained in the course of the consultations to think for himself in a scientific way then the amount of time spent on an introduction to independent studies diminishes accordingly and is devoted instead to the consolidation of knowledge and abilities. To this end, the use of didactically-prepared special teaching material (*Lehrbrief*), programmed study material or a written guide to the studies can reduce the time spent on an introduction to independent studies to a minimum and thus allow more time to be given over to the remaining tasks. Not the least of our tasks therefore, is to constantly improve the didactic preparation of the study materials for distance education. This applies both to study materials (*Lehrbriefe*) and textbooks, and will in the future certainly lead to the development of other modern materials. Although the amount of time needed for the introduction to independent studies can be reduced, it seems unrealistic to dispense with the introduction completely because a teacher will always be able to and will always try to pass on his own experience of studying to his students and will advise them as best he can on the organization of their work. In any case, it is wrong always to devote the same length of time to each part of the consultation, as is still sometimes argued.

As to determining the functions of each didactic part of a consultation, a few brief points can be made:

1 Assessment of knowledge and abilities

The essence of this part of the instruction is to set tests at regular intervals in connection with an objective evaluation of what knowledge and abilities have been acquired. This evaluation is used, among other things, in assessing the results of intermediate and final exams.

Important rules for such oral and written tests (such as oral reports, short papers, synopses) lasting not longer than ten to fifteen minutes are:

- they have to be carried out regularly

- they have to be well-planned and thoroughly prepared as regards organization

- they have to be corrected thoroughly and recommendations given concerning gaps and weaknesses and

- the following fundamental principle should be borne in mind when carrying out any assessment:

Each distance student has the right to ask questions in the consultation to clarify any points and to fill gaps in his knowledge.

It follows from this that tests for assessment purposes can only be held on subjects that have already been dealt with in the consultation. This is the basis for a realistic evaluation of the results.

2 *Consolidation of knowledge and abilities*

This part of the instruction requires the largest amount of time in the consultation. It serves

- to close gaps, to clarify problems that have not yet been understood, to help in overcoming students' difficulties in finding solutions and in mastering scientific methods, as well as

- the enlargement and logical ordering of knowledge, the emphasis of vital links and essential phenomena, plus necessary additions to, and the deepening of, the students' knowledge, and

- the emphasis of connections between theory and practice as well as the organization of theoretical and practically-orientated exercises, and finally the systematic reiteration of subject matter by means of questions and solution of tasks designed to consolidate knowledge and abilities.

3 *Introduction to independent studies*

A teacher cannot do justice to this part of the instruction by simply giving quick and superficial information about which part of the study material has to be read for the next consultation. His task is, based upon the study material,

- to decide exact aim

- to give a brief, clear outline of the topic covering certain fundamental aspects which are already known to the students,

- at the same time to emphasize main points,

- to point out difficulties which may crop up in private study,

- to set concrete tasks and possibly to indicate ways of solving them as well as

- to outline the results that must be achieved without fail and to speak about their significance.

Enumeration of the tasks which have to be carried out in each of the three parts of the consultation reveals how complex they are.

A teacher who is conscious of the complex nature of his work in distance education is aware at the same time of how thoroughly he must prepare for it. His preparation must embrace not only his specialist subject, but also his pedagogical and methodological approach to it. For this work he needs sound pedagogic training, because he will soon realize in his practical work that he can never fulfil his educational tasks with the help of a universal method or even a rigid set of rules.

It seems to us that the most important attribute of the university teacher is pedagogic receptiveness to the aims, tasks and problems of distance education, because from this grows a readiness to fulfil all his educational tasks. Great success is achieved by teams of teachers who purposefully contribute to the improvement of pedagogics and methodology in distance education by regularly sharing their experiences with one another. This represents an important pledge to constantly increase the intensity and effectiveness of distance education, a form of study to which we in the German Democratic Republic are devoting great attention.

SECTION 8: ECONOMICS

INTRODUCTION

It may well be asserted that the economics of education is
as old as economics - or perhaps education - itself in that
skills of all sorts have ever been seen as an investment
leading to a higher return either in wages or status or some
other currency. However, most people would agree that the
beginnings of major developments in the economics of education can be traced to the late fifties when economists began
to look at the developed and developing countries and to try
to relate education and economic growth and at the same time
to begin to assess investment in the education of individuals, the creation of "human capital", in relation to the
other more generally accepted forms of investment.

By the early sixties, development of these economic
theories had produced a general acceptance that investment
in education, and particularly in higher education, could
and would lead to economic growth. Since the opportunities
for higher education would also expand the opportunity for
individual potential, the requirements of the State and the
requirements of the individual were seen to be combined in
the expansion of public sector - and therefore "free" -
higher education. The sociological argument in favour of
equality of opportunity and the economic argument in favour
of investment in higher education both appear in the Robbins
report[1] which was the major influence on the expansion of
higher education in the United Kingdom at this time and
these arguments held sway in developing and developed countries alike. By the end of the seventies, some significant
challenges to theory and practice had developed but it is to
the sixties and seventies, two decades of euphoric partnership between social and economic theory, that the great
developments in higher education at a distance belong.

This social and economic theory alone created such a
climate, we might have expected higher education to flourish
by expansion along traditional lines. Certainly this was
seen, and in a worldwide context, but in addition the
technological climate was such that multi-media distance

369

teaching systems could be developed and evaluated and this, of course, could be done not only in relation to the feasibility of the technology as a servant of education but also in relation to the inputs and outputs of traditional higher education and these new systems, the education production function as it is sometimes called.

The three articles in this section are concerned with the education production function in higher education with particular reference to a comparison of distance education and traditional systems. The problems encountered in any consideration of this area are legion. In the first case, studies must be concerned with the inputs in relation to the outputs. But any comparison must be made to an input or output which is constant or for which an agreed value can be determined. Problems immediately arise when a comparative cost analysis is done of traditional and distance teaching higher education systems and even when the comparison is between distance teaching higher education systems themselves, since there is disagreement on the value of inputs and outputs.

In the traditional universities, the proportion of costs not related directly to output, the fixed costs, is small since the major ongoing cost of a traditional system is academic staff salaries which is related by a formula to student numbers, the output. The traditional higher education system is therefore very labour intensive and economics of scale, at least in relation to the major ongoing cost of staff time, are minimal. The same is not true of distance education where the preparation of the teaching material represents a considerable cost or input and does not stand in such a fixed ratio to the students. Thus, the distance teaching system is not labour intensive and costs per student are not so fixed but will vary very significantly in accordance with student numbers.

The argument in these articles is based upon the published costs and structure of conventional universities in the United Kingdom, the Open University in the United Kingdom and Athabasca University in Canada. Snowden and Daniel judge that the general cost equation and the methodological approach adopted by Wagner in relation to the large Open University system is appropriate to the small distance education system represented by Athabasca. Wagner has used the conventional university recurrent expenditure in 1973 and compared this with the Open University. His previous articles[2] had been based upon 1968/9 figures for the conventional universities and this new data confirms the significant cost advantages of the Open University which he had previously postulated and which had been supported by Laidlaw and Layard[3]. However, Wagner's later article, published here, interposes a number of new factors which became more clear as the Open University developed and began to show that the economies of scale reached in the Open University's first years could not be projected into the future indefinitely. Indeed, after some 5 years, the Open University had begun to settle down more closely to the conventional university pattern with little increase in productivity. It is this feature which is taken up by Rumble who notes that for the Open University a significant change in patterns of expenditure is required if unit costs are to be affected to any significant degree.

The articles by Snowden and Daniel and by Wagner have formed the basis for a methodological approach. They do not, however, provide an acceptable definition of constants for input or output, nor do they provide any formula for the comparison of such inputs and outputs. Their comparative cost analysis between conventional and distance teaching higher education systems are thus open to question in relation to some of the fundamental assumptions. Rumble notes that the assumption that the same academic quality can be attached to a United Kingdom Open University degree and that of a conventional university degree has been open to question [4]. Moreover, the higher age of Open University graduates in comparison to conventional university graduates lowers *prima facie* the value of an Open University degree to a graduate. While Wagner had based his calculations on an assumption of equality between conventional Open University students and graduates, he had himself suggested that a better measure of value would be the value added to a student. Such a factor would, of course, significantly alter the balance of the equation in favour of the Open University since, if the Open University and the conventional university degree are seen as equal, the Open University, by admitting in general a student population of a lower academic level than the conventional universities, would be adding a significant extra value to its students in achieving the same output standard of graduates. In his conclusions, Rumble begins to provide some useful qualifications which will doubtless form the basis of further research in this area. He notes that it is not only the number of students but more correctly the number of students studying a course i.e. the number of courses on offer, which produces the significant cost variable. Furthermore, the cost of the chosen media and the relative effectiveness of this choice is also significant. Mace [5] had suggested that a reduction in expenditure on broadcasting amongst other things might prove more cost-effective in the Open University context. Recently, and postdating these articles, the Open University has set some cost limits on its broadcasting activities and the average number of television and radio broadcasts per course has been reduced significantly. In addition, audio cassettes are rapidly taking over from open circuit radio broadcasts and video cassettes have begun to follow a similar pattern. The

question is further complicated by the educational effectiveness of these two systems. The cassette which can be stopped,
re-started and repeated at will is a totally different
medium from the ephemeral open circuit broadcast. It goes
without saying, of course, that the production costs follow
an entirely different course.

The three articles which follow represent a major
initial attempt at an economic analysis of distance teaching
systems in higher education and in comparison with conventional universities. They begin to point to a whole area of
work involving the comparative costs and cost-effectiveness
of different media and different systems in order to ascertain relative effectiveness. It would be valuable to see
more recent data from Athabasca University compared with the
conventional universities in Canada. A comparative study of
the Fernuniversität and the conventional universities in
West Germany is also essential as is an analysis of the dual
on campus and off campus (distance teaching) systems exemplified in certain Australian universities and particularly
Deakin University.

It is likely that the next decade will see significant
advances in this area of research. In Europe and in many
other parts of the world, the climate under which the
expansion in higher education flourished in the sixties has
changed. The needs of the State and the development of the
individual no longer appear in such perfect harmony. The
economic value of higher education to the State is now
questioned, not only in the confines of academia. Other more
pressing requirements for public sector funding are now
being advanced. Amongst students too, the economic value of
a degree is called into question as unemployment and redundancy, previously almost the exclusive preserve of the blue
collar worker, have taken a hold amongst white collar workers
and the graduate professions. The comparative cost-effectiveness of distance education demonstrated by Wagner and
others from the beginning of the last decade, had little or
no impact on policy at that time. The idea of higher
education as an investment in human capital was eagerly
accepted by educationalists as a support and a "proof" of
their own judgement of eudcation as a good thing *per se*. For
them, expansion in higher education meant expansion of the
traditional system. Cost benefit analysis and cost-effectiveness was an unwarranted intrusion. Educational opinion
weighed heavily against the Open University at its inception.
Its creation was seen as a political publicity stunt and it
was regarded with open contempt and its chances of success
dismissed out of hand. The fact that it was successful has
led to the acceptance of distance education by all educationalists as part of the total United Kingdom plan for higher
education by the end of the decade. Perhaps, however, this
happy state of affairs is to be of very limited duration.

The economic climate in the United Kingdom has led to cuts in the conventional higher education system. Perhaps even the present limited research on cost-effectiveness in this area will have more implications for higher education than has yet been realised and the results in these papers will begin to have a serious effect upon policy in higher education in the United Kingdom.

David Sewart

Notes

1 Robbins, L. (1963). Committee on Higher Education under the Chairmanship of Lord Robbins, HMSO.

2 Wagner, L. The Economics of thee Open University, Higher Education I (2). Wagner, L. (1973), The Open University and the Costs of Expanding Higher Education, Universities Quarterly, Autumn.

3 Laidlaw, B. and Layard, R., Traditional versus Open University Teaching Methods: a Cost Comparison. Higher Education, 3, pp.439-68.

4 See also Carter C.F. (1973). The Economics of the Open University: A Comment, Higher Education, 2, pp.69-70; Carney, M. and Levin, H.M. (1975), Evaluation of Educational Medium: Some Issues, Instructional Science, 4, pp.385-406.

5 Mace, J. (1978). Mythology in the Making: is the Open University Really Cost-effective? Higher Education, 7, pp.295-309.

THE ECONOMICS OF THE OPEN UNIVERSITY REVISITED

Leslie Wagner

1. Introduction

In Wagner (1972, 1973) some first calculations of the likely average cost per student at the Open University were presented and compared with data for conventional universities in the U.K. The figures were calculated for 1973 at 1971 prices by using the Open University budget for that year estimated in 1971 and the actual expenditure figures for conventional universities in 1968-69 (the latest year then available) extended to 1973 on an assumption of no change in productivity. Leaving aside more general objections to comparisons between the Open University and conventional universities which will be discussed in a moment, the method of calculation clearly left substantial scope for error. However, this was the best that could be achieved with the data available at the time.

It is now possible to present a cost comparison between the Open University and conventional universities based on actual 1973 expenditures. This is not only of interest in providing more accurate data but also enables a check to be made on the estimating methods employed previously and particularly on the extent to which the budgeted figures for the Open University and the assumptions about productivity made for conventional universities were realized in practice.

This paper, therefore, will first present the revised figures for 1973. These will show that the average cost per equivalent undergraduate at the Open University was slightly lower than had been forecast, largely due to the University enrolling more students, whilst for conventional universities the results support the assumption of no increase in productivity between 1968-69 and 1972-73. The rest of the paper is concerned with a detailed analysis of Open University costs from 1973 to the end of the decade. The figures indicate that whilst in 1975 average costs fell, a rise is likely to have occurred in 1976. Moreover, on the basis of anticipated expenditure and student numbers of 1979, average costs are unlikely to fall much below the level reached in 1976. Thus it would seem that further economies of scale arising from the Open University method of teaching are unlikely. The reason for this surprising conclusion will be analysed and the paper ends with an examination of some alternative policies which could yield further reduction in average cost per student.

2. Comparisons between the Open University and conventional universities

The Open University is of interest to economists because its method of instruction produces a different cost function from that for conventional universities. In preparing and presenting courses using correspondence material, broadcasting and personal tuition for part-time students at a distance, a large proportion of costs is incurred irrespective of the number of students. The ratio of fixed cost to variable cost per student at the Open University is much higher than for conventional universities. According to Laidlaw and Layard (1974) the ratio is in excess of 2000:1 for many social science courses at the Open University compared to about 8:1 in conventional universities. A cost comparison is useful therefore for indicating the implications of alternative production systems in higher education. However, in order to ensure that the comparison is made on a fair basis, a number of problems need to be overcome.

1. *Costs and outputs*

A paper comparing the economics of two different systems of higher education ideally should calculate both costs and outputs. In using student or graduate numbers as a measure of output, the assumption is made that an Open University graduate is the same in academic terms as a conventional university graduate. Is this correct? Certainly, when the Open University was established it made clear its intention to set academic standards equivalent to those of conventional universities and the setting up of the Academic Advisory Committee, the heavy use of consultants on preparing courses and part-time tutors from conventional institutions in teaching them, together with the work of external examiners were all designed to achieve this objective. Any judgement on this matter is likely to be a subjective one. Certainly, there has been little public criticism of the University's academic standards and it must be remembered that virtually all the teaching materials are openly available for others to criticize. By 1976, an increasing number of collaboration and transfer schemes with other institutions of higher education has been established and the evidence is that graduates with first class honours are competing on equal terms with others for research and postgraduate posts.

In any event, a true measure of output should measure not just the final standard achieved but value-added, the difference between initial and final standard. A university which creams off the most academically able, may not necessarily have a higher value-added if it achieves more first class honours graduates than another which has a less able intake. If indeed the final academic standard of an Open University degree is the same as that of other institutions, then its teaching output per student as measured by value-added must be higher. The open access policy of the University results in a lower average educational standard of entrant than in conventional higher education. So, if final standards are the same, the Open University can claim to have a higher value-added per student. No evidence for this claim exists at the moment but the University is participating in a research project with the Esmee Fairbain Economics Research Centre at Heriot Watt University to test students on economics courses to obtain a measure of value-added. The results will be compared with similar tests carried out on students at conventional universities (see Attiyeh and Lumsden, 1971, 1972).

Carter has raised another objection to the assumption that the teaching output of the two types of institution are the same. He argues that the Open University and conventional universities are "two quite different kinds of educational experience: one full-time, involving close relations with other students in a wide range of activities, free from the pressures of earning a living and from most other responsibilites; the other requiring the dedicated use of spare time, in a life subject to the discipline of other responsibilites" (Carter 1973).

Carter's point is that while the investment benefits of the two forms of higher education as measured by the standard of graduate and future contributions to national output might be similar, the consumption benefits enjoyed by the students will be different. This is clearly so and any student would have to weigh up these differences in any private calculus of costs and benefits that he might undertake. They are of less relevance in a social calculus of the investment costs and benefits which is the theme of this paper.

2. Teaching and research

Even if it is accepted that standards are the same, cost comparisons in terms of student or graduate numbers only measure teaching output. Universities, however, have other functions, notably research. Some would argue that teaching and research are joint products which feed upon each other so that resources devoted to research should have an impact on better quality teaching. Even if this is so, it will not be reflected in an output measure of teaching such as student numbers which assume that the quality of all students is the same. Graduate numbers might show some distinction as presumably better quality teaching should be reflected in lower drop-out rates. However, this too is not very satisfactory.

Research is not a very well defined area of an academic's job specification. Clearly, research designed to improve teaching can be viewed as a joint product and the resources devoted to such research can be related to teaching output. Research designed to advance knowledge of a particular subject has a stimulating and refreshing function for the teacher and may influence the quality of teaching in a number of ways but is largely in the short-run at any rate a substitute product for teaching. Any fair comparison of the teaching costs of two institutions should take into account the proportion of total costs devoted to teaching.

The enquiry into the use of academic staff time by the Committee of Vice-Chancellors and Principals in 1969/70 indicated that about 35 per cent of academics' time was spent on research and external professional work. The rest was spent on teaching and unallocable internal work, most of which was connected with teaching or its administration. Direct teaching and research costs take up about 65 per cent of total university costs but a large proportion of the rest can also be allocated between teaching and research. Thus a fair estimate would be that about 30 per cent of total costs are incurred on non-teaching or student related activities.

Staff at the Open University in principle have the same conditions of service in relation to research as staff in other institutions. It is generally accepted that in the first few years this was not operative as the major effort was devoted to producing as many courses as possible. Whilst more time is now being devoted to research, indeed the increase in average costs for 1976 may in part be a reflection of this, it is certainly true that in the period under consideration here only a small proportion of academics' time was devoted to research. It should also be remembered that academic staff costs at the Open University are a smaller proportion of the total than at conventional universities, and that there are large areas of expenditure – broadcasting, regional tuition and administration, and production of course material – which are solely concerned with teaching. On this basis, it is a fair assumption that research and external professional work has taken up about 20 per cent of the time of O.U. academics and thus about 5 per cent of total Open University costs. Whilst the main results will be shown on the basis of total recurrent expenditure figures, separate calculations will also be shown allowing for non-teaching expenditure on the basis of 5 per cent reduction for the Open University and 30 per cent for conventional universities.

3. *Standardized input*

The Open University is concerned almost entirely with undergraduate teaching. There is a small amount of postgraduate work involving research students. In addition, the post-experience programme provides courses on a one-off basis in particular areas. Both these activities however, have a negligible impact on costs and it is therefore reasonable to assume that total expenditure is related to a standardized group of students, namely undergraduates.

Conventional universities have a much more complex mix of students involving both undergraduates and postgraduates. These must be standardized to undergraduate equivalent student numbers to provide a fair basis for comparison. Some years ago, the University Grants Committee used to specify that educational diploma students were worth 1 unit of undergraduate load [1], arts and social science postgraduates were worth 2 units and science-based postgraduates were worth 3 units (UGC 1969). These ratios were used in the previous papers. Subsequently, the UGC revised their estimates and stated that the ratio of postgraduate to undergraduate costs was "between 1 and 2 with arts subjects towards the bottom and science subjects towards the top of this range" (UGC 1973). The revised figures for conventional universities will therefore be calculated on both the old basis to provide a comparison with the previous estimate and on the new basis to provide an updated figure.

4. *Price index*

The previous calculations were in 1971 prices and the UGC Tress-Brown index of university costs has been used to revalue the 1973 data and that for subsequent years on the same basis.

5. *Subject mix*

A further objection to comparisons between the Open University and conventional universities is that the latter contain relatively expensive medical and veterinary departments, whilst the former does not. This matter was dealt with in Wagner (1973) where it was shown that excluding expenditure on medical and veterinary students reduced the average cost per equivalent undergraduate in conventional universities by about £40 in 1971 prices or in other words by about 4 per cent.

3. Revised calculations for 1973

In the previous papers, four main calculations were shown
(a) average recurrent cost per equivalent undergraduate
(b) as in (a) but including the imputed rental costs of capital equipment
(c) average recurrent cost per graduate

378

(d) resource cost per equivalent undergraduate.

The results of these calculations are shown in Table I. Details of the revised calculations for each of these four types of cost are shown and explained in Appendix I. The results are summarised in Table II. These indicate that the Open University average recurrent cost per equivalent undergraduate was slightly lower in 1973 than previously forecast.

TABLE I

Open University and Conventional Universities Original Estimated Average Costs 1973 at 1971 Prices

	Open University	Conventional University
A. Average recurrent cost per equivalent undergraduate	£278	£940
B. Average recurrent cost including the imputed rental cost of capital per equivalent undergraduate	£300	£1200
C. Average recurrent cost per graduate	£1200 @ 50 per cent drop-out rate £4000 @ 85 per cent drop-out rate	£4000 +
D. Resource cost per equivalent undergraduate	£295	£1577

This arises as a result of the University enrolling more students than had been assumed in the earlier calculation. For conventional universities the figure is slightly higher than previously forecast but the assumption of no increase in productivity is generally borne out. So the Open University average cost advantage of about 4:1 is maintained. However, if the allowance for research previously mentioned is taken into account the advantage is reduced to about 3:1. Allowing for the rental value of capital improves the ratio in the Open University's favour.

However, the Open University's advantage in average cost per student would be of little value if a substantially larger proportion of the students failed to graduate compared to those in conventional universitites. The evidence of the early years of the University is that about 25 per cent of finally registered students do not survive a particular course. When this is related to the average cost per student course and the number of completed courses required for a degree the likely average cost per graduate can be obtained. If the drop out rate in the future does not differ significantly from the past then the average cost per graduate is likely to be below half that at conventional universities.

Finally the resource costs measure the cost to the economy and include therefore the output lost by full-time students not being in employment. This of course increases the Open University's advantage because all its students are part-time. The figures indicate a ratio of 6:1 in the Open University's favour.

TABLE II

Open University and Conventional Universities Revised Average Costs
1973 at 1971 Prices

	Open University	Conventional University
A. Average recurrent cost per equivalent undergraduate	£258	£960
B. Average recurrent cost including the imputed rental cost of capital per equivalent undergraduate	£272	£1111
C. Average recurrent cost per graduate	£2719 in 1973 £1842 in the long run	£4049–£4801
D. Resource cost per equivalent undergraduate	£272 minimum	£1647–£1947

4. Development of Open University costs

The data so far presented relate to 1973 only. How have costs and student numbers at the Open University developed since then? Table III presents the answer giving Open University recurrent expenditure and student numbers for 1974 to 1976. The 1974 and 1975 data are actual figures whilst the 1976 figures are estimates made in mid-1976.

The data in table III indicate that in real terms, average costs fell in 1975 because of a significant increase in student numbers, but are likely to have risen again in 1976 because student numbers rose much more slowly. Additionally in 1976 total expenditure increased in real terms although this was not reflected in new courses. The statistics here are misleading. In 1975, 43 full credit equivalent courses were presented whereas in 1976 this rose to 55.16 whilst the planned figure for 1977 is 62.66. At first glance, therefore, it would seem that there was a significant increase in course presentation in 1976. It must be remembered however, that a large proportion of the costs of producing a course are incurred in the year before first presentation. So a major element of the costs of the extra 12.16 courses presented in 1976 were incurred in 1975 when average costs actually fell. One explanation for this is that academic staff concentrated their teaching effort into 1975, taking a large part of 1976 for accumulated study leave and research. Part of the extra costs in 1976 involved extra staffing to compensate for this factor.

TABLE III

Open University Average Recurrent Cost per Equivalent Undergraduate 1974-76

Year	Recurrent Exp.£M Current Prices	Student Numbers	Average recurrent cost per student	Average recurrent cost per student 1971 prices
1974	14.6	42636	342	255
1975	19.6	49358	397	240
1976	26.1	50994	512	249

The analysis in the previous paragraph indicates that there is only limited value to studying the average cost figure. For the figure in any one year may be affected by short-term factors as explained for 1976 above, whilst the figure over time is a result of a combination of factors, none of which is fixed. For example, the same number of courses could have been presented to 60,000 students with a marginal increase in total costs. This would have reduced the average cost figure by about £20 per student in 1971 prices. The student number total of 50,994 in 1976 was determined by government decision on the intake numbers, whereas in terms of demand far more could have been accommodated. Alternatively, if student numbers were fixed at 50,994 the University could have reduced its expenditure by putting on less courses. A long-term policy to halve the number of new courses produced each year with a consequent reduction in staffing would reduce recurrent expenditure by some £2 million. If this had applied in 1976 it too would have reduced average costs per student by about £20 in 1971 prices.

It is necessary, therefore, to provide a more detailed analysis of Open University costs in order to analyse likely trends to the end of the decade and the implication of future policies. A first attempt at this was given in Laidlaw and Layard (1974) where costs in 1972 were separated into central university or course costs. Within each of these categories, costs were further allocated between those which were fixed and those that varied with student numbers.

Laidlaw and Layard calculated the fixed and variable cost for each course presented in 1972. The annual fixed cost was calculated by amortizing the total fixed cost of a course over 6 years including 2 years prior to first presentation assuming a 5 per cent interest rate. The average over all courses was an annual fixed cost of £113,000 and a variable cost of £70 per student in 1972 prices. The central university costs were estimated at £1.58M fixed + £44 per student.

A more detailed analysis was provided by Smith (1975) and this has been updated by Rumble (1976). They identified the two major cost initiators at the University as course and student numbers and established a linear function which identified those costs which are independent of these two variables and therefore fixed and those which depended on either course or student numbers. Thus

$$C = a + bx + cy$$

where a = fixed costs
    x = number of courses
    y = number of students.

The values b and c can be determined for any particular year by dividing the total costs allocated to students and courses by actual student or course numbers in that year. They thus represent average variable cost and will only be equal to the marginal cost of expanding student or course numbers, if it is assumed that average variable cost does not decline as numbers rise. It is likely however, that economies of scale do exist particularly in student costs, so that the marginal costs of increasing student numbers is probably a little below the figure given by average variable cost. Table IV indicates the allocation of expenditure in 1976 between fixed, course and student initiated categories.

The central academic areas include all faculty and library costs and are largely allocated to course production; regional academic costs which include the running costs of the 13 regional headquarters but not the actual costs of part-time tuition - these are covered by direct student costs - are almost all allocated to student numbers. Broadcasting costs are divided between the direct programme-making costs (including production staff costs) which are allocated to courses and all other costs which are regarded as fixed. The majority of administration costs are regarded as fixed but a significant proportion covering examinations, registry and administrative, postal and telephone costs are related to student numbers. Institutional services cover a miscellaneous group including capital expenditure out of income,

maintenance, research funds and staff-student facilities and
is largely allocated to overheads. Summer School costs although self-financing through student fees are still a cost
of the University's operation and these are allocated to
students as are direct student costs which cover the variable
print costs and packaging and mailing costs of course material together with the costs of part-time tuition and counselling.

TABLE IV

Allocation of Open University Costs in 1976 at 1976 Prices between Fixed,
Course and Student Initiated Categories

Area	Fixed	Student	Course
Central Academic	119	676	4366
Regional Academic	279	3699	
Broadcasting	2008		1666
Administration	2700	1515	190
Institutional Services	1861	869	103
Summer Schools		1409	
Direct Student Costs		4689	
Total	6967	12857	6325

It is clear that some of the allocations are likely to be a
little arbitrary but the overall result is thought to be a
fair reflection of the distribution of costs between the
three categories. Dividing the figures in the total column
for student and course initiated costs by student and course
numbers for 1976 gives the following equation:

$$C = 6,967,000 + 100,000x + 248y$$

where x = number of courses
y = number of students

This equation, however, is of limited use in postulating
future course and student numbers and calculating the effect
on total and average costs. The difference between average
variable and marginal costs on student numbers has already
been mentioned. Rumble (1976) has calculated that the marginal cost of small increases in student numbers might be as
low as £116 rather than the £248 given above because administrative and regional academic services would not be burdened
with many extra costs in such circumstances. This calculation
also assumes a linear cost function for those areas (direct
student and summer school) which do incur extra costs from

383

small increases in student numbers. However, it is likely that economies of scale do exist in these areas as well. In these circumstances, the marginal cost from small increases in student numbers might be as low as £100. For larger increases it is difficult to be precise. Certainly economies of scale should reduce the figure below £248 but it can also be argued that very large increases may produce diseconomies of scale as well. However, for the student numbers estimated to the end of the decade these are not thought very likely and a figure of £200 per student is assumed.

A further complication arises from the figure of £100,000 for the average variable cost per course. This covers both new courses being produced and old courses being maintained. In 1976, for example the total course related costs of £6.325M were incurred on producing 9 new full-credit equivalent courses (of which 1.5 credits are remakes of an existing course) and maintaining 55.16 full-credit equivalent courses. In future years an increasing proportion of total course-related costs will be incurred on maintaining existing courses rather than producing new or remade ones. Thus it is necessary to separate out these two different elements in order to estimate likely future course-related costs. Open University planning assumes that the maintenance of a course incurs 10 per cent of the cost of producing a new course. If this is accepted, then the breakdown of 1976 costs between new and maintained courses can be obtained as follows:

$$£6,325,000 = 9x + 55\frac{x}{0.1}$$

where x = cost of producing a new course
$\therefore 6,325,000 = 9x + 5.5x$
and $6,325,000 = 14.5x$
$x = £436,200$

Therefore, on the basis of 1976 data, a new course costs about £436,000 to produce, whilst the cost of maintaining a course comes to about £44,000. These figures will be used to calculate the cost implication of future course production plans at the Open University.

It is now possible to provide estimates of likely Open University costs to the end of the decade based on different assumptions about course and student numbers. The equation used is:

$$C = 19,824,000 + 436,000Cn + 44,000Cm + 200Sn$$

where C = Total Costs
Cn = New Courses
Cm = Maintained Courses
Sn = Extra students above the 1976 level

384

Total student costs in 1976 have been included in the fixed term to enable the effect of taking extra students above the 1976 level to be estimated. As explained above, these marginal costs are likely to be below the average variable cost figure. The number of new courses produced in any one year is not necessarily the same as the number of extra courses added to the academic programme because some new courses will in fact be replacing existing courses. This will be increasingly so in the future, so that whilst the University has a production capability at present of about 12 new courses per annum as more and more of these simply replace existing courses, the number of new courses added to the academic programme will fall. Table V indicates the assumptions made about new course production, number of courses maintained and student numbers for the years 1976-79. These are based on plans known at the time of writing and may of course change. However, the equation used allows the effect of any changes on total and average costs to be calculated.

TABLE V

Open University Plans 1976-79

(1) Year	(2) New Courses Produced	(3) Net New Courses ((2)-Replacement)	(4) Courses Maintained	(5) Student Numbers
1976	9	7.5	55.16	50,994
1977	13	9.5	62.66	56,550
1978	12	5	72.16	60,500
1979	12	4	77.16	62,500

Note: number of courses to be maintained in year t equals number of courses to be maintained in year t–1 plus net new courses in t–1.

On the basis of the data in Table V and using the equation given, Open University average recurrent costs per equivalent undergraduate can be calculated as shown in Table VI.

It would seem from Table VI that there is unlikely to be any significant fall in average costs in the next few years. Indeed, the 1979 figure expressed in 1971 prices is £240 which is less than £20 below the 1973 figure. It would seem therefore, that most of the economies of scale of the Open University had been reaped within the first few years of its operation and that since then it has been following the conventional university pattern of little increase in productivity.

TABLE VI

Open University Average Recurrent Expenditure per Student 1976-79 in £000 at 1976 prices

Year	Fixed Cost	New Course Costs	Maintained Course Costs	New Student Costs	Total Costs	Average cost per Student
1976	19,824	3,924	2,427	–	26.2	513*
1977	19,824	5,668	2,757	1111	29.4	520
1978	19,824	5,232	3,175	1901	30.1	498
1979	19,824	5,232	3,395	2301	30.8	493

*Due to rounding there is a slight discrepancy between this figure and that given earlier in the paper for 1976.

Why is this so? One obvious answer is that the rate of increase in student numbers has slowed down. This is, of course, true but on the other hand, it may well be that a figure of about 65,000 students is the maximum the present system of production and administration can handle and any increase above this figure would require radical reorganization and a rise in the element of cost now regarded as fixed. Moreover, at the 1979 level of expenditure for course production and maintenance student numbers would have to rise to about 85,000 to bring average costs per student to below £200 in 1971 prices. In other words, it would require a 36 per cent increase in student numbers to produce a 16 per cent fall in average costs.

The major reason for the small fall in average costs since 1973 is that the University has been using the economies produced by rising student numbers to increase the number of courses offered to students. However, as Table VI shows, with a static new production capacity and an increased number of replacement courses, the number of new courses offered to students is likely to rise more slowly in 1979. Indeed, it is only by virtually halving the number of new courses offered that the University is able to maintain its average cost per student in that year. The academic plan proposes a final target of 87 full-credit equivalent courses and it is the speed with which this target is reached that will determine the behaviour of average costs. If the University increases its production capacity to reach the target earlier than presently planned (1982) costs will rise. On present plans, however, it would seem that the University is planning little or no increase in its production capacity so that remade courses will increasingly take up a larger proportion of annual course production and extra courses offered to students will increase much more slowly than in the past.

386

5. Reductions in average cost

The average cost per student figure indicates what the University is achieving on the basis of its present policies. It offers little guidance on the potentiality for reaping economies of scale or on the cost implications of various alternative policies. This last section, therefore, discusses some ways in which average cost could be reduced.

One obvious way would be to change the components of the University's teaching system. For example, if all broadcasting were removed, fixed costs would be reduced by £2 million or nearly 30 per cent and costs per course by £115,000 per new course and £11,500 per maintained course, a fall of some 25 per cent. With no broadcasting in 1976, the average cost per student would have been £440 or £215 in 1971 prices, some 14 per cent below the actual figure [2]. Alternative options are available such as a reduction in part-time tutoring or summer school attendance or a deterioration in the quality of printing and presentation of the course materials. All these alternatives, however, would change the nature of the product offered to the students and clearly an Open University operating under such circumstances would be different from the present one.

These options are therefore not pursued further. Their consideration, however, emphasises that the actual average cost figure as presented above is a consequence of decisions taken early in the University's life about the mix of its teaching components and offers little guidance on the cost effects of alternative Open University type systems in different circumstances. An Open University type technology can be made more or less expensive than the figures resulting from the particular production components of the existing Open University. Increasing the number of courses, broadcast programmes and hours of part-time tuition will raise costs. Reducing these elements will cause costs to fall. It is, therefore, possible to make an Open University system as expensive or as cheap as the planners wish.

However, it may be possible to reduce costs at the Open University whilst maintaining the same basic system by changing the mix of courses between arts and sciences. The calculations are given in Appendix 2 and they show that whilst the average cost of producing a new course in the University as a whole is £436,000 the cost in different faculties varies between £340,000 in arts to £598,000 in science. It is difficult to be precise about the exact difference because of the nature of the assumptions behind the calculations but it is probably correct to say that there is a difference of about £200,000 in the production cost of an arts/social science type course and science/-technology type course.

In addition, science and technology courses incur a higher proportion of those costs which are related to student numbers particularly in relation to summer schools and direct student costs. The latter include the cost of home experimental kits which are used largely on science and technology courses. Whilst the average cost per student of summer schools and direct student costs amount to £120, the cost per student on an arts/social science course is likely to be nearer £95, whilst for a student on a science/technology course, it is likely to be nearer £155.

The University's present policy is to divide its total courses more or less equally between faculties, so that when the 87 credits total is eventually reached, arts will have 16, social science 17 and science and technology 15 each. The rest will be split between educational studies, maths and general university courses.

If this policy is maintained, it can be argued that the figures given earlier under-estimate the likely pattern of future costs. For arts and social sciences by 1976 were closer to their final total than science and technology. Arts had about 3, social science about 5, science about 7 and technology about 7 more courses to complete. If the majority of new courses to be produced in the next few years are to be in science and technology, then the average figure of £436,000 per new course and £200 per student will under-estimate the cost burden of putting on new courses and taking extra students.

Changing the mix of courses would reduce average cost. In order to gauge the bounds of any change, assume that only arts and social science courses are offered, so that the figures for cost per new course C_n in 1976 were £350,000, the costs for maintaining a course C_m were £35,000 and costs per student S were £190 instead of £248 as previously calculated.

The equation would therefore read:

$$C = 6,967,000 + 350,000C_n + 35,000C_m + 190S$$

and in 1976 when

$C_n = 9$
$C_m = 55.16$
$S = 50.994$
$C = 6,967,000 + 3,150,000 + 1,930,600 + 9,688,860$
$\quad = 21,736,460$

$$\frac{C}{S} = £426$$

So if the University produced only arts and social science courses, its average cost per student in 1976 would be about £426 or £207 in 1971 prices, some 17 per cent below its actual average costs in that year.

Such a change of direction, however, would involve a major policy decision and would be open to the same criticism as changing the production mix, namely that students would be offered a different product. With no science and technology courses, students would be entering a Liberal Arts College rather than a university. However, this is not to say that some change in emphasis from science and technology to arts and social sciences is not feasible. In broad terms, every switch from science and technology to arts and social sciences saves the University some £200,000 in new course production costs, £20,000 in maintenance cost and about £60 per student per annum for every student taking the course.

One way of reducing the production cost of science and technology courses would be to spread these costs over a longer number of years. University policy is that courses should be remade every 4 years, although many courses in all faculties in fact have a much longer life than this. For the amortized annual cost of science and technology courses to equal those of arts and social science courses, they would need to last about twice as long. Student costs of science and technology courses would still be higher but by doubling the life of these courses in relation to arts and social science courses, the University might be able to reduce its average costs by up to 10 per cent.

Conclusions

The analysis indicates that average costs per equivalent undergraduate at the Open University in the next few years are likely to stabilize at the 1976 level of about £500 per student in constant prices, and that this will only be achieved by slowing down the expansion in the range of courses offered to students. Nevertheless, this level of average costs will be little more than a quarter of those at conventional universities. Even if an allowance for differences in the amount of research is made, Open University average costs are still a third of those at conventional universities.

However, it is clear that average costs could be reduced by changes in policy. Whilst some of the more radical changes such as the withdrawal of broadcasting would imply that the nature of the product had changed, some change in emphasis from science and technology to arts and social science courses would have a favourable impact on costs.

Appendix 1: Revised calculations for Open University and conventional university costs in 1973

Average recurrent cost per equivalent undergraduate

Total recurrent expenditure at the Open University in 1973 amounted to £9.9M at 1971 prices. With 38,424 finally registered students, this gives an average cost per equivalent undergraduate figure of £258. Conventional universities recurrent expenditure in 1973 was £332.3M in 1971 prices. The number of equivalent undergraduates appropriate to this expenditure figure depends on the assumptions made about postgraduates as explained earlier. Table VII shows the calculations. Column 2 is based on the weightings used in the previous papers to allow a fair comparison to be made. Column 3 uses the new weightings indicated by the U.G.C. Using the same weights as previously gives an undergraduate equivalent total of 346,220 and an average recurrent cost of £960. Using the new weights gives an undergraduate equivalent total of 292130 and an average recurrent cost of £1138 [3]

TABLE VII

Conventional Universities: Conversion of Student Numbers into Equivalent Undergraduates

	1	2	3
	Student Numbers	Undergraduate Equivalent Weights	Undergraduate Equivalent Weights
A Undergraduate	196344	X 1 196344	X 1 196344
B Post-Graduates			
Education	11558	X 1 11558	X 1 11558
Science	30138	X 3 90414	X 2 60276
Arts	23952	X 2 47904	X 1 23952
C Total	261992	346220	292130

Average recurrent cost per equivalent undergraduate including imputed rental value

Almost all Open University capital expenditure is related to the Walton Hall central site and unlike that at conventional universities is not closely related to student numbers. It consists largely of office and catering accommodation for staff. By the end of 1973 the University had incurred capital expenditure of £5.2 million which with a 10 per cent imputed rental value implies an extra annual average recurrent cost per equivalent undergraduate of £14[4]. Since 1973 further capital expenditure has been incurred to provide purpose-built laboratories and office accommodation and by 1974 this had increased the imputed rental value of capital per equivalent undergraduate to £16. Although further capital work is scheduled to the end of the decade, it should have only a marginal impact on the recurrent cost figures and average rental cost per equivalent undergraduate is unlikely to be in excess of £20.

For conventional universities, the figure is a little more difficult to calculate because of the difficulty of obtaining an accurate estimate of capital stock. The Robbins Committee (1963, Annexe) calculated an imputed rent on existing buildings of over £2 per student per week based on a depreciation period of 60 years and a 6 per cent interest rate. This figure included teacher training and advanced further education and the figure might be higher for universities which have a larger element of capital intensive and scientific work.

The expansion of higher education since 1963 has reduced the age-vintage of total capital stock so that a larger proportion consists of newer buildings in 1973 than in 1963. This, together with the rise in building costs and a higher rate of interest might be expected to raise the imputed rent to about £200 per student year. This is two thirds of the figure given in the earlier paper which because it applied a 10 per cent imputed rental value to the estimated capital stock per new teaching place was based on the cost of *new* capital rather than the existing capital stock. Using undergraduate equivalents instead of student numbers gives a figure of £151 per equivalent undergraduate with the weights of column 2 of Table I and £173 per equivalent undergraduate using the weights in column 3. This raises the average recurrent cost per equivalent undergraduate to between £1,111 and £1,311 depending on the postgraduate weighting used.

Average recurrent cost per graduate

Students at the Open University drop out of courses rather than the University. A student failing to complete a course can retake it or can take other courses in subsequent years. Students also have the option of taking between one half credit and two full credit courses a year whilst the principle of credit exemptions for those with previous qualifications means that many students do not have to take the full 6 credits for an ordinary degree or 8 credits for an honours degree.

For these reasons, there is no established link as with conventional universities between intake and graduate

391

numbers. Some students may stay in the system for a relatively short period (2 to 3 years) before graduating, whilst others may stay much longer. And there is also a significant group of students who try one or two courses and then disappear.

The average cost per graduate in 1973 as measured by the average recurrent cost and total number of graduates in that year is calculated as £3,270 in 1973 prices and £2,719 in 1971 prices. However, this is not typical, as the University had not yet reached a steady state situation where graduates as a proportion of total student population becomes a more stable figure. In 1973, for example, there were 3,641 graduates out of a total student population of 38,424. In 1975 there were 5,890 ordinary degree graduates out of a total student population of 49,358.

A more accurate estimate of the likely average cost per graduate can be obtained by building up the figure from data on cost per student course and course drop out rates. An ordinary degree at the Open University involves obtaining 6 credits [5]. Students, on average, take slightly more than one credit per annum so the average cost per student *credit* is slightly lower than the average cost per student. In 1973 for example students took an average of 1.17 full-credit equivalent courses and the average cost per student credit was therefore £230 in 1971 prices. If one allows for the fact that about 25 per cent of students might not survive a course, the average cost per surviving student credit is £307. For an ordinary degree of 6 credits the average cost per graduate thus amounts to £1,842 whilst for an honours degree of 8 credits the figure is £2,456 both in 1971 prices. Both of these would be reduced by 5 per cent to £1,750 and £2,332 if research costs were excluded.

These figures are for the data in 1973 but it is possible to establish a formula which expresses the method explained in the previous paragraph and which enables data for subsequent years to be used to calculate the average cost per graduate.

Thus:

$$G = \frac{RC}{FP}$$

where G = average recurrent cost per graduate
  R = average recurrent cost per student
  C = number of credits in ordinary degree
  F = average number of full credit equivalent courses per student
  P = pass rate or number of students surviving the course.

If the number of credit exemptions is to be taken into account (see note) then the formula becomes

$$G = \frac{R(C-X)}{FP}$$ where X = average number of credit exemptions per student.

The calculation for conventional universities using the average recurrent cost and the number of graduates is complicated by two factors. If intake figures fluctuate, the graduate and recurrent costs figures for any one year may not be typical. In order to avoid this, a series of figures over the period 1969-70 to 1972-73 will be used. Secondly, in order to make an accurate comparison with the Open University, the various types of diplomas and postgraduate degrees must be converted into first degree equivalents. As most diplomas are taken by part-time students, it is assumed that they are equivalent to half a first degree. Postgraduate degrees are a little more difficult to evaluate. In any one year, a postgraduate costs more to teach than an undergraduate, but the time taken to obtain a postgraduate degree is often less than for a first degree. The cost also varies between subjects. In order to show the range of possible costs per graduate, the calculations will be made on the assumption of a postgraduate being the equivalent of a first degree and also being equivalent to two first degrees. These calculations are shown in Tables VIII and IX.

TABLE VIII

First Degree Equivalent Graduates in Conventional Universities

Year	First Degree Graduates	Diplomas÷2	Post Graduate		Total	
			x1	x2	PG x1	PG x2
1969-70	47855	6679	12009	24018	66543	78552
1970-71	51189	6976	12901	25802	71066	83967
1971-72	50054	5248	11050	22100	66352	77402
1972-73	50766	5563	12859	25718	69188	82047

Source: UGC Statistics of Education, Vol 6, 1970-1973.

The tables indicate a rising cost per first degree equivalent graduate in 1971-72 and 1972-73. This is probably accounted for by a higher drop out rate in these two years. As a rough guide, the ratio of graduates in year t to intake in year t-2 fell from 89.7% in 1970-71 to 83.8% in 1971-72 and 79.7% in 1972-73. The result is that in 1972-73 the average cost per

graduate was in excess of £4,000 and may have been as high
as £4,800. Allowing for expenditure on research reduces the
teaching cost per graduate to between £2,800 and £3,360.

TABLE IX

Cost per Equivalent First-Degree Graduate in Conventional Universities in
1971 prices

Year	Recurrent Expenditure	Total Graduates		Cost per Graduate	
		FG x1	FG x2	FG x1	FG x2
	£M				
1969–70	299.9	66543	78552	4507	3818
1970–71	313.8	71066	83967	4416	3737
1971–72	323.3	66352	77402	4872	4177
1972–73	332.2	69188	82047	4801	4049

Source: UGC Statistics of Education, Vol 6, 1970-73.

Resource cost per equivalent undergraduate

The resource cost measures the cost to the economy from the
provison of higher education. This not only includes the
resources lost for other purposes by their use in higher
education such as teachers, materials and buildings but the
resources lost by students not contributing to production.
The first can be measured by recurrent expenditure including
an imputed rental value for capital equipment and buildings.
The second is conventionally measured by average earnings on
the assumption that these reflect contributions to output.
Both these calculations, however, assume full employment for
it is in this situation that resources used for one purpose
cannot be used for another. However, if there is a significant level of unemployment, then staff and students may not
be able to find alternative employment by which they might
contribute to output and buildings may not be able to be put
to alternative uses. In this situation, the money of
these items will exaggerate their resource cost.

However, assuming full employment, the resource cost of
the Open University is measured by its average recurrent
expenditure including the imputed rental value of capital.
As indicated earlier this was calculated as £272 in 1973 at
1971 prices. Students at the University are part-time and in
principle there is no output forgone. However, it is likely
that some output is lost through the loss of overtime, and
part-time work. So the figure of £272 should be taken as a
minimum.

For conventional universities, the recurrent cost figures were given earlier. An additional calculation is required for output lost. The earnings of non-manual workers in

the 18-20 age group can be taken as a measure of earnings
lost by undergraduates whilst the earnings of the 21-24 age
group for non-manual workers can be taken as the figure for
post-graduates. An allowance needs to be made for the contribution to output of undergraduates during the vacation[6]. A
study by the office of Population Censuses and Surveys for
the academic year 1974-75 indicates that the mean income
earned during vacations was £167. If this is converted to
1971 prices and deducted from the total earnings figure, net
output forgone cost can be calculated. This is shown in
Table X.

TABLE X

Earnings Forgone by Students 1973 in 1971 prices

		Earnings Forgone £	Total £M
Students			
Full-time undergraduates	193,249	£ 788	152.3
Full-time postgraduates	46,117	£1244	57.4
Gross earnings forgone			209.7
Less vacation earnings	193,249	£ 123	23.8
Net earnings forgone			185.9
Net earnings per equivalent undergraduate			£536–£636*

* The variation results from the different weightings given to postgraduates
  (see Table I).

If the figure in Table X is added to the recurrent cost
figure including imputed rental value of £1111-£1311 per
equivalent undergraduate given earlier, the total resource
costs of conventional universities amounts to between £1647-
£1947 per equivalent undergraduate depending on the assumption made about postgraduate weightings.

Appendix 2. Faculty costs for producing 1 new full credit course in 1976

	A	D	E	M	S	T
1. Academic costs per man year (Total Faculty Cost÷Academic Staff)	13,722	13,831	13,767	13,760	17,336	15,561
2. Man years required to produce 1 full credit course	12.8	13.9	20	20	22.9	22.9
3. Academic staff costs per man year (2X1)	175,641	192,250	275,340	275,200	396,994	356,347
4. I.E.T. (Total Budget equally spread across faculties)	23,000	23,000	23,000	23,000	23,000	23,000
5. Course Team Budgets (Assume spread across faculties)	50,200	50,200	50,200	50,200	50,200	50,200
6. Broadcasting allocation of direct costs of £5000 per T.V. and £500 per radio programme A.D.E.—16 TV & 24 radio S.M.T.—24 TV & 16 radio	92,000	92,000	92,000	128,000	128,000	128,000
Total (3+4,+5,+6)	340,841	357,450	440,540	476,400	598,194	557,547

Notes

1 Load is defined as staff effort, library facilities and laboratory and equipment resources.

2 In addition, the absence of broadcasting would have allowed academic staff to concentrate on producing more courses.

3 If research costs are excluded as explained previously, the Open University recurrent expenditure figure is reduced by 5 per cent giving £9.4M and an average recurrent cost figure of £245. The recurrent expenditure figure for conventional universities is reduced by 30 per cent giving £232.7M and average recurrent cost figure of £672 or £797, depending on the postgraduate weighting used.

4 In 1971 prices, the figure would be slightly lower as the capital expenditure figure on which it is based includes spending in 1972 and 1973 at current prices.

5 As mentioned earlier, some students obtain credit exemption and the average number of credit exemptions per student is just under 1. Strictly speaking, therefore, over the University as a whole, students on average obtain about 5 credits for an ordinary degree. However, as the purpose of this calculation is to compare the Open University with conventional universities where in general, no credit exemptions are given, this factor will be ignored to provide a correct basis for comparison. The effect of including an allowance for credit exemption is to reduce the O.U. cost per graduate by about 15 per cent.

6 It is assumed that postgraduates have no vacation earnings.

References

Attiyeh, R. and Lumsden, K.G. (1971) University Students Initial Understanding of Economics: The Contribution of the 'A' Level Economics Course and of Other Factors Economica (February)

Attiyeh, R. and Lumsden, K.G. (1972) The Production of Economics Understanding: An Analysis of the First Year Course Economica

Carter, C.F. (1973) The Economics of the Open University: A Comment Higher Education 2:69-70

Laidlaw, B. and Layard, P.R.G. (1974) Traditional versus Open University Teaching Methods: A Cost Comparison Higher Education 3:439-467

Committee on Higher Education under the Chairmanship of Lord Robbins (1963). Cmnd 2267 (Robbins Report) Appendix

Rumble, G.W.S.V. (1976) The Economics of the Open University of the United Kingdom, Open University (mimeo)

Smith, R.C. (1975) A Proposed Formula for Open University Expenditure in a Plateau Situation, Open University (mimeo)

U.G.C. (1969) Statistics of Education, vol6, London: H.M.S.O.

U.G.C. (1973) Quinquennial Letter of Guidance to Universities, London:U.G.C.

Wagner, L. (1972) The Economics of the Open University Higher Education, 1:159-183

Wagner, L (1973) The Open University and the Costs of Expanding Higher Education, Universities Quarterly, Autumn

THE ECONOMICS AND MANAGEMENT OF SMALL POST-SECONDARY DISTANCE EDUCATION SYSTEMS

Barry L. Snowden and John S. Daniel

Introduction

All institutions and agencies engaged in distance education have benefited and acquired enhanced respectability from the worldwide attention that the U.K. Open University has attracted by its success. One benefit has been a new impetus for research which has already strengthened and expanded the conceptual framework on which distance education is based.

The study of the economics of distance education is important for a number of reasons:

1   Distance education requires the implementation and maintenance of complex systems. The management of distance education frequently requires systems analysis - which is little more and little less than another name for economic analysis. As Kershaw and McKean (1959) put it:

> Systems analysis is the comparison of alternative means of carrying out some function, when those means are rather complicated and comprise a number of interrelated elements. Such analysis could often be called 'economic analysis' since the aim is to find the best use of one's resources, but the word 'systems' is useful in calling attention to the complex nature of the alternatives being compared.

2   The economics of distance education are generally expected to be different from those of conventional education. Among ten characteristics of open learning systems Wedemeyer (1974) includes the following:

> As an operating principle the system is capable, after reaching critical minimum of aggregation, of accommodating increased numbers of learners without a *commensurate* increase in the unit cost of the basic learning experiences: i.e., costs must not be directly and rigidly volume sensitive. After reaching the necessary level of aggregation, unit costs should show a diminishing rela-

tionship to total systems costs.

Of particular importance in our analysis will be the identification of this 'critical minimum of aggregation'. This article is about small distance education systems which we shall define as systems fewer than 15,000 part-time students. We shall explore the conditions under which small systems can be cost effective.

3   During the sixties and early seventies the public funds made available to post-secondary education increased steadily and substantially. In most countries of the free world this growth has now ended. Since distance education systems are still facing a buoyant, often increasing, demand, it is their public duty to maximize internal efficiency in order to produce the highest output from the resources allocated to them.

The second part of the paper explores some of the alternatives in the management of distance education systems which arise from the analysis of internal efficiency. Management is the effective utilization of human and materials resources to achieve the objectives of an enterprise. Distance education systems, because of the inherent complexity and interdependence of their parts require 'tighter' management than conventional educational institutions.

The economics of distance education

1 Background

Since the concept of systems analysis has been a constant theme of the educational literature of the last decade it is noteworthy, in view of the close relationship between them, that the economic analysis of educational alternatives has attracted relatively little attention. The difficulties inherent in performing such an analysis at a general level are no doubt to blame. However, a number of U.S. articles on the economic analysis and cost-effectiveness evaluation of educational technology have at least served to identify some of these difficulties. Stated briefly the problems are, (a) to agree on a definition and a measure of output and, (b) to relate costs appropriately to different components of an educational enterprise.

        In the specific case of distance education we are fortunate in having two previous papers which, taken together, state the issues rather well. Wagner (1972,1973) has studied the economics of the U.K. Open University from its inception and summarized findings in a more recent paper (Wagner, 1977). Mace (1978), in an attempt to explode what he considers the growing mythology surrounding the Open University, has attacked some of Wagner's methodology and conclusions in an enjoyable polemical article. A brief summary of the points at issue between these authors will provide a useful introduction to our own analysis of the economics of distance education systems smaller than the Open University.

Wagner (1977) addresses two main issues. Firstly, how do the costs of the Open University (OU) compare to those of Conventional Universities (CUs) and, secondly, how will OU costs evolve in the future and what are the major factors which influence their evolution?

For measures of output Wagner uses both student and graduate numbers claiming that, since OU and CU degrees are of comparable standard, this is a fair measure. He suggests that a better measure of output would be the value-added (i.e., the difference between the academic level of a student on entry and the standard he must achieve for the degree) noting that if OU entrants are, on average, less qualified than CU entrants, use of such a measure would favour the OU in cost comparisons. Wagner also examines the argument that the full-time CU student is getting a very different educational experience from the part-time OU student. While admitting there is a difference from the consumer's point of view he doubts it has much relevance in a social calculus of investment costs and benefits.

In calculating costs Wagner uses the recurrent expenditure figures for the universities but adjusts them to take into account the lesser expenditure of the OU on research and graduate studies. He also excludes expenditure on high cost faculties (e.g. medicine) in CUs.

Using these figures Wagner shows that at the OU the annual average recurrent cost per equivalent undergraduate is less than one-third the cost at a CU. The cost of the OU graduate is less than one-half that of a CU graduate. Finally, comparison of resource costs to the economy per equivalent undergraduate favours the OU by a factor of 6:1.

In attacking this part of Wagner's study Mace (1978) claims that the economic benefits from second-chance adult education of the OU type are much less than those for CU graduates. He argues that the average OU graduate, in his late thirties, will have less time to enjoy higher earnings and greater difficulty in moving to a higher paying occupation than the 22 year old CU graduate. Mace also argues that the OU is doing less to provide education to disadvantaged groups than a cursory examination of the data might suggest. This has, of course, been a live issue in the U.K. ever since the OU opened for business (Perry, 1977).

Although this debate on the external economics of the OU is also of fundamental concern to small distance education systems, the argument between Wagner and Mace on the internal economy of the OU is of even greater interest.

After pointing out that the ratio of fixed cost to variable cost per student is about 2000:1 for the OU compared to about 8:1 in CUs Wagner goes on to develop an equation for the cost of the OU. Previous work had identified the two major cost initiators as course and student numbers so that the total cost equation is of the form:

$$C = a + bx + cy$$

where   a = fixed costs

x = number of courses

y = number of students

For the Open University in 1976 the actual equation (with C expressed in pounds) was:

$$C = 6\ 967\ 000 + 100\ 000x + 248y$$

Wagner then developed a more refined equation in which the variables were new courses, maintained courses, and extra student numbers beyond the 1976 level. He used this equation to show that the OU was unlikely to see any further decrease in average costs. It would take a 36% increase in student numbers to bring average costs down by 16% and since the annual expansion in the number of different courses offered was already small (and decreasing) little scope for economies lay in cutting back course development.

To this point Wagner took the OU teaching system and curriculum as a given. In the final section of his paper he explores briefly the economic consequences of changes in the teaching system (e.g., removing broadcasting) and changing the mix of courses to include a smaller proportion of science and technology courses. After showing which changes would reduce costs most Wagner stated that:

... consideration (of these changes) however, emphasises that the actual average cost figure as presented above is a consequence of decisions taken early in the University's life about the mix of its teaching components and offers little guidance on the cost effects of alternate OU type systems in different circumstances. An OU type technology can be made more or less expensive than the figures resulting from the particular production components of the existing OU. Increasing the number of courses, broadcast programmes and hours of part-time tuition will raise costs. Reducing these elements will cause costs to fall. It is, therefore, possible to make an OU system as expensive or as cheap as the planners wish.

Despite this disclaimer Wagner was roundly and unfairly castigated by Mace for not pursuing his cost-cutting analysis further. Mace himself went on to show how this might be done in a section entitled 'Cost-Effectiveness Analysis (CEA) and its Application to the OU'.

Mace states that CEA is a technique designed to take account of all objectives, whether economic or not, when choosing between different policies:' any objective will serve the purpose provided it can be expressed in terms of a numerical index or scale'. Application of the technique is described as follows:

So, if we establish the objectives of the policy, agree on ways of measuring these objectives, cost the methods of achieving these objectives, we will arrive at as many cost effective ratios as there are objectives. But, as the objectives may not be measured in the same units, it is necessary to rank the C.E ratios. This is achieved by eliciting from the decision-makers their subjective preferences. Then rational choice between alternative policies becomes possible.

Without attempting any serious analysis Mace did suggest some possible results of the application of the CEA technique to the internal economy of the OU. He argued that there was a strong case for reducing expenditure on broadcasting and that other candidates for CEA should be class tutorials, reduction in the number of central academics and extensions to the life of courses.

2 *Application to small distance education systems*

Wagner (1977) stated that in 1976 it cost the OU £436 000 to produce each new full credit course. Since such a sum would be a significant proportion of its total annual budget any small distance education system (SDES) has two choices if it wishes to offer its students a programme containing a reasonable number of courses. It can buy and use expensively produced courses from elsewhere, creating only a small number of similarly produced courses itself, or it must develop cheaper ways of producing courses.

In fact SDESS tend to implement both these options. For example the authors' institution, Athabasca University (AU), will, in 1979/80, offer some 40 home-study courses of which one-third have been purchased from elsewhere. These 14 courses, which came from eight different institutions, are, in general, offered with only the minimal adaptations necessary to fit AU's credit and delivery system. Of the remaining courses, which were developed by AU itself, none had costs approaching the OU figure and most were produced for less than $100 000.[1]   To give meaning to this figure we shall analyze the economy of SDESs in as general a manner as possible, taking into account the methodological issues raised by Wagner and Mace and using Athabasca University as a source of examples.

3 *Outputs*

It is unnecessary to dwell on the difficulties of analyzing the output of educational systems. How do we measure a particular institution's contribution to the 'creation of an educated citizenry' or the 'advancement of knowledge'? The compromise which the economist makes is to find a lower level of production which can give a useful measure of outputs. This process is called sub-optimizing.

In this analysis Wagner used two sub-optimal outputs, graduates and 'equivalent undergraduate years of study'. Although both he and Mace agreed that the measures of these outputs could be refined (e.g., by consideration of value-added) their discussion suggested that the refinements proposed reflected more the particular patterns and controversies within university education in the U.K. than a desire to produce a sub-optimal measure of general applicability.

For the economic analysis of SDESs we suggest that measures based on enrolments in individual courses provide better and more useful sub-optimal indicators than those used by Wagner. Our reasoning is as follows:

i   Not all SDESs have the production of graduates as their main objective. Some have an important 'way-station' function, enabling students to accumulate credits for use elsewhere.

ii   Even where the award of degrees and diplomas is a prime objective it is usually more difficult to compare these credentials between institutions than to compare the courses which make them up.

iii SDESs usually have more flexibility to change teaching methods than do large systems like the OU. It is useful, therefore, for cost-effectiveness analysis to be conducted at the level where changes can most easily be made, i.e., at the individual course.

iv   In their present phase of rapid growth most SDESs can only guess at figures for their annual production of graduates in the steady-state.

v   As conventional universities cater to increasing numbers of part-time adults the notion of full-time equivalent students is less and less useful as a descriptor.

In this article the units of learning activity most commonly used will be credits and courses. A credit is defined as a learning activity that takes the average student around 45 hours to complete (this includes all components of the activity-lectures, laboratories, assignments, homework, examinations etc). Courses commonly consist of either three or six credits, the latter being used as a standard in this paper.

Given this emphasis on courses we shall use course enrolments as a measure of the number of active students. Since most SDESs cater largely to part-time students who take only one or two courses at a time the number of course enrolments is often only slightly larger than the total number of active students in such systems. (e.g. At Athabasca University in 1978/1979 there was one active student to every 1.23 course enrolments.)

Strictly speaking course enrolments are an input, not the output measure which would be successful course completions. For studies of system efficiency this distinction is clearly vital and most SDESs use the following vocabulary:

- *initial enrolments:* all students who enrol in a course.

- *confirmed or final enrolments:* students who remain enrolled in the course after any initial period allowed for trial enrolment.

- *withdrawals:* students who withdraw from the course either (a) with a partial refund or (b) before paying the full tuition fee.

- *non-starts:* students who enrol but neither withdraw nor complete any exams or assignments.

- *drop-outs:* students who complete some assignments but do not finish the whole course.

- *completions:* students who complete the course and either pass or fail.

- *passes:* students who pass the course.

Given this diversity we have elected to use initial enrolments as a quasi-output measure since Keegan (1980) has warned against inter-institutional comparisons of drop-out rates.

4 *Costs and cost analysis*

TABLE 1 Athabasca University average operating cost per course enrolment 1975-1983

Year	Operating Expenditures (Current $)	Course Enrolments (Weighted)	Average Cost per Course Enrolment (Current $)	Average Cost per Course Enrolment (1979-80 $*)
1975-76	1 118 000	726	1 540	2 255
1976-77	1 986 000	1 257	1 580	2 023
1977-78	2 512 000	1 724	1 457	1 704
1978-79	3 773 000	3 169	1 191	1 288
1979-80	4 710 000	4 390	1 073	1 073
1980-81	5 706 000	5 925	963	963
1981-82	6 548 000	7 325	894	894
1982-83	7 234 000	8 440	857	857

*1975-76 to 1978-79 costs restated in constant 1979-80 $ using National Accounts (Canada) implicit price index for government services expenditures.

Before examining the economics of SDESs it may be useful to provide some indication of the organizational and budget-

404

ary context of the institution which we will use to represent a SDES. Athabasca University has operated with its current mandate since 1975.[2] Operating cost (recurrent expenditure), student enrolment and average cost data are presented in Table 1. The data for 1975-76 (the University's fiscal year, 1 April to 31 March) to 1978-79 are actual figures; 1979-80 data are budget estimates.

As should be expected, average costs decline at a decreasing rate over the 1975-76 to 1979-80 period and further but less dramatic decreases are anticipated through 1982-83. The University's 'average cost curve' is presented in Figure 1 in both current and constant dollars.

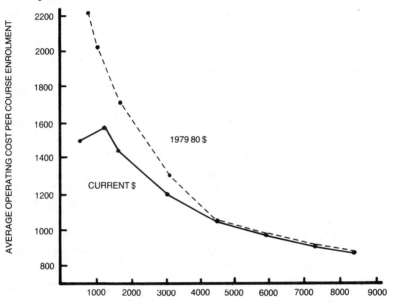

COURSE ENROLMENTS (WEIGHTED)

Fig.1 Athabasca University 'average cost curve'

Wagner (1977) indicates the limited information provided from average cost analysis of Open University data and reveals the degree to which reliance on the statistics so generated can be misleading. The same can be said for the SDES and here too it is necessary to use a more detailed methodology.

Much work has been done in the areas of programme and activity costing and financial modelling for the conventional university. This work has produced a 'language' which has gained considerable acceptance among financial planners and institutional researchers. Through this language the characteristics, operations and costs of programmes and institutions can be described in terms of staffing levels, student loads, class sizes, teaching loads, salary costs etc. To illustrate, what has come to be known as the 'elementary model of the instructional process' can be described as follows:

$$\text{Number of faculty (F)} = \frac{\text{Weekly student hours (WSH)}}{\text{Average class size (ACS)} \times \text{Average faculty load (AFL)}}$$

This model describes functional relationships among policy variables which are basic to the instructional process and in addition, provides a simple, objective means for comparing activities, resources and 'outputs' within and among departments, faculties and institutions.

This elementary model may be extended to account for financial allocations and to analyse costs. In the conventional university, faculty salary expense represents a major component of total costs and to the extent that total instructional cost can be expressed as a function of faculty members, the model can be used to represent the instructional cost equation. Multiplying both sides of the elementary model by average faculty salary (AFS) produces:

$$\text{Faculty salary expense} = \frac{\text{WSH} \times \text{AFS}}{\text{ACS} \times \text{AFL}}$$

which has been termed the 'fundamental cost model' by Sheehan and Gulko (1976). This kind of formulation is the basis for many of the cost analysis and allocation models in use in conventional universities, and coordinating or funding agencies. The approach can be readily adjusted to reflect total costs and/or resource requirements or the model can be extended to explain total cost behavior. It is easily understood by university planners and government officials and its utility is reflected in the format and wording of information requests etc., from government and other coordinating and funding agencies.

A problem for Athabasca University, which we suspect is shared with other SDESs, is the considerable difficulty we have in describing the institution's operations and its economics to officials in government and funding agencies, to members of other (conventional) institutions and, to some extent, to our counterparts and colleagues in other SDESs. In nearly all jurisdictions with which the authors are familiar, financial and operating reporting processes in general, and grant determination and allocation processes in particular, depend upon effective information exchanges between and among institutions and funding agencies. These exchanges, both formal and informal, require a relative degree of definition, standardization and understanding of the terms, terminologies and quantitive and qualitative measures employed. For the conventional universities which dominate most jurisdictions, the language described above satisfies these requirements to a large extent. The absence of an accepted and understood 'shorthand' is a problem for an SDES coexisting, as Athabasca University does, with conventional institutions in a relatively well developed post-secondary education system.[3]

5 *A cost model for small distance education systems*

SDESs share a number of operational characteristics in addition to their relative size. With a few notable exceptions they are newcomers to the world of higher education. Many have experienced rapid growth over a relatively short time period and this growth, together with the development and introduction of new technology has triggered high rates of organizational change. Few have extensive or sophisticated financial and operational information systems. In many it is hazardous even to compare expenditure data from one year to those of the next. Thus, for a costing model and methodology to have both validity and utility for a SDES, it will need to be sufficiently general to permit a relatively high level of aggregation of operational and cost data, yet sufficiently specific to the activities and relationships represented to enable the identification and analysis of costs and trends and the evaluation of policy alternatives.

As described above, models developed for conventional universities represent the instructional function and permit the identification and analysis of costs through a model which associates productivity with the faculty-student interface and relationship. Given the nature of instructional activities within the conventional university, it is not necessary and may, in fact, be impossible to separate the activities associated with instructional delivery. In the large distance learning system, to cite Wagner's work as an illustration, it would appear to be relatively easy to gather and refine the data necessary to develop and use a multi-functional model. For the SDES, where many staff members engage in both course development related and delivery rated activities and, using Athabasca University as an example, precise time/effort accounting data are not available, the uni-function model is attractive. The separation of the development and delivery functions is so much a characteristic of the operations of the SDES, however, that it should be safe to assert, without proof, that the explicit recognition of each as a function supporting the general instructional objective is fundamental to the development of a valid costing model.

Wagner's work at the Open University has already been described. Although our efforts at Athabasca University must at this stage be termed preliminary, sufficient progress has

been made to enable the authors to be confident that the
general cost equation and methodological approach reported
by Wagner is appropriate to the analysis of the economics of
the SDES.

Wagner (1976) has described the equation established by
Smith (1975) as a linear function which identifies costs
which are dependent on either course or student numbers and
those which are independent of these two variables and are
therefore fixed. The model being developed and used at
Athabasca University is similar; but before presenting the
basic equation it may be useful to define more precisely the
activity areas (functions) that these variables represent:
course development and services delivery.

Course development includes those activities which contribute directly to the planning of programmes and courses,
to the formation and creation of instructional materials
including activities which facilitate and refine course development processes and to the maintenance and replacement
of course and materials. Included as well are royalties and
fees paid for rights and permissions to use materials developed by others.

Services delivery includes those activities associated
directly with the delivery of instructional services to
students including materials production, transportation, regional tutorial services, library services, communications
etc., and those activities which facilitate the student's
learning experience including academic and career counselling, orientation, learning centre operations etc.

The basic cost equation which has emerged from our
analysis of operations and costs at Athabasca University is:

$$TC = a_1 x_1 + a_2 x_2 + by + c$$

where x_1 = course credits 'in development'

x_2 = course credits 'in delivery'

y = 'weighted' course enrolments

and a_1 = course development costs per credit

a_2 = course/revision/maintenance/replacement costs per
credit

b = 'delivery' costs per 'weighted' course enrolment

c = institutional costs (overheads)

An important feature of this model is that it incorporates
separate identification of the costs associated with maintaining existing course offerings and the costs and activities
associated with 'new' course development. Because Athabasca
University has been engaged almost exclusively in the development and delivery of new courses, cost and activity data do
not exist to enable direct determination of a_2 or x_2. This

408

difficulty can be overcome, however, by introducing a depreciation model into the basic cost equation. If it can be assumed that the total accumulated cost of maintaining the currency of a course over a variable lifetime $(\mathcal{L})$ is not greater than its replacement cost and if it can be further assumed that this cost is not greater than the cost of developing a new course then the maximum revision/maintenance-/replacement cost per course credit per year can be represented by:

$$a_2 = a_1 /\mathcal{L}$$

By substitution, the basic model becomes:

$$TC = a_1(x_1 + x_2/\mathcal{L}) + by + c$$

The activity data required to illustrate the costing application of the model to Athabasca University operations for the 1977-1979 period are provided in Tables 11 and 111. Actual data can be used for the 1977-78 and 1978-79 fiscal years and planned levels of course development activity (1978-80 budget) and estimated student volumes are used for the current year.

Table 11 Athabasca University course development 'load' 1977-79

Year	Course Credits (In Development) x_1	Course Credits (In Delivery) x_2
1977-78 (Actual)	33	60
1978-79 (Actual)	75	135
1979-80 (Budget)	69	192

Athabasca University offers three-credit and six-credit courses, the latter being roughly equivalent to one-fifth of a full-time undergraduate student load at a conventional university or one-twentieth of a four-year undergraduate degree program. The student activity (course enrolments) data in Table 111 have been obtained by applying the following formula:

$$\text{Course enrolments (weighted)} = \frac{3e_1 + 6e_2}{6}$$

where $e_1 =$ enrolments in 3 credit courses

$\quad\quad e_2 =$ enrolments in 6 credit courses

Table 111 Athabasca University student related activity 1977-79

Year	Weighted Course Enrolments y	Full-time Equivalent Students* $y/4$
1977-78 (Actual)	1725	431
1978-79 (Actual)	3169	792
1979-80 (Estimates)	4390	1098

*Although five courses are usually regarded as a full-time student load, a part-time to full-time weighting of 1/4 is generally accepted for the conversion of course enrolments to full-time equivalents, thus recognising those operational and cost factors which are not variable with respect to course load.

Table lV represents a summary of Athabasca University's operating (recurrent) expenditures for the 1977-79 period. A financial information system which will provide for direct accounting of expenditures against the activity areas (functions) identified in the basic cost model is currently under development. In its absence, our work to date has relied heavily on a rather crude cost allocation procedure which is indicated in Table V.

TABLE lV Athabasca University operating expenditures 1977-79

Year	1977-78 (Actual)	1978-79 (Actual)	1979-80 (Budget)
University Development	36 900	40 800	117 200
Staff Development	25 600	42 800	56 000
Institutional Management	411 800	438 700	523 900
Learning Services Planning		56 200	42 600
Course Development	386 200	408 000	451 700
Regional/Tutorial Services	193 100	282 400	367 200
Student Development	113 300	181 500	231 000
Registry	65 300	166 300	236 700
Liberal Studies	260 900	453 600	507 300
Applied Studies	66 900	130 800	166 400
Library Services	123 400	133 700	154 700
Computing Services	135 400	182 000	219 000
Media Services	255 300	400 000	432 500
Financial Services	42 800	66 300	86 300
Personnel Services	42 400	58 800	93 100
General Services	41 200	93 900	121 300
Student Materials Administration	26 100	66 000	127 100
Course Materials Acquisition	53 200	247 500	245 000
Institutional Operations	232 700	328 700	531 000
TOTALS	2 512 500	3 773 000	4 710 000

TABLE V Athabasca University cost allocation assumptions

Budget Line	% Cost Allocation		
	Course Development	Services Delivery	Institutional Costs
University Development	–	–	100
Staff Development	–	–	100
Institutional Management	–	–	100
Learning Services Planning	50	–	50
Course Development	100	–	–
Regional/Tutorial Services	–	100	–
Student Development	–	100	–
Registry	–	100	–
Liberal Studies	50	50	–
Applied Studies	50	50	–
Library Services	50	30	20
Computing Services	30	30	40
Media Services	40	50	10
Financial Services	–	–	100
Personnel Services	–	–	100
General Services	–	–	100
Student Materials Administration	–	100	–
Course Materials Acquisition	–	100	–
Institutional Operations	–	–	100

Application of the cost allocation assumption (Table V) to the operating expenditure data (Table lV) produces allocation of expenditures to the activity areas recognised by the basic model (Table Vl).

TABLE Vl Athabasca University Cost Allocation 1977-79

Year	Course Development	Services Delivery	Institutional Costs
1977–78 (Actual)	754 500	820 200	937 800
1978–79 (Actual)	1 007 250	1 528 100	1 237 650
1979–80 (Budget)	1 125 900	1 872 200	1 711 900

The results of this admittedly arbitrary allocation procedure should be examined carefully. In the three year period course development costs appear to have increased by 49%, services delivery costs by 128% and institutional costs (fixed costs?) by 83%. In terms of proportion of total

411

expenditure, course development activity accounts for 30% in 1977-78 which decreases to 27% in 1978-79 and 24% in 1979-80 and student delivery activity 33% in 1977-78 which increases to 40% in 1978-79 and 1979-80. Given the stage of development of Athabasca University, these shifts confirm intuitive judgement.

Using the cost allocation figures in Table Vl, the activity data in Tables ll and lll, and making the assumption that the average life-time of courses is 5 years (setting $\ell \approx 5$), total cost equations for 1977-78, 1978-79 and 1979-80 can then be written in the basic model form as:

$$TC\ (1977\text{-}78) = 16\ 775x_1 + 3\ 555x_2 + 475_y + 937\ 800$$
$$TC\ (1978\text{-}79) = 9\ 880x_1 + 1\ 975x_2 + 480_y + 1237\ 650$$
$$TC\ (1979\text{-}80) = 10\ 425x_1 + 2\ 085x_2 + 425_y + 1711\ 900$$

One of the important uses to which we intend the costing model to be put is the projection of future costs, given a development plan for the University which can be expressed in terms of the 'primary planning variables' (x_1, x_2, y) around which the model is built. On the basis of even cursory examination, the area presenting the most significant difficulty is that of institutional costs. As indicated previously, the basic cost equation treats this as a fixed cost area. While there is some evidence that those costs identified as institutional costs have declined as a proportion of the total cost, a strong argument can be presented that, at least in the developing years of a SDES, such costs are a fixed proportion of total cost. To accommodate this using financial volume as a basis for allocation of institutional (fixed) costs, the model can be rewritten:

$$TC = (a_1 + c_a)(x_1 + x_2/\ell) + (b + c_b)y$$

where
$$c_a = \frac{(a_1x_1 + a_2x_2)c}{a_1x_1 + a_2x_2 + by}$$

$$c_b = \frac{byc}{a_1x_1 + a_2x_2 + by}$$

$$a_2 = a_1/$$

The resulting cost equations, with ℓ set equal to 5, become:

$$TC\ (1977\text{-}78) = 26\ 650x_1 + 5\ 330x_2 + 760y$$
$$TC(1978\text{-}79) = 14\ 695x_1 + 2\ 940x_2 + 715y$$
$$TC(1979\text{-}80) = 16\ 380x_1 + 3\ 275x_2 + 670y$$

To facilitate the reader's interpretation and comparison of these 'full-cost' results with those presented earlier, both are provided in Table V11.

TABLE V11 Athabasca University unit costs 1977-79

Cost Initiator	1977-78 Actual	1978-79 Actual	1979-80 Budget
'Variable and Fixed' Cost Model			
'New' Course Development (per credit)	16 775	9 880	10 425
Course Revision/Maintenance (per credit)	3 355	1 975	2 085
Services Delivery (per weighted enrolment)	475	480	425
'Fixed' Institutional Costs	937 800	1 237 650	1 711 900
'Full' Cost Model			
'New' Course Development (per credit)	26 650	14 695	16 380
Course Revision/Maintenace (per credit)	5 330	2 940	3 275
Services Delivery (per weighted enrolment)	760	715	670

6 *Using the basic model for cost projections*

To use the basic model for cost projections, estimate must be made for the cost coefficients $[(a + c_a)]$, $[(b + c_b)]$ and for the course life-time variable ℓ described in the previous section. These estimates need to be informed by cost analyses, but also require additional judgemental and/or analytical input. To highlight a degree of independence, the costing model can be restated as a projection model as follows:

$$PC = p_1 x_1 + p_2 x_2 + p_3 y + p$$

If institutional costs are to be projected as fixed costs or:

$$PC = p_1 x_1 + p_2 x_2 + p_3 y$$

where $p_1 = (a + c_a)^1$ = projected full cost of course development activity per credit

$p_2 = (a + c_a)^1/\ell^1$ = projected full cost of course revision/replacement activity per credit

$p_3 = (b + c_b)^1$ = projected full cost of services delivery per course enrolment

Our preference is for the latter, not only for the reasons that the 'full-cost' format was adopted previously but also because it acknowledges the variability of 'fixed' costs in the long run. To illustrate projection application, we will use the following estimates:

413

$$p_1 = 16\ 400$$
$$p_2 = 3\ 300 \quad (\ell^1 = 5)$$
$$p_3 = 650$$

As much as the utility of the model as a projection tool depends upon well informed estimates of costs, it relies even more heavily upon a carefully developed academic plan for the projection period. The authors do not claim that the primary planning variable estimates in Table Vll have such basis. We hope however that their derivation from what we regard to be a reasonably realistic future for Athabasca University will satisfy our need to illustrate the projection application.

The results of a cost projection using the cost projection equation

$$PC = 14\ 400x_1 + 3\ 300x_2 + 650_y$$

are given in Table 1X. The general results of this projection were presented previously in Table 1 and Figure 1. Average costs per course enrolment (weighted) continue to decline over the projection period, at a declining rate, producing an average cost curve indicative of an expanding operation with increasing economies of scale.

TABLE Vlll Athabasca University 'academic plan' 1980-1983

Year	Course Development Load		Services Delivery Load (y)
	New Course Credits (x_1)	Course Revision Maintenance (x_2)	
1980–81	66	234	5 925
1981–82	54	273	7 325
1982–83	45	306	8 440

TABLE 1X Athabasca University 'cost projection' 1980-1983

Year	Course Development Costs			Service Delivery	Total
	New	Maintenance	Total		
1980–81	1 082 400	772 200	1 854 600	3 851 500	5 706 100
1981–82	885 600	900 900	1 786 500	4 761 500	6 548 000
1982–83	738 000	1 009 800	1 747 800	5 486 000	7 233 800

7 *Using the model to evaluate policy alternatives*

Athabasca University is currently engaged in a detailed review of its academic plan. Among the products of this review, we hope to define a 'steady-state' curriculum for each program of study and to derive a course development schedule which will bring course offerings to the steady-state level in a long-term cost effective fashion. In the previous section we noted that for projection purposes the model requires input data from an academic plan. It can also be used, however, to assist the academic planning effort. To demonstrate, of Athabasca University's 1979-80 budget $1 768 800 can be attributed (via the cost allocation including institutional costs methodology) to the course development function. From the projection results in Table 1X, total course development costs increase in 1980-81 and then decrease through 1981-82 to a 1982-83 level slightly below the current budget. These costs are treated as variable costs in the model, but in the real world operation of the University, course development costs have the tendency to be like prices, upward variable but downward 'sticky'. Thus operationally an academic plan which enables course development capacity to be held constant at the 1979-80 level may be preferred. Course development capacity may be defined as:

$$d = x_1 + x_2/\ell = \frac{TC - (b + c_b)y}{a_1 + c_a}$$

For 1979-80, planned capacity can be calculated to be approximately 107 credit equivalents. Making the assumption that one-half of the credits developed in any year are available for delivery in the same year (the remainder in the next), the relationship $x_1 + x_2 \ell$ can be used iteratively to produce the course development schedule in Table X.

By setting x, equal to zero in $x_1 + x_2/\ell = 107$, the steady-state curriculum level given 1979-1980 course development capacity can be calculated to be 535 course credits. But it can be shown further that this full curriculum would not be reached until after the turn of the century. While the constant course development capacity policy may satisfy certain cost and operational objectives, it may not enable the University to respond sufficiently to student progress in the curriculum and demand for increased offerings.

TABLE X Athabasca University course development schedule under constant 1979-1980 capacity assumption

Year	Course Development Load (d)	Course Development Schedule	
		New Course Credits x_1	Course Revision Maintenance x_2
1979–80	107	69	192
1980–81	107	56	252
1981–82	107	46	303
1982–83	107	38	345

One of the assumptions made in calculating the projection shown in Table 1X is that the average lifetime (ℓ) of a

course is 5 years. This assumption represents current planning policy at Athabasca University. Table Xl indicates the
total cost effects of adjusting to ℓ = 4 and ℓ = 6. Such
adjustments may be found desirable on the basis of course
development and institutional operations policy analysis or
may be considered necessary as a response to external demands
or constraints such as funding limitations, low enrolment
demand, availability of required expertise etc. In addition
to providing an indication of the cost impact of this policy
change, the data in Table Xl indicate the sensitivity of
projection methodology to changes in the course lifetime
variable.

**TABLE Xl Athabasca University cost projection effects of
alternative lifetime assumptions 1980-1983**

Year	Total Cost ℓ = 4	Total Cost ℓ = 5	Total Cost ℓ = 6
1980–81	5 893 300	5 705 850	5 573 500
1981–82	6 676 400	6 548 000	6 393 300
1982–83	7 478 600	7 233 800	7 060 400

A policy objective of reducing average cost (in constant $)
is implicit in the academic plan data presented in Table
Vlll. Were this to be adjusted to a policy of maintaining
the 1979-80 average cost level ($1 073), an increased rate
of course development would be permitted, all other things
being equal. Application of the model produces the results
indicated in Table Xll which indicate a much more rapid
growth in course offerings than under the current plan.

It must be noted, however, that unless course development capacity can be reduced or new programs developed when
the curriculum goal for a given set of programs is reached,
such a change in policy may introduce serious operational
problems. To illustrate, were the goal for the current
Athabasca University program set to be 500 credits, we have
already shown that 1979-80 course development capacity is
sufficient to maintain the steady-state. Nevertheless, it
may be necessary to increase capacity to meet other objectives including the addition of programs and it is useful to
be able to determine, in advance, the average cost impact of
alternative program mix and schedule assumptions.

TABLE Xll Athabasca University cost and activity projection under constant 1979-1980 average cost assumption

Year	Total Cost	Course Development Costs (Total)	Course Credits 'In Development'	Course Credits 'In Delivery'
1979–80	4 710 000	1 768 800	69	192
1980–81	6 357 500	2 506 000	102	252
1981–82	7 859 700	3 098 200	120	342
1982–83	9 056 100	3 570 100	128	449

8 *Productivity relationships*

Most cost analysis and projection models developed for conventional universities incorporate a fundamental relationship which may be defined as 'average class size' or 'student-faculty ratio'. This relationship is often referred to and used as a gross measure of productivity. In a SDES this precise measure is not available. However, a ratio with similar characteristics can be stated:

$$\frac{y}{x_2} = \frac{weighted\ course\ enrolments}{course\ credits\ in\ delivery}$$

In terms of the model we have developed at Athabasca University, this relationship is not so much a productivity ratio as it is an indicator of the relative balance between the two primary functions of the institution. For this reason, we will call it the 'enrolment ratio'. Athabasca University enrolment ratios for 1977-78 to 1979-80 and the three 1980-81 to 1982-83 projections are presented in Table Xlll. While we have not examined this relationship in any great detail, it would appear to be as useful an indicator in the planning and management of SDESs as its counterparts are in the conventional environment.

TABLE Xlll Athabasca University enrolment ratios

Year	Actual & Budget Data	Basic Cost Projection (Table lX)	Constant Capacity Projection (Table X)	Constant Average Cost Projection (Table Xll)
1977–78	29	–	–	–
1978–79	23	–	–	–
1979–80	23	–	–	–
1980–81	–	25	24	24
1981–82	–	27	24	21
1982–83	–	28	24	19

The management of small distance education systems

Management is a process aimed at the effective utilization of human and material resources to achieve an institution's objectives. In the introduction to this paper we suggested that SDESs require tighter management than is common in conventional educational institutions and we believe the results of the cost analysis bear this out. In this section we shall examine the four major facets of management, i.e. planning, organizing, leading and evaluating, in commenting on some of the key issues in the administration of an SDES.

1 *Planning*

Planning enables an institution to anticipate and adapt to a changing environment. Although forward planning does not appear to have influenced educational administration greatly in the past, evidence from business indicates that enterprises which plan outperform consistently those that do not. An SDES should have a formal plan for a 3-5 year future and a more detailed action program for the 24 months immediately ahead.

In forecasting external conditions, which must precede planning, SDESs should pay attention not only to the social, political and economic developments affecting all education, but especially to technological and market changes. How will satellites and video discs change the delivery of educational TV? What could be the effect of computerized word-processing on course development? How strongly will the private sector move into distance education? The answers to these and many other questions have major implications for SDESs.

Another important step for an SDES planning its future is to ask itself regularly: *What business are we in?* It is easy to miss opportunities by misdefining the key thrust of the institution. For example, by equating enrolling students in courses produced by the institution itself, opportunities for providing other services (e.g. career advice) and for brokering courses from elsewhere may be neglected.

The complexity of both the environment and the internal workings of an SDES require a high degree of creativity in the planning process. Fortunately those conditions known to stifle creativity, such as narrowly defined jobs, clear authority relationships, formal rules and impersonal relationships tend not to be characteristic of SDESs. However, where an SDES is relatively young it is likely to have many staff who are not only unfamiliar with distance education but also expect the SDES to operate like a conventional institution. Setting detailed and explicit objectives for the year ahead in a participatory manner, sometimes called a 'bottom-up formal' planning process, can be a good way of focussing the staff. The level of specificity of the objectives will depend on the particular situation; precise goal setting is called for when there are severe time or resource limitations and a relatively stable environment, whereas broader, directional goals are more appropriate in the formative period of an institution, in conditions of uncertainty, or when there is little consensus among the staff. In either case, for management by objectives to be effective it must have the support of the senior administration which must be able and willing to operate a reward system keyed to the attainment of the objectives that are set.

2 *Organizing*

The four basic concepts on which the organizational structures are built are division of labour, span of control, departmentation and unity of command.

While SDESs share with all modern organizations a degree of division of labour, this division will be less developed than in larger institutions of either the conventional or distance type. The cost allocations of Table V, which show the involvement of most of Athabasca University's departments in both course development and services delivery probably underestimates the versatility of some units. The diversity of tasks facing each staff member in an SDES militates against the job monotony which is a prime drawback wherever the concept of division of labour is highly developed.

In terms of the span of control (the number of subordinates reporting to a manager) SDESs of which the authors are aware are somewhat unusual. While the span of control of senior executives is, at between six and nine, slightly larger than is common for small enterprises, the span at the next level is significantly narrower, at an average of around four. It is more usual for the span of control to increase at lower levels of an organization. The existence of the opposite tendency in SDESs reflects the fact that many functions must work together for successful operation although the number of staff attached to any single function is small. Distance education is not a labour intensive activity. The relative youth of these SDESs also helps to explain this anomaly.

Reference to function leads naturally to an analysis of departmentation. Function is not the only basis on which to divide an organization into departments. Simple numbers, product or service, client, geography and process are other criteria commonly used. An SDES, like most complex organizations, will in fact departmentalize by several or all of these methods. While some aspects of departmentation are likely to be uncontroversial (e.g. the creation of a registry for the records function) other forms of grouping are less easily decided. An SDES at the postsecondary level will usually display something of the product departmentation (by academic program or discipline) characteristic of conventional institutions. In such institutions it is usual for

419

each academic department, indeed each instructor, to teach, via the simple technology of the classroom, in a fairly autonomous manner. In distance education such autonomy is hardly possible. We have shown that the distinction between course development and services delivery is important in economic analysis and, at least in Canada's three SDESs, this distinction is reflected in the organization of the institution.[4] However, although there are usually few difficulties when functions such as warehousing or printing are organized as departments, instructional staff may see themselves threatened when departmentation by function or process is used to organize the areas of course development and services delivery. Since these functions and processes involve these staff directly the existence of such departments, alongside the academic 'product' departments, may indeed violate the principle of unity of command which holds that 'no man can serve two masters'.

However, in breaking the unity of command concept SDESs are similar to many complex modern organizations using a matrix structure in which a project framework is superimposed on a departmental grouping. Although there are clearly considerable opportunities for conflict between project and departmental administrators in such an arrangement its advantages are impressive. It can generally respond more quickly to program needs and the conflict it stimulates, if functional rather than dysfunctional, can help generate creative solutions to problems. In short, use of a matrix structure allows an SDES to combine the advantages of bureaucracy and adhocracy.

3 *Leading*

External and internal factors combine to create an unusually strong need for good leadership in SDESs. Many SDES are fairly new and have not reached steady-state stability. At present most free world governments, after the rapid university growth of the sixties, are no longer giving much priority to higher education. This situation can create a climate of insecurity for SDES staff which the much reduced job mobility in conventional institutions does nothing to alleviate. It is not surprising that SDES staff are tending to organize into collective bargaining units, nor that the demands of these units are for the job advantages that conventional institutions offer (e.g. sabbatical leave, institutional research funds).

Given the novelty and uncertainty that any SDES experiences in its infancy, motivation of the staff is a particularly important aspect of leadership. By severely restricting an institution's ability to motivate people via monetary rewards for good performance, bargaining units oblige the administrators of SDESs to motivate their staffs through higher order needs, such as the needs for esteem and self-actualization. This is entirely healthy, although far from easy. Attempts to match performance objectives to the personal goals of individuals, to take an autonomy-oriented approach to management, and to encourage participative decision-making must often be tempered by the unusual degree of synchronized team-work required for successful operation of an SDES. The fact that SDES staff operate as team members rather than as individual entrepreneurs like the faculty in conventional universities creates an especial difficulty with the concept of 'due process' in the resolution of difficulties. In a conventional institution resolution of a conflict involving an individual need not interfere with the ongoing business of the institution. In an SDES such interference is much more likely since the conflict usually impacts directly on the team in which the individual is working.

The administrators of SDESs should ideally be leaders with deep concern for both production and people. Between the two key dimensions of leadership, namely 'initiating structure' and 'consideration' (Stogdill and Coons, 1957), sometimes abbreviated as autocracy and democracy, an SDES will, like any organization, require change in emphasis from time to time. Our experience is that in SDESs these changes must occur in more frequent cycles than elsewhere, implying that administrators must be proficient in both dimensions of leadership.

4 *Evaluating*

SDESs require tighter administration than other educational enterprises and this is particularly true of the evaluative function of management. Although we treat this function last it is, of course, an activity that permeates all the others.

The three steps of the evaluation process are measuring, comparing, and correcting. Each presents special problems in an SDES. Measuring the learning activity of students is complicated by distance, for even determining such apparently straightforward indicators as rates of student progress or drop-out is surprisingly difficult to do on a continuous basis, especially in SDESs which enroll students throughout the year. Only in the vital areas of academic quality is measurement in an SDES easier than elsewhere, for the team approach to course development and services delivery both encourages quality and ensures a wide awareness of any shortcomings. It is rather ironic that, although the team approach gives distance courses more quality (and usually quantity) than their conventional counterparts, the notion that home study is substandard dies hard in traditional circles.

In the area of economic evaluation this article has hinted at some of the measurement difficulties. These difficulties are even greater when we consider the second aspect of evaluating, namely comparing performance measurements to standards. The relative newness of distance education means there is little basis for such standards and we have shown that, at least in the area of economic performance, standards borrowed from conventional education should be used with caution. To cite but one example, it is certain that the 'standard' proportion of total operating budget spent on fixed salaries, which is now at around 85% in conventional Canadian universities, would be a recipe for disaster in any SDES which adopted it.

Thus, while an SDES must set standards in order to evaluate its performance, the proper response to a discrepancy between the measure and the standard may often be to revise the standard rather than to initiate corrective action.

Where corrective action is required, the highly integrated and complex nature of an SDES can make the implementation a difficult matter. Although an SDES usually has greater flexibility to modify its sub-systems than a large operation like the Open University, this flexibility should not be abused. Neither students nor staff appreciate being part of an experiment in which all variables undergo constant modification. In implementing corrective action it is useful to think of instructional changes as a shift in the mix between the independent and interaction learning activities that make up distance education (Daniel and Marquis, 1979). We believe that the economic analysis presented in this paper, which has identified the somewhat analagous 'teaching' activities of course development and services delivery, provides a good basis to assess the financial implications of the correction action proposed.

The analysis may also be helpful in modelling the relative importance of three important characteristics of performance: quantity, cost and time. The fourth characteristic, quality, is by the nature of distance education rather visible.

A final aspect of evaluation, cost-benefit analysis, brings us back to some of the general issues raised in the introduction to this paper. While all SDESs should engage in cost-benefit planning when they assess alternative means of answering the service opportunities facing them, cost-benefit analysis of the institution's activity cannot be the exclusive preserve of the institution itself. Most SDESs receive support from public funds and their external economy should be a matter of public interest.

Conclusion

This article has examined the economics and management of small distance education systems with an emphasis on those providing services at the post-secondary level. We have shown that, in both economic and administrative terms, such systems require different treatment from conventional education institutions. The authors believe that the analyses are sufficiently general to provide an improved conceptual base for the operation of small distance education systems.

Notes

1 An Athabasca University course is roughly equivalent to 2/5 of a full credit Open University Course. Thus the comparable costs for course equivalents are $100 000 for an AU course and £175 000 ($315 000 CAN in 1976) for an OU equivalent.

2 Athabasca University was first established in 1970 as a conventional undergraduate institution to offer degree programmes in Arts, Sciences, and Education. Planning was suspended in 1972 following a change in the provincial government (education is a provincial jurisdiction in Canada). A re-examination of demand for conventional undergraduate programmes led to Athabasca University's reorganization as a pilot project in open learning. The results of the pilot project were evaluated in 1975 and the University was given a permanent distance education mandate under which it has since operated.

3 The Alberta post-secondary system includes four universities, ten public (community) colleges, two technical institutes, four adult vocational centres, and two special purpose training institutions. The Province has a population of approximately 2 million, 1 million of which reside in two major urban centres. System enrolments total approximately 70 000.

4 Athabasca University, Alberta: La Télé-université, Québec; and the Open Learning Institute, British Columbia.

References

Daniel, J.S. and Marquis, C. (1979) Independence and interaction: getting the mixture right. Teaching at a Distance, 14, 29–44

Keegan, D. (1980) Drop-outs at the Open University. Australian Journal of Education, 24, 1, 33–45

Kershaw, J.A. and McKean, R.N. (1959) Systems analysis and education. Santa Monica, California: The Rand Corporation RM-2473-FF

Mace, J. (1978) Mythology in the making: is the Open University really cost-effective? Higher Education, 7, 295–309

Perry, W. (1977) The Open University. San Francisco: Jossey-Bass

Sheehan, B.S. and Gulko, W.W. (1976) The fundamental cost model. In Mason, T.R. (ed.) Assessing computer-based systems models. San Francisco: Jossey-Bass

Smith, R.C. (1975) A proposed formula for Open University expenditure in a plateau situation. Open University, mimeograph

Stogdill, R.M. and Coons, A.E. (1957) (eds.). Leader behaviour: its description and measurement, Research Monograph No. 88, Columbus: Ohio State University

Wagner, L. (1973) The economics of the Open University, Higher Education, 1, 150–183

Wagner, L. (1973) The Open University and the costs of expanding higher education. Universities Quarterly, Autumn

Wagner, L. (1977) The economics of the Open University revisited, Higher

Education, 6, 359-381

Wedemeyer, C.A. (1974) Characteristics of open learning systems. In Open Learning Systems, Washington, D.C.: National Association of Educational Broadcasters

ECONOMICS AND COST STRUCTURES

Greville Rumble

Introduction

Cost Functions of Distance-Learning Systems

Cost analysis is concerned with establishing cost functions which attempt to relate costs to some measure of output. In educational systems student numbers are the usual measure of output, but other measures (e.g. graduates, student credit hours, courses) are sometimes used. The purpose of cost analyses is to identify the main generators of cost, and to study how costs change as key input or output variables change.

Most campus-based teaching costs are traditionally treated as variable costs, directly related to the output of students. Indeed, one of the major cost components of conventional universities (academic staff time) is commonly related by a ratio or formula to student numbers or student credit hours. The proportion of fixed costs (i.e. those not directly related to output) to total costs in campus-based universities is therefore very small.

In distance-teaching universities, however, very significant expenses are incurred in the preparation of teaching materials (print, television and radio programmes, and other media). The costs are incurred *irrespective* of the numbers of students in the system. As a result, such costs can be regarded as a fixed cost in relation to the output of students. On the other hand, the course materials themselves represent a very significant output in their own right, for they are the product of a multi-media publishing enterprise. The investment of manpower in the development of courses is, then, analogous to capital investment in business, and represents a move away from the labour-intensive nature of conventional educational institutions.

It follows, then, that in any consideration of the cost per student, a much higher proportion of the costs of a distance-learning system is fixed irrespective of the level of output (students). Some of these costs will in fact vary with the level of output of courses (or course materials) in the system. It therefore becomes necessary to consider at least two major outputs as variables, one related to students and the other to courses. However, once an institution has achieved its planned level of course output (by, for example, completing its academic profile of courses), then the costs involved in the initial development of its courses are no longer being incurred, and the costs of maintaining the profile may be regarded as a fixed cost.

Thus at its simplest, the cost function of distance-learning systems can be expressed in the form:

$$TC = F + VN \qquad (1)$$

where TC is the total cost and F is the fixed cost of the system; V is the variable cost per unit of output, and N is the unit of output (students, student hours, etc.).

When the total cost function is linear, the average cost (AC) is simply equal to the fixed cost divided by N plus the variable cost V, so that

$$AC = F/N + V \qquad (2)$$

and the marginal cost is equal to V.

Figure 1 illustrates the cost structure of conventional and distance-learning systems, where:

F_1 is the fixed cost of a distance-learning system
F_2 is the fixed cost of a conventional system
V_1 is the variable cost per student of a distance-learning system
V_2 is the variable cost per student of a conventional system

and where S is the break-even point, found by applying the formula

$$S = \frac{F_1 - F_2}{V_2 - V_1} \qquad (3)$$

for the intersection of two lines such as in Figure 1, at which a distance-learning system has a unit cost per student equal to or lower than (as one moves to the right of the graph) the conventional system.

Economists point to the economies of scale that are achievable in distance-learning systems, for, as the number of students N increases, so the average cost AC declines (by spreading the fixed cost F over more units) until, when N is very large, the average cost is close to the marginal cost (V). Plotted on a graph the result is a rectangular hyperbola as illustrated in Figure 2 (which is derived from Figure 1).

Figure 1: The Cost Structures of Conventional and Distance-Learning Systems

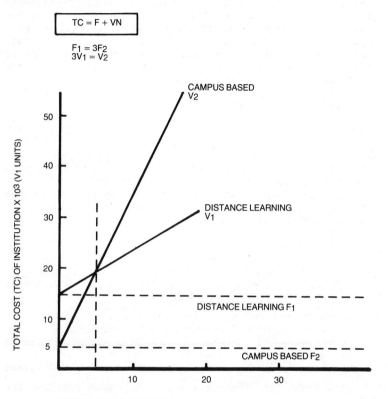

$$TC = F + VN$$

$$F_1 = 3F_2$$
$$3V_1 = V_2$$

Factors Affecting the Costs of Distance-Learning Systems

Eicher (1978) has summarised some of the factors which affect cost levels in media-based distance-learning systems. These show that design and production costs are generally much higher than the costs of transmission and reception. The fixed costs are much higher for television than for radio (of the order of 10:1), although they vary considerably with geographical coverage and the number of broadcasting hours involved. However, fixed costs can be lowered, significantly, if existing broadcasting installations are used.

Production costs are particularly high for film, whatever the size of the system. They are relatively high for television, but economies of scale are rapidly achieved as audience size moves from 2,000 to 200,000. Production costs are low in the case of radio.

Figure 2: Student Numbers and Unit costs in Conventional and Distance-learning Systems

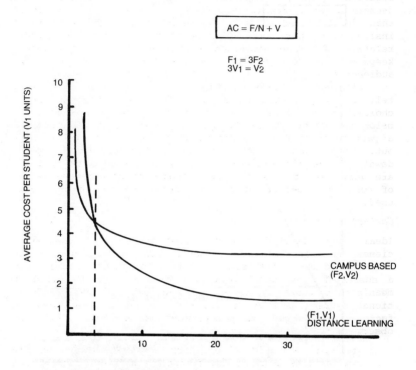

$$AC = F/N + V$$

$$F_1 = 3F_2$$
$$3V_1 = V_2$$

AVERAGE COST PER STUDENT (V_1 UNITS)

CAMPUS BASED
(F_2, V_2)

(F_1, V_1)
DISTANCE LEARNING

NUMBER OF STUDENTS (N) X 10^n

Transmission and duplication costs are very high for video systems. Unit costs for open-circuit television transmission are high for audience sizes below 200,000, but thereafter drop rapidly and then rise slightly from 1 million upwards. Unit costs for radio transmission are moderate below 100,000 students, and very low above that number. Generally speaking, the variable costs drop very quickly with the size of the system. However, the variable programme costs of television are always much higher than is the case for radio.

Eicher concludes that the media giving the greatest potential economies of scale are television via satellite, open-circuit television, closed-circuit television and radio. The media giving the least or no economies of scale are language laboratories, computer-based teaching and films. The media for which unit cost increases with the magnitude of the project are films (once a certain level of population dispersal is reached) and video systems, the cost of which

428

quickly becomes prohibitive because of duplication problems.

As a general rule, the 'little media' (that is, those requiring simple, inexpensive equipment such as slide projectors and tape-recorders) offer far greater cost advantages than the 'big media' (such as television and computer-based instruction) where small audiences are concerned, but their relative advantage diminishes subsequently. Radio, however, keeps a relative advantage over the 'big media' whatever the audience size.

Although Eicher's conclusions are of importance, they tell us very little about the effect of different media choices on the costs of particular projects. When we consider below the costs of the UKOU, we are looking at the costs of a particular system. As Wagner (1977) and Mace (1978) point out, these costs could change significantly (both up or down) if the mix in media is changed. Unfortunately, there are very few studies that have looked at alternative levels of cost in a particular system, given changes in the media used.

Cost-effectiveness

Ideally any cost study should consider not only the cost-efficiency but also the cost effectiveness of the system, in relation to the benefits derived from it. However, there are a number of conceptual problems which have to be faced in meaningfully comparing the effectiveness of alternative educational systems, and, in particular, how one derives a satisfactory overall unit of measurement. As Woodhall (1972) has observed:

> There is a world of difference between accepting the similarities between investment in physical capital and investment in human skills and capabilities through education and training, and actually applying the criteria and techniques of investment appraisal, such as cost-benefit analysis, to expenditure on education.

Certainly there is no evidence that distance teaching per se is less effective than conventional teaching. Eicher (1978) notes that generally speaking it seems that students who follow and complete a cycle of education at a distance learn as well or as badly as students who follow the same cycle in a traditional system. What is not as yet clear is whether multi-media systems are in general more or less effective than, or of equal effectiveness with, single -media systems. Overall, it seems that the use of distance teaching as opposed to traditional forms of teaching is not a critical variable in comparing effectiveness. More important factors seem to be student motivation and the quality of the teaching given. It is generally assumed that the benefits of distance education are equal to those of conventional learning systems, and so existing studies concentrate on costs. This assumption will be looked at more closely when we review the cost studies on the UKOU.

Specific case studies

Two of the universities with which we are concerned in this book have been the subject of important cost studies. These are Athabasca University in Alberta, Canada, and the Open University of the United Kingdom. In this section we briefly review these studies.

Athabasca University, Alberta, Canada

AU offers a wide variety of courses. Many have been adapted from courses developed by other institutions such as the UKOU, Coastline College in the United States and the Laurentian University in Canada. However, the University also produces many of its own courses using a course team typically consisting of an external consultant in the subject-matter of the course, an instructional designer, a subject-matter expert on the University's own staff, a visual designer and an editor.

Although some conventional courses relying on face-to-face teaching are offered to AU students in certain locations, the University chiefly offers home-study courses, designed and packaged for self-instruction. All require textbooks, study guides, student workbooks and other materials such as audio-tapes, directly mailed to the student's home. Some have television programmes; others have laboratory components that are available in certain locations. The student also has the chance of free telephone access to a tutor. The television programmes are transmitted on local channels, often on cable. They can also be viewed at some of the local centres located in various towns in the Province.

These local centres are open at convenient hours and stock a supply of most course materials. The economics of AU are described in Snowden and Daniel (1979), who have developed a simple cost equation based on the two functions of course development and services delivery:

$$TC = a_1 (x_1 + x_2 /l) + by + c \qquad (4)$$

where

x₁ = course credits 'in development'

x_1 = course credits 'in development'
x_2 = course credits 'in delivery'
l = the lifetime of a course in delivery, where it is assumed that the total cost of maintenance over the life of a course is equal to that of developing a course. l is taken to be 5 years in practice
y = weighted course enrolments. Course enrolments are weighted on the basis of a standard 6-credit course, such that a student enrolled on a 3-credit course is equal to 0.5 of a standard course enrolment

a_1 = course development costs per credit
b = delivery costs per weighted course enrolment
c = costs of institutional overheads

Snowden and Daniel comment that the weakness of the model is that it treats institutional costs as fixed, whereas a more realistic assumption in the developing years of an institution is that institutional overheads are a fixed proportion of total costs. They therefore adjust their basic equation (4) to take account of this factor and, on the basis of 1979/80 data and price levels, estimate the full cost of course development to be Canadian $16,400 per credit (45 hours of student learning activity); $3,300 per credit for the full cost of course revision and replacement; and $670 for the cost of services delivery per course enrolment (on a standard 6-credit course).

Figure 3: Athabasca University: Average Recurrent Cost per Course Enrolment

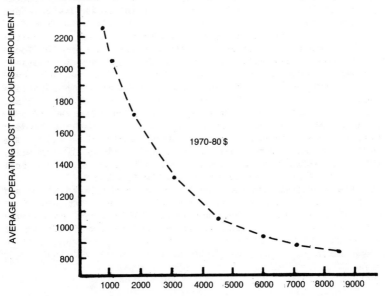

NUMBER OF COURSE ENROLMENTS

Source: B.L. Snowden and J.S. Daniel, 'The Economics of Small Open Universities', paper presented to the Open University Conference on Distance Education, Birmingham, UK, 18-23 November 1979.

The average recurrent cost per course enrolment declines as the number of course enrolments increases, but at a declining rate, such that once AU has about 10,000 course enrolments, further economies of scale cannot be expected to be significant (see Figure 3). The unit costs per student hour are within the range set by comparable programmes at the three conventional universities in Alberta Province.

The use of small course teams, the smaller emphasis on expensive media, and the practice of buying in courses developed in other institutions have meant that course development costs at AU are significantly lower than in some other distance-learning systems (e.g. UKOU). However, Figure 3 suggests that the average cost per student at AU is not very different from the average cost per student at the Open University, even at the lowest point.

Open University, United Kingdom

The UKOU's course materials include correspondence texts and supplementary materials; radio and television programmes; and related audio-visual and experimental materials. Students can attend local centres for counselling and tuition. They are required to submit assignments (both tutor-and computer-marked) and sit a final examination.

The course materials are largely prepared by the full-time academic and related staff of the OU, and the professional broadcasting staff of the BBC's Open University Productions, although in some cases external consultants are used.

The economics of the UKOU have been more extensively studied than those of any other distance-teaching university, and a number of studies have been published (Laidlaw and Layard, 1974; Lumsden and Ritchie, 1975; Mace 1978; Wagner, 1972 and 1977).

Laidlaw and Layard (1974) studied the relationship of fixed and variable course costs. They included in the fixed costs of course development the cost of full-time central academic faculty and their support staff, and of consultants employed by the University; expenditure on art and design work and the fixed print costs of compositing, machine preparation and the like; the cost of broadcast and audio-visual production; and some administrative costs not clearly related to student numbers. They annualised these fixed costs over the number of years a course would be used, assuming an interest rate of 5 per cent. The variable costs include expenditure on printing (paper and machine time), tuition, counselling and summer-school costs; the cost of experimental kits and computing services used by the students; and administrative costs such as those of examinations and course-materials despatch.

Laidlaw and Layard showed that while the variable cost per student-course was, with one exception, lower in the UKOU than in conventional campus-based universities in the United Kingdom, the fixed costs were much higher. They concluded that

> the real strength of the Open University teaching system, aside from its social aspects, is the potential economies of scale which can be reaped by substituting capital for labour. This means that a major part of the costs of the course became fixed and invariant with respect to student numbers.

Application of formula 3 on page 426 provides a break-even point at which the average cost per student on an Open University course is the same as that for a student on a campus-based course. From then on, any increase in the number of students results in a fall in the average cost per student, and this constitutes the case for the expansion of student numbers at the UKOU. On the other hand, the case for developing and presenting higher-level courses with relatively smaller numbers of students has to be justified 'on the ground that they are an integral part of a system providing wider access to complete degree courses rather than on the ground that they are a cheap way of doing this' (Laidlaw and Layard, 1974).

Laidlaw and Layard's general conclusion that the UKOU is cost-effective in comparison with conventional British universities bore out Wagner's 1972 study based on budgeted expenditure and planned student numbers for 1973. This study suggested that the average recurrent cost per equivalent undergraduate at the Open University was about a quarter that at conventional universities, although it fell to about one-third if allowance was made for the greater research activity at conventional universities. On the other hand, Wagner shows (1) that the cost per graduate at the UKOU was likely to be only about one half that of conventional universities owing to the higher drop-out rate of UKOU students; and (2) that the resource cost per UKOU undergraduate (that is, the cost of his or her education taking into account earnings forgone as well as total costs of the education) is likely to be only one-sixth the resource cost of an undergraduate in a conventional university, given the part-time nature of the UKOU students' studies, and the fact that many of the students are in gainful employment.

These early papers constituted convincing grounds for the rapid expansion of the UKOU. On the other hand, the nature of the average cost curve (a rectangular hyperbole) means that at a certain point further economies of scale cannot be achieved without a significant change in patterns of expenditure and hence in the cost structure of the institution itself. This conclusion is borne out by Wagner's 1977 study. Wagner first of all checked and broadly confirmed the conclusions he had reached in his 1972 paper concerning the relative cost advantage of the UKOU on the basis of planned expenditure and student numbers of 1973. He then went on to consider the average cost per undergraduate student for the period 1974-6, for which figures existed, and for the period 1977-9, using a simple equation for projecting UKOU expenditure:

$$C = a + bx + cy \qquad (5)$$

where C is total recurrent expenditure, a are fixed costs, x and y are the number of courses and the number of undergraduate students respectively, and b and c can be determined for any particular year by dividing the total costs allocated to students and courses by actual student or course numbers for the year. The number of courses x reflects both those in development and those being maintained - the latter weighted as being equivalent to 0.1 of the former.

Figure 4: Average Cost per Year per UKOU Undergraduate Student at 1976 Prices

Year	Average Cost £	Status
1973	560	Actual
1974	525	Actual
1975	494	Actual
1976	513	Budgeted
1977	520	Projected
1978	498	Projected
1979	493	Projected

Source: L. Wagner, 'The Economics of the Open University Revisited', Higher Education, vol.6 (1977),pp.359-81.

Wagner's figures (at 1976 prices) are given in Figure 4. This suggests that 'most of the economies of scale of the Open University were reaped within the first few years of operation and that since then it has been following the conventional university pattern of little increase in productivity' (Wagner, 1977).

Wagner advances several reasons why this should be so. The rate of increase in student numbers had slowed down significantly. However, the main reason is that the additional numbers of students in the system had been matched by an increase in the number of courses offered to students, as the UKOU sought to implement its plans for a minimal academic plan based on providing a range of undergraduate courses equivalent to 87 credits.

However, although the average cost per UKOU undergraduate was likely to stabilise at about £500 per year (at 1976 price levels), Wagner could still point to economic advantages over conventional universities. In the UKOU, average recurrent costs per undergraduate student were about a quarter those in conventional universities (a third with an adjustment for research activities); the average cost per UKOU graduate of the order of one-half the cost in conventional universities (about 3/5 this if an adjustment is made for research activities); and a resource cost of about one-sixth that of conventional universities.

Throughout these studies there is an assumption that a UKOU graduate is the same in terms of academic quality as a conventional university graduate. This assumption was first questioned by Carnoy and Levin (1975), who suggested that the cost savings of the UKOU system might be 'obliterated by a smaller educational product'. They argued that the average university student 'receives not only instruction and instructional materials, but he receives substantially more tutorial services, contact with fellow students, access to libraries, computers and campus lectures than does his Open University counterpart'. They therefore argued that

> a more realistic premise is that the limited nature of the Open University education as well as the credential effect of particular institutions on earnings and occupational attainments would suggest that the Open University graduate is not likely to receive either consumption or income benefits from his education that are as high as those of the person from the more conventional university setting (Carnoy and Levin, 1975).

Further criticisms are put forward by Mace (1978). He suggests, for example, that the economic value of a UKOU degree to a student (in terms of increased earning power) will be less than is the case for a conventional university student, because the average age of UKOU students is higher than that of students in conventional universities, and because by then there are powerful institutional forces such as internal labour markets which inhibit UKOU students' job mobility, and hence the possibility of their benefiting economically from the education that has been gained.

Mace also queries whether or not the Open University is internally cost-efficient. Could not the same output be achieved by an internal reduction in costs? Although the necessary data to answer such a question are not publicly available, Mace suggests, for example, that broadcasting may not be a necessary component in the UKOU's teaching system, or at least that it could be used less extensively than is the case. In support of his case he cites an internal report in which radio had been consistently ranked by students in the last three places of importance in relation to ten other teaching aids, while television had been ranked in the last five by students in five out of the six faculties of the University. He also mentioned that only some 60 per cent of students watch the television programmes, and only 30 per cent of all students (18 per cent of viewers) find television 'very helpful'. Mace concludes, therefore, that there is a need to question the cost structures of the UKOU, and not to regard them as given; and that moreover, if such analyses were done, then the institution's cost-efficiency could be raised substantially.

Clearly, changes in the media used would affect the cost structure of courses. However, although abandonment of broadcasting or tuition (both of which are significant items within the total budget) would lower absolute costs and increase the cost-efficiency, it is not clear what effect this would have on the UKOU's cost-effectiveness.

Conclusions

Studies of cost-efficiency are concerned with the economical use of inputs relative to the output produced, where the *quality* of the output is held to be constant. Generally, the assumption in studies concerned with the comparative cost-efficiency of two systems is that the effectiveness of the two systems under consideration is constant, and attention is focused on the costs of the different ways of producing the output. The least expensive way is held to be the most cost-efficient way. Thus Wagner (1972,1977) and Laidlaw and Layard (1974), in their papers on the UKOU, assume a consistency in the quality of the graduates produced by the UKOU and conventional UK universities, and, on the basis of the data available, conclude that the Open University is cost-efficient relative to conventional UK universities.

This conclusion needs to be qualified before it can be applied generally. While distance-learning systems catering for high student numbers are cost-efficient, their cost advantage is reaped at the expense of limiting the number of courses on offer. What evidence we have suggests that in high-technology systems the investment of resources in learning materials (where these are designed only for teaching at a distance) and the cost of establishing production and transmission systems can only be justified on grounds of cost-efficiency if there are sufficient students to bring average costs down. At the higher-educational level, where student numbers tend to be smaller, the results of such studies for the development of academic programmes would seem to be the following:

- the restriction of the distance-learning system's academic programmes to areas where there is known to be a significant level of demand (e.g. teacher training);

- the development of courses in a wider number of subject areas, but with a severely restricted course choice in each discipline, thus forgoing the possibility of turning out graduates with a single honours degree;

- a conscious decision to ignore comparative unit costs

and to embark upon a programme for social or political reasons, or because it is the *only* way of fulfilling specific goals and needs (e.g. to reach previously deprived target populations), irrespective of the cost.

Thus the UKOU has had to restrict on cost grounds the number of courses which it can offer. The UKOU graduate is not able to take an honours degree in a single subject area. The most he can achieve is to major in two subjects. Moreover, because average costs fall at a declining rate (the nature of the cost curve is, as we have seen, a rectangular hyperbola), at a certain point in the development of a system the economies of scale achievable as a result of increases in student numbers cease to be significant. In such circumstances only a change in media, and particularly away from high-technology media, or a reduction in the number of courses on offer, will lower unit costs signifi- cantly. As we saw, Wagner (1977) held that the stabilisation of unit costs at the UKOU resulted largely because the cost advantages to be reaped by taking in more students had been offset against an expanding course profile. However, the UKOU is now at a point on the cost curve where additional student numbers cannot affect unit costs to any significant degree, and the scope for expanding the profile of courses while maintaining unit costs (by balancing additional expend-iture on courses with additional students in the system) is limited.

The most significant cost variables, then, are the media, the number of courses on offer, and the number of students studying courses. In some cases (e.g. video-casse-ttes or tutorials) the number of locations at which facili-ties are made available will also be an important variable. It is in the relative cost of media, and in their effective-ness, that future research is needed. In particular, we need to consider whether the teaching advantages of high-tech-nology media (television, audio-cassettes, films and so on) are sufficient to warrant expenditure on them or whether the little media (print, slides, audio-tapes and in some situa-tions radio) will not do as effective a job far more efficiently. This suggests that we need to have more inter-institutional studies looking at the order of costs incurred in different systems using different media (or using the same media in different ways) and at the relative effective-ness of these systems.

It is clear that the absolute costs of a project (both in terms of the fixed expenditure on capital items and overheads, as well as variable expenditure per student or student-hour), are critically dependent upon the choice of media and their distribution or transmission systems.

This suggests that before planners and decision-makers embark on the establishment of a distance-learning system, very careful consideration must be given in the light of student number projections to the cost implications of media choices and the number of courses to be developed and presented. Certainly, for low student populations, conventional teaching methods are likely to be more cost-efficient than high-technology distance-learning systems.

References

Carnoy, M., and Levin, H.M. (1975) Evaluation of Educational Media: Some Issues. Instructional Science, 4, 385-406

Eicher, J.C. (1978) Quelques réflexions sur l'analyse économique des moyens modernes d'enseignement. Paper presented to the International Conference on Economic Analysis for Education Technology Decisions, University of Dijon, Institut de Recherche sur l'Economie de l'Education, 19-23 June 1978

Laidlaw, B., and Layard, R. (1974) Traditional versus Open University Teaching Methods: a Cost Comparison. Higher Education, 3, 439-68

Lumsden, K.G., and Ritchie, C. (1975) The Open University: a Survey and Economic Analysis. Instructional Science, 4, 237-91

Mace, J. (1978) Mythology in the Making: is the Open University Really Cost-effective? Higher Education, 7, 295-309

Snowden, B.L., and Daniel, J.S. (1979) The Economics of Small Open Universities. Paper presented to the Open University Conference on Distance Education, Birmingham, U.K., 18-23 November 1979

Wagner, L. (1972) The Economics of the Open University. Higher Education, 2, 159-83

Wagner, L. (1977) The Economics of the Open University Revisited. Higher Education, 6, 359-81

Woodhall, M. (1972) Economic Aspects of Education. A Review of Research in Britain. Slough: National Foundation for Education Research in England and Wales

441